'I've never met Kate Bush. But on occasion we may have shared the same dream about the afterlife of Elvis Presley – a fact I learnt while reading this wonderful book. She's beguiling and eccentric and in thrall to a singular vision. She's also smart in not dispelling her mystery. Over the years she has come to occupy a unique place in the British psyche. She's now part national treasure, and part pop-Athena with her devoted acolytes. *Under The Ivy* is respectful, but it gets us pretty close to the temple. This is the perfect book for aficionados or even the merely curious.' **Paddy McAloon**

'Graeme Thomson peers deep into the weeds of this extraordinary woman's work. *Under The Ivy* brilliantly fleshes out the stories behind the Bushcraft, without reducing any of her music's enduring magic.' **Rob Young**, author of *Electric Eden* and *All Gates Open: The Story Of Can*

'Graeme is a fantastic biographer, warm and wise. He brings Kate's interior and exterior lives to life, in vivid colours, in this wonderful book.' **Jude Rogers**, author of *The Sound Of Being Human*

'Such a well written and detailed book. It's satisfyingly in depth and revealing and just as its title suggests a door to a secret garden, we get unseen glimpses of a private life and the connections of that world to one of the most influential and important artists of my lifetime. Absorbing, revealing and immersive.' **Kathryn Williams**

'This is writing about music, and one of the key songwriters and performers of her or any time, that demands to be read not only by fans and connoisseurs, but by anyone interested in art and those who make it.' **Laura Barnett**, author of *The Versions Of Us* and *Greatest Hits*

'Written in prose that from time to time seems linked umbilically to the very same "otherworld" from which Kate Bush's art manifests, Graeme Thomson's style of storytelling penetrates the surrounding truths and myths. In doing so he presents us with the rarest of things: a portrait of Kate Bush incarnate.' **Jim Kerr**

T0182423

'There is no shortage of books written about Kate, but when *Under The Ivy* first appeared it felt like the definitive text. Probing, exhaustively researched, with a huge attention to detail, it was immersive and engaging. Graeme Thomson is clearly an admirer of the work, but avoids any hagiography.' **Sinéad Gleeson**, author of *Constellations* and *Hagstone*

'*Under The Ivy* is an absolute joy for the Kate Bush fan, indeed any music fan, delving deeply and passionately into the world of one of our most important and cherished artists. A fascinating and richly rewarding read, this book explores in exquisite detail a truly unique vision and uncompromising approach in what has been the creation of some of the most incredible and intoxicating music ever recorded.' **Emma Pollock**

'Smart and respectful.' *New Yorker*

'The best music biography in perhaps the past decade . . . an absorbing, painstakingly researched and downright fascinating book . . . After this magnificent read you will come to appreciate her work that much more. And if that isn't the point of music biography, what is?' *Irish Times*

'Mapping a path through the life of this enigmatic writer is not easy, but Graeme Thomson's superb book manages to do just that . . . A compelling examination of an artist in a constant state of becoming.' *Mojo*

'Meticulously reconstructs Bush's career through diligent research and fine writing.' *Uncut*

'Thomson's book sheds a light on the woman behind the inspiration of many a modern-day chanteuse.' *NME*

'*Under The Ivy* presents a different portrait [than] the tabloid press caricature . . . A plausible picture emerges of a hippyish, perfectionist individual, single-minded in her artistic vision and unaffected by fame.' *Financial Times*

'[An] excellent biography . . . expertly unravelling her contradictions and motivations. In addition to his faultless research. Thomson's prose is often as rich and as eloquent as Bush's own writing.' **Record Collector**

'A thoughtful and rewarding book.' **Classic Rock**

'Respectful, fascinating and full of insight . . . Thomson gets beyond the traditional party line [and] challenges the perception of Bush as some waif-like ingénue.' **Q**

'An exhaustive and engaging account of Bush's career . . . Thomson proves an insightful critic, weaving cohesive threads from Bush's scatter cushion themes.' **Metro**

'Sensitive, empathetic and exceptionally well-researched biography.' **The National**

'Meticulously analyses outstanding moments . . . debunking myths of the ethereal sprite and the dotty recluse.' **The Herald**

'A masterful biography. Thomson's descriptive language is gorgeous . . . he delves into lost parts of her career with glee.' **The Word**

'Graeme Thomson has vast knowledge of his subject . . . Media perceptions of Kate as fey or eccentric are challenged and the stories he has gleaned from countless sources shape a more accurate picture of a fascinating creative talent. A must-read for fans and recommended for any fans of biography.' **The Anti-Room**

UNDER THE IVY

GRAEME THOMSON

UNDER THE IVY

THE LIFE AND MUSIC OF

KATE BUSH

OMNIBUS
REMASTERED

Contents

For my father

Foreword By Sinéad Gleeson

The world is not short of auteurs. *Ne plus ultra* creators who exist on the hinterland, moulded only by their own vision. To exist on the thin line of such a margin means that one becomes adept at occupying a very singular space – and there's only room for one. An unquantifiable number of words has been written to try and capture the essence of the ultimate creative outlier, Kate Bush. A performer who resists genre and classification, whose musical and production choices have always tended towards precociousness and risk-taking. If there is a vast storyboard for her output, it's crammed not just with music, but with art, film, culture, folklore and history. Lean in and there is Powell & Pressburger, the gothic, the choreography of Lindsay Kemp, folk songs, Leonora Carrington, mime, Irish literature and English pastoral. Listen to *The Kick Inside* or *The Dreaming* or *Aerial*, and it's immediately evident that this is the work of a chameleon; an artist who knows the value of independence and the power of creative control.

Growing up in a house where *Top Of The Pops* was an unmissable Thursday night staple, I remember Kate appearing – first in videos, later in lip-synched performances. Each one varied and elemental, from the roller-skating dunce caps of 'Sat In Your Lap' to the Amazonian figure of 'Babooshka'. The aesthetic and costuming was rooted in camp and theatricality, but often a serious point was being made, about the horrors of war or environmental catastrophe. What was even more striking was the voice; octaves of sibilant sensuality that could swoop from gothic whisper to oscillating wail. St Vincent (the professional name of Annie Clarke) once described it as being "like fire coming out of her mouth". When Bush declined to attend the 2023 induction ceremony at the Rock and Roll Hall of Fame, it was Annie Clarke who performed 'Running Up That Hill'.

No matter how many times I go back to the albums, something new presents itself. A note used in a way no one else would dare, unusual instrumentation, and a rogue production decision. It's impossible to unpack here why and what I admire in this vast body of work, but the album I find myself returning to most is *Hounds Of Love*. It is that rare thing, a perfect record, and I can't recall an album with a stronger first side – of songs that managed to be both critically revered and commercially successful. These are the tracks other bands cover; the ones people who aren't overly familiar with Bush know the words to. For some, *Hounds Of Love* is about a rain-making machine, or a deal with God intoned over erotic, intricate choreography, and while each song lines up in its own monolithic way the record is, for me, all about the flip side.

The Ninth Wave song cycle was originally conceived as a conceptual film about a woman lost at sea. Disconnected, stricken, it sounds anguished and eulogistic but also works as an apt summation of her entire catalogue: experimental, consistently and surprisingly filmic – a deeply cinematic songwriter. It crests from the emotive swell of 'And Dream Of Sheep', to the sonically glitchy 'Waking The Witch'. Quietly tucked away amid these brine-soaked songs is what I consider to be one of Kate's best and most under-rated tracks, 'Watching You Without Me', a supernatural lament for loss and love; a deep whirl of sadness. The album celebrates its 40th anniversary in 2025 and still sounds as invigorating as it did back then.

Bush's music is never one thing – a deep, lone furrow of audio – it embodies a synaesthetic, multi-disciplinary quality. It gravitates to the physical and visual, and within the universes of her albums, all the characters she creates and the narratives she spins coagulate into one tentacular opus. For all this scale, there is intimacy between artist and listener. We believe Kate when she says, "It's you and me".

There is no shortage of books written about Kate, but when *Under The Ivy* first appeared in 2010, it felt like the definitive text. Probing, exhaustively researched, with a huge attention to detail, it was immersive and engaging. Thomson is clearly an admirer of the work, but avoids any hagiography. Bush fans tend to be completist, often territorial about the singer, and while no new music has been released since 2011, there have been events to update in this new edition. The live shows of 2014 – an unbelievable spectacle to witness, more theatrical than a music gig –

the resurgence of interest after 'Running Up That Hill' appeared in *Stranger Things* and her induction into the Rock and Roll Hall of Fame in 2023. Admirers live in hope of new material, but Kate Bush doesn't owe the world anything else. In a career now stretching into its sixth decade, there is enough to sustain us, thanks to a catalogue of music that is timeless and immediate, as distinct as any "little light shining" on the horizon.

Sinéad Gleeson
Dublin, February 2024

Preface To 2024 Edition

I first started work on *Under The Ivy* in 2008. It was published in May 2010, almost five years after Kate Bush had returned with her eighth album, *Aerial*, following a twelve-year hiatus. I thought the timing was good. A sufficiently lengthy period had elapsed to allow a degree of perspective on her latest record, an outstanding piece of work which reveals more of its riches with each passing year, and its relationship to the rest of her catalogue. Yet its release was still close enough to qualify – at least in the off-the-clock world of Kate Bush – as recent news.

There had been a flurry of promotional activity at the end of 2005 around the announcement and arrival of the album, but Bush soon retreated into customary media silence and public non-visibility. Quite quickly after this biography was published, however – and not for a second to suggest a case of cause and effect – her work rate began to pick up pace. In 2011 came *Director's Cut*, then *50 Words For Snow*. I duly updated *Under The Ivy* in 2012 to include consideration of these records and wondered, as we all did: whatever next? If Kate Bush could release two new albums in the space of a single calendar year, surely all bets were off.

A steady tick-tock of minor activity followed, little tremors in the highly sensitive Bush ecosystem. She recorded a new version of 'Running Up That Hill' for the London Olympics in 2012 and publicly collected a Sky Arts award. In the background, something far more significant was formulating. By the time Bush received a CBE from the Queen in the spring of 2013, the idea of her performing again after an absence of thirty-five years was already solidifying into fact. Fast forward to March 2014 and the thunderbolt announcement that, in the summer and autumn of that year, Bush would headline concerts for the first time since 1979. The seemingly unthinkable had become reality: the most stage-averse artist of her generation was breaking cover. Fans around the world spent hundreds, often thousands of pounds on tickets, flights and accommodation.

The 'Before The Dawn' residency at the Eventim Apollo in west London spanned several weeks and twenty-two shows. I was fortunate enough to attend one of the earlier concerts, and it was unforgettable, as much from an anthropological viewpoint as a musical or theatrical one. On the night I attended, 2 September 2014, and no doubt on all the others, the Apollo was filled not just with Londoners, or Brits, but with scores of other nationalities, all of whom had made the pilgrimage – some more than once – to witness what had become the most eagerly anticipated and widely reported music story of the new millennium. People wept. Strangers hugged and high-fived. Some wide-eyed, nervous, childlike energy seemed to have taken hold of the theatre. It was easily the most emotionally charged, keyed-up, expectant and downright odd atmosphere of any concert I have ever experienced. And all this before Kate Bush had even stepped onstage.

No serious biography of Kate Bush could fail to include analysis of this event. *Under The Ivy* was therefore revised again in 2015, adding a chapter on the strange magnificence of the 'Before The Dawn' experience.

This "remastered" 2024 edition marks the third occasion that the book has been updated. There is perhaps less to add than I would have hoped. As time passes, it appears 'Before The Dawn' may be remembered as an unforgettable one-off rather than, as I had envisaged at the end of 2014, perhaps still a little giddy from the thrill of it all, the start of a creatively vibrant "third act" for Kate Bush. Then again, I have been wrong enough times in the past to remain open to any and all possibilities. Only one person knows what happens next.

In the decade since those shows, Kate Bush's standing in the world has again shifted. There has been no new music nor any public appearances, yet much has happened to push the narrative along. With that in mind, the text of *Under The Ivy* has again been revised and made current. In doing so, I am immensely grateful to Sinéad Gleeson for writing a new foreword, and to Omnibus Press for giving the book an elegant makeover and fresh impetus. If not quite "*The Whole Story*" – for who, really, would want that? – *Under The Ivy* is once again as complete and current as it can be.

Graeme Thomson,
Edinburgh, February 2024

Introduction

"You Never Understood Me. You Never Really Tried"

IT starts with a question. Two questions. The absolute shock – was this art-rock, pantomime, musical theatre, novelty or left-field genius – of hearing and seeing 'Wuthering Heights', feeling the perceptible thud of its instant impact upon popular culture, was immediately followed by these simple queries, heard in offices and pubs, in schools, shops, cafes and building sites, spoken over breakfast tables, in front of televisions and from behind crackling newspapers: My God, who is *she*? And where did she *come* from?

Good, enduring demands. This book doesn't promise to supply all the answers so much as revel in the act of delving deeper inside them. The truly tantalising thing about Kate Bush is that the whole has always been somehow greater, more dazzling, more mysterious, than the sum of her many parts.

Who is she? Every time you look you get a different answer.

She is the 19-year-old who fought EMI General Manager Bob Mercer tooth and nail in order to ensure that the stupendously strange 'Wuthering Heights' would be her first single rather than his preferred choice – the more orthodox 'James And The Cold Gun' – and won.

She is the astute million-selling rock star and reluctant sex symbol who knocked Madonna off the top of the album charts in 1985, who has successfully controlled every aspect of her career and who once called herself the "shyest megalomaniac you're ever likely to meet,"[1] admitting "I'm probably quite calculating behind my creativity."[2]

She is the Celtic spirit-child who sings of witches and phantoms, who

1

has been known to give her friends sealed jars containing 'essence of the day': some air, a few twigs, some grains of earth, a flower; and she is the relentlessly tenacious studio artist, playing the same piece of music over and over and over again as though lost in some Shamanistic ritual, cajoling, caressing, chipping away at the chrysalis of her art until the longed-for butterfly of emotional truth emerges. "She would do lots and lots of takes and I could never understand why," says Max Middleton, who played organ on *Never For Ever*. "Normally with other musicians we'd do it again because it was too fast or slow or you're playing the wrong chord – something very definite – but she was looking for something nebulous that was hard to pinpoint. She wasn't doing it again out of sheer belligerence. She was looking for something [that no one else could see]."

She is the unguarded young woman who once walked down a south London street and saw a lady waving at her from some distance away, through the window of a first floor building. Smiling and waving back as she continued down the street, Bush finally reached the house and realised that the woman was, in fact, cleaning her windows.

She is the visual icon, an inspiration for countless creative artists for more than three decades; and she is the reluctant pub singer, performing The Beatles' 'Come Together' and The Rolling Stones' 'Honky Tonk Women' in a Putney pub to a bunch of heroically inebriated Scottish football supporters who were, according to her old bandmate Brian Bath, "playing catch the whisky bottle, throwing it at each other, climbing up the pylons. They were getting up onstage. Some guy was all over Kate. . . ."

She is the powerful multi-millionaire who flew the director of the 'King Of The Mountain' video, Jimmy Murakami, by helicopter from London to her summer home in Devon for lunch and then promptly flew him back again afterwards.

She is the down-to-earth den mother, bustling around making cups of tea for her family, her musicians and producers, phoning out for curry and pizza when hunger strikes; the fearsomely loyal woman who has frequently helped out her friends financially and who is described by her former Abbey Road engineer Haydn Bendall – echoing a sentiment shared by almost everyone interviewed for this book – as "very sensitive and aware and gentle and loving. It's an intoxicating mixture."

She is the artist so ruthlessly dedicated to her vision that she is prepared to exist within strictly defined physical parameters in order to explore fully the vastness of her interior landscape. She is both the semi-mythical 'recluse' of tabloid lore who has lived on an island – and in her head – and the very model of sanity in a world where celebrities accumulate children from around the globe and subject them to the full glare of the media machine, delegating their 'management' to a well-drilled team of nannies, minders, publicists, dieticians and private tutors, and for whom nothing in their life is deemed real or worthwhile until it is observed by millions of strangers and projected back at them. She is the woman who, at 56, proved capable of turning the industry on its head with a return to the stage as creatively triumphant as it was unexpected.

She is all and none of these. And she is more. There are several parts of her we will never be permitted to see: the "ferocious mother"[3], the lover, the composer, cocooned in silence and solitude. Each fractured snapshot captures a portion of her, some more revealing than others, but none are defining. Piecing them together to form a single picture often feels like trying to complete a jigsaw when some of the pieces are missing, or simply don't fit.

★　★　★

"Let Me In-A Your Window!" Given the swarm of rumours and decades spent in retreat, it's worth recalling the moment of arrival. Bush started her career in full flight, already airborne at 19, pitched headfirst into the kind of unforgiving spotlight that can leave much of the world beyond its glare dark, shadowed and forever changed. Rarely has any artist made such an immediate impact upon public consciousness. Within a month of releasing her first single in January 1978 Bush was as famous as she ever would be, her image plastered on buses, tube station billboards and TV shows, her songs – one in particular, so precocious it practically dared you to ignore it – all over the radio, her somewhat gauche pronouncements to the media printed in every variety of magazine and newspaper, her breasts a topic of national debate.

Her life, such is the way of instantaneous fame, was subjected to a brutal and entirely unexpected *coup d'état*. The ferocity of the success of 'Wuthering Heights' took everyone by surprise. Buffeted off course, blown into the wider pop slipstream, Bush didn't really locate her artistic true north until the early Eighties, while those observers who attempted to define her through the rather limited critical vocabulary of the pop lexicon were usually stumped, opting for either fawning hagiography, open hostility, or a kind of benign patronisation.

Little wonder. Many of the misunderstandings that have grown up around Bush could be better addressed by absorbing the implications of the following exchange, undertaken during an interview in 1993.

Q: "What's the worst thing about being a musician?"

A: "I don't think of myself as a musician."

Q: "What then?"

A: "As a writer, I suppose."[4]

Or, to boil the question down to its essence: *Who and what are you?* Her answer ("A writer", the "I suppose" tacked on to signify her reluctance to describe herself as *anything* in such concrete terms), is not primarily meant to signify the form and content of her work – which is clearly musical, with significant leanings in the early days towards poetry and dance and, latterly, film and theatre – but, instead, it reveals how she perceives what she does and, more particularly, the way in which she chooses to do it.

In terms of her overall aesthetic, her creative instincts, her work ethic, her attitude to fame, as well as the way she insists on living her life, Bush has always been far closer to a poet, novelist or playwright than a pop musician. She began by writing poems. When she embraced the piano – privately, passionately – it was not in order to perform in a band, or master her favourite pop songs to impress her friends, or to play a technically complex solo. It was purely a writing tool, a conduit for self expression. It was her pen. Later, technological advances made the Fairlight, the earliest form of digital sampler, her word processor, allowing her to cut and paste sounds, to transcribe more accurately the murmurs in her heart and head. Despite her obvious musical gifts, she has never made a serious effort to learn to play any other instrument. She has sufficient skills to facilitate her needs.

Bush *writes in sound*. For her, the creative act lies not in the initial seed of songwriting. That is simply the beginning of the compositional process, containing the germ of the idea; in the studio, she drafts and redrafts, plots a path, finds new stories and edges towards something definitive. Onstage, she has twice toiled over the creation of a carefully constructed spectacle designed to live in the imagination long after the curtain fell. Every piece of work is laboured over for years, hewn slowly into shape, and then handed over to posterity. She returns again and again throughout her career, with decreasing frequency, to this one primary purpose: to create a single artefact, fixed, tangible and everlasting. It is her statement to the world but, more pertinently, to herself.

As far as the audience is concerned, there is no work in progress. She carries within her the remnants of intense self-consciousness – few are permitted to watch her creative struggles. She is no Icarus, striving publicly and failing heroically. Instead, her work simply appears, like Zeus' thunderbolt.

In the 35 years between 1979's 'Tour Of Life' and 'Before The Dawn' there was virtually no meaningful revision of her work in the form of live performance, nor has she embraced the increasingly prevalent culture of reissues, deluxe packages and endless compilations. Until *Director's Cut* appeared from leftfield in 2011 her recording career was almost entirely without retrospectives. Like the witch-woman celebrated in Bob Dylan's 'She Belongs To Me', Bush is "an artist, she don't look back". She has created and moved on, the majority of her work defined by a novelist's wish for the final full stop, the definitive ending, which is almost unique amongst her peers.

Where did she come from? In plain biographical terms, too, it's striking how little common ground Bush shares with the archetypal rock star who is, we often find, propelled by a degree of rage, their childhoods typically characterised by disruption and domestic instability, perhaps a combination of parental loss, pain, poverty and frequent uprooting, the urge to make music motivated by a sense of frustration, anger and rebellion against family, against authority, against the social and political mores of the age.

There is very little of that impetus in Bush's background. She did not start creating music in order to confront some deep fissure in her upbringing, or to rebel against her social conditions. Comfortable and permissive, filled with love, unfailingly polite, not a little eccentric and unapologetically devoted to artistic expression, her childhood is closer to that of Jane Austen – another pioneering female writer from a close-knit, progressive brood, with elder brothers, particularly James and Henry, who inspired and encouraged her – than a Lennon, Bowie or even a Bono. 'Art for art's sake' could have been the Bush family mantra.

"It was a very bohemian upbringing," says Charlie Morgan, who played drums in the latter stages of the KT Bush Band and has appeared on many of her albums. "A bit like Virginia Woolf, like a modern day Bloomsbury group. Bohemian but with this kind of underlying normality. The life you led was fairly mundane and middle class, but it was what you were *thinking* about – your philosophical and artistic and emotional thoughts – that was incredibly creative."

It brought undeniable privileges. Bush has never had to make a living away from music; she has never experienced the standard rites of passage of slogging from town to town to sustain her career, fathoming out what songs will work in front of a disgruntled, drunken crowd on a wet Wednesday in Wigan; her sole tour to date, as well as the 'Before The Dawn' residency, were both organically realised theatrical productions, a million miles away from the spit and sawdust of the Hope and Anchor or the quasi-Messianic stadium rock experience.

But although she has never had to bow down to the inescapable logic that drives most music careers – studio, album, press, tour; studio, album, press, tour – her art has never been a luxury. A compulsion rather than an elective, her music comes from a sense of "poetic *necessity*,"[5] and her material comforts and domestic stability have simply enabled her to be as adventurous as she wishes in her imagined life, the wild world of her musical forays. Her music acknowledges precious few conventions. Unable to confine it within standard pop formats, she has stretched the form to suit her own needs rather than shrinking or compromising her vision to fit into existing templates. She has rarely adhered to orthodox song shapes, there are no clichéd three-chord rock tricks, very few blues-based notes, indeed almost no trace whatsoever of any American influence in the structures, themes, chords or harmonies. When she does tune into a specific genre it usually comes from somewhere out on the margins: the soft reggae of 'Kite', 'Rocket Man' and 'King Of The Mountain'; the Balearic smudges of 'Nocturn'; the Weimar melodrama of 'Coffee Homeground'; the Madagascan sway of 'Eat The Music'; the hard, Hellenic folk rhythms of 'Jig Of Life'.

Lyrically, she has rarely leant on the standard singer-songwriter crutch of confessional autobiography, preferring sly humour, knockabout slapstick, child-like wonder, unbuttoned sensuality, impressionistic storytelling, unconventional philosophising and a taste for horror and the supernatural. As a singer, she has constantly pushed her voice into uncompromising shapes, disdaining melisma and button-pushing over-emoting in order to use her vocals as another instrument, never simply plumping for conventional beauty when something more interesting, primal and challenging might be available. She has sung in Australian, Irish, French and German accents, she has impersonated a donkey, a witch, a bird and an enchanted house. She has an aversion to drawing straight lines.

She exists entirely and gloriously outside the orthodoxy of the rock lineage. Many artists – from Tori Amos and Bjork to relative newcomers such as La Roux, Bat For Lashes and Florence & The Machine – have been likened to her, but such comparisons are unfair and unflattering to others. Her music simply sounds like Kate Bush, some wondrous alchemy of *musique concrete*, folk roots, post-punk, world music, progressive rock and an ancient, long forgotten siren call. She is unafraid to make mistakes, but her willingness to seem ridiculous is more of a strength than a weakness. For over three decades she has held onto a kind of heroic artistic blindness that allows her to pursue her most outlandish ideas to their conclusion without feeling restricted by popular opinion or current trends. She is certainly the only musician who, having persuaded Prince to play on one of her songs, would then decide that what the track *really* needed was a contribution from Lenny Henry. And it's hard to imagine any other artist returning to the stage after 35 years with a show that featured the line "HP and Mayo – the badger's nadgers." Being a mere 'pop star' has never been enough, but if pop music lays claim to harbouring any geniuses, her name must be somewhere near the top of the list.

For those who never did understand, who have always found her self-indulgent, self-absorbed and dippy, who corralled her within the confines of their own limited imaginations – the worst of all possible things: a female pop singer with ideas above her station – she was dismissed as a twittish hippie girl, the suburban doctor's daughter with a thing about mime and mysticism, all too easily mocked on *Not The Nine O'clock News*. Wow. Amazing. Like all great artists, she is easier to parody than to understand.

For the rest of us, 'Wuthering Heights' was simply the opening pistol crack in a mystery tale that has negotiated myriad twists and turns and has rarely failed to grip.

After countless contemplations of songs like 'Moving', 'Babooshka', 'Breathing', 'Night Of The Swallow', 'Under The Ivy', 'Rocket's Tail', 'Mrs Bartolozzi', 'Lake Tahoe' – the list rolls on and on – we're still waiting to find out whodunit. Those initial two questions hold true, with only a slight shift in emphasis: Who *is* she? And where *did* she come from?

And at certain points in our story comes a third, and then a fourth: Where did she go? And why, after so long in retreat, did she chose to return?

1

All The Love

A WHITE, solid stone farmhouse. Sprawling but homely, a jumble of uncertain angles, its belly full of battered black beams, sloping floors, unlikely stories and all manner of mysterious nooks and crannies. Upstairs, a warren of bedrooms, private dens, a library with a coal fire. Downstairs, a large kitchen, the wooden table serving as the thrumming engine at the hub of the house; a living room, its open fireplace almost tall enough to swallow a man, gazing down onto exotic rugs and well-used furniture; a study here; a grand piano over there, French windows opening out to a self-contained micro-world, thick with trees, honeysuckle and cobwebs, hiding within its heaven and earth an eighteenth century rose garden, a Victorian pond, a scattering of sheds and outbuildings offering secrecy and sanctuary. Literally and metaphorically, a place in which to lose yourself.

Where did she come from? We could do much worse than begin here, a refuge to which Bush has returned again and again in both body and song. East Wickham Farm was always more than just a patchwork quilt of bricks, mortar and dense foliage. A 350-year-old plot situated just off Wickham Street in Welling, Kent, to the south-east of London, it was once the focal point of the local community and even at the turn of the twentieth century remained extensively rural. By the time the Bush family settled there in the Fifties there had been some relatively minor augmentations and cosmetic additions, but the basic footprint had remained unchanged for centuries. Though no longer a working farm, and no longer surrounded by acres of open land, it still had a palpable presence.

In the compact but densely packed grounds stood a brick duck pond, later converted into a swimming pool, a circular rose garden, a dovecote, a Wash House and a mice-riddled grain store known by all as the barn, which would later become Bush's private studio and in childhood, too, served as a kind of refuge. With its dilapidated pump organ, its cracked, uneven brick floor and its wooden steps edging upwards towards a loft with a distinctive round window looking down onto the farm, for Bush it was a "mouse's nest",[1] both a retreat and a favoured launch pad for her imagination long before she recorded songs like 'Running Up That Hill' there.

Once the farm would have stood in splendid isolation among the surrounding countryside, but by the time Bush had started primary school in the early Sixties only the back of the property looked onto open ground, as it does today, the scrubland of 'Fanny on the Hill' stretching away to the north-east towards Plumstead Cemetery. By the mid-Sixties Wickham Street, the road lying at the end of the short front drive leading to the farm, was buzzing with traffic and its flanks lined with new houses. On the same side of the road as the farm entrance stood a number of modern properties, low-level blocks of flats to the west and neat suburban houses to the east. London, that most voracious of cities, had crept up and devoured it.

And yet a sense of solitude remained. The farm was protected from public view by a large outer fence and a dense thicket of trees on all sides of the main house; nestled in greenery, rooted deep in its own history, the modern encroachments all around served only to emphasise East Wickham Farm's sense of somewhere out of time, a hushed oasis in a sea of bustling modernity, with half a foot and most of its oaken heart in another world.

It offered numerous opportunities for concealment and countless sirens' calls to escape, imagine, create, pretend. In her brother John Carder Bush's book *Cathy*, published in 1986 and again in 2014, containing more than 30 briefly annotated photographs of his sister taken when she was between seven and 12 years old, we can see her at play in this magical place. The book – a simple collection of evocative black and white images – is both beautiful and revealing. There she is, dressing up, posing, preening and role-playing beneath the black roof beams, made out of wood scavenged from old warships broken up at the docks at nearby Woolwich; or draping herself over deer- and goat-skins plundered from the Scottish Highlands and Iceland; or gripping old swords, almost her own height, wearing her brother's over-sized motorcycle boots and a quizzical expression; or twirling near a shed that housed two unexploded World War II bombs, a legacy of Bush's grandfather Joe, who had moved into the farmhouse for the remaining 13 years of his life after his wife Annie died in 1950, and retained an unaccountable fondness for the incendiaries.

Some of the pictures in *Cathy* bring to mind The Cottingley Fairies, the celebrated photographic hoax of 1917 which showed two young sisters playing with nymphs at the bottom of the garden; others showcase her eldest brother's love of the great early twentieth century book illustrators, Eduard Dulac and Willy Pogany; others still are clearly partly a homage to Charles Dodgson, better known by his literary pseudonym Lewis Carroll, and his vivid photographic portraits of children, specifically young girls like Xie Kitchin and Alice Liddell. Where some of Dodgson's portraits had obvious sexual overtones, the ones in *Cathy* are by turns playful, melancholic and sensual, at their best hinting at the woman within the child, capturing the surreptitious weighing out of knowledge and innocence, a girl on the cusp of something she can feel even if she can't yet put a name to it.

These kinds of complex ruminations on childhood are potently late Victorian and Edwardian obsessions, and crop up in some of the keynote works of literature that Bush loved as a child and continued to love as an adult, among them J.M. Barrie's *Peter Pan*, Kenneth Grahame's *The Wind In The Willows* and Oscar Wilde's *The Happy Prince* (the latter celebrated in 'December Will Be Magic Again'). They are obvious touchstones for the aching sense of loss and deep-rooted Englishness in much of her music. It is not the impish, chimbley-sweep Englishness of The Small Faces' 'Lazy Sunday', nor the detailed kitchen-sink vignettes of The Kinks, nor even the Blakeian Albion of The Libertines. It's certainly not the diluted, warm-beer-and-cricket version pined for by the likes of John Major, nor the mock-Tudor chintz framing the suburban dream.

Half Irish, Bush connects with a harder, more mythical England, a pre-Christian Celtic land, a deep, green dream of a country that has never truly existed except buried deep within our own minds. As a child she went hunting for it in on Sunday afternoons in the beautiful old gardens at Hall Place in Old Bexley; she sought it in Ealing comedies, dark folk songs, dusty old children's novels and cheesy TV dramas. It's a country populated by ghosts, ghouls and phantoms roaming among wild flowers, brambles and mossy graveyards, much more a half-remembered feeling than a physical place, wet with the tears of lost innocence, scented with a whiff of greasepaint. Filled with a glorious nostalgia, it's both ecstatic and desperately sad, full of beauty, mystery and horror.

It's the world she inhabited as a girl, and the one she has strived to hold onto as an adult: the delicious – if painful – heightened awareness of youth, the yearning to return to uncomplicated, instinctive modes of behaviour, an acute sensitivity to the crackle and static of real life. The desire to break down the barriers we erect in adulthood can be felt in many of her songs, and can be traced back to those early photographs of her at East Wickham Farm, among the ivy and tall stone walls, the decrepit barn and shady, leaf-strewn pool, the open fires and old bellows, the wooden Wendy house with the windows of real glass.

It is indisputably the same world depicted on the front cover of *Lionheart*. The farm bequeathed to the child the kind of intense feelings – melancholia, innocence (and its inevitable loss), a fear and attraction to horror and dark corners, peace, solitude, sensuality – as evoked in later songs like 'Oh England, My Lionheart', 'In Search Of Peter Pan' and in the almost unbearable sense of sadness found in the words to 'Under The Ivy'. In 'Suspended In Gaffa' she sings "out in the garden there's half of a heaven", while both 'Warm And Soothing' and 'A Coral Room' recall coming into the house from the garden, through "the back door."

In one of her earliest – and best – unreleased tracks, 'Something Like A Song', she plugs into 'The Piper At The Gates Of Dawn' section of *The Wind In The Willows*, telling of an embodied spirit voice, a muse, calling her from the grounds of the farm. She sings about seeing a piper "by the willow", only visible at night when all the lights in the house are lit low. She calls out to him as he moves across the pond, but he "won't answer me." This house, it is clear, is one of the deepest pools from which her songs spring. In 'The Fog', a song about having the courage to step away from the certainties of the past, she looks into the mists of her childhood and sings: "Just like a station on the radio, I pick you up."

The past is her constant companion, and one of the most compelling narrative strands of her career has been the fight to maintain contact with this place, to keep it continually alive in her present.

★ ★ ★

The Bushes moved into East Wickham Farm in the Fifties and it remains in their ownership today, filled with the memories of over half a century of rich family life. Catherine Bush, the youngest member of the household, was the product of a marriage of understated English scholarship and vivid Celtic spirit, with each side of the union bequeathing many shared qualities, not least among them eccentricity, kindness and a love of music.

Her father, Robert John Bush, was born on April 4, 1920 in South Ockendon, a village in Essex, just east of London, dating back to mediaeval times but long ago subsumed by post-war prefabs and modern housing estates. His was not a privileged start, but he was bright and worked hard to win a scholarship to the highly regarded Grammar School at Grays, a few miles south, and later won a place at medical school to train to become a doctor.

In early 1943, at the age of 22, the newly qualified General Practitioner married Hannah Patricia Daly at St Joseph's Roman Catholic Church in Epsom, Surrey. An Irish staff nurse two years his senior, born June 20, 1918, Hannah worked at Epsom Grove Hospital and was one of 12 children who originally hailed from the harbour town of Dungarvan in County Waterford.

A little over a year after the marriage, in the spring of 1944, their first child was born and named John Carder Bush. The unusual middle name, which the oldest Bush brother has always used professionally, is in honour of Dr Bush's maternal grandfather, John Carder. To friends and family he would always be simply Jay.

Dr Bush spent the remainder of WWII serving in the army in India, while Hannah looked after the new baby. When the doctor returned he began working in Welling as a GP and settled with his new wife and family at East Wickham Farm. Patrick followed eight years after Jay on December 9, 1952, and finally Catherine arrived, almost six years later, on July 30, 1958, born in Bexleyheath Maternity Hospital in south-east London. She was known as Cathy or Catherine throughout her childhood; the shift to Kate after she left school seemed to have some small but worthy significance.

She was born when her mother was already 40, late in the day even by today's standards and exceptionally so by those of the late Fifties, by which it might be speculated that her arrival was not entirely planned. (Bush also became a mother very late, just shy of 40). As a consequence, by the time she had started school Jay was already at Cambridge University studying law – though he never qualified – and Paddy was attending St Joseph's Academy, the local Catholic grammar school. The quirk of having three children arrive at such irregular intervals did much to dictate the sibling dynamic. Her brothers not only became a profound influence on Bush through their pioneering forays into books, music, philosophy and art, but there was little in the way of rivalry or the kind of turf wars that frequently break out when siblings are born close together. It was a harmonious unit, and if they were each highly protective of one another, it's hardly a wonder that Jay, in particular, became such a fierce defender of a sister who could almost, in terms of the 14-year age gap, have been his daughter.

Her looks have always been closer to her mother, the Celt – tiny but shapely, dark hair, pale skin, rather elfin – but her voice is her father's: the same slow, southern English accent, the same charmingly weak 'r's. She also inherited his sense of patience and outer calm, while internalising her mother's energy and crackling vivacity, stored up for use in her work. Dr Bush ran his surgery from home and in time Hannah stopped nursing and effectively became a housewife, answering the phones when required but generally serving as the dynamo of the household, constantly on the move: singing, laughing, making cups of tea and offering sustenance, occasionally snapping at the mess her children made or their lack of activity. Dr Bush, with his pipe, his armchair and his considered manner, was the ballast.

It was a winning combination. Everybody loved them. "Kate's mum was universally accepting of everybody, she was just one of the sweetest human beings ever," says Charlie Morgan. "And Kate's dad as well, the Doc. He was a sweetheart, a real nurturer of his kids' creativity. Her family were so functional and so nurturing and so loving. Her brothers being very close to her and her parents being very close to her, it [was] such a great luxury to have." The KT Bush Band's original drummer, Vic King, recalls his first visit to the house late in 1976. "Very friendly family: 'Come into the kitchen!' It was cups of tea, cake and biscuits until you couldn't move. Kate's mum was lovely, she floated around; Dr Bush was really nice, made you welcome."

In a rare 1979 film clip we see them all together, sitting in the garden at Wickham Farm. Faced with her parents' obvious pride – although as ever it is quietly expressed and understated; there was never anything brash about this family – Bush, aged 20, still seems very much the baby of the brood despite her star status. She sits with her head bowed, half-embarrassed, half-overjoyed. When her father speaks a few simple words of kindness, you can see her affection and respect for him radiate from her. Almost 40 years later, for those who witnessed the onstage interplay between parent and child during 'Before The Dawn' it was acutely apparent that she had spent a significant part of the past 20 years building a similarly nurturing relationship with her own son, Bertie.

Much was later made of Bush's 'privileged' background. So prevalent is the notion that pop stars are forged in the fires of dysfunction, her childhood looks like an anomaly by comparison, the kind of upbringing which offers no imperative to challenge or create or push for inner change. At times, the stability and constancy of her early life has been used as a stick to beat her with, as though it somehow negates her claim as an artist. She has even pondered the thought herself. "I've had really quite a nice life, actually,"[2] she said, rather apologetically, in 1979, later adding. "I often think people are looking for something in my life that they can't find. A number of performers, I suppose, come from working-class families, or their parents were divorced. Perhaps that gives them the urge to go out and struggle for something."[3]

Her struggles were real enough, but they were never immediately obvious. She was usually ferried around in her father's car and money was never a problem – she always seemed to have it and never had to earn a living by any conventional measure, nor did she seek the kind of temporary work that teenage girls often take on, like waitressing or baby-sitting, for pocket money. From an early age, she was free to carve out her vision of the world as she saw fit, but that fact doesn't make her urge to create any less urgent, or somehow invalidate the importance of what she is saying. Bush had a favourable start, perhaps, but the important thing is what she did with it. How many other all-singing, all-dancing daddy's girls have knuckled down and come up with such astonishing results?

In fact, her parents were both from solid, unshowy country stock; they were not born into wealth, but they did become extremely comfortable. A doctor in the Fifties and Sixties was at the higher end of the social scale, and the Bushes not only had Wickham Farm, but came to own a property in the village of Birchington-on-Sea – a small, secluded and rather sedate seaside resort close to Margate in north-east Kent that looks out onto the North Sea and is much favoured by the retired – where family holidays were often spent, as well as a three-storey house in Lewisham, divided into three large flats, where first Jay, then Paddy, and finally Bush herself all later lived.

There was also a grand adventure to the Antipodes when Bush was aged six. The family – minus Jay, studying at Cambridge – travelled by boat to Australia and New Zealand to visit members of Hannah's family and, it seems, to investigate the possibility of emigration. In the end they stayed for about six months, putting a serious dent in both her and Paddy's school attendance; she was seasick on the way there and had measles on the way back. Her hazy, hallucinatory recollections of the trip stood out as an exotic memory of childhood, but more important than the money that enabled it was the general atmosphere of creativity and knowledge that surrounded her; and always that sense of a vaguely Bohemian permissiveness, that alluring pull of a faintly mystical 'other' life tugging at her hemline.

Although she was given an astonishingly sensible upbringing – she was protected and cared for without ever being spoiled, she was given freedom without being over-indulged, she was treated with respect without being made brattish – it was by no means an ordinary childhood. Loving and calm, yes, but hardly conventional. Her school friends recall Dr Bush taking surgery in a flowered smock; when the house ghost, a Victorian serving maid who would swish past in the hall, became too troublesome the family had her exorcised; Bush later recalled how her mother, when ill, had "taken off like a balloon and hit the ceiling."[4] There was nothing sinister in this, it was simply evidence of a very real engagement with unseen realms of influence. "The whole family were very unusual and artistic and spiritual, but all completely different," says Stewart Avon Arnold, Bush's long term dance partner. Other descriptions of the Bushes range from "eccentric and lovely", "bonkers, great fun, very charming" to "mad as a bat"[5], but every single one brims with very genuine affection.

To outsiders, they seemed somehow divorced from the mundanities of Sixties and Seventies suburban life. The evidence in support might be esoteric – they practised karate and Kyudo, Japanese Zen archery, which Jay still teaches all over Europe – or prosaic: they had their groceries delivered each week rather than lugging them home from the shops. An alluring mixture of nouveau-hippie Sixties sensibilities, scholarly pre-Raphaelite sensuality, and solidly pre-war middle-class family values – there were rabbits called Winkle and Took hopping around the farm, and various other furry things in hutches, including a hamster – the Bushes appeared to exist in their own rather rarefied bubble. Inside, the influences came thick and fast. "I think being brought up in a situation where music is there, people are being creative, it feels natural for you to do that too," said Bush. "I think that was a very big opening for me at a very young age to have that kind of energy around me."[6]

★ ★ ★

Where did she come from? Almost all her significant early creative strides were incubated in the febrile environment of Wickham Farm. "It felt like a college," says David Jackson, the set designer on her 1979 'Tour Of Life' who visited during preparations for the tour. "The farm is genuinely old, in the middle of this conventional neighbourhood, and when you go in it takes you by surprise. It's like Doctor Who's time machine, you step through a time warp into this old, old farmhouse. It's a family of serious intellectuals, from daddy on down, and the boys were into renaissance music and all these ancient instruments. It was quite intimidating, in a way. I was so terrified of meeting the whole clan I went to the pub on the way there and got drunk as a skunk. I just remember this collegiate atmosphere – books everywhere, shelves and shelves in every room – and very spiritual. Not religious, but a general [spiritual] interest, obviously with Kate in her lyrics and in John's poetry."

There was also a spiritual connection to music. In Hannah's childhood home in Waterford there were always fiddles and accordions on the go, much singing and dancing. Though many of her brothers and sisters had also moved away from Ireland, the family would go back and visit from time to time and the trips made a lasting impression on Bush. Music in Ireland was considered an essential part of the domestic fabric, and it was also deeply woven into life at Wickham Farm. Pop music leaked in, often uninvited, as pop music tends to. One of her favourite singles was 'They're Coming To Take Me Away, Ha-Haa!', the 1966 novelty hit by Napoleon XIV; you can see how its sense of silliness and contrived derangement might have appealed to her eight-year old self. Later, she would buy her first album, Simon & Garfunkel's *Bridge Over Troubled Water*, and formed allegiances to Elton John, Dave Edmunds, Marc Bolan, King Crimson and particularly Bryan Ferry and Roxy Music.

As a listener as well as a future performer, she was rarely more than two steps away from the pop mainstream, even if she favoured the arty, intelligent end of the marketplace. She loved David Bowie and attended his final Ziggy Stardust show at the Hammersmith Odeon on July 3, 1973, but she didn't fall for The Beatles until well into the Seventies, and even then she rather eccentrically decreed *Magical Mystery Tour* to be her favourite. And although she remembers being "fascinated"[7] by The Rolling Stones' 'Little Red Rooster', struck by the rude swagger of Jagger's voice, tellingly she heard it not in the house but via the radio in a car. At home, classical music and folk predominated. "We weren't really involved in the pop thing at all at that time," recalled Paddy Bush. "We had an incredibly staunch approach towards traditional folk music."[8]

Dr Bush practiced Schubert, Beethoven and Chopin on the piano, interspersed with a smattering of the great American songbook of the Thirties and Forties, and he also played church organ and composed his own songs, diligently rather than with any great spark of inspiration. It was he who first showed his daughter the all important middle 'C' note on the instrument and encouraged her at first tentative, then rapidly improving, attempts at songwriting.

An exposure to classical music later informed her unorthodox song structures, which have rarely acknowledged the conventional patterns of most rock music. Fold into the mix her love of the more theatrical side of pop culture (a dash of Bowie, some Roxy, a little prog-rock) and an abiding love of folk music and there emerges at least a vague inkling of the direction from which she arrived at her unique musical style.

From her mother's heritage she discovered a direct line into the pure emotion and narrative instinct of Irish folk song, traditional Irish jigs, airs and standards like 'The Lark In The Morning' and 'She Moves Through The Fair'. There was nothing intellectual about this: it was pure instinct, as natural as breathing, and all the children picked up the baton. Jay drank up the heritage, loving the sense of layered story-telling and timelessness in the songs, and banged happily around with his folk band in the farm's Wash House. Paddy dived perhaps even deeper into the dark waters of traditional music. He played concertina in the local folk clubs for the English Morris Dancers, and also worked for the English Folk Dance and Song Society. It became "a way of life you can't stop," he said. "In my case, the folk tradition was constantly there."[9]

In time, Paddy became a fixture on the south London music scene, always popping up with a mandolin or guitar slung over his shoulder. Brian Bath, a local musician and later a member of the KT Bush Band, recalls first bumping into him around 1970 at a house party in Wood Hill, where all the hippies used to congregate. "I walked up the stairs one night and there was a guy standing there with a mandolin," says Bath. "I had my acoustic guitar with me and we started jamming. He said, 'Fancy coming back to my place?', so I hopped in his car and we went back to Wickham Farm. Upstairs there was a big room, like a library, with a coal fire, and we just sat there and jammed all night. I took my tape recorder and I've got a recording of some of it. I got on really well with Paddy. We'd meet once a month and jam, I always used to want him to come round and get involved. We used to have a really good time."

With his widely spaced eyes, easy smile and mass of tightly curled hair, Paddy was an amiable eccentric with a passion for old music. He became synonymous with all sorts of weird and wonderful instruments, from Pan pipes to the Strumento da Porco, which "looked like a sea crustacean", according to Bath, and which he built himself from plans that dated back to Egyptian times. He became fascinated by how things were made, where they came from, what odd sounds could be achieved. "Paddy was like the Mad Professor!" laughs Stewart Avon Arnold. "He reminded me of Catweazle, in the nicest possible way. Every time I went around to his house he'd have these new bells from Tibet, or gongs from some farm in the Outer Hebrides. Such an interesting character."

After unsuccessfully seeking an apprenticeship in harp-making he eventually won a place at the London School of Furniture, studying Music Instrument Technology between 1973 and 1976, later describing himself as "an artist of weirdness. . . . Making instruments with arms and legs, and out of very unorthodox materials."[10] The depth of his knowledge and his enthusiasm for the ancient and experimental has proved an enormous boon for his sister, first as a guide to discovering music, then later as both a general sounding board and a member of her core band of musicians. Naturally shy, never a man for drawing attention to himself, he beavered away industriously in her shadow for many years.

The Bush brothers' interest in traditional music coincided with the booming folk revival of the late Fifties and Sixties, and both Jay and Paddy owned impressive collections of UK and US music, which their sister would happily plough through on wet afternoons. Sometimes they would all travel together around Kent looking for traditional dances, and she recalls being introduced to a deep, varied pool of British music. The works of those two great English folklorists and Communist custodians Bert Lloyd and Ewan MacColl sat alongside "dirty sea shanties" and long, unwinding tragic tales like 'Tam Lin' and 'Lucy Wan', which in turn led to the phantasmagorical psychedelic folk of The Incredible String Band, whom they all revered, and Bob Dylan's lysergic poetry.

The old British folk songs often mined a subtly different seam from traditional Irish music, which was more concerned with matters of the spirit. Here, by contrast, was grittier fare: ancient myths and legends, tales of murder and madness, death and despair, infanticide and incest, women transforming into swans, the gender twists and fluid sexuality of songs like 'The Handsome Cabin Boy', old ballads so acute and vivid that to listen was almost to experience time travel. Folk music acts as a bridge between conscious and unconscious worlds, between the known and unknown, the stated and the implied, the guts and the imagination, the past and the present: there are disquieting narrative blips, daring flights of fancy, leaps in imagery and scant regard for temporal and spatial formalities. It is both vivid and deliciously mysterious.

With very few exceptions, Bush has never made what could be regarded as 'folk' music in the conventional sense, but the influence of its impact upon her runs deep in her writing. From her first album onwards we are introduced to strange characters, twisting storylines, and ghosts and spirits singing from beyond the grave. Deep, important connections between the living and the dead ring through 'Wuthering Heights', 'The Kick Inside', 'Houdini', 'Cloudbusting', 'Jig Of Life', 'How To Be Invisible', 'A Coral Room', 'Lake Tahoe' and many more.

This is not, however, the world of *Dungeons And Dragons* or even *The Lord Of The Rings*. "All those characters that she sings about, the fairies and goblins and witches, all that stuff *is* her world," says producer Nick Launay, who worked closely with her as engineer on *The Dreaming*. "I imagine as a little kid her room was full of that kind of stuff. That's what it's like working with her, you're entering into this wonderful world of fantasy."

This is a slight but crucial misreading. Bush's songs do indeed tap into other realms but they don't exist in a Tolkeinesque world of pure fantasy; they aren't peopled with strange beasts – goblins, unicorns and orcs. She once said her songs were "mostly about myths, spirits, that kind of thing.

Not fairies, stronger than that."[11] *Not fairies. Stronger than that*: there's a fine phrase to bear in mind. Her lyrics are about the things that drive, or repulse, or empower the human spirit. Not escapism, in fact, but its exact opposite. They're about using the magic of the imagination to open up as many avenues of real emotional and physical connection as possible. This was an alchemic freedom she found in folk – and later, through mime and dance. "Kate's subject matter for her lyrics has always been extraordinary," Jay once said, "which I think comes from an ability to empathise with life forms that is unusually sensitive."[12]

Traditional songs were also one of the few places in the Sixties where Bush would have heard convincing, complex representations of female sexual desire. Albums like Anne Briggs (perhaps the only female British singer with a claim to being even less attracted to the glare of publicity than Bush) and Bert Lloyd's *The Bird In The Bush* contained frank songs of lust and sensuality, such as 'The Wanton Seed' and 'The Bonny Black Hare':

> *"I felt her heart quiver and I knew what I'd done.*
> *Says I, 'Have you had enough of my old sporting gun?'*
> *Oh, the answer she gave me, her answer was, 'Nay,*
> *It's not often, young sportsman, that you come this way.*
> *But if your powder is good and your bullets play fair,*
> *Why don't you keeping firing at the bonny black hare?'"*

She wouldn't have found much of *that* sort of thing in the pop music of the time, though she would certainly have been exposed to similar urges via Jay's poetry. If Paddy was the music man, then working with words and images was Jay's true love. "Our lives were filled with the trappings of the Celtic Twilight, its poetry and its music," he said. "The Pre-Raphaelites and the turn of the century book illustrators were an obsession for me long before the fashion machine born in the Sixties plastered Beardsley all over Europe, the Brotherhood into every home."[13]

It's possible to detect a whiff of superiority in that statement, a tinge of artistic arrogance. Jay was a serious man, almost aggressively devoted to the power of ideas, the sacredness of Art with a capital A. Dismissive of the conventions of modern life, he dropped out of Cambridge to explore the lost teachings of the past, rummaging around in ancient mythology, outré philosophy, the Golden Age, spiritualism and mystical cul-de-sacs in an attempt to uncover some deep, atavistic truth. Very much an educated product of the liberal, progressive Sixties, he "was a super-hippy; he was old enough to be a *real* hippy," says David Jackson. "Paddy was younger brother hippy-in-training, and Kate was the baby sister. All hippies."

Attracted to everything from Greek mythology to Nordic folklore, he would scrawl the mouth of the devil on the farm's barn wall and add vivid poetic augmentations. He was wary, often didactic, and in the early part of Bush's professional career his input aggravated many people at EMI and several others creatively involved in her work. "There were tensions between me and Jay," admits Bob Mercer, the man who signed Bush to EMI in 1976. "He was a poet, and he and she were very, very close. Jay got very involved for a while and eventually I had to kind of lay the law down and have her keep him away from us."

These difficulties can be explained through a combination of Jay's strong, perhaps rather superior sense of his own artistic vision colliding with the ephemeral pop world (family motto: Kerching!), and his understandable protectiveness as an older brother. In truth, he was shy, and those who know him well lay claim to a much softer private side. He has been notably accessible and helpful to many Kate Bush fans throughout the years, and a bulwark of love and support to his sister. "What worries me is that sometimes Jay is portrayed as a Svengali who is black and evil," said Bush. "And he's not at all. He's very beautiful and sensitive and I love him very much."[14]

Jay and some compatible souls founded Salatticum Poets (derived from a Latin term for 'wit'), through which he distributed pamphlets of their work, organised readings and met with his friends to debate intensely the pressing artistic matters of the day. Brian Bath recalls some *ad hoc* musical performances where he and Paddy improvised behind a screen at readings, often as far afield as Hastings, involving Jay and other like-minded poets such as Tony Buzan and Jeremy Cartland. "Different," he says diplomatically. "Not really my cup of tea, but it was good."

He published slim books of his poems *The Creation Edda: A Poem* in 1970, and *Control: A Translation* in 1974, while his work has appeared in *The Poetry Review, Tracks, Samphire, The Sceptre Press, Catholic Education Today, Poets' Workshop Pamphlet*, and has been heard on BBC Radio 3 and BBC Radio London. He self-published his novel, *The Cellar Gang*, in 2005. When the Bush family formed their company, Novercia Limited, in

1976, Jay stated his occupation as 'writer'. How he managed to actually earn a living from it was less clear.

Though he too loved music deeply, his over-riding significance in terms of Bush's career was becoming her unofficial tutor in the deep stuff, opening many doors into the wide world of ideas. His very existence had a huge influence on her writing, her use of words, and her exposure to poetry, philosophy and spiritual doctrine, many of them deeply esoteric – and erotic. Some of his work still resides in the British Museum's pornography collection.

> *"She straddles Hekla's mouth,*
> *he sucks the boiling mound:*
> *copulation brings screams,*
> *the volcano dribbles" ['The Creation Edda']*

Alongside the unabashed folk songs and "dirty sea shanties", Jay's poetry indicated to the young Bush that expressing explicit desire was a legitimate artistic endeavour; certainly nothing of which to be ashamed. From early on, her songs were full of unambiguous sexuality. The unreleased 'The Craft Of Life', recorded at home in 1976, is a prime example, positively revelling in the imagery of "silvers in our dark hair" and the bed sheets "soaked by your tiny fish."*

It's admirably forthright, if rather clumsy. Later she would find more subtle ways of expressing sensuality, but 'The Craft Of Life' is by no means the sole example of such directness. Around the same time, Bush and Jay collaborated on 'Before The Fall' (sometimes known as 'Organic Acid'), a story poem he had written and which he narrated, interspersed with Kate's chorus melody and piano backing. With its references to "mutual masturbation", "cunt" and "wet hair", it is explicit, eroticised poetry – and remains one of the odder examples in the pantheon of brother-sister collaborations.

It was not a prudish family. An understanding of one's own sexual urges was simply viewed as another means of breaking free from chains of self-consciousness, of becoming more alive to one's own true nature. The title of 'Sat In Your Lap', after all, suggests the possibility of experiencing enlightenment through sex. Ian Bairnson, who played guitar on the

---

* Thirty years later, she was still using fish to convey an erotic charge, in 'Mrs Bartolozzi'.

majority of *The Kick Inside*, recalls Bush showing her father the newly written words to 'L'Amour Looks Something Like You' during the album sessions in 1977. "There were certain lines that jumped out at you," he says. "I remember her dad came in, he would stop by, and she had just completed the lyric to 'L'Amour Looks Something Like You'. She said, 'Oh yeah, here's dad. Look, I've got these lyrics I've been working on', and she gave him the lyrics. That's the song with the line about "sticky love inside", but he didn't bat an eyelid. He was very relaxed, 'Yeah, that's really good!'"

★ ★ ★

Where did she come from? It's possible to pick up direct echoes of Jay's stylistic influence in her work, but Bush was equally as inspired by the big picture, his utter immersion in art and his seeming rejection of the conventional world. In many ways Jay's pursuits legitimised her own ambitions. Her crucial skill was an innately populist instinct, harnessing some of the energy of her brother's restless intellectual curiosity and giving it a clear purpose and an accessible edge.

Who else could have smuggled Joseph Campbell, Wilhelm Reich and G.I. Gurdjieff into the charts? Just after Bush became famous some of the press latched onto her interest in Gurdjieff in particular, the Greek-Armenian Sufi mystic and spiritual teacher who died in 1949 and whom she mentioned – perhaps unadvisedly – a number of times in interviews and namechecked on the first album as an inspiration. She was almost certainly introduced to him through Jay, who has often sported a suspiciously extravagant moustache, *a la* Gurdjieff.

It's not hard to see and hear threads of Gurdjieff's broad – and, to non-adherents, woolly and unconvincing – belief system popping up in Bush's work. Music and movement ("the sacred dance") were two of his favoured methods of imparting his philosophy but, perhaps more significantly, one of his central tenets was the belief that mankind lives in an almost automatonic state of permanent 'waking sleep'. He desired that people shake themselves out of their torpor to experience life more fully, to truly connect with their own consciousness and remake the world through their own subjective experience. The ultimate aim of existence is the full development of one's potential, to fuse the body, the mind and the emotions in what was later termed 'The Fourth Way'.

This was clearly inspirational to the young Bush, as she quite specifically relayed in 'Them Heavy People', an uncommonly direct thank you to all the teachers who "rolled the ball" of knowledge and wisdom her way and forced her to look deeper, who "read me Gurdjieff and Jesu" and showed her the "heaven inside."

Yet the idea that she was pursuing one dedicated path towards enlightenment seems overly simplistic. There was always much more going on than that, and so it remains. For many years, Stewart Avon Arnold has enjoyed intense conversations with Bush about a range of spiritual and philosophical matters. "We talk about different philosophies on the phone for hours," says Arnold. "She mentions karma a lot, and reincarnation, and witchcraft and paganism and Buddhism. We always end up in these conversations about life in general and spiritual life in particular. Both of us have a fascination about spiritual life; we used to question each other and we still do. She'll phone me and say, 'What do you think about this, Stewart?' It always comes round to the spiritual questions in life, Man's place on the planet and what we're doing to it. The other thing that I talk about with Kate is End of Days. Not Revelation, because neither of us believe in the Bible as such, but in terms of what Nostradamus was saying about 2012. The Hopi Indians, too. We're in for a global meltdown of some kind, the planet will change drastically in the next 10, 15 years. That's something that Kate and I talk about quite a lot."

In her songs, videos and interviews it is possible to discern a clear love of ritual and to pick up on influences as diverse as Vedic, Sufism, Catholicism, Krishna, Buddhism, paganism, karma, reincarnation, astrology. It's an entirely bespoke, self-sufficient search for meaning – and one in which the search is at least as important as the meaning – and a clear continuation of a learning process that began at Wickham Farm. As often as not these influences filter into the music at a subconscious level. Most religious stories, spiritual philosophies and classical myths can be interpreted in a variety of ways. Their influence constantly bubbles away beneath the surface with shifting emphasis, to be called up and used at any time, often in a highly impressionistic manner.

As a girl significantly younger than her two male siblings, naturally Bush had her own private interests. Her brothers may have drawn her into a whole world of art, philosophy and music, held her hand as she ambled through it and pointed out notable landmarks, but she wandered off and took what she needed from a wide spectrum of sources. In *Cathy*, John Carder Bush notes at the foot of one image: "Splashed by the obsessions of her brothers she was masking her own secret conclusions." Perfectly expressed. Like any decent artist, she has a knack for dipping into a subject, finding out what interests her about it and incorporating elements of it – sometimes heavily disguised, sometimes more obviously – into her work. "All the stimulus comes rushing in and I pack it away in the back, and it will come out maybe a couple of years later," she said.[15]

In the earliest years of this holistic approach to creation, everything became fodder for her music. Books – Kurt Vonnegut, John Wyndham, Oscar Wilde, though *not* Emily Brontë – dance, 'heavy' spiritual ideas, disposable TV shows, the pre-Raphaelite art of John Millais, snatches of conversation, her friends, the sea, the sky. She loved Billie Holiday, Judy Garland, Gene Kelly, the whole business of show, and although it was an academic house, television was also a major influence. "I was always in front of the television instead of doing my homework," she said. "I wasn't off reading books, I was watching television, and cinema."[16]

From television songs such as 'Wuthering Heights' and 'Delius (Song Of Summer)' arrived; from film, the inspirations are multitudinous: 'The Infant Kiss' (*The Innocents*), 'Hounds Of Love' (*Night Of The Demon*), 'The Wedding List' (*La Mariée Etait En Noir*), 'Get Out Of My House' (*The Shining*), Michael Powell's *The Red Shoes* and many, many more. She had a real knack for responding to visual stimulus, much more frequently, in fact, than to the written word.

All the things she loved and absorbed as a child poured into her songs, and the songs in turn inspired her own ideas for film, dance routines, striking photographic images. Bush has the power of *conversion*. "You eat what you steal, digest it and it becomes part of you."[17]

In the end, it comes from her gut as much as her head. There is real beauty in the fact that she has never distinguished between high and low brow. Bush has always displayed a complete absence of preciousness about the things she loves and which have inspired her: it could be *Pinocchio*, it could be Wilhelm Reich; it could be a camp old horror flick or *Ulysses* by James Joyce. She treats them all equally, because at heart her music has always been about what triggers her emotionally rather than intellectually. She had no compunction, for instance, about admitting that she had no idea who Doris Lessing or Angela Carter are. Perhaps the most persistent error certain fans and critics make about her is that she is somehow an *academic* or difficult songwriter, forever cramming her music with ancient mythological codes or wrestling with weighty literary references. In fact, one of the great things about her music is that her small, silly thoughts – "That cloud looks like Ireland!" – are equally as compelling as her profound ones. Her music, especially as time has passed, is about serving the mood of the emotion that first inspired her. There's nothing consciously 'clever' about the best of it.

It is certainly possible, therefore, to get too high-falutin' and precious about her childhood, to get lost in the Gurdjieff and forget the Alec Guinness, as it were. There was a great deal of laughter at Wickham Farm, much fun, silliness and uncomplicated joy. What is of enduring significance, more than any single mode of influence, is the fact that she was permitted her secret, internal life, developing from an early age an artistic vision, a growing idea of herself as being apart. Perhaps her biggest single inspiration was simply the notion, validated by Jay and Paddy and endorsed by her parents, that she really could spend her life among words and music, expressing herself as an artist.

What you can't actually *see* in the *Cathy* photographs but which is equally clearly on view is the space her home environment afforded her to explore who she was and wanted to be. A tangible atmosphere of creativity and validation seeps through the lens: nobody here was going to mock her ideas, precious though they may have been, or laugh at her aspirations, or tell her what she could or couldn't be. From a young age she was allowed and indeed encouraged to poeticise her life, to create a world all of her own. Her family seemed to have made some kind of deep, unspoken creative pact with her long before the likes of David Gilmour came on the scene. Already they were dedicated to her artistic endeavour in some indistinct but quietly profound way. Indulged? Probably. But also liberated.

2

Somewhere In Between

THERE are two distinct sides to Bush's childhood. "Before I was going to school, before I was reading, I was singing along to songs, to traditional music," she once said. "And in a way I think it got my soul before the education even got near me. I think really when you are that young. . . . The sparks of what you really want to do are there some-where."[1]

Allowed to roam free at home, at school she was forced to keep herself and her imagination rather more buttoned up, holding her creative side in check. It created a tension that became more pronounced as her school years progressed and later led her to describe the experience in unusually blunt terms. "I was unhappy at school and couldn't wait to leave," she said.[2] "I couldn't express myself in the whole system."[3]

Until the summer of 1969 Bush attended St Joseph's Convent Prepara-tory School on Woolwich Road, Abbey Wood, after which she sat her 11-plus exam and moved up to St Joseph's Convent Grammar, on the same site, where she stayed until early 1976. There was nothing particu-larly remarkable about Catherine Bush the schoolgirl. Most of the omens and portents have been spied retrospectively, spotted only through the gift of hindsight.

When she appeared, as a rank and file third former, in the school's 1972 production of Gian Carlo Menotti's one-act opera, the Christmas parable *Amahl & The Night Visitors*, she was given a bit part as a shepherd-ess. Those who saw it recall that the lead girl stole the show, with her "fantastic operatic voice," according to Bush's school friend Shealla Mubi. "She was the star, a bit of a diva." By comparison, Bush's performance made a minimal impression. Only brief mention was made of her in the review in the school magazine, which noted the 'entrance of the shepherds and shepherdesses, members of the Senior and First and Second year Choirs, who tripped in all rosy-cheeked and healthy-looking, bringing gifts for the kings. Two of these, Catherine Bush and Sarah Brennan, later gave a short dance in honour of the kings, which was both pastorally graceful and imaginative.'

It's safe to say that nobody at St Joseph's saw 'Wuthering Heights' hovering on the horizon, or guessed at the "wiley, windy moors" lurking beneath her placid disposition. When they were later revealed it was a colossal shock to the school's collective system. "After we left school [my friends and I] all kept in touch," says Bush's school friend Concepta Nolan-Long. "I can remember them contacting me and saying, 'We need to listen to the radio because Catherine is going to be on.' We honestly thought it would be something classical, and we were absolutely bowled over when we heard 'Wuthering Heights'. Can you imagine!"

"She was a very likeable, quiet personality," recalls Mubi. "These huge big eyes, huge dimples. My sister always talked about Kate even before she became famous: 'Oh, I love Kate! Those eyes! She's so sweet, so cute, like a little elf!' The way she smiled, her face just lit up, that's something I always remember. She was a very, very nice girl. Very nice in a warm way."

It's a description echoed by many. Most friends and acquaintances recall a pretty girl, self-contained, bright, overwhelmingly *nice*. "My only memories are of someone quiet who certainly didn't stand out as someone destined to be a rock star," recalls classmate Jane Wilkinson. "Her dark hair was usually covering her eyes, she was shy and unassuming." However, although she is remembered as a pleasant, studious girl, outwardly calm and accommodating, her time at school was inwardly mutinous and ultimately defining. It was largely characterised by a process of, at best, marking time and, at worst, feeling acutely inhibited, overtaken by a sense of being steered down a road she didn't wish to travel.

★　★　★

A short hop on the 96 bus from Wickham Farm, or more often a ride in Dr Bush's car, St Joseph's stood at the top of the hill at Abbey Wood. An academically selective convent school, it was run by nuns with the help of lay staff, also mostly women, with a small but significant male presence. Other than the fact that the convent building symbolically tied together the lower and upper schools, each school was self-contained, with separate teaching blocks and playgrounds.

The main body of the grammar school was Victorian, smelling vividly of polished wood and scrubbed righteousness, its corners cast in long, cool shadow. Prior to Bush's arrival a modern block had recently been added, three stories high, and with it came six new classrooms, an assembly hall and a new entrance. Despite these jarring additions the school maintained an element of mystique and mystery: secret doors that only the nuns could use connected the two school premises, "a bit like going through the looking glass, or down a rabbit hole," according to Nolan-Long.

Surrounded by woods, with its own hockey pitch and tennis courts, the spruce, ordered environment was a reminder of the school's "expectation of the standard to which you should aspire," says Nolan-Long. "You should have nice things around you and have the best. There was a sense of a beautiful atmosphere and things being kept really nicely. There were gardeners, lots of green and grass, very well tended. I remember [head teacher] Sister Margaret saying, 'Whatever you do you should do it to the best of your ability.'" Whatever else may have frustrated her about the school, it's an ethos Bush has continually held onto, even if the means and methodology of her execution transpired to be rather more idiosyncratic than most.

St Joseph's was certainly highly regarded locally, a sought after school for middle-class families and an aspirational one for less monied children smart enough to win scholarships. 'A good education for young ladies' was the mantra. Each year's intake was split into two classes, divided alphabetically with some aptitude streaming later on. There was a reasonably diverse social mix from all over South-east London, from the plusher locales to the rather more rough and ready Thamesmead estate. Although the school roll was predominantly white and Catholic, and there were prayers before and after each lesson and Mass on St Joseph's day, it did not necessarily conform to the stereotype of a Catholic girls school. There was a smattering of Asian and black pupils, as well as some non-Catholics who were attracted by its single-sex ethos, secure environment and high educational standards.

"The nuns who taught us at St Joseph's were proto-feminists, they were not *Sound Of Music* nuns," says Nolan-Long. "Nuns are always strict, but there were no beatings or anything like that. You were spoken to in terms of 'letting people down'. They were looking for an expected level of behaviour and they were generally met." There was very little misbehaviour and discipline was generally self-regulated. "It was a school that was very strict, you had to obey the rules, down to the hat you had to wear, the colour of your socks; inside and outside shoes," says Nina Brown, also in Bush's year. "We got on with our school work. It wasn't a very sociable time for any of us. If anyone was slightly different they certainly could not have shown it off at that school." During Bush's time, the names of transgressors were read out at assembly by the head teacher, first Sister Elizabeth, later Sister Margaret.

Shealla Mubi remembers the school – not without affection – as "a weird environment. I had friends from other schools and I would tell them about things we did that I thought were normal, and they would laugh." It was not unknown for the nuns to lift up the girls' skirts to check that they were wearing their regulation red knickers. There were different sports kits for hockey, tennis and netball, and the uniform – grey skirt, white blouse, maroon jumper and tie – was strictly enforced: no jewellery, no short skirts, no make-up, no heels. The school song, 'Potius Mori Quam Foedari' ('Death Before Dishonour') portrayed the girls from St Joseph's going out into the world and fighting to retain their honour against the advances of rapacious and dishonourable men: 'Honour and purity', they sang, 'Shall guard our way!' The girls rather liked it.

"Within the school, the worst thing you could do was behave in an unladylike manner, that brought a very stern rebuke," says Nolan-Long. "I'm sure the nuns felt it was their mission to educate young women so they would be able to function in society." Preparing the pupils for a sexually fulfilling adult life wasn't high up on the agenda: there was some furtive talk about placing telephone directories on one's lap before letting a boy near you, and some hearty advice about the way to a man's heart being through his stomach. For Bush, who harboured a fascination with all things masculine from a young age, this kind of attitude, combined with the lack of male company at school, was less than inspiring.

More promising, at least in theory, was the fact that music was an integral part of the curriculum. Every pupil had to learn an instrument, and individual tuition was augmented by a choir, an orchestra, lots of hymn-singing and frequent shows. The principal music teacher, Miss Slade, was an eccentric but rather stolid presence. She was, recalls Mubi, "quite powerful in the school. A single woman, highly strung, a bit manic, almost." "Oh God, talk about a traditional music teacher," adds Nolan-Long. "The thing I remember about her is that she used to *attack* the piano. Not arty-farty at all." According to another pupil, Oonagh McCormack, "when she worked she did it with gusto!"

Catherine Bush, however, was already beyond her reach, trying to negotiate a less rigidly defined path. Even before she started at primary school she was enchanted by music, and had an ingrained sense of it being something extraordinary that held transformative powers. Although she periodically enjoyed studying music at St Joseph's, the school never added to the bubbling sense of magic cultivated by her family at Wickham Farm. Indeed, the general perception of music as a rather dull duty seemed directly at odds with the "sparks" of her ad hoc home education. But she tried. She sang in the choir, competently if without any great acclaim, and took up the violin in the orchestra. "I played violin in the school orchestra as well, and she was always better than me," says Connie Nolan-Long. "Kate was a good girl, she would always practise."

She did indeed fulfil her obligations, 20 minutes practise a day, prodded along by private lessons, but she chafed against the formality of the tuition. Brian Bath recalls that often he would be upstairs at Wickham Farm playing music with Paddy and "Kate used to pop in: 'Paddy, I've got a violin lesson and I don't want to go!' 'OK, hide behind the sofa, we won't tell anyone!' She was only about 12." In 1976, not long after leaving school, she wrote 'Violin', later recorded on *Never For Ever*. It's a spirited reclamation of that most virile of instruments, dragging it "out of the realm of the orchestra" and back to the "Banshees", the female spirit of Irish mythology who traditionally appeared as an omen of death from the Otherworld. The implication is clear. Here is both a rejection of the fettered formality that made school so stifling for her, and also an unambiguous declaration of where her loyalties have always lain when it comes to music: gut feeling over prissy technique every time. Like music, dancing – which she came to love – was little more than a perfunctory sideline as taught at St Joseph's. "I didn't really get on with the dance teacher at school," she later said.[4] Simply *doing* these things wasn't enough; they had to mean something, touch her in some way.

She later claimed, "I think kids learn more from their parents than their teachers."[5] While in Bush's case this is undeniable, a few tutors challenged that assumption and did their utmost to make learning fresh and inspiring. The Religious Education teacher, Luke Connaughton, was a highly regarded Catholic journalist and writer who composed many hymns, often pseudonymously, and displayed a more spiritual, searching take on music 'coming from within', a notion which would have appealed to Bush.

The English teacher Mrs Prime, née Miss Helena Organ, was a particular stand-out for the girls. She loved to animate her lessons by reading aloud from texts like Chaucer's *Prologue* in order to make the characters live and breathe. She was very much one for acting out the words, plunging into the world described in the text; a very Bushian approach. "She was amazing," says Mubi. "If anybody ever wants to have a love of literature they should have a teacher like her. She encouraged you to see the characters come alive. If she read you any passage of a book you wanted to go and read that book. She was the kind of person who instilled life into the subject."

What most of the pupils didn't know was that their English teacher was embroiled in a private tale of emotional betrayal and political intrigue worthy of any future Kate Bush song. Between 1969 and their divorce in 1974, covering almost all of Bush's secondary school career, she was the first wife of Geoffrey Prime, one of Britain's most notorious spies, who for many years passed on state secrets to the Soviet Union and who was sentenced to 38 years in prison in 1982 for espionage and sexual offences against children. Little wonder the English teacher at St Joseph's sought to fully disappear into a world of books.

Bush later recalled a fondness for her English classes, and felt that they helped her find new ways to express herself, but Mrs Prime's unconventional, inspirational brand of teaching was the exception to the rule. Though Nolan-Long claims that "independent thought was very much prized, and so was creative endeavour," most other former pupils recall a safe, rigorous, reasonably kind but not terribly stimulating atmosphere at St Joseph's. Mubi describes the general class routine as "regimented. For example, you couldn't write your own notes into your book. The teacher would dictate everything, and in that environment there's not that much discussion. We all got good grades, but some who wanted to experience a more discussion-orientated environment felt constricted."

All in all, it certainly did little to stimulate Bush who, feeling bored and patronised, retreated. "I found [school] wasn't helping me," she said. "I became introvert. I guess it was the teachers' system, the way they react to pupils, and I wasn't quite responsive to that."[6] In fairness, this wasn't entirely attributable to anything specific at St Joseph's, but rather a deeper symptom of the institutionalised modes of learning that practically all schools employed. An individualist by nature *and* nurture, she didn't want to be told what to read, or handed information by rote. It was the precise opposite of the kind of free-spirited and sometimes eccentric education she was receiving at home, where opinionated discussion was always encouraged and available, liberal sensibilities abounded and there were definitely no set-texts.

The feeling that school life was pale and uninteresting in comparison to her other life became entrenched as she moved through the years. It was exacerbated by the social aspect, the traditional trial by fire of childhood and adolescence. Years later, she recalled many moments of sadness, acts of cruelty, sarcastic put-downs, brashness and bragging, the kind of ruthless social engineering in which teenage girls in particular excel. "My friends sometimes used to ignore me completely, and that would really upset me badly," she later recalled.[7] It was nothing unusual, and indeed St Joseph's Grammar School was a relatively genteel environment in comparison to the roughhouse atmosphere of many comprehensives in the Seventies. There was very little physical intimidation, although Bush later recalled being bullied and Connie Nolan-Long remembers a "very nasty" isolated incident where "some older girls picked on a group of younger girls . . . Kate might have been [a victim] of that."

Academically "very bright, noticeably so" and "privileged; Kate never had a problem, she always had the right kit for everything,"[8] it's not diffi-cult to imagine how some pupils might have regarded her as a too-pretty goody-two-shoes and acted accordingly. She found it all a little hard to comprehend after Wickham Farm, where kindness and courtesy were the norm, sarcasm was non-existent and her siblings protected her. She felt older than both her years and her peers and regarded herself as thinking too deeply about things, fascinated by matters of the spirit and the soul.

But although she often felt lonely, alienated and emotionally cut adrift, she was by no means physically alone, nor was she the kind of crushingly shy girl that has sometimes been portrayed. Friends recall a quiet con-fidence, a highly developed sense of humour, a love of silliness – she adored *Monty Python* – an infectious giggle, all married to a kind of serene detachment. "Thinking, dreaming, hoping, waiting patiently, Cathy was never hurried," recalled Jay.[9] Ultimately, school probably toughened her up, rubbed off a few of her more idealistic edges.

"She wasn't shy," says Nolan-Long "If she had something to say she would say it, but I always got the impression she'd think, 'Well, somebody else has said that, I don't need to make a noise about it.' She would merge into the background. She was always a pretty girl, but she was quite content to let other people speak unless she had something to say."

Bush was neither at the centre nor adrift on the outskirts. At primary school she'd had good friends such as Janet Willmot, but at nine she became tight with Lisa Bowyer – later Bradley – with whom she remains extremely close; Bradley still runs her fan club today, and has done so since 1978. She was gregarious enough for both of them, and to an extent Bush sheltered in her shadow. "Kate and Lisa were very close, and still are, and if anybody had said to me that one of them was going to be a rock star I'd have put my money on Lisa, absolutely," says Nolan-Long. "She was the extrovert of the pair."

Aside from Lisa she had her small social group, and there was a blurring of lines between home and school. Friends loved coming to the farm, relishing its sense of space and mystery, its offer of escape: there were parties around the swimming pool, Guy Fawkes Night fun with fireworks, the odd confidence shared in the fields about crushes: always older boys, often elusive. Bush had her own den, filled with books, records, posters, dressing up clothes, an old sofa and cushions. It was a private spot, cut off from the rest of the house, a place for her and her friends to talk, play music, read magazines and indulge in typical teenage experiments: séances, ghost stories, role-playing. In the barn they would secretly smoke, scribble poems on the ancient walls, sing and wait for their futures to unfold.

Outside of home and school, she would meet friends in the We Anchor In Hope pub in Welling or at St Lawrence's Youth Club, which promised a heady mix of music and ping pong. Physically, she was already instantly recognisable as Kate Bush, pop star. She looked remarkably similar to the way she appeared throughout the early years of her career: tiny, slim, pretty, her face framed by long, auburn hair, not so much styled as attractively *arrived at*. Not hugely interested in clothes, she wore jeans, jumpers, cheesecloth shirts, smocks, with the occasional leaning towards the weekend hippie – black velvet capes, oversized thrift-store jackets – and the odd lurch into flowing dresses and gaudy, incongruous high heels, bought with a giggle from Ravels in Lewisham. Even as an adolescent there was something innately organic and essentially earthy about her.

Only Lisa really gained her trust. As became characteristic in her life post-'Wuthering Heights', where she quickly learned to adopt a battened-down public façade in order to protect herself from media intrusion and personal invasion, she hid her true self from view at St Joseph's. It seems astonishing that practically no one at school – that most febrile of arenas for boasting, bragging and social one-upmanship – was made aware of her recording at David Gilmour's house in 1973, nor her subsequent session at AIR studios in 1975, both of which occurred while she still trotting off to Abbey Wood in her regulation red knickers.

Lisa would have known, but no one else at school did. Partly it was plain good manners – none of the Bush clan was predisposed to making a big noise about themselves – and partly it was because she didn't want to "alienate" herself by seeming too different or precocious.[10] A self-conscious fear of failure, too, is not to be discounted. Even today, all the hard work is done out of view. "She doesn't do work in progress, I don't think, because, well, it's work in progress," says Tony Wadsworth, her CEO at EMI between 1998 and 2008. "She's so proud of her work that she wants people to hear it in the best possible setting." But mostly it signified an ingrained natural instinct to keep her most precious pursuits to herself. From early on she displayed an innate understanding of the value of secrecy, of invisibility. In a rare moment of true candour she once admitted: "The real me . . . no one will ever see that. There is part of me I will always keep to myself."[11] She came early to the realisation that the finished article is all she wants us to see of her music; the journey leading up to it is too personal, too exposed.

As a result, at school she stayed close to the shadows. She was nobody's idea of superstar material. "I wasn't aware of anything special about her," says Nina Brown, and although everybody knew she played music – another former pupil, Chrissie Ashley, recalls that she was "always in the music room with Miss Slade" – nobody had any real inkling about the depth of her talent, nor caught a glimpse of the ambition whirring away beneath the surface.

"She was not the kind of person to broadcast what she doing at all," says Shealla Mubi. "Lisa might have been more aware of her ambitions, but as a topic of discussion in the common room, or in class, never. I suppose because her music was so personal, she wouldn't say, 'Listen here, chaps, I'm going to try out this song.' It wasn't like that. I'd be lying if I said I thought she would get seriously into music. Kate wasn't part of that 'serious' musician scene. I don't think the school was even aware that she was writing songs and trying to get into music. I can understand that. There were so many depths that she kept hidden, because the school would perhaps not have given her room for that to be expressed. There was really no arena for that."

★ ★ ★

The greatest impression she made on the collective school consciousness was through her writing. Between Form I and III she had several poems published in the school magazine. It did not go unnoticed. "The magazine was important, and not everyone who put work in had it chosen," says Nolan-Long. "It was quite an honour."

The handful of published poems fall into two distinct categories: introspective examinations of her own private nature, and more descriptive narratives primarily focusing on death and religion, both perfectly natural areas for teens (and pre-teens: she was only 11 when the first, 'The Crucifixion', was published) to feel compelled to explore. Some of the connections to life at Wickham Farm are obvious. One of her earliest poems was called 'Blind Joe Death', published in the school magazine when she was in Form III and clearly inspired by the first John Fahey album of the same name, no doubt snapped up by one of her brothers when it was reissued (twice) in either 1964 or 1967. 'Epitaph For A Rodent', meanwhile, sounds suspiciously like a terribly solemn lament for a deceased hamster.

'You' is more directly personal, an acknowledgement of her dual nature, addressing her public and private selves and the conflict of expressing her true feelings in an unforgiving environment. "Yet inside you there may be great feelings / Of beauty and love fighting to appear. . . . A laugh, a jeer / The feelings are trapped and you / You – disappear."

Her poems are the first tangible public evidence of the overpowering excess of emotion that, hidden away, characterised her private childhood, later described in an unreleased song, 'Frightened Eyes', as "latent hysteria". In 'I Have Seen Him' this duality is even more candidly expressed:

"I have noticed him seven times or more
But he has not seen me.
He may have seen a girl called by
My name –
But neither he, nor anyone else will
Ever really see ME."

The other prevalent strand in these poems is a dramatic channelling and fusing of the stories, dark fables and endlessly fascinating characters who crop up in old folk songs and classical myths, with a particular fixation on death. 'The Crucifixion', 'Death', 'Blind Joe Death' and 'Epitaph For A Rodent' all confront mortality, with some striking imagery: "Silence ceases and murmurs gather quickly, like the grabbing of a hand." "The blood red sun sinks into the skull of a dead man." Together, the lines recall the end of 'The Dreaming': "See the sun set in the hand of the man."

Jay's influence is clear, but this is a very distinct voice. Not yet fully formed, sometimes precious, over-ripe and clumsy, but impressive nonetheless. What was notable to all was the sheer quality of her writing, her grasp of the form, the ability and self-confidence in her expression, so at odds with the almost painful sensitivity of the words. The earliest of her songs, and even many of the tracks on *The Kick Inside*, are very much a continuation of the themes of these early poems, though stripped of much of the youthful morbidity. We hear the secret identity and the deep longings of a young girl growing into adulthood. There are many covert assignations, shared moments, fears about going "too deep", huge sweeps of emotion and, above all, the difficulty of truly seeing, of connecting with the real person, which has remained threaded throughout her work. In 'Sunsi', one of her earliest recorded songs, never officially released, she sings, "You appear so many ways."

The poems stopped appearing in the school magazine almost as soon as her musical vision began developing. She had an epiphany on discovering that the piano offered a more attractive, fluid outlet for her words than plain paper. She had pawed happily at the mice-riddled church organ that lived in the barn, but when her father showed her the rudiments of piano structure aged 11 or 12, and when she discovered it had a logic to it that she understood and embraced, she felt a profound sense of homecoming, a direct outlet for the expression of her private self. "It's the only thing that I can do where I can really let myself go," she said. "It gives me great comfort, whenever I'm at the piano, because for the few times that it happens I feel like I'm part of something."[12]

While the violin had symbolised the restrictions of the school's dedication to learning by rote – what was the point of music if it didn't allow you to be free? – the piano was a front door into the inner life she had already glimpsed through music, books, films, dance and television. "The piano was a way of exploring music in dimensions diametrically opposite to what the violin must have represented to her," said Paddy Bush. "Escapism, pure escapism! You know, the command would be, 'Go and practice that violin, Kate', but the piano came out instead. I think perhaps we Bushes are a bit like that."[13]

And that was how it started. She began writing voraciously, reams and reams of songs, utterly infatuated with her emerging gift. It was a "release. I found something that I don't think I've ever really found since when I first started writing songs; that I could actually create something out of nothing. It was a very special discovery."[14] There was an immediate and significant epiphany: this was another world. There were no limits beyond those of her own imagination.

As soon as she became serious about setting her poems to piano, her family afforded her the space and silence to develop at her own pace. She was given that essential artistic privilege from an early age. "To cultivate music you have to spend a lot of time by yourself," said Paddy Bush. "When there's a family all in one house and you're getting your music together, normally the others close the door and try to keep the sound out. When Kate began working on the piano, she'd go and lock herself away and wind up spending five or six hours, seven days a week, just playing the piano."[15]

It was obvious to the whole family that Bush was musically precocious in a manner that went beyond both her father and her brothers' talents. "There's a world of difference between my own plodding compositions and Kate's fusion of gifts," said Dr Bush modestly. "She has 'it' and I don't."[16] At first this 'fusion' – absolutely the right word for what Bush does – was inexact and unbalanced. She had a clear instinct for composition, though not for performance. Indeed, those who sang with her in the school choir were not terribly impressed with her voice; she sang in tune, but she lacked – oddly, considering her later style – a clear top end. One friend even likened it to a foghorn. "When I first started my voice was terrible," Bush said. "But the voice is an instrument and the only way to improve it is to practise."[17]

And improve she did, through dedicated rehearsal. Her parents were encouraging without being pushy. Her father in particular would listen attentively when she sought him out to play him a new song, but he did not go knocking on her door. She sailed on the strength of her own determination. "We simply helped her to get her imagination working," said Dr Bush. "Her songs seemed to write themselves – whole stanzas in her head at a time – while I struggle to put one word after the next."[18]

Given time and space to develop, Bush by the age of 14 had amassed an impressive catalogue of songs which she recorded in batches on her father's AKAI tape machine. Impressed with the mounting evidence, the family decided to seek the advice of Ricky Hopper, a friend of Jay's from his days at Cambridge University who was now working as a record plugger.

With his long blond hair and palpable music biz aura, it was Hopper who really made the initial inroads on her behalf. Unicorn, a progressive rock band signed to Transatlantic Records, would often bump into him on the lower rungs of the industry ladder. Bass player Pat Martin recalls Hopper frequently beating the drum on Bush's behalf. "Ricky was a really nice guy who I think never gets his dues, because he was always banging on about her," says Martin. "First of all, he said that her brother kept trying to get him to listen to her, and I got the impression he was a bit worried that she might not be very good and it would be a bit embarrassing. Eventually, he went round there and listened to some tapes of her playing the piano and singing. He just seemed really impressed with her, I think he liked her innocence. He was always trying to get people to listen to her."

It was Hopper who hawked her first, painfully lo-fi recorded efforts around all the major music publishers and record companies. For a period of time there was a belief that Bush, already a prodigious writer but not yet a truly assured singer nor – it seemed even then – naturally inclined to the limelight, might become a composer rather than a performer. In a sense, that's how it has eventually turned out. However, the manner in which her songs were presented to the industry – she had up to 100 of them distributed over a number of cassettes, around 30 on each, all featuring just piano and vocal – alongside her obvious rawness meant it would have taken no small amount of dedication to spot a distinctive talent. There were no takers.

"You wouldn't be able to hear a thing, just this little girl going 'yaaaaa yaaa' for hours on end," she later said of the tapes. "[The songs] weren't that good. I could sing in key but there was nothing there. It was an awful noise . . . terrible. My tunes were more morbid and negative . . . too heavy. You're younger and you get into murders. . . ."[19]

She was being overly hard on herself. Certainly, the handful of songs dating from this period that exist in bootleg form are far more than mere curios. Brian Bath, who had been in a number of bands since the late Sixties and whose group, Conkers, had their own record deal, remembers hearing her compositions for the first time. "One day Paddy said, 'Kate's got lots of songs. Would you like to come around and have a listen, bring your guitar and play along?'" recalls Bath. "She played all these really strange chords, I couldn't fathom it out. They were really odd songs, but she was great. She would have been about 14 or 15. I sat and worked with her a little bit, but I felt I couldn't really add anything. I went away from there and thought, 'God, I've got so much more to learn.' She was brilliant just on her own, she sounded fabulous."

At the very least, the songs announced a bold and unusual artistic voice, filled with a strange, seductive poetry. 'Eddie The Queen', aka 'The Gay Farewell', has a hauntingly sad melody, a song of homosexual love that looks forward to 'Kashka From Baghdad', while 'Something Like A Song', with its ululating siren call – "Oohoo, ahoo, oohoo, ahoo, oohoo, ahoo, hoooo" – is a truly wonderful piece of music that merited further development. Already a distinct sensibility is taking form; polished and knocked into shape, some of these songs would not have sounded out of place on *The Kick Inside*. But taken as a whole there is an undeniable one-dimensional quality to the rhythms and themes, a cumulative lack of pace and a certain uniformity in the melodic structures not helped by the fact that these are simple piano-and-voice recordings made on fairly rudimentary equipment. With the benefit of hindsight, listening with the knowledge of what Catherine Bush would *become*, it's easy to convince oneself that any A&R man would be mad to reject this material, but it's equally easy to hear how this might have been a hard sell commercially. Listening to them in a continuous sitting they tend to merge into an extended, mellifluous single entity without a cutting edge.

Hopper played the songs to David Gilmour, the Pink Floyd guitarist and another old friend from his Cambridge days.* Gilmour's interest was immediately piqued, but he was pragmatic. "The demo was not saleable," he later recalled. "The songs were too idiosyncratic: just Kate, this little schoolgirl who was maybe 15, singing away over a piano. You needed decent ears to hear the potential and I didn't think there were many people with those working in record companies. But I was convinced from the beginning that this girl had remarkable talent."[20]

The idea that Gilmour 'discovered' Bush or deliberately sought her out is not quite true. Pink Floyd had just gone stratospheric with *Dark Side Of The Moon*, released in March 1973, and, like good hippie-god patriarchs, were looking to spread the sunshine all around. Bush became one of several pet projects Gilmour was pursuing. He installed an eight-track recording studio at his home in Royston in Essex and was actively looking for talent to foster. Unicorn was another of the lucky recipients. They had played at Hopper's wedding and, after Gilmour and Chris Jagger got up and jammed on a Neil Young song, Gilmour offered the band some free recording time at his studio. Later they signed with Floyd's manager Steve O'Rourke.

If he was generally playing the philanthropic rock patron, there's still no doubt that Bush's raw demo tape, placed in his hands with a personal recommendation from a friend, made an impression on Gilmour despite its commercial limitations. It's likely that he went around to East Wickham Farm at least once around this time, possibly to record Bush, certainly to meet and hear her music. "Absolutely terrified and trembling like a leaf, I sat down and played for him," she recalled.[21] "He was great, such a human, kind person – and genuine."[22]

In the late summer of 1973 Gilmour called bassist Pat Martin with a suggestion. Keen for Bush to have a better quality recording to "punt around", he asked if Martin and Pete Perrier, Unicorn's drummer, would help him record a demo as a favour. In August the three musicians assembled at Gilmour's home studio where, after about an hour, Bush

---

* Former EMI chief Bob Mercer claims the Bush family had another connection with the Pink Floyd guitarist, suggesting that Dr Bush was friendly with one of Gilmour's guitar technicians.

arrived with Ricky Hopper. "She came in more or less looking at the floor," says Martin. "She was dreamlike, she had this distant look in her eyes. She didn't know how to go about things but David was really good: 'Just play them like you're at home,' he said. 'We'll just listen to them and as we think of things we'll bring them in.' I remember her sitting at this Wurlitzer electric piano with her legs crossed, she looked very demure, this schoolgirl. She'd never played an electric piano before and she was quite fascinated by the sound and feel of it, she really liked it. I was immediately impressed. I was worried in case she wasn't very good and it would be embarrassing, but it wasn't."

The men did their best to make her feel at ease. Bush had never played with other musicians before, indeed she had barely played her music in *front* of anyone else. "We made her laugh quite a few times, little quips and musician jokes to help her relax," says Martin. "There were a couple of times where we might have said something very, very slightly risqué, in no way obscene or anything, and she was slightly sort of pretending that she wasn't quite as innocent as she made out."

They ran through four or five numbers and recorded the ones that gelled most quickly. They certainly played 'Humming' – also known as 'Davy' and 'Maybe' during its lifespan – and a very lovely song, particularly in its solo piano incarnation. The most notable recording, however, was 'Passing Through Air', simply because it's the only recording from that day that has survived, unexpectedly turning up many years later on the B-side of 'Army Dreamers', like a long lost child suddenly reunited with its more sophisticated family.*

'Passing Through Air' is a strange beast. It's a catchy little song but lacks spark. The arrangement is generic and the performances are solid but stiff, betraying the fact that the players were effectively feeling their way into the song as they went along. Only on the unvarnished solo piano version

---

* The occasion revealed another example of Bush's innate sense of decency. Pat Martin: "Years later she put out a single ['Army Dreamers'], and one of the additional tracks on it was 'Passing Through Air', and I remember getting a cheque for it. She organised to send us some money out of the blue, which was a nice gesture. She was that sort of person, a really nice, unaffected person. I remember after 'Wuthering Heights' came out and Unicorn was killed by punk, just after we'd had the fateful meeting, we went home and put the telly on and she was sat there talking and she actually mentioned us. She said she'd really like to thank the guys from Unicorn for helping her."

of the same song – often called 'Need Your Loving' – which can be heard on bootlegs can you really hear a glimpse of something hinting at greatness. Even then, it is faint.

On the band version Bush's voice is pretty but unremarkable, and though recognisably *her* it's very firmly in the mould of other female singer-songwriters of that time: there's more than a little Kate & Anna McGarrigle, a touch of Judee Sill, Laura Nyro and Joni Mitchell, even a little Elkie Brooks and Linda Lewis. Certainly no great swoops and soars. "When 'Wuthering Heights' first came out a few years later I was a bit surprised, because I don't remember her sounding quite like that," says Martin. "I don't know if they did something to it or deliberately made it sound weird, but that's not how I remember how she sounded in those sessions. It was more Joni Mitchell-like, that was obviously an influence."

But think of the thrill! After only a few hours she came away with a tape of herself playing with a professional band, one of whom was a member of Pink Floyd, her songs coloured in, beefed up and fleshed out, springing to life outside of her own head and home. She even got to overdub for the first time. "I put this little electric piano thing down, and I remember thinking: 'Ooh! I like this!' "[23]

Afterwards they all sat down in another room, had some tea and, flushed by the experience, Bush "opened up a bit more, she was gaining in confidence," according to Martin. "It was hard to make small talk. It was on a musical level, about the fact that the electric piano had a vibrato and stuff like that." Straightaway she loved the input of other musicians, hearing the drum and bass lock the song down, stretching the parameters of what she could achieve, even if at this point she didn't have the time, confidence or the capability to articulate what it was she wanted. From that point on, making a record became something close to an obsession. For the first time she began to get an inkling of the almost limitless possibilities of the recording process, and began to experiment at home, beginning a process that could later be heard on songs like 'Leave It Open' and 'Watching You Without Me'. "Her dad had this other machine – if you pressed one button, it played everything at exactly the same speed but backwards," says Brian Bath. "It was amazing, and Kate used to try to learn how to sing backwards. She'd go, 'Nygg Haaa Shy Woo', record it, then play it forwards. I think she still does it now! She used to do things like that."

Bush and Gilmour kept in touch. Martin claims that some short time after the band session Gilmour went "in a room with just her and her piano and recorded everything she could play on a TEAC four-track. I did have that tape at one point and there's some amazing stuff on there, some of those famous songs in really early form." If this is the case, this solo session, usually thought to have happened at Wickham Farm before the band demo, actually happened shortly afterwards. Certainly, it seems that between 1972 and 1974 she made several different recordings of her huge stockpile of songs, only a fraction of which have ever surfaced.

She might pop in to see Gilmour at Britannia Road Studio in London, where she got to prod around on Rick Wakeman's mellotron and was amazed – "Wow!" – at the sounds it could make, or visit him during the sessions for *Wish You Were Here*, Pink Floyd's follow-up to *Dark Side Of The Moon*, recorded at Abbey Road in St. John's Wood during the early months of 1975. He in turn kept abreast of her progress, but there wasn't much to tell. She had no profile other than the songs: she didn't perform live, she had no band, and her tape was making no waves. Often, it went unheard. "In the early-to-mid Seventies, David Gilmour asked me if I wanted to hear a tape of this amazing girl singer he'd discovered," recalls celebrated folk-rock producer Joe Boyd. "I was trying to be a film producer then and avoid getting sucked back into the studio, so I told him not to even play it to me. That, of course, was Kate's demo tape." In the end Gilmour offered, with enormous generosity and foresight, to pay for a professional recording session at AIR studios on Oxford Circus. Bush, ever mindful of the correct way of doing things, later paid him back.

"We spent a bit of time working on what was the best way of moving her forward, or getting her what she wanted, which was to make records," he said. "[We] made some demos, proper ones. I mean, we didn't make them as demos, we made proper master recordings of three tracks. I didn't actually really work on that stuff myself. I chose the songs out of piles of stuff that she had and then employed other people to do the work. And it worked brilliantly."[24]

Gilmour picked six songs and phoned his friend Andrew Powell, a hugely talented player, arranger and producer with a classical background, perfect pitch and a degree in music from King's College, Cambridge, who had edged into the pop world, working with Cockney Rebel, the Alan Parsons Project, Al Stewart and Gilmour himself. Powell agreed to meet Bush at Floyd's offices. "She was shy but quite intense and very impressive," he remembers. "Dave played me the songs he had recorded, but I went away with just Kate's voice and piano demos. That's the way I prefer to work, just strip it down to the song without any other preconceptions. Dave said, 'Look, go into the studio and do it and I'll listen to it when I get back', or words to that effect. He put up the money for the initial sessions, he just thought she was something really special."

In June 1975 they convened at AIR Studios on Oxford Circus in central London. She was 16, approaching her seventeenth birthday and, not surprisingly, "very nervous, [but] Andrew was fantastic. He was completely in control of it."[25] Powell confirms that, of course, Bush was nervous, but it was an excited, anticipatory nervousness. "She was fascinated by everything that was going on around her, absolutely intrigued."

He had recruited some quality session players. Bruce Lynch, not long arrived from New Zealand and a regular with Cat Stevens; Barry De Souza on drums; Paul Keogh and Alan Parker on guitars; and Alan Skidmore blowing some rather freeform sax on 'Berlin' – later called 'The Saxophone Song' – a slinkily erotic nightclub fantasy of "a sensuous shining man being taken over by the instrument"[26] while the sole observer of this emotional striptease, Bush, is happily seduced. Powell played keyboards.

For some, the session made no great impact and was just another day at the office. "I got a call – 'D'you wanna work?' 'Does Dolly Parton sleep on her back?' – and you'd just turn up and get stuck in," recalls Lynch. "She was young, but I've never taken much notice of age, really." Skidmore's recollections are similarly blank. This was, after all, 35 years ago. Engineer Geoff Emerick, on the other hand, recalls the day vividly. "She was a breath of fresh air," he says. "Me and Pete Henderson, my assistant, were sitting there and this sweet little shy girl came in and said, 'Have you got something to drink?' She was very thirsty and wanted some water. We sat in the control room waiting for Andrew, making small talk."

When Powell arrived they recorded three songs in two three-hour sessions: 'Berlin,' a new version of 'Maybe', and, crucially, 'The Man With The Child In His Eyes'. 'Wuthering Heights' may have been the song that catapulted Bush to stardom, but it was 'The Man With The Child In His Eyes' that really made the people who mattered sit up and listen. Early, embryonic versions of the song dated back to at least 1973, possibly earlier. "Fragments of her early songs which became hits were already finding their way out of Kate's head by the time she was just 13," said Dr Bush.[27] Mysterious, secret and sensitive, it certainly shared many characteristics with the poetry she was writing in her first few years at St Joseph's. David Gilmour mentions the song as being among the early batch he heard, and Pat Martin recalls running through a "basic version" of the song at the 1973 session. "It didn't sound the way it did when she finished it," he says. "It was just her and a piano, and I vaguely remember the chord sequences were different. It wasn't the one that stuck out to me."

She chipped away at it until a final version was ready. As soon as Andrew Powell heard it in piano-and-vocal form he was riveted, describing it as the "outstanding one. I was very impressed at that song. When you think about it, it's an extremely mature song for someone of that age, and rather odd. Definitely not a band song. I think drums would have killed it." True to his instinct, he decided to record it live at AIR studios with just Bush and her piano accompanied by string players from the London Symphony Orchestra, conducted by David Katz. "I insisted upon it, and it really did work," he says. "I wouldn't have made her do it if I didn't think she was up to it, but she was. It's a fantastic vocal performance and I think that's partly because of the whole tension there."

For Geoff Emerick, a man who had worked on all the major Beatles recordings post-1966 and would go on to produce Elvis Costello and Paul McCartney among many other luminaries, it was a revelation. "That was one of my favourite recordings of all time," he says. "We knew when we recorded it that it was one of the most beautiful records we'd made in a long time. Those sort of things happen once every eight or 10 years for me. It made a very deep impression."

Aside from its luminous melody and swooping chorus, 'The Man With The Child In His Eyes' is one of the first examples of the extraordinarily positive way in which Bush views men. She is surely unique among female songwriters in that her canon contains not a single song that puts down, castigates or generally gives men the brush off. She has never been feminist in the bluntest sense – she wants to preserve and embrace the differences between the sexes and understand the male of the species. Many songs display a desire to experience fully what it is to *be* a man; she invests them with power, beauty and a kind of mystical attraction which is incredibly generous. "It's not such an open thing for a woman to be physically attracted to the male body and fantasise about it," she once said. "I can't understand that because to me the male body is absolutely beautiful."[28]

Of the song itself, she said: "A lot of men have got a child inside them, you know, I think they are more or less grown up kids. It's a very good quality. It's really nice to have that delight in wonderful things that children have."[29]

It has been dismissed as mere adolescent fantasy, but like many of her best songs 'The Man With The Child In His Eyes' successfully blurs the lines between reality and imagination, between romantic and platonic love, sex and sensuality, between the woman and the child. And once again there is that familiar, tugging hint at a secret life: "Nobody knows about my man." There has been much speculation over the years about who inspired her to write the song. David Gilmour's name has often been thrown into the ring, alongside her brothers. While it transcends specifics and is unlikely to be wholly 'about' any one person – it's an elusive song, and she once claimed it "had something to do with one of my nephew's books"[30] – it seems likely it was written with her first serious boyfriend in mind.

Steve Blacknell was another older, formative figure in Bush's younger years, who later became a record plugger, a DJ and VJ, a TV presenter on Live Aid and many other music shows, and latterly has worked in PR. An old friend of Lisa Bowyer and her boyfriend Rob, at the time he met Bush he was a toilet cleaner, but she saw beyond the bleach and Brillo. "I'm told I'm 'The Man With The Child In His Eyes'," says Blacknell today. "Kate never told me that, but I was told through the family and Lisa. I know it's true. I've got the handwritten lyrics here, they're dated and it's [dedicated] to me. I'm very proud of that. I think it's one of the greatest songs ever."

A few years her senior, Blacknell first met Bush in Dartford. "We were each others first loves, and first loves are always special," he says. "The fact that they go on to be a star means fuck all. She was a true genius. I can recall her playing in the farm, hearing these incredible songs and thinking, bloody hell! I have some very personal memories of that kind of thing. I'm privileged, but more than that she was my first love. That's more important than anything."

Later in their relationship, when they were "going strong", Blacknell tracked down Robin Williamson of The Incredible String Band, one of Bush's favourites, and scored a job with them, living for a while in the group's commune at Glen Row in Innerleithen, near Edinburgh, working as roadie, chief cook and bottle washer. "She was a big String Band fan and I think that probably influenced her somewhere, in her tribal, percussive ways," says Blacknell. "But she drew from so many sources. Just bloody stunning."

Blacknell was a self-confessed "hippie", deeply immersed in that lifestyle. Bush's social group away from school was diverse and rather exotic, which probably reinforced her feeling of alienation at St Joseph's. Many of her songs were inspired by the interesting, eccentric people she met or saw around the farm, her own friends or Paddy's or Jay's. When she first arrived on the scene much was made of Bush's 'little girl lost' persona and apparent naïveté, but "she wasn't innocent by any means", according to Jon Kelly, who engineered *The Kick Inside* and *Lionheart* and co-produced *Never For Ever*. "Her brothers were quite bohemian, mystical, open to the ways of the world, and her parents were very open minded. Not innocent, our Kate, but very sweet. You don't write those songs if you're innocent!"

She later said she smoked her first cigarette at the age of nine, and has maintained a love affair with smoking throughout most of her adult life. And although she was never particularly keen on alcohol, she was well aware of drugs and their impact. In one of her unreleased songs, 'Cussi Cussi', she sings of getting "really stoned, really amazingly", and in an 1978 interview in *Record Mirror* with the novelist-to-be Tim Lott, she was uncharacteristically direct, if not exactly open, about her experiences: 'She experimented,' wrote Lott, but "I've never taken acid," said Bush. I don't think I'm into things like that. I've seen a lot of people screwed up through it. The idea of it is really fascinating, though – to be able to see the room breathe, and stuff like that." '[31]

She may well have had contact with people who had a taste for stronger stuff – "there was a lot of acid flying around," says one friend – but for Bush marijuana was as far as it went. The great keyboard player Max Middleton, who played on *Never For Ever*, recalls attending a party at the farm on New Year's Eve 1979. "Midnight came," says Middleton. "There were several rooms, and one of them was filled with balloons and the TV was on playing all the Scottish songs, but there was not a soul in there. I walked into the kitchen and everybody was sitting around the table smoking and it was absolutely silent because they were so stoned. And in another room it was silent because they were all listening to seventeenth century recorder music. Just your typical New Year's party! It was a bit odd. They were eccentric and lovely, the whole family were."

She wasn't one of the brash girls, ostentatiously picked up from school in their boyfriends' car, but she was no wallflower. Later she said she had "lots" of boyfriends. "I really liked boys . . . I was popular with them."[32] Maybe she did and no doubt she was. In early interviews she scattered many seeds of obfuscatory misinformation about her romantic life, not just on the grounds that it was nobody's damn business, but also to deflect attention away from the fact that by early 1978 she was already living with her bass player, Del Palmer. Only in 1985 did she fully acknowledge Del as her partner; later, quite understandably, she clammed up completely.

She did reveal that she had her first boyfriend at the age of 11 – someone called John, who lived "around the corner". Like most teenage girls, she developed "terrible crushes on boys, always much older than me."[33] Hardly surprising, considering her own emotional maturity and her many older male role models. Her early romantic life seems a typical teenage mix of rich fantasy and some direct experience, all of which *felt* real and fed directly into her songs: excitement, trepidation, longing, disappointment, secrecy. A decade before she wrote 'Hounds Of Love', the idea of love was already a kinetic speedball comprising of equal parts thrill and terror. Unlike many of the girls at St Joseph's, she was not naïve, dismissive or, conversely, overly rash when it came to men. "Some fell pregnant not long after going to university, some got into marriages very quickly which they regretted," says Shealla Mubi. "You didn't have that much exposure to men. Kate was lucky, she had much older brothers. When I left I'd not been kissed and never had a boyfriend, and I viewed the opposite sex with fear mixed with, 'Oh, you don't need men!' I think Kate had a more rounded experience."

Whether it was directly inspired by Blacknell or not, by the time she had recorded the definitive version of 'The Man With The Child In His Eyes' at AIR studios in June 1975, Bush had embarked upon another relationship. Alastair Buckle, known as Al, was another slightly older boy whom she dated seriously. Like Blacknell and Paddy's steady girlfriend of the time Teresa Fox, he was made an honorary member of the Bush family and was a frequent visitor to the farmhouse during the period they were together, plonked down at the kitchen table and fed tea, cake and good will.

Buckle was a polite biker, with shoulder length hair and a leather jacket. She didn't quite fit into his social set, and often felt shy and self-conscious. Once, according to her schoolmate Francis Byrne, rather than venturing into the We Anchor In Hope pub to meet Buckle and his friends she left a single rose on the petrol tank of his motorbike parked outside, an almost quintessentially Bush gesture that could have come straight from one of her songs or videos. From an early age, clearly, she had an instinct for the powerfully romantic and dramatic, with a twist of Celtic melancholy.

Bush and Buckle had a typically intense on-off relationship with the usual measures of heartache and rapture. They split up after a year, and for the next couple of years there was no one steady. After the AIR demo she was getting serious about her work and her music, thinking about leaving school, leaving home and living alone for the first time. She wasn't ready for commitment and indeed chose not to confide in any of her boyfriends when it came to her music. Steve Blacknell, for instance, recalls being only vaguely aware of the recordings sessions. "I knew about [them] . . . but that's about it," he says.

It was a post-feminist world, but only just, and she feared her male companions might be discouraged or intimidated by her talent, perhaps even regard her as a "threat to their masculinity".[34] As she progressed, she "tended not to tell my boyfriends about my music. My family and my close friends knew about it and that was OK, but I didn't want anyone else to share it."[35]

Again, there is evidence of that understated but steely single-mindedness, the sense of playing for high stakes and placing an appropriate value on her most precious pursuits. Around her, friends like Diane Carman and Lisa Bowyer, who would soon marry Rob Bradley and start working as a telephonist, were already finalising their wedding plans. She decided it wasn't for her.

* * *

The 1975 AIR recording session turned Bush's life around. Such was its quality, it not only secured her a major label deal with EMI but two of the recordings – 'The Man With The Child In His Eyes' and 'The Saxophone Song' – ended up over two years later, unadorned, appearing on her debut album, *The Kick Inside*.

When he heard the demo, Gilmour "loved it", according to Powell. "He was very happy." Shortly afterwards, he was in the studio with the rest of Pink Floyd, in the final throes of completing *Wish You Were Here*, finished on July 19, 1975 and released in mid-September, when EMI General Manager Bob Mercer popped in for a visit. In Abbey Road's Studio Three Mercer was given his first, unexpected introduction to the music of Kate Bush.

"It was two or three o'clock in the morning, and David said he had paid for these demos that Andrew Powell had produced and that he wanted me to listen to," recalls Mercer. "We went into another studio and had a listen. He had [three] songs, extremely high-end demos, string sections, the whole lot, and one of those songs in particular really got to me: 'The Man With The Child In His Eyes'. I listened to it a few times and the next day I called Dave and Steve O'Rourke to find out what was in their minds. Were they going to sign her and record her? Dave said, 'No, no, I just wanted to help her out, so if you're interested go ahead.'"

Mercer says he called Dr Bush straight away and asked him and his daughter to come and see him the following day. "We talked it over a fair amount, and I told him I was happy to sign her but I wouldn't want her to go into the studio for a couple of years, and her dad was obviously not against that at all," says Mercer. "He was a very level-headed GP and they weren't short of money, there was absolutely no showbiz promotion coming from that side at all. So that's what we did."

It wasn't quite that simple. EMI's head of publishing Terry Slater was also involved, and negotiations were protracted, probably because Bush had not yet even turned 17 and her family, notably Jay, became heavily involved in the whole process. The final contract was sealed in July 1976, a year after the AIR session, which suggests that all parties may have been waiting until Bush was 18 before committing to anything formal.

There was also the small matter of school. She had achieved an outstanding 10 'O' Level passes in 1974 and was now in the sixth form, taking her 'A' Levels. Everything at St Joseph's was geared towards the top pupils attending university. This was an assumption rather than a hope or expectation: the question was not, 'Will you go to university?' but 'What will you be studying?' For the brightest – which included Bush – the Oxford entrance exam beckoned. She had harboured vague ideas about becoming a vet, a psychiatrist, a social worker – always, it seemed, a profession that helped someone or something – but deep down she recognised that she had no great passion for any of them. In her heart, she knew there was only one thing that would satisfy her. "She was good, she was bright, she had other options to follow, she could have led a very professional life," says Mubi. "Coming from a school like ours it took a lot of courage to follow that [musical] line and say, 'OK, I'm going to pursue this.' She must have been extremely brave to buck the expectations that the school had instilled in her over all these years."

Her mother and father, so steeped in academic excellence and true believers in the value of education, were at first against her dropping out of school. They had already been disappointed when Jay had chosen not to be a solicitor. "My parents were very concerned I was leaving school and going into something that was completely insecure," she said. "They had a tremendous amount of faith in me. They wanted me to be happy and they understood that I wasn't just spending my time doing nothing."[36]

It is to their eternal credit that they saw her argument and subsequently backed her to the hilt. Having spent so long exposing her to a rich and varied world of art and creativity, when it mattered most they were prepared to put their money where the mouths were. They were also fans. Highly impressed with her talent, in the end they were content to trust the evidence of their own ears. "I remember the first time I heard 'The Man With The Child In His Eyes', not long after she recorded it," says Brian Bath. "I went round to the farm [and] Kate's dad said, 'Do you want to hear something Kate has recorded?' He took me into the front room and put it on, I stood there with him, it started and, honestly, the hairs on my neck were tingling. I could not believe it was so beautiful. I looked at him and he said quietly, 'Good, you like it? It's beautiful, isn't it?' "

How could they have stopped her? She left school early in 1976, soon after sitting her mock 'A' levels and midway through the final year of Upper Sixth, before her deal with EMI was concluded but with the promise of it glinting on the horizon. "I knew I had to leave school then," she said. "I wanted to do something in music and I had to get away from the alternative career opportunities being rammed down my throat."[37]

A small inheritance from an aunt assuaged any immediate financial concerns, although they were hardly pressing: she would not – God forbid – ever have to get anything as troublesome as a job, a prosaic but highly significant point. There was, naturally, no general announcement to the masses. She simply left. The teachers thought she was "a bit foolish".[38] According to the relatively low readings picked up on the school's rumour radar she had gone to pursue dance, not music.

"It was like, 'Where's Cathy?'," recalls Shealla Mubi. "Somebody mentioned that she was doing dancing – Oh! A girl had left before to go to ballet school, but I don't remember [Cathy] doing any ballet, so it was a bit of a shock to hear that she'd gone to do that. It didn't really make sense. I'm sure Lisa would have known, but there wasn't a big, 'Oh, I'm leaving to go and do this and this.' That wouldn't have been her way."

The canny, low-key negotiation of her time at St Joseph's reveals much about Bush's personality and the way she has conducted her career ever since. "I was too shy to be a hooligan, but inside I had many hooligan instincts," she said.[39] She practiced a prolonged and unfailingly polite internal rebellion, all the more effective for the fact that few saw it or even recognised that it was happening at all. A cool patience underpinned a great confidence. She didn't make a fuss and then ultimately conform, like many of us. She got on with school, studied hard, did as she was asked – "never gave any lip"[40] – and then went off to pursue her own singular vision, defying the expectations not only of her teachers but, initially, her friends and parents.

There are echoes of this low volume, maximum yield approach to patrician authority throughout her subsequent career: in battles with EMI chief Bob Mercer and the record company in general, in skirmishes with producer Andrew Powell and various video directors, in jettisoning an unwanted manager, in continually defying the lumpen expectations of the media or the public in general to pursue her vision. Voices are rarely raised, but she invariably emerges victorious. Actions and results, not words, are what matter. It could be said that – subconsciously, no doubt – she has consistently used the reserved, polite, very English side of her nature as a Trojan horse, a vehicle for smuggling in the wild, uninhibited Celtic part of her lurking beneath, begging for release, freedom and flight. Her schooldays ended in an act of *proper* rebellion, much more deft than those routinely mapped out by surly young men in artfully distressed clothes mouthing second hand, lazily confrontational platitudes. They revealed an inner strength that has served her well ever after.

3

Room For The Life

"IT wasn't until I left school that I found real strength inside," Bush later said.[1] The events of 1976 and 1977 bear out these sentiments a hundred times over. The next two years are a blur of creative evolution in fast forward, and each time the show reel stops spinning it throws out a host of seemingly conflicting images.

When the light falls a certain way an unlikely pub singer comes into focus, embarking on an enforced, somewhat delayed apprenticeship. Fronting the KT Bush Band, she was a characteristically vivid turn as a lounge bar chanteuse, singing the likes of Hall & Oates' 'She's Gone', Steely Dan's 'Brooklyn', Arthur Conley's 'Sweet Soul Music' and Free's 'The Stealer' to a less than select crowd of lager drinkers, corporate low-rollers and sports aficionados. "We played Tottenham Football Club, where they thought she was the stripper," says the band's drummer, Vic King. "At a pub in Putney on the day [before] Scotland beat England at Wembley we had dry ice machines that set off the fire alarm. There was a bit of a riot and a panic. It was a really good evening!" He pauses. "But not really her thing, no."

Look again and she has become the profoundly private writer, largely hidden from sight, pouring herself into an almost unending stream of superb new songs, sometimes writing all through the night. Prior to going into the studio in July 1977 to make *The Kick Inside*, Bush handed producer Andrew Powell a vast amount of material which gave him – in football parlance – a serious selection headache. "I've still got some of the cassettes," he says. "I must have 100 songs here, pre-*Kick Inside*, some of which I still wish she'd done. The process was difficult."

This picture, too, dissolves to reveal another view: the dedicated dance and mime student of tutor Robin Kovac's recollection, the girl with the "beginner's body" who "made herself wonderful. I have a picture of her in pigtails, of all things. She was really sweet, she still had baby fat in her face, [but] she was determined to be a dancer."

Yet another angle shows the deceptively "calculating" – her word – careerist, setting up with her family a series of limited companies with which to keep tabs on her song publishing rights, her future earnings, setting in place her control strategy long before fame and fortune struck. "She ain't daft," says Brian Southall, EMI's former Head of Press and later in charge of Artistic Development. "People shouldn't be fooled by the mystical, hippie stuff. This girl is very, very tough."

At the centre of it all, unifying these diverse characters, is the independent young woman, leaving the family home at 18 and pushing out towards freedom. Hers was a characteristically sensible departure, reasoned and well planned. Owned by her father and divided into three spacious flats, 44 Wickham Road* in Brockley was a rather grand red-brick Victorian building set back off the road, far enough from home to enable independence, close enough to maintain family ties. In any case, it was already a fiercely tight-knit Bush fiefdom in the south of the city: Jay lived on the ground floor with his teacher wife Judy and their two children; Paddy occupied the middle apartment; and Kate moved in to the top floor with a second-hand upright piano and a couple of cats, Zoodle and Pyewacket. In time, boyfriend and bass player Del Palmer would join her. For now, she luxuriated in her freedom.

Emerging from a period where she wondered whether she would ever be able to break free and channel her feelings into something truly liberating, suddenly she found she was able to do everything all at once: dancing, writing, exploring mime, even performing live. Leaving an old way of life behind and embarking on a new phase, the sense of transformation was vividly, almost physically, apparent to her. Embracing vegetarianism at 16 – "I don't believe in eating life"[2] – leaving school, throwing herself into dance, learning to drive (though she rarely did), living alone; all these steps forward were synthesised in what she regarded as symbolic change in her preferred Christian name. "I used to be called Cathy and I became Kate,

---

* The similarity of the address to Wickham Farm is confusing but, presumably, mere coincidence. The two properties were several miles apart.

and that was a very different stage for me," she said, adding. "The first part of my life was so difficult."[3]

In hindsight it all happened rather quickly, though at the time it didn't seem nearly fast enough. All her pursuits were leading towards one inexorable conclusion: recording an album. In 2005 she looked back and claimed she felt she was on a "mission from God."[4] It's a purposely tongue-in-cheek phrase, but it accurately captures her drive and sense of growing momentum. Suddenly, the future was wide open, and she stepped gratefully inside. She later remembered it as one of the happiest times of her life.

★ ★ ★

After nearly a year of to-ing and fro-ing, in the summer of 1976 Bush finally concluded a deal with EMI. Initially, it was a straightforward direct artist agreement: EMI paid for all the recording and up front costs and owned the results. The deal included Europe and Canada but not the United States, where EMI America would have first option on Bush's albums but were under no obligation to release them.

At Bob Mercer's insistence recording expenses would not be deducted from Bush's advance on the grounds that such a practice was "immoral", a concept not normally acknowledged within the industry. A straight-talking, humorous, larger-than-life figure, Mercer was widely regarded as a decent man who, after joining the company in 1971, had somewhat belatedly ushered in the era of T-shirts, long hair and growing artist power at Manchester Square following several decades of suits, ties and received pronunciation. He rapidly became an avuncular figure in Bush's life, a role he happily fulfilled, from a distance, until his death in May 2010. He was another in the line of significant, powerful, kindly older men who made up her extended musical 'family'.

EMI offered a four-year contract paying an initial, non-recoupable advance of £3,000, with an additional £500 for publishing, with options at the end of the second and third year. This last detail was crucial. It enabled Bush to renegotiate her contract from a position of strength following the huge success of 'Wuthering Heights' and *The Kick Inside*, with the result that she was able to retain ownership of all her later record-ings, only leasing them to EMI for agreed periods of time. This move, allied to a stubborn adherence to her unflinching vision, gave her real power and has allowed her to retain tight control of her music throughout her career, as well as protecting her image and her legacy. "It was re-negotiated very early on so she owned her own music," recalls Brian Southall. "That was unheard of for an act that early on in their career. To their credit, when she started selling records they rewarded her. Bob was very fair in that respect, he was a good man. It was unusual for EMI to do a license deal. Many other acts wanted similar deals and they were turned down."

How did she pull it off? The immediate success of 'Wuthering Heights' certainly afforded her enormous bargaining power, but even before then every move was made with deliberate and careful forethought. Pink Floyd had carved out significant creative independence, albeit only after pro-longed ascendency, and the family sought advice from their manager Steve O'Rourke and David Gilmour, as well as taking advantage of Jay's legal learning and his experience in publishing. They set up a company, Novercia Holdings Limited, later expanded to include Kate Bush Songs Limited, Noverica Limited and Novercia Overseas Limited. All five principal family members were named as directors and Bush, Paddy and Jay became shareholders, the brothers owning ten per cent each and Bush the remaining 80 per cent. They brought on board an accountant and a top industry solicitor, Bernard Sheridan, in advisory capacities. All con-tracts went through this route, discussed by the family and rubber stamped by the suits. "The whole thing is really to just structure it so that the final decision on anything becomes Kate's, which tends to be unusual in rock music – especially when somebody has just become popular," Jay explained.[5]

This was not an uncommon set-up among established rock stars with real clout, but it was almost unheard of among new acts. It was designed to ensure that Bush would never be one of the industry's hard luck stories, either artistically or financially. The accounts of her company show highly astute financial management, with substantial sums (£223,000, for example, in 1992) set aside for pension contributions, establishing a considerable nest egg, a significant factor for someone who has paused as long between releasing records as she frequently has. They also show that all the company directors have been well rewarded for their roles in helping to run her career. The money has always been kept firmly within the family. The Bushes may have had a pronounced bohemian streak, but like many other middle-class artists they understood the absolute necessity for control. In this regard they were unsentimental and clear-sighted in negotiating contracts and helping her stick to her guns. If she made mistakes, she was determined that they would be her own. "The most important thing seemed to be that I had control," she said. "Because one of the worst things that can happen to one's product – that terrible word – is that you become manipulated."[6]

She couldn't call the shots just yet. EMI didn't want her to record straightaway, and Bush spent much of the next two years in a strange kind of limbo: *something* was going to happen – but what? And when? The gap, though frustrating, enabled her to think long and hard about her appearance, her expression, her songs, her body, her style. Andrew Powell, for one, thinks that "it was inordinately helpful that we didn't straight away make an album. She discovered a lot about herself in that time, working a lot of stuff out. She certainly wasn't wasting time."

The big surprise, and in retrospect one of her most astute moves, was that she focused the greater part of her energy on dance and physical movement, not simply for its own sake but quite consciously in an attempt to make it work in tandem with her music. Though she had danced at St Joseph's – it was another compulsory step in the great quest to become A Lady – the tuition had, once again, been rather formal and she "didn't really get on with the dance teacher".[7] At Wickham Farm she could at least move freely to her own internal pulse. Retreating to her room, she would work out routines to songs like 'Eleanor Rigby' – hardly the most upbeat material – showing typical dedication, practising for days and days until it was right.

She loved dancing, but it was another private passion. The penny didn't really drop until she was knocked sideways by Lindsay Kemp's *Flowers*, an intensely powerful re-imagining of Jean Genet's *Notre Dame Des Fleures*. A world away from the niceties of ballet, *Flowers* was populated by drag queens, pimps, murderers and sailors; it was orgiastic, erotic, oppressive, violent, funny and thoroughly homosexual in its aesthetic – Kemp played 'Our Lady'. It would not have been allowed within 100 yards of the gates of St Joseph's. In its earliest showings it was often raided by the police.

Bush went to see the show when it played at the Collegiate Theatre in Bloomsbury in 1975 and again during its later, long run at the

Roundhouse in Chalk Farm, north London. This was no teenage girl trotting off dutifully to Covent Garden to gaze at *Swan Lake*, and even for an adolescent as accustomed to the *avant garde* as Bush, *Flowers* felt thrilling and even slightly illicit. And tremendously powerful. The visceral impact of her first viewing directly inspired her to leave school and follow her burgeoning love of physical movement. "I couldn't believe how strongly Lindsay communicates with people even without opening his mouth," she said. "It was incredible, he had the whole audience in his control . . . I'd never seen anything like it, I really hadn't. I felt if it was possible to combine that strength of movement with the voice then maybe it would work, and that's what I've tried to do."[8]

She had already realised that "there was something missing from the expression" in her music,[9] that just sitting down and playing her songs at the piano wasn't going to be enough. She was influenced in this regard by Gurdjieff's 'Fourth Way', the idea that mind and body are not separate creative entities and that the key to personal and creative breakthrough lies in learning how to fuse the two, using the one to feed off the other. Seeing Lindsay Kemp in action vindicated the notion of using movement as "as an extension of my music"[10] and, crucially, gave her practical instruction as to how it could actually be achieved. After leaving school she had tried to enrol at dance school, but without any formal qualifications nobody would admit her. Instead, in 1976 she began taking mime lessons at Kemp's drop-in classes, 50p per session, each one lasting as long as three hours at a time.

Kemp was no stranger to the music world. A 38-year-old former *enfant terrible* whose previous highlights included studying with Marcel Marceau, starting his own dance company and making a splash at the 1968 Edinburgh festival, he was a teacher, choreographer, dancer and actor whose style – a unique and seductive blend of Butoh, mime, burlesque, drag and music hall – was highly personal and often confrontational. His teachings had already had a profound influence on another of his students, David Bowie. "I taught him to exaggerate with his body as well as his voice, and the importance of looking as well as sounding beautiful," said Kemp in 1974. "Ever since working with me he's practised that, and in each performance he does his movements are more exquisite."[11] Kemp wasn't interested in escapism or pretence. His central mission was to "free what is already there. Everybody has that dove flying around inside them, and to let it fly is a fabulous experience. That's why Isadora Duncan danced, and Pavlova danced – because they loved the moment when they actually *became* swans, not just impersonating them as actors do."[12]

It's also why Bush danced. The sense of transformation is what she keyed into. It wasn't about who or what you were; it was about what you could become. The experience of freeing from within her a series of multi-faceted personae was profoundly liberating and had an obvious affect on the way she has both written and presented herself throughout her career. "For me, the singer is the expression of the song," she said. "An image should be created for each song . . . the personality that goes with that particular music."[13] It's not acting, it's emotional amplification; finding the right part of her character to accentuate in order to represent the emotion of the songs, dissolving the fixed parameters of the corporeal into an amorphous, ever-changing "moving liquid" alter ego, bursting through boundaries and rolling over obstacles. "She's a lot stronger [than me]," she once said of her other self. "I wouldn't be as daring as her."[14] What may look like an escape into other characters is, in actual fact, the direct opposite: a means of deeper self discovery and release.

Guitarist Ian Bairnson recalls being particularly struck by this aspect of her work when they were recording *The Kick Inside*. "She did everything with such conviction, and she seemed to adopt different personas within the album," he says. "She'd sing the lead vocal with one voice and do the backing vocals in a completely different character and you'd think, 'There's a cast of people in there!' That's what so amazing about her – everything she does hits home. Whether she is putting on an unusual voice, it still comes across as genuine and we accept it, and that's what makes her stand apart. The fact that her talent has so many facets to it and each one is so believable."

When Kemp went off to tour Australia, Bush started studying with the American mime artist Adam Darius, another renowned performer with a global reputation who, between professional engagements, taught at the Dance Centre on Floral Street in Covent Garden. When Darius left the Dance Centre and began taking smaller private classes in Elephant and Castle, she followed him. It was here that teacher first really noticed pupil, recalling an "eagerness and enthusiasm about her. Not in an attention-grabbing way, not at all, but she was very absorbent in the best way that a student can be. One sees things in a person's eyes, and she was drinking in a very thirsty manner."

Like Kemp, Darius worked in the area of expressive mime and his methods – though different – were also designed to unlock something personal from within each individual. "I cultivated this rippling, liquid quality where the movement begins centrally, in the solar plexus, and radiates outwards to all the extremities, to the head and the hair follicles, and the arms, hands, fingertips and beyond," he says. "When done well, it's a very hypnotic way of moving. Kate absolutely absorbed it, to the manner born."

At the same time, and for the same reasons, she began taking dance classes, also at the Dance Centre. For over a year she studied with several tutors, attending a number of drop-in classes five days a week. The classes gave a new shape and purpose to her life; she would later talk about how much she loved travelling into central London every day, how she felt herself becoming an individual for the first time, taking control of her own life, shaping her future. Afterwards she might dive into Watkins' occult bookshop at Cecil Court on Charing Cross Road for a root around, or head off for vocal practice.

Although dancing taught her "discipline and humility"[15], she characteristically gravitated towards the visceral rather than the formal. She tried ballet but found it "very hard to get on with the people in the room."[16] She came to the conclusion that she was willing to sacrifice a degree of classical technique in order to get to the raw emotions, that "feeling of movement and freedom . . . like suddenly breaking through a barrier."[17]

One of her key tutors in this regard was Robin Kovac, a graduate in English Literature, Dance and Drama from Florida State University. Kovac remembers Bush as "a gentle soul, a special person. I was fond of her from the beginning, I loved having her in class. You love anyone who is keen and determined and working hard. A teacher recognises someone dead keen and concentrated, [and] even at the time I thought the best of her."

The classes at the Dance Centre attracted students of all levels. Initially, the standard of Bush's dancing was not impressive. "I was useless," she said. "I looked an idiot for months and I used to get very depressed because I couldn't do it, but challenge is very important to me and I was really tough with myself."[18]

She was being characteristically harsh, and applied herself unsparingly. She soaked up everything and improved rapidly, although Kovac recalls "a real beginner's body. She came straight fresh in, and the feet have to be trained, the legs, the arms, everything has to be trained. It takes 10 years to be a good dancer. She jumped out before she was fully trained, but she was a wonderful, fluid mover."

Kovac taught a contemporary style, with touches of jazz, heavily influenced by Martha Graham's 'contractions'. Anyone who has seen Bush's early videos and live performances will immediately recognise the following description. "Contractions begin in the stomach, as if someone knifed you, and you just press back, rounding the back," says Kovac. "It's not that you're getting smaller, you're actually getting bigger in the back, like a bow, but it's called a contraction because you're lifting up and away from the legs. The body must flow through that, because you've started an impulse, spreading ripples through the body."

It was "creative movement", within a clear dramatic context. Kovac also taught drama at Rose Bruford College in Sidcup, not far from Welling, and her class at the Dance Centre attracted many actors. It made sense, therefore, that it was Kovac to whom Bush turned when she later needed to work out a routine for the 'Wuthering Heights' video at extremely short notice. Kovac charged her £30, and in her tiny flat in Archway Road they worked out the soon-to-be famous routine as Bush sang the song a cappella for her tutor.

"It was her tiny little voice and nothing else, on the spot and we worked on movements that would match what she sang," she says. "Breaking in the window and doing the cartwheel. She didn't say, 'This is for a video clip that's coming out in a short time that's going to launch me.' She just said I need you to choreograph [something] for me. Next thing I know she's flashed all over television with my choreography! In an interview where she was asked who choreographed 'Wuthering Heights' she said she was influenced by Lindsay Kemp, which I do think is not in order. Shame on her! It wasn't that I would have asked for more money, but I would have liked to have had the credit."

If true, it's a rare example of an uncharacteristic lack of good manners and scrupulous accreditation on Bush's part. It does, however, highlight an early instance of her enduring gift for *using* – in the nicest possible sense – the talents of her peers and mentors. She has an eye for spotting talent, and absorbing it into her own work; nothing goes to waste. Soon after the 'Wuthering Heights' episode, Kovac moved to Switzerland, where she remains today, producing, directing and choreographing her own musical theatre productions. In the early Eighties, Bush learned of her sense of aggrievement and "wrote a very sweet letter" of apology; she also made a point of mentioning Kovac in a couple of major interviews around the same time. Her old tutor, Bush recalled, was a "wonderful lady"[19] who "had a big influence on me. She certainly gave me that strength to develop my own style."[20] How typical of her to try to right a perceived wrong. There appears to be no lasting hard feelings. "Kate is a creative genius," says Kovac. "I'm thrilled if I was any influence on her at all."

The ability to harness the physical side of her creative energy was terribly significant. Perhaps no one thing about Kate Bush is as misunderstood as her dancing. Easily mocked as the physical manifestation of an apparently floaty, flighty brain, whatever its objective merits her movement has never been a mere adjunct or afterthought, nor a simple matter of routine. Certainly, it allowed her to embellish the songs in her videos and to enrich and enliven her rare public performances, but it would be a mistake to focus on the skimpy costumes, swirling arms and big, round eyes and overlook the underlying impetus.

"My father told me I used to dance to music on the telly," she said. "I remember it vaguely. It was completely unselfconscious and I wasn't aware of people looking at me. One day some people came into the room, saw me and laughed, and from that moment I stopped doing it. I think maybe I've been trying to get back there ever since."[21]

Dancing, then, became a means of defeating her inhibitions, of accessing her inner emotions as a writer, of returning to a pure source. Through movement she was better able to circumnavigate her sense of self-consciousness (initially non-existent, as with most children, but which grew and became quite acute in grammar school) and fully access her feelings. "Suddenly I became a human being – just learning to move!"[22]

This chimes perfectly with Adam Darius' overarching ethos. "What I teach is emotional release," he says. "Most people, once they're not children any more, become more and more restricted by the teachings of societies, and if you want to be an artist this is the death knell. You can't be an artist if you can't express fully what you feel. Kate was grateful for that philosophy of my teaching, helping her to release herself emotionally.

When you get that release in one area, then you are capable of releasing it in other areas. It infiltrates whatever area they are pursuing, and Kate is a marvellous example of that."

As Darius implies, the invigorating effects lingered and were channelled directly into her music. It is surely no coincidence that Bush's most productive, and arguably most accomplished spells as a writer – between 1976 and 1977, and again from 1983 to 1984 – occurred during spells of intense, almost regimented dance instruction.

She was certainly writing in a torrent throughout this period, stimulated by a happy balance of all her artistic pursuits, perhaps a little lost in her own creative world, oblivious to the practical concerns of the comparatively mundane lives ticking over all around her. "I'd practise scales . . . on the piano, go off dancing, and then in the evening I'd come back and play the piano all night," she recalled. "The summer of '76 . . . we had such hot weather, I had all the windows open, and I just used to write until four in the morning. I got a letter of complaint from a neighbour who was basically saying 'shuuut uuup!' because they had to get up at five in the morning. They did shift work and my voice had been carried the whole length of the street, I think, so they weren't too appreciative."[23]

Almost every day something would emerge, if not a fully fledged song then *something*. There were songs about 'Dali' (with one superbly Austenesque line: "'Oh, I prefer absence," said she, "My heart grows fonder alone'."), songs about Rinfy the Gypsy, Joan of Arc and being stranded at the moonbase; lovely, romantic, beautiful songs, most of them containing at least a grain or two of magnificence. Dozens of the recordings she made at 44 Wickham Road are preserved on bootlegs, good quality voice-and-piano recordings, some of them early attempts at future favourites: 'Hammer Horror', 'Violin', 'Kashka From Baghdad', 'Oh, To Be In Love', 'The Kick Inside', its lyric based on 'Lucy Wan', the traditional ballad of incest and death, and a song called 'Pick The Rare Flower' which has most of the melody of 'James And The Cold Gun' but a completely different set of lyrics.

In 'Them Heavy People', also written at this time, she related with great candour her ongoing personal transformation, describing how her teachers entered her life at an "inconvenient time", forcing her to stop "hiding" and instead encouraging a process of intense self-examination. After the lows of St Joseph's here is an explicit account of her restored faith in the power of knowledge, of being shown rather than told, revelling in the gift of opportunity and acknowledging the importance of taking it.

Compared to the songs taped in 1973 there is a world of difference in the detail. The adolescent angst and cinder-smudged melancholy of yore have been overtaken by a palpable verve and spark in the writing, stronger melodic hooks, clear improvements in her voice and piano playing, and a greater sense of humour (although the initial version of 'Hammer Horror' didn't yet end in that flurry of corny puns: "I've got a hunch" and "get your own back"). She is also learning to project fragments of her own personality into the songs, to take on roles rather than surrender into the will of the music and words.

Given the quality and quantity of the material she was, not unexpectedly, in a rush to get going. "Once I got the contract I presumed things would happen," she said. "I didn't go on holiday in case they called me to do some recording. But nothing happened."[24] The official line about this waiting game is that it constituted a mutually agreed strategy between EMI and the Bush camp, mainly because of her age. More likely, it was instigated by the record company, who weren't entirely sure what they had or what to do with her. Bush herself later felt they signed her simply so nobody else would get her first, and they felt in no rush to hustle her into the studio. For a small investment they were prepared to bide their time and see what unfolded. In the event, the strategy, whether intended or not, worked to perfection.

She was undoubtedly fortunate in her long term relationship with EMI, specifically with Bob Mercer and later his successor David Munns, but they were, after all, running a multinational business, with all that that entailed. Brian Bath recalls having conversations with Bush around this time where she complained that "EMI want me to write a hit." The idea, according to Brian Southall, was to "get her to write less but more. She was prolific, but maybe it was a case of calm it down a bit and write ten songs as opposed to 100." She was always regarded as an albums artist and Mercer actively embraced the fact that her "songs were obviously tremendously personal and unique to her, that was what I liked and it was certainly what I encouraged," but even before she signed a deal he was closely monitoring her progress, trying to nurture her potential into something more solid and commercial. Less air. More hooks. "I bought her tape-recording equipment, a simple Grundig thing, and left it with her to come and see me every couple of months or so with whatever she'd been writing," he says. "That's what we did for the next year or two."

Partly it was a question of technical ability. Unicorn's Pat Martin recalls thinking during the 1973 session that she "wasn't a brilliant piano player, not accomplished or anything, but she had her own style," and Mercer claims that she later "spent quite a lot of that time, at my suggestion I must say, having formal piano lessons." She also visited a vocal coach, Gordon Farrell, for 30 minutes each week to practise her scales, improve her breathing, stretch her range and play him her new songs. "She needed to broaden her musical scope, which would obviously benefit her writing," says Mercer. "Her musical skills weren't that developed at that time – her musical *instincts* were tremendous, but not her skills at that age. That's what she did over that year, 18 months. And then I let her go into the studio." The word 'let', in this instance, is a small but significant one.

Aside from the matter of honing her musical skills, hanging in the air was that familiar question: *Who is she?* Whether or not they were directly expressed, there were significant disagreements and tensions on this score. EMI saw her as a serious songwriter with a pretty face who would perform in an uncomplicated, straightforward manner. Bush, on the other hand, ever the shape-shifter, felt her musical urges came from a very 'male' place. "Being brought up with two brothers I'd sit philosophising with them while my girlfriends wanted to talk about clothes and food," she said. "Maybe it's the male energy to be the hunter and I feel I have that in me."[25]

She talked often of this primal 'hunting' instinct, and was rather disparaging about female singers who would "sing about heartbreak and keep a big smile on their faces."[26] Specifically, she cited Lynsey DePaul and Carole King . . . "that lot. When I'm at the piano I hate to think that I'm a female because I automatically get a preconception. Sweet and lyrical."[27] She saw herself as doing something quite different, something that didn't neatly fit with any preconceived notions of what a female artist should or could be. Much more David Bowie than Joni Mitchell.

Given her looks, her high voice and obvious femininity, this caused EMI a degree of consternation and indeed confusion. "She was with the record company but she was shelved, and I do remember her telling me that she was disappointed that they wanted her to be a 'Joni Mitchell' and sit at the piano and sing," says Robin Kovac. "That's why she was doing classes. She was not just going to [do] as they wanted. She was determined to get her body together to be a mover and not just a singer."

The hiatus led her to consider her options. At one stage, she was approached by friends in her dance class with an offer to go to Germany to work in nightclubs. Unsure if the longed-for album was ever going to appear, she momentarily contemplated throwing in her lot with dance as a profession. In the end, she decided – probably correctly – that she wasn't good enough, but she looked at other escape routes. Her ex-boyfriend Steve Blacknell had begun working for Decca as a record plugger, and he passed on her demo tape to his friend and colleague Jeremy Thomas, who had also worked at Decca and now ran his own label, Electric/Cube Records. "Steve, who either was or had been going out with Kate Bush, played me her tape, saying she was unhappy with EMI and perhaps I could sign her," says Thomas. "I listened to the tape, thought it pretty good but, then again, it was only my friend's girlfriend. Later, 'Wuthering Heights' was released and I was gutted for not having taken him – and her – more seriously."

Above all, EMI wanted to see her perform. In fact, they insisted upon it. Selling records, of course, was still all about putting the hours in on the road. "This was an artist that I'd worked with for a couple of years and never, *ever* seen perform live," says Mercer. "You'd naturally assume in those days that anybody you signed would have to be able to do a live show. I was anxious to get her out there and working her chops." With little room for manoeuvre, for once she did as she was bid.

★ ★ ★

One of the most delicious anomalies of Kate Bush's entire career is the short period of time she spent singing live in the pubs and clubs around London. The KT Bush Band in their initial incarnation existed as a gigging entity for only a matter of months, between April and June, 1977, and apart from Bush comprised Vic King on drums, Del Palmer on bass and Brian Bath on guitar, three old friends from Charlton Secondary School who bonded back in the late Sixties over an almost irrationally obsessive love of Free. Even today, they excitedly recall the night they witnessed the first ever performance of 'All Right Now'.

Between four and five years older than Bush, the trio were already veterans of the south London music scene by 1976 and had played in numerous groups – both with and without one another – and experienced the industry's standard doling out of brief highs and crushing lows. From clattering around in bedrooms and youth clubs to enduring bad record deals, good bands that petered out and promises that came to nothing, they had always retained their love of playing music.

Bath, of course, had known Paddy Bush for several years and was well aware of his little sister's talent. She was also aware of his attributes. Aside from his frequent jam sessions with Paddy at the farm, Bush had seen Bath play with a hastily assembled band consisting of Vic King and another friend, bass player Barry Sherlock, at the Whitechapel Art Gallery in 1976. She was there to perform at Paddy's final year show for his course in Music Instrument Technology at the School of Furniture, which was situated just across the road, and as part of the presentation she danced to classical music "wearing some woollen type suit with a big trumpet thing coming out of her head," recalls Bath. "You couldn't actually see her. Paddy had some wacky ideas, he really did. He wanted us to do duelling basses with a band."

This showpiece was an early prototype of the memorable routine later reprised during 'Violin' on Bush's 'Tour Of Life'. Indeed, although her time with the KT Bush Band proved to be her sole experience of the dubious, stale-sweat-and-watered-down-beer romance of small scale live performance, and although it was an essentially contrived exercise in which, considering she had already signed a record deal, very little was actually at stake, nonetheless a line can be drawn between what she was doing in 1977 in places like the Rose Of Lee in Lewisham and what she did almost exactly two years later to wild acclaim in the theatres of Europe.

Vic King recalls that after their "basic rock'n'roll" performance at Whitechapel, Bush came up to the band, said that she enjoyed their set, and asked whether she could sing with them. Bath remembers the approach somewhat differently, as a clear response to Bob Mercer's diktat about the necessity for Bush to perform live. "Paddy left a note at my house with my mum, saying 'Get in touch, something has come up,'" he says. "I phoned him up and he said, 'I've got to see you, it's about my sister. She wants to form a band because she needs the experience of playing live. Could you do it?' I said, 'Yeah, I think so!'"

One of Bath's previous bands, Shiner, had recently split up and he decided to enlist Del and Vic and stick with a similar set: Motown, Beatles, some rockier material from the likes of Free and The Rolling Stones;

songs that everybody knew and which made few demands on the audience. The first band practice was in a boiler house in the local swimming baths at Greenwich, in "a little dungeon of a rehearsal room they used to hire out," says King. Bush arrived fully prepared, having learned the lyrics to ten songs, including 'I Heard It Through The Grapevine' and 'Sweet Soul Music'. They all enjoyed themselves but agreed that a boiler room in the public baths wasn't necessarily conducive to locating the creative spark, so Bush suggested they relocate to the barn at the bottom of the garden at the farm. "We went up there, moved all the furniture out, swept the floors, cleaned it up and played all afternoon," says King. Once again, the old grain store became her creative playground.

Through the late winter of 1976–77 and into spring the group rehearsed regularly at Wickham Farm, drumming up a 20-song set. Working on their music, fortified by Hannah Bush's legendary hospitality, breaking off for games of football and as much tea and cake as they could reasonably consume, they got to know one another. King was the oldest of the male trio, socially set slightly apart (he was dubbed 'Nosmo King' for his aversion to cigarettes), and he became the band's de facto organiser: buying the equipment, organising rehearsals, picking up, dropping off. He often collected Bush from her dance classes in his Hillman Imp and brought her to gigs or rehearsals. Bath was the musical dynamo, a gifted player and songwriter who had won a deal with Essex Music, one of those vastly talented musicians always just a whisker away from seizing their big chance. Many years previously he had taught his close friend Del the rudiments of 12-bar blues on the bass, and Palmer had progressed from there. A plain speaking extrovert with a lively sense of humour, Del "was naturally rhythmic, he won dancing competitions," laughs Bath. "He used to do Mick Jagger impersonations. Del was obviously up for it. Del's just really solid, you know there's a bass player there when Del's playing, he's got such a heavy anchor point. A tremendous player, he can really hold it down."

The 18-year-old Bush made an immediate impression on her new bandmates. "She stood out from other girls, she was different," says King. "Not overtly sexual, [but] there was something about her. Shy as shy can be, wouldn't say boo to a goose. She just wanted to sing and play without all the trappings." Palmer, meanwhile, later recalled that he fell for her almost immediately.

None of them, perhaps with the exception of Bath, realised initially how deep her involvement with EMI went. It was not a frequent topic of discussion. "It didn't come out at first, it came out later that she had been paid some money to stay at home and write," says King. "We didn't have to pay for anything at the time, I remember that. The petrol was all paid for."

They rehearsed, according to Bath, for "ages". In common with most fledgling bands, they argued most vociferously over what to call themselves. Bush wanted to give the band "some strange name", and when King came up with the KT Bush Band she shrieked, 'Ooh no, that's terrible!' But that's what it became. Her opposition may have been simple diversionary tactics. There was a certain reluctance on her part to leave the age-old sanctuary of the barn and surrender herself to her first ever taste of live performance, but finally Bath used his contacts to organise a residency at the Rose Of Lee, a popular local pub at 162 Lee High Road in Lewisham*, beginning in April 1977.

"I went down and said we were getting a new band together, we've got a fabulous looking girl singer, we'd got a really strong band," says Bath. "I said the first week you'll get a handful of people, but by the fourth week you won't be able to get them in the door. And sure enough, it was exactly as I predicted." Around 20 people turned up to watch the first Tuesday night gig, split into two 45-minute sets, for which the band were paid the princely sum of £27. "I was so scared, I really was," Bush later recalled of her live debut.[28] "The first time was a little bit daunting [for her], but it got to be great fun," says King. "The following week you couldn't move – and then the week after that you couldn't get *in*. It was just heaving. It was great!"

The KT Bush Band very quickly became a success on its own terms, and their nights at the Rose Of Lee were highly anticipated by both the crowd and the rest of the group, if not necessarily by Bush. Bath tended to handle most of the talking and general audience interaction, traditionally the role of a band's lead singer. Bush – mostly just standing and singing, without the natural defence of a piano and keyboard – was reluctant to communicate directly to the crowd. "She was very nervous," says King. "Sometimes you had to push her on there, but once she was on she was

* It's still there, now called Dirty South.

fine. Singing in these smoke-filled rooms . . . wasn't really her scene, she didn't really frequent pubs. I don't think it was 100 per cent enjoyable, but she wanted to do it because she had to learn stage presence and projecting and playing in front of a band of musicians."

There's little doubt that if Bush had been willing to perform earlier she would have found a more direct route to a record contract, though at what price creatively it's hard to say. Although King says he envisaged the KT Bush Band progressing along the lines of a group like The Pretenders, more straight ahead and rocky, with less emphasis on the arty angle, even in 1977 they stood out. At the time pub-rock was all the rage, its foundations laid deep in US roots music – blues, folk-rock, country, R&B – and a set of aesthetic values that stopped at jeans and plaid shirts. The emphasis was on raw energy and accomplished – solid as opposed to flashy – musicianship over anything so presumptuous as a performance or spectacle. In this landscape, the KT Bush Band was a strange beast indeed.

Bush's involvement brought an extra tantalising twist to standard pub fare. Her innate Englishness made everything from across the Atlantic change hue rather charmingly. They even tried to turn 'Nutbush City Limits' into 'Kate Bush City Limits' but it "didn't quite work!" According to King, "We had this strange little way of playing and performing. The vocals were very high, she was very young and the strength of the vocal wasn't quite there, but people's eyes were popping because she used to wear very flimsy, floaty dresses, rather than jeans and a T-shirt. It was something south-east London hadn't seen, especially the Rose Of Lee."

As word spread and the gigs at the Rose Of Lee and other venues like the Royal Albert in New Cross Road became more successful, they began to feel energised by the group's progress. Although for Bush the experience was ultimately just about "doing [some] thing so my time would be full"[29] while she waited for the moment of ignition, along with her bandmates she took it seriously and invested considerable reserves of time, energy and emotion into it.

"We formed very strong links between us all," she recalled.[30] It was like an extended family, "a good, kind of chummy thing", according to Brian Bath, and everyone mucked in. Lisa Bowyer and her boyfriend Rob became unofficial roadies; Rob worked for a printing firm and offered the services of his van for shifting equipment and personnel. Paddy helped out with the lights and would drop in on guitar and mandolin. Del and Brian cooked up some hand-drawn posters for gigs and had T-shirts printed with the KT Bush Band daubed on the front – the singer, sadly, wouldn't wear one – while King splashed the group's name across his kick drum. In honour of Bush's great love of *The Muppet Show*, he was tentatively nick-named 'Animal'.

Rather quickly, Bush's natural urge to push the envelope and her burgeoning notions about performance – which were being fed daily by her sessions at the Dance Centre – began to rise to the fore. They had rehearsed her song 'James And The Cold Gun' right from the beginning, and it was so cold in the barn that sometimes they would decamp to the front room at Wickham Farm, putting the drums on the hearth rug and playing with acoustic guitars. Because there was a piano in the room, they started rehearsing more Bush originals, and the band of seasoned semi-pros was given a direct insight into her astonishing gift.

"Kate used to write a lot each week and come up with these ideas and bounce them off you," says King. "I don't know how many songs she had for the first album that weren't used. [I remember] some strange song about 'tick tock the clock . . .' She had a unique style of writing and com-posing music. Books, stories, films – she loved *The Red Shoes* – it was that world of art and portraying characters, detectives with trilby hats and old raincoats, old Forties and Fifties films. It became something to write about. From our point of view, it was just chords and rhythms and beats."

Del Palmer, meanwhile, was also impressed and intrigued. "The songs always started off in a way I found instantly familiar, but then suddenly they'd leap off somewhere completely different and I'd think, 'How could you possibly think of going to there from where you were originally?'" he said. "I would never have thought of doing that, and yet it always works! . . . I've never had any desire to work with anyone else since."[31]

There was no shortage of material, but only the songs that most obvi-ously lent themselves to the standard band format – and the ones that stood the most chance of being easily digested by a pub crowd – made it into the set. The strange beauty of 'Them Heavy People', 'James And The Cold Gun' and 'The Saxophone Song' insinuated themselves into the cracks between Marvin Gaye and the Stones. On these songs, Bush would bring her plastic portable keyboard to the front of the stage and add her piano playing to the band; her own songs somehow seemed to require her direct musical participation where 'Honky Tonk Women' did not.

On other numbers, she started putting into practice some of the things she was learning through Lindsay Kemp, Adam Darius and her teachers at the Dance Centre. 'James And The Cold Gun' in particular became a showpiece, complete with fake gun. "Rob got a dry ice machine from somewhere," says Bath. "We used that onstage for 'James And The Cold Gun' and it looked great. We had a bit of a show going! Kate did a costume change, she'd put on a bloomin' Western cowgirl dress for the second set! The theatrical thing was starting to get there. She wasn't shy onstage. She would move around, she didn't stand there like a prop. She was pretty dynamic, she used to live it all." Del Palmer recalls that "she was just brilliant, she used to wear this big long white robe with coloured ribbons on or a long black dress with big flowers in her hair. She did the whole thing with the gun and [the audience] just loved it. She'd go around shooting people."[32]

As the band's circle grew wider, they began amassing more equipment, a bigger PA system, and signed a contract with Len Fletcher's South Eastern Entertainment Agency to play nightclubs at £60 a show. "Once they came to see us they were just ringing up all the time," says King. "We did build up a following, especially in the London scene. It was great driving around and seeing our posters on the hoardings." At Tiffanys in Harlow they played a Sunday afternoon cabaret spot in a restaurant where fake palm trees gazed back at them forlornly and faded photographs of distant beaches adorned the walls. They were asked back but declined. If they were playing places like the Target in Greenford, west London, on the way home they would park Vic King's Hillman Imp and Bath's Morris 1000 van and stop off at Mike's Diner, an all-night eatery in New Burlington Street, off Regent Street. Over 4 a.m. omelettes and cups of tea and strong coffee, they would dissect the night's gig and discuss plans for the next day: Shall we meet tomorrow at the farm? Does Kate have any new songs?

Aside from meeting to play and rehearse, there wasn't a huge amount of this kind of social interaction. They would sometimes pop around to Bush HQ in Wickham Road for a plate of spaghetti and a pow-wow, but she retained a customary detachment between the band's life and her own existence. "She liked to turn up, hide as much as possible, hide again and then go home," says King. "She didn't really drink, she might have had a glass of wine but when we were doing the gigs I don't remember any of that. She didn't really like to hang around and talk to lots of people. She had her little entourage, always secluded. Lisa and Rob, Jay or Paddy, her parents came along to the gigs sometimes. She didn't have a boyfriend that I knew of. I think she might have been seeing a few people, but nothing serious."

That was to change when she and Del Palmer became an item. Neither of them, it seems likely, were initially aware that this was going to be a long lasting attachment. "I felt Kate was more dedicated to singing and writing, to being on her own, rather than being attached to someone," says Vic King, bearing out Bush's earlier feelings about settling down too early. Palmer, however, was to become one of the key figures in her life story. Their romantic relationship would last 15 years, and their working relationship still thrives today.

Palmer recalls feeling an instant attraction from the very first rehearsal at Greenwich Baths. "I felt a little nervous because, you know, I felt a particular emotional involvement coming on right from the word go," he later said.[33] "Kate used to travel with Vic in the Hillman Imp and I used to travel with Brian and we'd follow along and I used to sit in the van raging because I was so envious of Vic that she was travelling with him."[34] When he began hearing her compositions these feelings only intensified. In some deeply subconscious way his love of her work and the woman were bound together. "It was a phenomenon because it was so completely different from what anyone else was doing," he said. "I knew I just had to get involved in some way because this was going to be mega."[35]

The initial steps of their *pas de deux* are long forgotten, but Brian Bath and Vic King recall two separate moments of ignition. "We played a nightclub in Lewisham, the Black Cat or something like that, and [afterwards] we were all talking," says King. "Then they started talking a bit more between themselves than me and Brian. We assumed something might be happening, and obviously at the next gig something *was* happening."

"After a couple of times at the farm you could see there was something going on between Kate and Del," says Bath. "Really quickly they just ran at each other and that was it, they were off – during one of the rehearsals, I think. I thought, 'Oh my God, there's going to be trouble here!' She was just a member of the band, and this was the first time we'd ever had a woman in the band, but it worked out OK. We all got on with each other."

She was 18, he was 24, born on November 3, 1952. When he moved into her flat on Wickham Road later in 1977 it was "all a bit hush-hush and keep-it-careful," says Bath. Charlie Morgan, who had played with Del in one of their previous bands, Conkers, and later drummed for Bush, recalls that the prospect of another male entering the tight-knit Bush circle wasn't necessarily welcomed by all the family. "I think there was a bit of friction between Del and John," he says.

Palmer's influence, however, was unquestionably good for her, both personally and professionally. Talented as Bush undoubtedly was, there was a tendency towards a blanket acceptance of everything she did as being outstanding, particularly when it came to her family's views. Even her mother occasionally made interjections on Bush's behalf if she felt her daughter's interests weren't being represented as well as they might be. "I do remember Kate coming to me after we'd mixed 'The Man With The Child In His Eyes' [in 1975] and saying that her mum didn't think the strings were loud enough!" says Andrew Powell. "And I said, 'Mmm, OK, but I think it's all right.' If I thought they weren't loud enough I would have turned them up."

Charlie Morgan recalls another time, shortly after *The Kick Inside*, when "everything that she did was just amazing according to the family and everyone around her: 'Kate, that's incredible!' We were listening to these [new] songs and everyone was going, 'Oh, that's great! That's *got* to be on the album! That's *fantastic!*' But nobody writes fantastic songs all the time, and a couple of times I said, 'You know, that one's not as good as that one.' I got these horrified looks from the family, that I'd dared to imply that one of Kate's songs was substandard. I was just trying to be pragmatic and as objective as possible. I think Del was able to cut through some of that adoration factor . . . and say, 'Well, I don't think that's the best thing you've ever done. You've got better in you.'"

This would sometimes result in a butting of heads. "I don't like hearing very truthful things about myself," Bush admitted. "I get really indignant, I put a lot of defences up, and I can be stubborn."[36] The fact that Del remains her engineer and sounding board today, long after the end of their personal involvement, suggests that unlike many at the higher echelons of rock and pop she has learned the value of hearing the unvarnished truth on occasion, no matter how unpleasant it may be. She can also be severely self-critical.

Like her best friend Lisa, Palmer was another of those funny, no-nonsense extroverts who took the lead socially, whose behaviour allowed Bush, to a certain extent, to take the back seat in public situations. A working-class south Londoner with few airs and graces, he was able to balance the more serious, academic and 'arty' side of her family's input with a more grounded, pragmatic route to creativity. "Well, Del swears a lot," laughs Bath. "Del just knocks it right down to the basics, he's very blunt with it. He can bring it down to normality, but at the same time it could bring the whole thing down. It can get on your nerves, but he does push it down to reality, which is a good thing, a good attribute for a bass player. He's an anchor point all the way across."

From the outside, it looked like an odd pairing. With his passion for motor racing and fast cars – Hugh Padgham, the producer who worked with Bush on *The Dreaming*, recalls, "My friend several years later sold Del a Ferrari S40, a pretty happening car, and he crashed it on the way home" – there were certainly those who always found Bush's relationship with Palmer a little perplexing, and who were not immune to pondering aloud what exactly it was she saw in a man who would talk excitedly about 4 × 4 cars while wearing a double-breasted suit and sporting a lavish moustache. Everyone agreed he was a nice guy, but he didn't particularly seem her type.

In fact, as much as Bush has ever had a 'sort', Del seemed to fit the bill. From as far back as her earliest romances she has preferred older men – "I don't think I could find a younger man attractive," she once said[37] – from backgrounds often very different to her own. Even their names give off a solid, no-nonsense ring: Steve, Al, Del. Her current partner and the father of her son, Danny McIntosh, falls into a similar category. Direct, grounded, supportive but unafraid to offer criticism of her work.

"Danny and Del – they're both very down to earth," says Stewart Avon Arnold. "I think she needs that. I call her a space child – if she was with someone who was similar to her I think they'd be on another planet by now, mentally. I think Del and [now] Danny ground her, in a sense. Like all couples it works if there's the right combination of energies. It does seem to work for Kate, because she went out with Del for many years, and he is the kind of person that calls a spade a spade. Del was a normal cockney guy, very talented musician, and also very funny, a right laugh. And Danny is very similar, in a sense. Very down to earth. A fantastic

"People confuse the strangeness of the songs with the way she lives her life." – Jon Kelly.
Washing up in the kitchen at East Wickham Farm, 1978. (EVENING STANDARD/GETTY IMAGES)

"A refuge to which Bush has returned again and again in both body and song."
In the gardens at East Wickham Farm, 1978. (EVENING STANDARD/GETTY IMAGES)

"The whole family were very unusual and artistic and spiritual, but all completely different." – Stewart Avon Arnold.
Hannah, Paddy, Kate and Jay, with canine friend, at the farm in 1979. (BBC)

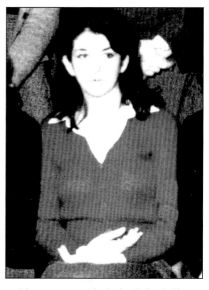

"A fiercely tight-knit Bush fiefdom in the south of the city." 44 Wickham Road. Bush wrote 'Wuthering Heights' while living in the top floor flat. (G. THOMSON)

"There were so many depths that she kept hidden, because the school would perhaps not have given her room for them to be expressed." – Shealla Mubi. Bush in Fifth Form at St Joseph's, pursuing her music largely in secret.

"Within the school, the worst thing you could do was behave in an unladylike manner; that brought a very stern rebuke." – Concepta Nolan-Long. The girls of St Joseph's in their first year. Bush is fourth left on the top row

Poster advertising the KT Bush Band's final gig at The Ship in Brighton: "A lager-drinking pub which wanted something completely different to us. After an hour we were asked to stop." – Vic King.

"I said the first week you'll get a handful of people, but by the fourth week you won't be able to get them in the door. And sure enough…" – Brian Bath. The Rose of Lee in Lewisham, now called Dirty South, where the KT Bush Band played a residency in 1977. (G. THOMSON)

"The theatrical thing was starting to get there. She wasn't shy on stage. She was pretty dynamic, she used to live it all." – Brian Bath. The KT Bush Band at the Rose of Lee, 1977. Vic King on drums, Bush on vocals, Brian Bath on guitar, and (out of shot) Del Palmer on bass. (COURTESY OF VIC KING)

"She jumped out of dance lessons before she was fully trained, but she was a wonderful,
fluid mover. I loved having her in class." – Robin Kovac.

"She was regarded by many as part of the axis
of orthodoxy, the Prince's Trust and BPI set."
With Cliff Richard, Labi Siffre, compere Russell Harty
and members of the London Symphony Orchestra
on the steps of the Royal Albert Hall, publicising
a show in aid of the LSO's 75th Anniversary Appeal,
November 14, 1979. (GRAHAM TURNER/KEYSTONE/GETTY IMAGES)

(MIKE STEPHENS/CENTRAL PRESS/GETTY IMAGES)

"She was harvesting gold and platinum discs from around the globe, and armfuls of awards from the industry and
music magazines." Weighed down with acclaim at the 1979 Capital Music Awards (RICHARD YOUNG/REX FEATURES)
and, above right, celebrating success with Bob Geldof at the *Melody Maker* Reader's Poll Awards, November 28, 1979.

Scenes from the 'Tour Of Life': "She was incredibly nervous, but the show was just extraordinary. We didn't quite know what we were letting ourselves in for, this extraordinary presentation of her music." – Brian Southall.

"For all the flash and grab of the theatrical spectacle, in the end the show really was all about her extraordinary face. One minute she was Douglas Fairbanks, the next Lillian Gish, the next Lolita." Copenhagen, April 26, 1979. (JORGEN ANGEL/REDFERNS)

musician, but not a Keith Moon type character, let's put it that way. He's very organised!"

★ ★ ★

The KT Bush Band's reign of glory lasted for a grand total of 20 gigs. Their last few engagements were, at least, memorable. On Friday June 3, 1977, they played the Half Moon in Putney, a well established music venue, on the eve of the England v. Scotland football international which ended, famously, in the victorious Scotland fans rampaging over the Wembley turf and breaking the goals. "They were mad, they were just mad," said Bush, recalling a night that may well have put her off performing for good. "They had flags waving everywhere, and no one could see the stage because all the guys were getting up on the stage and putting their arms around you!"[38]

"Oh, it was a riot!" remembers Bath. "They were getting up onstage, some guy was all over Kate. I'm not a hard nut, but I went over and pushed him out of the way, off the stage area. Del didn't do anything! It was mental, but we got through it. We did OK." The following Monday, June 6, they were at The Ship in Brighton, a "lager-drinking pub [which] wanted something completely different to us," says King. "After an hour we were asked to stop."

And stop they did. EMI were finally calling their terribly patient prodigy into the ring. Brian Southall was the first representative of the record company to see the band, and he had come away convinced that she was ready for active service. "I went to some pub in Lewisham and I remember having a long conversation with her mum, who kept giving me sausages," he says. "Lovely lady. Mad, eccentric Irish woman. I left the pub and drove with some excitement – we're talking midnight, 1 a.m. – straight to the Royal Garden Hotel in Kensington where we were having a reception for The Shadows, to tell my boss Bob Mercer and other colleagues that I had just seen a little magic moment."

Mercer and Andrew Powell later ventured to south London to check up on Bush's progress and the former, at least, seemed to concur with Southall's verdict. (Powell was less than impressed. "It's what people do early on in their careers," he shrugs. "Stockhausen spent his early years playing piano for a conjurer.") Mercer was happy with her ability to cut the mustard, even if he already sensed a reticence, something held back.

"Those gigs were great, just great," he says. "I always wanted her to do an album of covers, and the main reason for that was having seen her do some covers in her show and realising how good her voice was just as a performer, away from her material. [But] she was never that comfortable. You always knew that she was 'performing' the performance, if you know what I mean. Other artists you'd see bound on to the stage and everything took over. She didn't have the obvious enjoyment of it."

Bush was scheduled to go into the studio in July 1977. As her career snapped out of the leisurely camaraderie of playing pubs and suddenly became serious again, there was a lingering sense, however unfair, that she was simply a little rich girl merely 'playing' at being in a noisy rock group. This was bound to create a degree of resentment and confusion among some of her bandmates as things wound down.

Vic King claims that there was an expectation that they would play on *The Kick Inside*. They had made four-track recordings at De Wolfe studios in Wardour Street which King calls "the pre-demo of the first album: 'Them Heavy People', 'James And The Cold Gun'. . . . One day she had a really terrible cold, she's done better things than that, but it was to hear her songs and her voice maturing so they could be taken to whoever was producing the first album with a view to orchestration and ideas for the final album." In this respect, at least, the session was a success. The arrangement of 'James And The Cold Gun' used on *The Kick Inside* – where the tempo is reduced to half pace at the end and comes out with a guitar solo – was King's idea and was first used at KT Bush Band gigs. "Being her band [on the first album] was mentioned, but then they started getting session guys in," he says. "Bye bye band! Word came across: 'I've got to go into the studio and I'm sorry to say they are going to get session musicians in. I have tried to fight it, but they insist.'"

Colin Lloyd-Tucker, who later befriended Bush and Paddy and collaborated extensively with them both, was working at De Wolfe studios at this time and recalls the session was booked by EMI, so perhaps there was some discussion of the possibility of her band playing on the album. Brian Bath, however, recalls being made clear about the limited life span of the enterprise from the very start. "I think her dad said at the beginning, because he had a lot to do with things, that this is not going to go on forever," he says. "It's probably going to last a few months. I don't think there was [any talk of us doing the album] because that process had already begun. But what a shame. It was a really good band."

It's probable that Bush would indeed have preferred to use her band on *The Kick Inside*, given that she lobbied hard for them to appear on the follow-up, *Lionheart*, and kept them on board for promotional duties after the album's release. There was also the fact that her boyfriend was the bass player. At the time, however, she lacked the power to call those kinds of shots.

Other issues left a less than sweet aftertaste. Aside from the studio recordings, many of the band's gigs were filmed, taped and photographed, but almost none of this material has ever come to light. According to Brian Bath, an attempt to release a single of the KT Bush Band's "really good" version of Johnny Winter's 'Shame Shame Shame', which they had cut at Graphic Sound studios in Catford during a recording session designed to capture some of the highlights of their live set rather than Bush originals, was later halted because "there was some opposition about it." He may be being diplomatic. "Everything had to be confiscated – '*or else*', I think the phrase was," says Vic King. "They were all confiscated and disappeared. I was told at the time that nothing else could be put out, they didn't want anything ruining her impact. Whether it was EMI or the family, word got around. I think Del said to Brian that if anyone has anything hiding they're not able to use it for profit or gain. 'If you've got anything could you hand it back.'"

Bush wasn't at all keen on her earliest experiments in live performance being unearthed and held up to the world, although she was in no way dismissive of the band members themselves or their contributions. In an expanded incarnation the band would go on to play a significant part in her early career, she made sure of that. For now, however, the focus shifted to the studio. At last, it was time.

4

Pull Out The Pin

"I CAN remember saying to Kate, 'You're going to be so famous you're not going to be able to walk down the street,'" says Jon Kelly. "I said that to her after the first week of recording, though she wouldn't have believed it."

It was the kind of premonition guaranteed to give her nightmares. It was also true. *The Kick Inside* was recorded in AIR studios over a period of six very happy weeks in July and August 1977, with Andrew Powell producing and Kelly, the house engineer, as his right hand man. From the very start, everything seemed to click into place. "It was a fantastically creative atmosphere, we cut three or four tracks in the first day," says Powell. "I remember we started off with 'Moving' and that got done in about two hours or less, and I thought, 'Hmm, this is good!' I think we did 'Kite' next, to mix up the fast and slow tracks. I remember . . . Jon Kelly said he came out of that first day and thought, 'That's it, I've peaked, it can never get any better than this!' It was that kind of feeling."

Indeed it was. "It was fabulous," says Kelly. "It was what I had gone into the business to do, to have those moments. They are few and far between. I remember her sitting at the piano singing those songs and it was just mesmerising. You could have put the mike anywhere in the room and recorded it on anything. It was an absolute joy, there was nothing to fix."

The musicians were a bespoke quartet assembled by Powell, pairing up two halves of two successful bands: David Paton on bass and Ian Bairnson on guitar, from Scottish group Pilot; and Stuart Elliott on drums and Duncan MacKay on keyboards, from Cockney Rebel. Powell had worked with both bands as an arranger and was aware that these players were far from the weary, clock-watching session musicians of rock lore. They had both had number one singles in 1975 with, respectively, 'January' and '(Come Up And See Me) Make Me Smile', and were empathetic to a young songwriter with unique sensibilities. "I had no say, so I was very lucky really to be given such good musicians to start with," she said. "And they were lovely, 'cause they were all very concerned about what I thought of the treatment of each of the songs. And if I was unhappy with anything, they were more than willing to re-do their parts. So they were very concerned about what I thought, which was very nice. And they were really nice guys, eager to know what the songs were about and all that sort of thing."[1]

It was the first of many times that the four would come together as a session band, and it proved an instantly fruitful blend. So much so that Bush worked with them all again – collectively and separately – several times over the coming years, and in Elliott she found a drummer who has provided her music with its polyrhythmic pulse all the way through to *Aerial*. "I knew Stuart Elliott would work well with Kate, he had a light touch," says Powell. "He's someone who really listens. He'd shout 'Stop!' in the middle of a take and say, 'Can't you *hear* what she's singing? She's singing this and we're all bashing away.' That's what you want, someone who is really locking in and listening. He's a very sensitive musician."

The musicians hadn't heard any of Bush's music prior to the session, and the fact that they came in cold made their subsequent reaction all the more emphatic. Paton recalls Powell had told him that her songs were "a bit wild, a bit wacky even," but he wanted them to enter the studio without any firm preconceptions. Just as David Gilmour had done back in 1973, the producer said to Bush on the first day of recording, 'Just play them the first song.' It was 'Moving'.

"She sat down at the piano, said, 'It goes like this,' and just played," recalls David Paton. "We were all gathered around the piano with our jaws dropped, because it was a stunning performance. Faultless, absolutely faultless, and she could do that time and time again. Every song she introduced was just faultless. I'd worked with a lot of musicians in the past and solo artists and it's not very often you get that wow factor, [but] she had that as soon as she played the first few notes. Even her piano playing was so accomplished. I knew right away. I think we all did."

Most of the group performances on the album were cut this way – live, with overdubs added later. Bush would play a song at the piano and the band would "wrap ourselves around her, looking for ways to embellish it or give it direction," says Ian Bairnson. Some direct stylistic touches – like the light reggae rhythm on 'Kite' – tended to evolve as the musicians bedded in the song. Others, like the half-tempo breakdown towards the end of 'James And The Cold Gun', were remnants of the KT Bush Band's pub arrangements.

Andrew Powell was very much the senior partner in the relationship, although early on there was a need for some gentle recalibrating of the producer-artist dynamic. Powell "at first treated me like a session musician,"[2] said Bush, but "eventually gave me an incredible amount of freedom. I was lucky to be able to express myself as much as I did, especially with this being a debut album. Andrew was really into working together, rather than pushing everyone around."[3] Morris Pert, the eccentric Scottish musician brought in to add percussive touches such as the delightful Boo Bams (how could Bush have possibly resisted such an instrument? They are, a little disappointingly, merely tuned bongo drums) on 'Room For The Life', recalls that there was a general settling in period while everyone – including Powell, who of course had worked with Bush in 1975 – readjusted their expectations in light of the evidence in front of their eyes. "Even Andrew at the beginning was a bit flummoxed as to what direction she should be going in," says Pert. "He let her take over gradually, because he was just a little bit flummoxed. It would have been criminal to bring in a producer who said, 'Don't do this, do it like that'. That would have been a nightmare, and Kate would have collapsed in a heap."

EMI left Powell to get on with things. He wasn't even given a budget, another example of the record company's largesse and faith in its debutante. Bob Mercer visited the studio only once, and on that occasion he telephoned ahead to say, 'Do you mind if I do? I don't want to disturb anything.' Such a careful, hands-off approach was astute – anything else was likely to have made Bush self-conscious and even resentful – but they were keeping a discreetly close eye on the proceedings all the same. Brian Southall recalls dropping into AIR to have "long conversations with Andrew." Members of her family also frequently popped in.

Generally Powell was sympathetic to both her sensitivity and her music, allowing the songs to grow and the arrangements to evolve. His presence was nonetheless a powerful one. He was, says Kelly, a "dominant producer". He wrote parts for the rhythm section, played a variety of instruments, and generally had strong ideas about how the album should proceed. Bush may later have concluded that her debut album reflected – perhaps inevitably – at least as much of Powell's artistic vision as her own, but whatever misgivings she had (and it later transpired that she was unhappy with much of *The Kick Inside*, but wasn't yet able to do very much about it) were kept to herself, stored away for future experience. She also recognised, as did everyone else in the room, that she was essentially in good hands. "Andrew was a very, very talented man," says Kelly. "His writing and his musicianship, and his appreciation of Kate and his astuteness at getting the best out of her when she was so young and naïve – knowing what I know now of the business, that could have easily all gone so wrong. Andrew. . . . loved Kate and the songs, but he was determined to get it right."

She absorbed everything. She listened and watched and asked questions, showing infinite patience and enthusiasm. When it came time for mixing and sequencing, she was there every day, drinking it all in, spooling forward to the day when she could do it all herself. At the time, primarily she felt relief at finally being able to unburden herself of at least some of her vast store of songs, and not a little grateful that she was able to daub the canvas with her own stylistic touches. Her beloved whale song acted as a prelude to 'Moving' and effectively opened the album; she brought Paddy in to play some of his esoteric instruments and sing with her on several songs; and she was able to introduce her cast of vocal characters on backing vocals, growling and chiding to great effect in the background on 'James And The Cold Gun', rumbling theatrically on 'Them Heavy People', and generally adding much depth, flavour and personality to the tracks.

All those present were immediately struck – and rather captivated – by the dichotomy revealed through working with her, the seemingly huge gulf between, as Paton puts it, this "very quiet girl, very down to earth, the first person to say, 'Do you want anything, do you want a cup of tea?'", and the hugely assured artist singing these songs of sex, love, lust, ghosts and cosmic philosophy, imploring and declaiming in a variety of strange, enchanting voices. It was a wholly alluring mixture of innocence and experience; the combination of, on the one hand, an understated personality and a vastly amplified performing persona. "After we did a couple [of songs] we were thinking, 'What's coming next?'" says Ian Bairnson. "She pulls out these characters that aren't there when she's not singing or performing. There was no formula there, they were all truly original songs, and the thing that pulls it all together is *her*."

Unlike her work at the Dance Centre, which she continued until right before the recording sessions and for a short period afterwards, there was no overtly physical side to her musical expression. Paton recalls, with a distinct gleam in his eye, the way she used to limber up in the studio during sessions, but when she was singing she stood still and concentrated. She wasn't one, says Powell, "for doing the dance of the seven veils while she was doing her vocals." Somewhere deep inside, however, gears were shifting. She consistently delivered, indeed exceeded, the expectations of what her producer and her fellow musicians asked her to do, but she found ways to make the process a little smoother, to ease the metamorphosis. "I remember her smoking an awful lot of joints in the studio," says Paton. "That was a strange influence for such a 'public school' girl. I think she needed it to relax. Dope was kind of taboo then, it was still 'illegal'."

"She did smoke quite a lot," adds Jon Kelly, while Andrew Powell, three decades on doing a convincing impression of a sighing, eye-rolling but essentially indulgent schoolmaster, recalls: "It did definitely happen. It was just a fact and you had to work with it. There were times when one had to hide the stuff: 'You can have it back when you've finished this vocal!' What can one do? Most of the time it didn't get in the way, but sometimes you could hear the voice starting to suffer and drying out – so it was sometimes hidden! It could have been [nerves]. A confidence booster? Dutch courage? It's hard to judge."

The sense of camaraderie and respect in the room grew as everyone realised that this was no ordinary singer songwriter and that they were working on something truly special. There may have been a vague feeling among the band of mind-your-language, but nobody was standing on ceremony. She was, says Bairnson, "just one of the lads. She's a very modest person, anyway, she's not an extrovert. She definitely leant on us, and we supported her. Whenever she got a bit nervous we came out with various strains of humour, generally based on *Monty Python*, which always seemed to do the trick. Her getting nervous, there was no drama to it, you just sensed it."

Despite her innate quietness, her inner strength, her sense of poise and self-assurance was apparent to everyone. "I didn't think she was vulnerable at all, I thought she was very intelligent, a lot more intelligent than your average musician, and I thought she'd be able to look after herself," says Paton. "I think you have to be confident to carry that off, to sit in front of these accomplished session musicians and say, 'This is what I do.' I would find it daunting myself. She must have known how good she was to be able to do that in front of us."

Once again, there was a reluctance – part shyness, part manners, part something more primal, some deep protective instinct – to let too much light into her motives and ambitions. Already well versed in the standard patterns of behaviour within the music business, the musicians all appreciated her lack of prattling self-obsession, and the absence of the kind of hollow boasting that afflicts the truly insecure. "If you just met her as a stranger you would have no idea what she is capable of, and she has never thrust that in your face, either," says Bairnson. "If you're absolutely comfortable with what you do, then there's no need to start blowing your trumpet."

"She didn't say, 'I want to do this and that, me, me, me, me . . .'," adds Paton. "She wasn't that kind of person at all and that in itself was very refreshing. A lot of artists you work with you usually find that they're besotted with themselves. Like Freddie Mercury, all he could do was talk about himself all the time, but she wasn't like that at all. She kept her vision to herself."

Her songwriting had never been open to general scrutiny, and on *The Kick Inside* she was consummately prepared, having been working privately towards this specific moment for many years. The songs were topped, tailed and more than ready before they were publicly presented. Nobody saw her extemporise or improvise – not even the lyrics would be altered once the song was being played in the studio. She was very careful not to reveal anything until she was certain it was complete.

There was an astonishing depth of material, even after Powell and Bush had met several times to cull the 120 songs she had available into a less unwieldy shortlist. "The songs just appeared, she seemed to have an endless supply," says Paton. "She would sit at the piano sometimes and play songs and say, 'I might do this, I might not.'" According to Powell 'Wow' was already written, and was considered for *The Kick Inside* but not pursued, which "tells you the quality of what we had to keep off. I've often tried to think where I would have put 'Wow' on that album. I just don't think it would have fit. And I know one day we did three voice and piano tracks, only one of which, 'Feel It', ended up on the album." In the end it was decided to add two of the three songs from the 1975 AIR session, 'The Man With The Child In His Eyes' and 'The Saxophone Song'. They recorded another version of 'Maybe', the third, but it didn't make the cut, a good song destined to always be the bridesmaid.

Another track recorded but never used during the sessions was 'Scares Me Silly', preserved on tapes of the early album outtakes. Musically it's unremarkable, the kind of song the record company may have been encouraging her to write. A chugging, upbeat track with a rather clunky new wave intro, a reggae breakdown and a clear, uncomplicated chorus hook, it was probably only included on the shortlist to make sure there were enough up-tempo numbers in the running. Lyrically, however, 'Scares Me Silly' is extremely interesting, a real-time depiction of Bush's mental, physical and emotional processes as she is singing – or more accurately recording – a song.

Numerous artists have been afflicted by stage fright through the years and some, such as The Band, have even written about it, but far fewer have ever described so graphically being affected by *studio* sickness, which here takes the form of acute self-consciousness. 'Scares Me Silly' begins in the studio, just as the lights are going down. Bush licks her lips and begins singing the opening line, but already she is overtaken by the idea that in order to perform she must become somebody else ("How can this girl be me?"), as though her everyday self is in danger of obstructing her performing alter ego as she strives to "keep the mood".

The sensation of singing is not depicted as a pleasant experience: it's a tightrope walk. Bush describes a sense of "vertigo" and a feeling of sickness as she tries to balance her emotions and force herself into another take – and yet, though it scares her half to death, it also "gets her going".

There's much on which to chew in there. The mix of terror and pleasure that performing – even in the studio – engenders mirrors the act of love (indeed, the chorus phrase of the song is a rather less poetic echo of the impulse behind 'Hounds Of Love'). Then there's the necessity of "goading" herself to keep going; the "need to lose"; the idea of holding the mood, like an actress, for the length of the take. Fascinating. An early unveiling of the complex and draining ritual she goes through in trying to honour the exact requirements of each song she sings. No mention, oddly, of sitting primly at the piano with a big fake smile for the cameras.

In terms of her songwriting, nobody had any real inkling about where it was all coming from. This was the summer punk went pop, but musically *The Kick Inside* was very much pre-Sex Pistols in its leanings: a bit flared, a bit hairy, weed rather than speed, a little bit prog-rock, even, with its floating melodies, classically influenced piano, shifting time signatures, tight musicianship and poetic, occasionally cosmic lyrics. It was beautifully played, but what *was* it exactly? Some elements the casual observer could objectively attribute to acknowledged sources. The "big brass bed" in 'James And The Cold Gun' is also part of the furniture in Dylan's 'Lay, Lady Lay'; Om Mani Padme Hum was a Tibetan Buddhist prayer, uttered in 'Strange Phenomena' as an ode to the unseen "hand a-moulding us"; the 'Goose Moon' is a concept from Native American Cree culture, where the flight of the geese heralds the coming spring. The nods to Gurdjieff, traditional folk songs, classic literature and lilting reggae, very much the hop-on-hop-off genre of choice at the time, all place it in pre-punk lineage, but already at its core her work was without obvious precedent, bearing the distinct mark of a unique psychic imprint.

"You can't say she comes from Carole King or Joni Mitchell or Kiri TeKanawa," says Powell. "There's bits of everything. The backing vocals on 'Moving' sound like 'Queen Of The Night' from *The Magic Flute*. There are all sorts of things going on there, [but] she didn't talk about it a lot." 'Moving' and 'Kite' both reflected the physical release and psychological transformation she experienced through dance. The "moving stranger" is Lindsay Kemp, and the fact that he "crush[ed] the lily in my soul" is a positive thing, reflecting the way that movement has empowered, rather than weakened her.

However, control room chit-chat and canteen conversation rarely touched on such matters, while the band generally steered clear of discussing her lyrics. Songs like 'Strange Phenomena' tended to put the frighteners on the session men. "I didn't like to ask her, 'What's this song about – tampons and things like that?'" says Paton, although Jon Kelly remembers vague discussions about whales and, in reference to 'L'Amour Looks Something Like You', "her love". He was most struck by the title track, a truly beautiful song of forbidden passion between a brother and sister, sung moments before the pregnant girl commits suicide, "giving it all in a moment for you." "I remember mixing that in Studio One, it was one of the songs that was left until last because we'd done some orchestra on it," he says. "As I'm mixing it the lyric just hit home to me. It got to me, it was so powerful. I found it quite an emotional song to listen to and to work on."

The album has a generous scattering of these moments. Heard today, *The Kick Inside* is simply an extraordinary record, most particularly in terms of its lyrical content. Her desire to 'masculinise' her muse, to sing from a strong, bold place, is clearly evident, and yet it is one of the most profoundly female albums ever made. She is the 'hungry' woman of Dylan's songs – fully awake, sensual, quiveringly alive – utterly without shame, astoundingly bold in her declaration of her appetites and fears. This is raw femininity in mind and body, but expressed in a very muscular way. It's an astonishing alchemy. She sings as the woman she is inside and out, and also as the child she often seems to want to remain. It has all the deep wisdom of youth, of experiences real and imagined, earned and unearned, of knowing without knowing, but this is not the realm of fantasy. It's all real. It's all emotionally true. "I wasn't a daydreamer," she later said. "Writing songs and poetry is putting into words and music my real feelings."[4]

The language is something new for a female artist. *The Kick Inside* is lit up with the ecstasy and fear of puberty and sexual awakening – everywhere you look there's a sense of a body growing, changing shape, immensely powerful but also terrifying: "Beelzebub is aching in my belly-o"; "Room for a life in your womb"; "This kicking here inside"; "Sticky love inside"; "Stars that climb from her bowels"; "Your warm hand walking around." Elemental, primal. The title track is a sympathetic gaze at an incestuous relationship; 'Strange Phenomena' ties in the menstrual cycle to the waxing and waning of the moon; 'Wuthering Heights' is a supernatural psychodrama. These are no run of the mill boy-meets-girl songs. Even the many romantic shadowplays are sensually drawn, with a fine eye for lace and stockings, fire and candlelight, fact and fancy, almost teetering on the edge of Mills & Boon erotic-cliché ("My stockings fall onto the floor"; "We move into the boudoir") but usually saved by a poetic turn of phrase or a flash of genuinely inspired imagery ("You came out of the night wearing a mask in white colour"), or a dash of daft, endearing humour.

The album's crowning glory almost missed the boat. 'Wuthering Heights' was written on the eve of going in to record the album, beneath a full moon on a clear, midsummer night in 1977, looking out through the open window over the rooftops of south London. "It was only written a few days before we went into the studio," says Powell. "Kate came round to my place and said, 'What about this one?', and sat down at my piano and played it. I said, 'Um yeah, I think we should use that!' It hit me straight away as really extraordinary. She's doing some very interesting things with her voice. I loved it."

It was one of the final pieces in the jigsaw, a bold confirmation of her intent. The song wasn't directly inspired by reading Emily Brontë's novel of 1847, but rather by catching the final ten minutes of a 1970 movie adaptation starring future James Bond, Timothy Dalton. Indeed, she wrote 'Wuthering Heights' before she had read the book in its entirety. Interesting that, even with this most seemingly literary of songs, it was direct – and accidental – visual stimulus that, as so often seemed to be the case, provided the initial creative spark. "I'd just caught the very end of [the film]," she said. "It was really freaky, 'cos there's this hand coming through the window and whispering voices and I've always been into that sort of thing, you know, and it just hung around in my head. I *had* to write a song about it."[5]

With its stirring combination of the supernatural and the sheer bloody-minded power of obsessive love, with a not insignificant personal connection ("It's me, Cathy!") thrown in for good measure, 'Wuthering Heights' is a fine insight into the how and why Bush writes. It was the instant connection, rather than the detail, that was important. The impetus isn't intellectual (it's a world away from someone like Sting name-dropping Nabokov for pure effect), but entirely emotional. Brontë's novel doesn't tiptoe around the pretty feelings on the surface, but rather digs around amongst the churning currents below. Bush related to Cathy's hidden depths, her youthful passion, her violence. Once hooked, she climbed inside and truly embodied the song. "This young girl in an era when the female role was so inferior and she was coming out with this passionate, heavy stuff," she said. "Great subject matter for a song."[6]

And so it transpired. When it came to recording the song at AIR, Andrew Powell pulled rank and wrote and played the bass part, much to David Paton's chagrin. "As a consolation prize he says, 'Davie, you can play 12-string.' Hmmm!" Powell knew a good thing when he heard one. The piercingly high vocals were partly the result of Bush's attempts to improve her vocal technique. She had started writing in keys beyond her range in order to expand her vocal reach. The songs started climbing; she wanted them to fly. But the vocal is also a deliberate piece of characterisation, signifying Cathy as a spirit rather than flesh and bone. The track was topped off by Ian Bairnson's stunning solo, stretching out over the horizon and disappearing deep into the mists, ringing into eternity.

However impressive the results, 'Wuthering Heights' was never intended to be the first single. EMI wanted 'James And The Cold Gun' because, according to Bob Mercer, "I thought it was a cleverer song and more accessible. She didn't agree with me and nailed me to the floor. She asked to come and see me and burst into tears. I backed off, and I said at the time, 'Look Kate, it's of no consequence or importance to me what the first fucking single is. I don't think you're a singles act, you're an albums act, and I think it could take at least three albums for us to gain any traction at all. So by all means put 'Wuthering Heights' out first. It's not the most important thing.' She was an albums act as far as I was concerned, in those days there tended to be a clear distinction between the two. Frankly I wouldn't have minded if someone had suggested we didn't put out a single at all. Thank God we didn't [do that]!"

Bush has always disputed Mercer's claim that she "burst into tears", but whatever way the drama unfolded, it was a significant dust-up for several reasons. It showed that this 'girl' who attracted any number of unintentionally patronising adjectives from her peers – 'innocent', 'sweet', 'shy', 'lovely' – possessed deep reserves of strength and fortitude when it came to fighting for her art, even with those within the EMI family for whom she had great affection. It also gave her instant power. Once 'Wuthering Heights' became a number one single, a hit as unlikely as it was all-encompassing, her insistence on it being the first single seemed like a stroke of genius, almost spooky in its prescience. Who was going to have the courage to argue with her next time? It bought her a freedom she used, usually wisely, always wilfully. "There was really never another fight," says Mercer. "To be honest, I pretty much lay down after that. After the fight, I realised what kind of artist I was dealing with and that my role here was to keep out of the way and not knock over the scenery. I didn't have any [more] disagreements with her." When it came to the second single Bush wanted 'The Man With The Child In His Eyes', in order to showcase her singing and songwriting talents and prove that she wasn't a mere gimmick. EMI, who favoured 'Them Heavy People', said – 'Sure, whatever you want.'

Of course, Bush hadn't fought for 'Wuthering Heights' because of her certain belief in its innate commerciality, but primarily because she felt it was far more representative of what she did – *who is she?* – than 'James And The Cold Gun' which, though a decent theatrical rock song which neatly broke up the mood of the album and really came into its own onstage, was a little two-dimensional and formulaic. She burst into public consciousness at almost exactly the same time as Debbie Harry and Blondie, whose 'Denis' was working its way up the charts at the same time as 'Wuthering Heights', and she intended to set herself apart from the start. She had an inkling 'Wuthering Heights' might turn a few heads, for better or worse. Far from the doe-eyed hippie chick with nothing but disdain for commercial considerations, she was acutely aware of the importance of making a splash. "I felt that to actually get your name anywhere you've got to do something that is unusual, because there's so much good music around and it's all in a similar vein," she said. "It had the high pitch and it also had a very English storyline which everyone would know. . . . I'm into reaching more than the ordinary market."[7]

She did not become a star by mistake. Who ever did?

★ ★ ★

'Wuthering Heights' was finally released on January 20, 1978, after all manner of eleventh hour hiccups. Originally scheduled for November 4, 1977, it was delayed to avoid being trampled by the Christmas market – Wings' 'Mull Of Kintyre' was coming out on EMI the following week, devouring all in its path – and also to allow the sleeve to undergo a complete revision as Bush wrestled for the first time with the realities of projecting herself to the public. Rather than sinking it, the delay in its release lent the single a crucial momentum. Promotional pressings had been sent out some two months before Christmas, direct from the factory to key radio stations and journalists via EMI's Automatic Mailing List. They then attempted to put the genie back in the bottle, but it was rather like trying to thumb a plum Pontefract into a slot machine. "We did, for the first time in my knowledge, send the promotion people out asking them *not* to play our record," laughs Brian Southall. "Most people obliged, bar two, one of whom was Eddie Puma, the producer at Capital Radio, and the other was his presenter Tony Myatt. They weren't having any of it and continued to play it."

Myatt's dogged and genuine support of 'Wuthering Heights' ensured the song was an airplay hit over a month before it was released. "They said the switchboard lit up with people ringing up asking who it was, and they told people it was coming out in January," recalls Southall. Bush never forgot this stroke of good fortune. Myatt and Puma were later given a gold disc by EMI and were guests of honour at the launch of *Lionheart*. As the snowball thickened and gathered pace, Bush observed its progress with a mixture of detachment and excitement.

"I remember going round to her flat when 'Wuthering Heights' was first played by that DJ on Capital and Kate said, 'Oh, they're playing my song tonight,'" recalls Brian Bath. "We were all sitting round there and [Myatt] said he'd found this really odd song. She couldn't believe it was coming out of the radio. And he kept playing it. You could phone Capital to vote for the song you wanted to hear each day. I was round at the farm pretty much every day, there was always something to do, and Kate's mum would say, 'Have you phoned Capital radio yet? Use the phone, do it now!' It kept getting played and played and all of a sudden it just exploded."

In those days, there was such a thing as a gradual explosion in the music industry. Within a fortnight of its eventual release 'Wuthering Heights' entered the charts at number 42. It crept up, week-by-week: 27, 13, five, as the attendant clamour grew louder. *The Kick Inside* was released on February 17 and climbed to number three, further increasing the momentum. On March 7, the single reached number one and stayed there for a month. The media interest was astonishing, moving far beyond the music press and encompassing the tabloids, broadsheets, television and radio. Auberon Waugh weighed in appreciatively. Bush had already sold over 250,000 records and was, according to one of those great immeasurable statistics by which fame is measured, the most photographed woman in Britain. Suddenly all hell was breaking loose and she was wanted in a million different places simultaneously.

"As soon as 'Wuthering Heights' became a hit . . . my whole routine was just blown apart," Bush recalled. "It was extraordinary how suddenly everything changed. . . . It happened, it was instant. It [was] frightening."[8]

★ ★ ★

She had rounded up a revamped KT Bush Band to handle promotional duties and, one suspects equally as importantly, to lend her some much needed moral support. Since the recording of *The Kick Inside* Brian Bath had spent considerable time writing charts of all Bush's songs, knocking them into shape for some future, as yet unspecified purpose. Vic King was still put out by the way the band ended – when *The Kick Inside* came out he refused to even look at the credits – and in his absence Bath had recruited Sergio Castillo on drums, who played in "a busy, Latin American style", which must have done wonders for 'Moving'. With Paddy occasionally joining in on guitar and mandolin, prior to the single and album release the band performed with Bush at some key EMI functions, notably a "pretty nerve-wracking" showcase of songs from the forthcoming album for EMI executives at the White Elephant on the River, a plush restaurant on the Thames Embankment in Pimlico, which "went down well,"[9] as well as a "bun fight up at Turnberry"[10] in January for record company representatives from all around the world. These cemented her reputation within the company, confirmed her as a cause well worth fighting for.

With 'Wuthering Heights' climbing the charts all over Europe, suddenly they were all swept off on a great adventure. When the last minute call came to go to Germany for the music show *Bio's Bahnhof*, it became apparent that Castillo, a Cuban, wouldn't get a work permit in time. Vic King was asked to rejoin the band but declined. "I said I was doing something else," he recalls. "I was a little bit annoyed about being kicked out of the band, and I was thinking, 'Should I help out and then be kicked out yet again?' There was the abrupt ending, and not being involved on the first album, and then suddenly you get a phone call. Looking back I probably should have said 'yes' but the pride said 'no'. If Kate had rung up to explain the situation it may have been a bit different." Charlie Morgan – an old friend and a member of Bath and Palmer's former band Conkers – took Castillo's place with less than a day's notice. Most of the group didn't even have passports, but within two hours of visiting EMI HQ at Manchester Square they were ready to leave.

It was Bush's first time in an aeroplane, an experience she never learned to love and quickly came to dislike and, in time, avoid if at all possible. It was her first ever television performance, too, consisting of a live version of 'Kite' played with the band on the back of a train – "poor Kate was *so* nervous", says Charlie Morgan – and singing 'Wuthering Heights' to a backing tape, before battling gamely through an interview conducted entirely in jaunty German. The backdrop – supposed to evoke the rough majesty of the Yorkshire moors – featured a volcano. Welcome to the joys of European music promotion. For now, her smile, her giggle and her sense of wonder at this new, ridiculous world got her through.

And so it began. For Bush, it was the start of a year of utter mayhem. Off to ITV at seven o'clock in the morning to record a performance for *Magpie*; playing on *Saturday Night At The Mill* and chatting briefly to presenter Bob Langley; off to Ireland for the legendary *Late Late Show*; introduced by Peter Cook on the short-lived music show *Revolver*, appearing on the current affairs programme *Tonight*, and being gently patronised about her 'O' level results on *Ask Aspel*.

Top Of The Pops was the big one. She made her first appearance on the BBC's flagship music programme on February 16, when 'Wuthering Heights' broke into the Top 40 at number 27. What should have been a happy occasion turned into a nightmare. She discovered just prior to taping her performance that the show's arcane rules dictated that, as a solo artist, she was not allowed to play with her band. Instead she would have to sing solo to a new, markedly inferior backing track of her song, knocked off that afternoon by the BBC orchestra. It was all dictated by stringent Musicians' Union regulations. Robin Nash, the programme's producer, came from a variety background (he was the man behind *Terry And June* and *The Les Dawson Show*, no less) and was unsympathetic to Bush's plight. "He threw his weight around," according to a member of the Bush entourage. "It was not a nice experience for someone who has bust a gut creating things properly and wants to be able to do it with backbone and honesty."

All her band were there but they could only stand at the front and watch helplessly as the misery unfolded. "She had a terrible time with *Top Of The Pops*," says Charlie Morgan. "If you had a sound like Kate had on 'Wuthering Heights', with this wonderful guitar solo by Ian Bairnson, and you want to use your own band but the BBC says, 'Absolutely not, Kate is a solo artist and she will sing with the house band,' – well, it was a really, really unpleasant experience for her. She had a horrible time, she was practically in tears. Her band would have given her huge moral support, if nothing else. We all felt for her and we were really dejected, because we knew she hadn't done a fantastic performance and it wasn't really her fault. It's one thing being out of your comfort zone, but if you have an element of control it's OK. But if you're completely out of control and you're 18 years old [in fact, she was 19] that's not a very good experience." She later memorably described seeing the performance played back as "like watching myself die."[11]

These were merely the brutal opening skirmishes in her long battle with that most strange, destructive and vertiginous phenomenon: fame. Coming to terms with the odd process of observing yourself as seen from several different angles, losing control of your art, frequently feeling like a tin of beans rattling along a conveyor belt, besieged by doubt and self-loathing, the contours of your old life warped by the push and pull of constant motion. She had to learn quickly, chalking up the negatives to experience and making mental notes in her little black book: don't do *this* next time. Avoid *that*. The fact that her career has always been defined as much by the things she refuses to do as those she embraces can be traced directly back to this time. Before the end of March she had appeared again on *Top Of The Pops*, a much more assured performance, this time from a number one artist. But she didn't forget. "She was once bitten, twice shy, and she vowed never to let that happen again," says Morgan. "Typical Leo: 'I'm *not* going to let that happen again.'" Despite numerous invitations, she didn't appear on the programme again until 1985, when she could do whatever she liked.

Dealing with the printed press proved perhaps her steepest learning curve. "That was when things started getting very difficult for me because until then it had all been very creative work, writing, recording, learning to dance," she said. "[Now] I was talking to press . . . and I couldn't express myself easily. I was up against a different beast."[12] She was thrown into the bearpit, offered to everyone from *The Sun* and *NME* to *Vogue* and *The Vegetarian*. Reading back over the multitude of interviews, much is made of her cigarette smoking and her high voice, her rather comical habit of punctuating each statement with a sincere 'amazing', a solemn 'heavy' or a simple, breathy 'wow'. Gurdjieff's name starts popping up, as does her vegetarianism, her belief in astrology, ghosts, ESP and reincarnation. Already you can see the outline of a caricature forming. Penny Allan, a columnist in the *Guardian*, castigated her for "cultivating a childlike voice and encouraging her audience to act like voyeurs."

The tabloid hounds soon started sniffing around her private life. Only once, very early on, does she name Del as her beau. Thereafter, she throws out a number of red herrings. She will say she lives "alone" when in fact she was co-habiting; she invents a boyfriend – "an artist", someone "not in the music industry" – for the benefit of *Company* magazine and the *Evening Standard*, while for others she breezily announces she is seeing lots of people and no one in particular. Always, she plays down marriage and kids, any hint of a "heavy" relationship. How much of this was down to protecting her privacy and how much to creating a sense of mystique – perhaps even an aura of availability – is open to debate. "I escorted her to lots of things as a kind of pseudo-boyfriend," says EMI's Brian Southall. "I don't remember who made the decision – maybe it was Bob, maybe it was her – that she shouldn't have a boyfriend and wouldn't be seen with Del. It was a very Sixties thing to do. Del was very much in the background, which he seemed quite happy with, but of course we all knew."

She was no shrinking violet. Self-possessed and opinionated when the mood struck, she often came across as genuine, ambitious and savvy. At times she seemed blessed with an intense self-awareness far beyond her years, watching herself constantly from some far away point, both fascinated and perpetually on guard against betraying any rock-starry traits; at other times she seemed astonishingly naïve in some of her comments. On her vegetarianism: "I do eat plants, and I know they're living, and I'm fond of them, but . . . I don't think plants mind being eaten, actually. I think they'd be really sad if no-one paid that much attention to them."[13] When asked about the songs she had written about incest she conceded, with inadvisable honesty, that "I see [my brothers] as men and I see them as attractive, but there is no sexual content in the relationship. I suppose there's never been much physical contact."[14]

Seeing her words thrown back at her having undergone various contortions was not a particularly pleasant experience for someone as essentially open and honest as she. "She got very wary of the media," says Southall. "They didn't dislike her, though they did take the mickey a bit, but she just wanted privacy. She was always obliging and friendly and affable, but she didn't really want to do it. I don't recall one specific thing that caused her to be resentful or mistrusting, but she grew up and realised that the world isn't quite as nice as you think it is. It's a fact of life. There was a kind of naïveté: 'He said he was going to ask me about my video, but then he asked me some other questions . . .' Well, yes! But that threw her I think. And there were a few bitchy writers."

The extent to which her fame broke beyond the confines of the musical world and into mass culture hit her with the force of a mugging. The success of 'Wuthering Heights' made her a tabloid entity, when normally an artist of her type and inclination would not have been subjected to that kind of exposure. The strength of her image and the sheer eccentricity of the song and video made her easy prey. And she was a gift for comedians. To a bastardised version of 'Them Heavy People' entitled 'Oh England, My Leotard', she was mercilessly spoofed by Pamela Stephenson on *Not The Nine O'clock News*, the BBC's hippest alternative comedy show. Some of it was clever and very funny.

> *'Went to Cairo and I read the Gnostic*
> *Apocryphon of John in the original Coptic*
> *Korsakoff's psychosis theories*
> *And the Fibonacci series*
> *Studied acupuncture and the Bible . . .*
>
> *My cauliflower quiches were better than the bought ones*
> *And I was thicker than two short ones.'*

Impressionist Faith Brown parodied, much less subtly, her love of mime, her voice, and her use of language – "I've learned what 'amazing', 'fantastic' and 'incredible' are in 85 languages" – on her LWT show, before performing another rather accurate spoof called 'Three Little Fishes'. She was a perfectly legitimate target for satire, but although Bush had a robust sense of humour and professed that she found this kind of thing more funny than upsetting, the implication in both cases that she was somehow stupid and contrived would have rankled.

The media preoccupations essentially boiled down to three things: sex, age and class. The fuss made over her age was baffling. She was 19, no longer a babe in arms when it came to the pop industry, certainly not in comparison to her male contemporaries at that time: Paul Weller was 18 when 'In The City' went into the Top 40; John Lydon was still only 21. But the discrepancy between the maturity of the songs and her physical youthfulness and occasional gaucheness was emphasised again and again, particularly coming from someone from such an apparently 'sheltered' background, the dancing doctor's daughter from the suburbs who had never had a 'real' job. She was a young woman with big ideas, and thus someone, somewhere, must be pulling her strings. "The thing with her career is that it started off, and people were thinking there was obviously some man behind her success," says producer Steve Lillywhite, who worked with her on Peter Gabriel's third album. "With 'Wuthering Heights', you thought she had a lovely voice, but somebody else was doing all the work." It's hard to believe now, but there was no comparable artist on the British scene at that time: a young, beautiful female who wrote and performed her own words and music to great popular and artistic success. As the first through the gates, she took many brickbats.

It's equally astonishing nowadays to recall the amount of emphasis placed on Bush's sexual side, her erotic charge. She constantly sought to dampen down her sex symbol status, almost to the point of obsession. The kind of 'Sexy? Who, me?' disingenuousness she often displayed in these early interviews was rather ridiculous but understandable. It's as though she was so wary of being defined by her sexual identity she would rather try and deny it entirely, put it down to a combination of unknowing instinct on her part and subjective interpretation on the part of the audience. This, of course, was nonsense. Her sexual presence is a very real and important part of her work as, occasionally, she has acknowledged. "So much of it comes from a sexual need, from inside me," she said. "I'm very basic."[15] Jon Kelly, who worked closely with her on the first three albums, recalls a conversation about the *Never For Ever* album cover, which depicts a parade of beautiful and demonic beasts flying out from under her skirt. "That's where she said her songs come from!" says Kelly. "That's what she told me – that's where all her ideas come from."

Her attitude to sex and the senses was that of a poet, not a pop star. She certainly wasn't ashamed of expressing her sexual side in her work, sometimes graphically, but she couldn't seem to understand why those words and images would then seep into the public's perception of her as a person. What she dreaded most was being defined by her looks, but if she wanted parts of her audience, and the British tabloid press in particular, to make the fine-toothed differentiation between the natural, earthy, instinctive sensuality of a 'poet' and the brash, blatant, come-and-get-it display of a 'pop star' she was in for a rude awakening. It was a problem she was still encountering when she stepped back onto the stage in 2014.

It was always going to be an area where some difficulty would arise. Early on a Dutch photographer 'tricked' her into posing for a bondage-style photo, in which she was shot wrapped up in rope, presumably in the belief that this was art, not sex. Money was offered to stop the picture being printed in *Record Mirror*, but it was not accepted. "We had no idea, it was all a bit unfortunate," says Brian Southall. "It was a warning to be a bit careful: people were looking for headlines."

One picture in particular proved defining. Late in 1977, EMI had asked renowned rock photographer Gered Mankowitz to shoot their new protégé for the 'Wuthering Heights' single sleeve and the ensuing promotional campaign. Mankowitz heard the song, thought it "extraordinary", and set up a session at his studio in Great Windmill Street. Learning of her love of dance he proposed a shoot themed along those lines, something very natural and raw. "I simply suggested we got leotards and woollen working socks and all that gear, and she seemed to like it," he says. "I did a whole series of pictures, full length, three-quarter length and portrait, she looked absolutely stunning. When they were processed, the advertising agency that EMI had employed to promote the single came up with the campaign of putting the posters on the buses, and selected the one in the pink leotard and the nipples. The rest is history."

The picture was used extensively. Several designs were rolled out for the poster campaign, the same infamous picture on each, with her name and *The Kick Inside* prominently displayed above the portrait in pink writing against a black backdrop, each one flaunting a single superlative below the picture: WONDROUS, AMAZING, MAGNIFICENT . . . These were cut to fit the front corners of London buses, and all four were combined to create a full-size poster for underground sites and billboards. They made a colossal impact and caused an extraordinary fuss, and not only in places like the *Daily Express* and *Private Eye*. Even before it was seen publicly, the picture divided opinion behind the scenes.

"There's been a lot of controversy about it since, and I think the root of it is simply that her family didn't like their daughter and sister being seen in a sexual way, they felt it was a distraction from her music," says Mankowitz. "One of the brothers – I don't think I met him and he certainly never came to my sessions, his input was in the background as far as I was concerned – but my understanding was that he objected to what I think they saw as a sexualising of her. The family did find it offensive, though nobody ever said anything to me and nobody ever stopped me working with her again."

As Mankowitz suggests, the 'nipple' portrait became a kind of symbolic battleground for the playing out of the many tensions between the Bushes and the record company. From the very beginning the family had been her sounding board, and as the stakes grew higher their influence became more pronounced. In interviews, she would constantly refer to what 'we' were doing or planning next, 'we' being the Bush clan. "She had got herself into a situation where she had the protection of her family . . . who believed utterly in what she was doing and were willing to follow her to the ends of the earth to get the result," says Charlie Morgan. "They all believed she was breaking new ground – and she was. EMI were fighting it all the time."

For a few years early on there were many occasions where heads bumped and tempers frayed, when boundaries were crossed and roles became confused, when the conflicting interests of art and commerce and business and pleasure collided. The Mankowitz portrait became a trysting point for all these frustrations and misunderstandings. "I remember Jay objecting to the photograph we were using, and he stormed into my office saying we were sexualising her and so on, stuff that frankly had never fucking occurred to me," says Bob Mercer, perhaps disingenuously. "Of all the things that you could have described her as, blatantly sexual wasn't one of those in my mind. God knows, I was in the record business and perfectly capable of thinking that way, but not in this instance. I got very cross with him about that, because it was below the belt. We had a big row over that."

Jay has since said that "to see every business meeting as a karate competition was probably silly", but remains unrepentant about fighting for the protection of a "clear vision of Kate the Artist."[16] Partly it was about artistic control – the poet's innate urge for complete autonomy – and partly an understandable sense of filial and parental protectiveness in an often cut-throat environment. From the moment EMI made advances, her eldest brother in particular played a central role in what he called the "coordinating process" of her career.[17] The motives may have been honourable, but they didn't always translate well. "The mafia! The bruvvers!" says Vic King. "The brothers might have been a bit [heavy-handed]. Never had any trouble with the parents, just as long as she was happy. It was mainly Jay, or Paddy. *Very* protective of their little sister." Says

Mankowitz, "I was aware of what was known as the Bush Family Mafia. I didn't have any direct dealings with them. I have a vague recollection of meeting a brother at an EMI reception, and I remember a not very friendly person. They were very precious and protective."

When it came to Mankowitz's image, Jay also felt a professional as well as personal sense of aggrievement. As a photographer, he felt that this was, somehow, his natural habitat. The only person who appeared less than flustered by it all was Bush herself. She was uninhibited about her own body to the point of occasionally and inadvertently causing severe palpitations in others. "Kate never had any concerns about her body at all," says Southall. "She could not work out what all the fuss was about – 'Well, we've *all* got those things.' Before one [awards ceremony] we were in the small rehearsal studio at Manchester Square and I said, 'Come on, Kate, get a move on! There's a car outside,' and she just took her top off [to get changed]. There was no embarrassment at all. I was in the corner quivering! She never understood that at all."

Sticking to her early line of downplaying any sexual content in her work, she was initially relaxed about the image. "I suppose the poster is reasonably sexy just 'cos you can see my tits, but I think the vibe from the face is there," she said in March 1978, seemingly convinced that the public would see beyond the surface titillation to the artist beneath.[18] A signed print of the photo, sent in 1978 from Paris to a 14-year-old fan and accompanied by a note and her handwritten lyrics to 'Wuthering Heights', underscore the fact that she clearly had no issue with the image at the time. By 1985 she had wised up considerably. "I didn't really see it objectively at the time, and I think now, when I see it, it's quite embarrassing," she said of the portrait. "It should have been cropped, and that's something that we would certainly do now. Looking at it retrospectively, I can see that it was suggestive."[19]

In this case, the family lost the battle but won the war. The photo wasn't used, as originally intended, for the 'Wuthering Heights' single sleeve. Instead, it was replaced late on with a similar design to the album sleeve, which nobody outside of Bush's circle much liked, featuring a red and orange Oriental theme – "concept by Kate Bush" – with a very small off-centre image of the artist flying on a kite. The back cover of *The Kick Inside* was designed jointly by Del and Jay. "Del played bass, and I didn't know what John Carder Bush did," says Mankowitz. "All I knew was that it was a dreadful cover, and everybody knew it. They didn't understand what you have to have to make a good cover – you certainly had to have the artist up front." Mankowitz's photograph, on the other hand, remains genuinely iconic, revealing a stunning mixture of animal instinct and great intellect; the potential for the unleashing of great energy, but also classical repose. And, yes, it was sexy, but anyone who ended up lingering longer over her chest than her face was missing half the fun.

In order to try and prevent repetitions of these kind of scuffles, around the time of the release of 'Wuthering Heights' EMI became convinced Bush needed a manager to act as a buffer and field the enormous number of demands on her time. After a few options were considered – Steve O'Rourke, Marc Bolan's former agent Tony Howard – Peter Lyster-Todd was hired, without much enthusiasm on her part. A photographer's agent moving into the music industry, he had managed Sky but was, he readily admits, still "learning on his feet". Though charming, well-spoken and genuine, Lyster-Todd was not quite attuned to the Bush family ethic. "He turned up with a big fur coat on," recalls Brian Bath. "I thought, 'Blimey, who's this?' He was really showbiz. I don't think there was really any need for him at the time. I think Kate had enough support from everyone around her to do what she wanted to do."

So it proved. Novercia Ltd. was already in existence and the company, with the help of Bernard Sheridan, dealt with all Bush's contracts and royalty payments. It was a closed shop, and unlike virtually every other manager in the history of popular music, Lyster-Todd was never involved in the underlying financial aspects of his client's career. His brief was simply to liaise with the record companies in Europe, organise promotion, sift through tour offers, and generally try to push his act as far as possible. This was what EMI wanted, but it seemed to the Bush family – who liked him, but this was business – that he had merely inherited a promising artist and was earning a healthy percentage on each deal without having to do terribly much. When 'Wuthering Heights' took off, after all, the momentum was generally self-perpetuating. In the end, their misgivings were encapsulated by two thoughts: What could any manager do that they couldn't do themselves? And a deeply ingrained distrust of the species of Rock Manager in general. "I think most managers are crooks, greedy and non-musical," Bush said on the eve of Lyster-Todd's arrival, before adding less than convincingly, "I think Peter will be amazing . . ."[20]

He was gone by the end of May. "I was never able to establish that [article of faith] with the family, and what I did begin to notice after taking this or that meeting on behalf of Kate and EMI, was that one would arrive at conclusions and forge ideas and try to turn them into something – and thus, *managing* – and then in a kind of overnight way one would get the feeling that it was all being redistilled back in Welling and it would all be undone," says Lyster-Todd today. "I did get the feeling I was managing by post-mortem. I don't want to sound in any way grumpy or bad tempered about it. Kate is by definition unique, and I don't think she would ever fall into that mould of an artist who is comfortable or happy to row the boat in tandem with their manager. That's just a reflection on her nature creatively and intellectually. In a way, for Kate there isn't a manager. It's not pertinent for her, and the proof of the pudding is in the eating; look at everything she has accomplished."

The end was swift and decisive. A note arrived from Bernard Sheridan "giving me the bum's rush: 'One way or t'other, we feel that this relationship is not exactly what we want. . . .' – I can't remember all the details. Kate – and I guess the people immediately around her – felt that what I was doing wasn't really the way they wanted to do things or the way they saw things going. That was sort of the gist of it. I couldn't really give you a definitive reason. I remember getting back in touch with Bernard Sheridan, who was a very decent sort altogether, and making a case, but it became apparent that the die was cast and there was no going back. I was disappointed and hurt and perplexed, but you've got to stand up and accept it."

With the benefit of hindsight, regardless of the details of each skirmish or the manner in which they may or may not have been conducted, one thing is overwhelmingly clear: the way the Bush family handled her career, the way they advised her, protected her, cared for her, loved her and fought for her artistic integrity all the way down the line was remarkably effective. It may often have been a distinct pain in the neck for those trying to drive her career from outside of that unit, but undeniably it *worked*. "Without any experience of the business we applied common sense, instinct and a determination not to get ripped off," said John Carder Bush in 2004. "With the help of a courageous lawyer we braved the giants."[21]

"I have to say with hindsight I think the family did a really good job," says Charlie Morgan. "They didn't do everything according to the book, but that was probably a good thing for Kate." It's hard to think of anybody who has dictated the narrative of their career so precisely, from start to present day, and has done so largely for the sake of her music rather than her ego or bank balance. To her credit, she never made EMI jump through hoops for the sheer hell of it. "She wasn't bothered about the stuff of normal rock stars," says Southall. "If you gave her a car she'd take it, but she didn't care what it was. When she toured she wanted a nice room, but she wasn't bothered whether it was the biggest or the suite on the top. It was quite refreshing. She wanted to be comfortable, to have quiet and peace and time to dance, that was all very important, but she didn't need a manager to ring up and shout that it wasn't a big enough car."

Those kinds of hollow, ego-gratifying demonstrations of power would never mean a thing. She was fixated on a greater prize.

5

Rocket's Tail

THE success of 'Wuthering Heights' was a distinctly double-edged sword, each side rapier sharp. The rewards were sweet and tangible: a £7,000 Steinway piano gifted to her from EMI, who also flew her to Paris for dinner on March 7, 1978, the day the single became number one, and splashed out on a champagne reception. Acclaim, financial security, creative clout, Top 10 hits in Germany, France, Denmark, Sweden, Finland, Brazil, Argentina and South Africa, and more number ones in Australia, New Zealand, Holland, Belgium and Japan. The problem was that she was expected to visit all these places, a "round the world in 80 days sort of thing," she said. "I don't know how I did it."[1]

This, it seems certain, hadn't really been reckoned upon by either EMI – who envisaged her as a slow-building albums artist – or Bush. Indeed, she spent the next few years trying to negotiate the demands success made on her time, on her work, on the way she was perceived and objectified. The great irony of the extraordinary impact of 'Wuthering Heights' is that, yes, it *made* her, but it also blew her entirely off course, and for a couple of years unplugged her from her source. She was wracked with guilt about her lack of writing. She had very little time to practise her dancing, precious opportunity to spend time at home or catch up with her friends and family. She was denied access to all the things that inspired her.

She made her first, brief promotional trip to the United States in May. *The Kick Inside* had been released in the US and Canada at the end of March, with a new picture cover, also by Gered Mankowitz, that seemed determined to sell her as the new Linda Ronstadt: jeans, gingham shirt, big, sensible socks – nice and cosy, down on the farm. The few reviews in places like *Creem* were positive, and she later consented to return again towards the end of the year, flying over on Concorde to perform the new

US single, 'The Man With The Child In His Eyes', and 'Them Heavy People' on *Saturday Night Live* on December 9, as the guest of host Eric Idle. The single crept to number 85 on the *Billboard* chart, but without undertaking a tour she was limited in what she could achieve. She didn't much care. She has never possessed that all encompassing ambition, and already fatigued and growing disillusioned with her itinerary, she was unwilling to endure the gruelling promotional workload required to achieve that mythical Grail sought by most emerging British acts: cracking America. "I've never seen it in terms of you make an album and then conquer the world," she said. "I must say it's never really worried me that I've not been big in America."[2]

She was offered the opening slot on the closing leg of Fleetwood Mac's enormous *Rumours* tour, covering stadium and arena shows throughout the US in July and August 1978, while the American record company also wanted to showcase her over three nights at Radio City Music Hall in New York, where the US media would be invited to come and bask in her brilliance. She declined both offers.

"She was having none of it," says Brian Southall. "She had an idea [to tour] with the dancers and jugglers and all that, which obviously wasn't going to happen in 20 minutes playing before Fleetwood Mac in Tucson, Arizona. It would have required compromise, and one thing Kate isn't good at is compromise: 'I don't do my music in 20 minute sets with a trio, that's not how I present my music.' People in America were desperately frustrated. She made a couple of small trips, but America needed to see her perform. It's a big country, the only way to break America is to tour, and Kate wasn't prepared to do so. She wasn't bothered. To her credit, she never bitched about people in America not selling her records." She was always relatively successful in Canada, where the head of EMI, Dean Cameron, remained a tireless champion of her music, but none of her post-*Kick Inside* albums were even released in the US until 1984.

'The Man With The Child In His Eyes' came out in the UK at the end of May, and as the new single and the album continued rolling out through Europe and beyond she was sent off like a piece of package mail, the itinerary expanding dangerously like a water balloon. A few snapshots catch the mood of scores and scores of promotional events: she shot a six-song promo at De Efteling, a fairy tale theme park in the Netherlands, where she was filmed by the pond, singing to the ducks in a karate outfit;

she appeared on *Top Pop*, Holland's 'premier music show'; and she visited Japan – a trip faithfully reported back home on John Craven's *Newsround* – where she played with a band of Japanese musicians at the Tokyo Song Festival and, between endless, disjointed interviews, squeezed in a rather brief and bizarre TV appearance in which she performed The Beatles' 'The Long And Winding Road' and 'She's Leaving Home', the latter sung in a manner which suggested it was a tribute to Margot Leadbetter from *The Good Life*.

Her year as a travelling salesman is characterised by the experience of performing at the San Remo Film Festival, early in 1979. "It was bizarre," she later recalled. "Up in the morning, over to Verona, and walk out on this stage. I'm facing the cameras and a few hundred people who I assume are the audience. Then the stage and the whole set starts to rotate and I realise that it's a huge circular stadium and out front there are thousands and thousands of people. I've never seen so many people in my life! Anyway I mimed 'Wuthering Heights', bowed, and flew off home again."[3]

It was like being part of a circus, and was entirely at odds with what she wanted to do. However, the idea that from the outset she habitually loathed all forms of promotion isn't quite true. "I think she did quite enjoy the promotion," says Brian Bath. "There wasn't the pressure of doing it all live, and if you can mime you can do other things: dress up and start to introduce all your other ideas and mime and things from a visual point of view. That's what counts on TV."

She was fascinated with shooting the early videos, rushing off to make 'Wuthering Heights' in the middle of the night with the innovative director Keith MacMillan and seeing the results broadcast on *Top Of The Pops* only a few days later. She quickly came to regard the embryonic art form as an essential part of what she did and therefore longed to control it. That would come. For now, she was learning from "an early pioneer, a creative genius," according to MacMillan's lighting engineer John Henshall.

She also enjoyed attending some of the awards bashes back home, where she could chinwag at length with comedian Rowan Atkinson or have to be rescued from the clutches of Bob Geldof and Phil Lynott – "these two wild Irishmen", says Southall, "leching after this young lady, and her naively going to chat to them not realising that they didn't have the best of intentions!" – at the *Melody Maker* 1978 Poll Awards, where she won Best Female Vocalist and Brightest Hope. And there was always room for a little covert radicalism. Previewing a new song on mainstream TV show *Ask Aspel*, she politely explained that she had intended to sing 'In The Warm Room' but, on reflection, felt its sexual subject matter was perhaps inappropriate for the show. Instead she sang 'Kashka From Baghdad', a song about two homosexual lovers. On *Saturday Swap Shop*, she even managed to cajole Noel Edmonds into a halfway intelligent conversation about Emily Brontë.

But the novelty quickly began to pall. She hated flying, and the long trips later in 1978 to Japan, Australia and New Zealand sapped her energy. They were made without her band and she missed their company, and Del. Above all, she hated the impact it had on her work. By Christmas 1978 she was already lamenting, "I miss being by myself very, very much but it's very difficult because you can't just ask people to leave, they don't understand. I can't remember the last time I was alone for any length of time, even a day. It must be well over a year."[4] This most intensely private of artists, who once said she couldn't contemplate writing a song with somebody else in the room, no longer had the time, space or sense of inner and outer quietude to write. The sanctuary of Wickham Farm and her flat in Wickham Road seemed a long way away.

There was no peace. There was no time. And there were no songs. For a writer like Bush, this was all a kind of nightmare. The very thing she had been determined not to do – get snagged in the riptide of the music industry, allowing the strong surface currents to dictate the direction of her art – was happening in front of her eyes. "I was really taken away from making music, which was a very hard thing to come to terms with," she said. "I kind of had to take a hold of that and reverse the whole situation."[5]

That reversal happened too late for *Lionheart*. Somewhere amid all the self promotion she had to write and record her second album, a tightrope walk she never quite managed to master. Loose plans for a UK tour had already been shelved due to lack of time and a feeling that it would be more beneficial to concentrate on making more 'product'. "We talked about dates," says Brian Southall. "She had performed as the KT Bush Band, she had a band, but she wanted to focus on making records. She wasn't keen, and we were happy to focus on the second album."

Eager to capitalise on the enormous success of *The Kick Inside*, EMI booked Bush into a favoured haunt of Pink Floyd: Superbear studios in the mountain village of Berre-Les-Alpes in the Alpes-Maritime region, near Nice in the south of France. With recording due to start on July 7, she found she had less than four weeks in which to get material for the album together. In the end, there was precious little in the way of new songs. 'Coffee Homeground', written in the US in May, was a rare example of her being able to compose while in transit. She had also written 'Symphony In Blue' and 'Full House', but the rest of its 10 tracks were by necessity reclaimed from the past: 'Wow' had been considered for *The Kick Inside*; 'Don't Push Your Foot On The Heartbrake' had been demoed with the band in 1977; 'Hammer Horror' and 'Kashka From Baghdad' dated back to the solo recordings of 1976, while 'Oh England, My Lionheart', 'In The Warm Room' and 'In Search Of Peter Pan' were very obvious reshapings of earlier songs: slow, beautiful piano ballads, by turns sensual and sad, of which she had a plentiful supply.

In May, and again in late June and early July after returning from Japan, she and her band demoed the songs for the album. While she had been ful-filling her promotional duties around the world, her father, Paddy and the group (who had been kept on modest retainers: "We were just paid here and there, it was a bit of a struggle," says Brian Bath. "Her dad paid us bits and pieces") had been constructing a studio at Wickham Farm. "We would turn up every day and while Kate was away we built the studio in the barn at her parents' place," says Charlie Morgan. "The summer of 1978 we were there doing all this work – it was quite an idyllic situation, we were all so wrapped up in Kate's talents." Armed with hammers and saws, they put in the stud work, built screens, filled the studio door with sand and put Rockwool in the walls to soundproof the building. Dr Bush did all the wiring. "Then we started messing around doing demos," says Morgan.

Brian Bath was very much the musical director. "When Kate had a few songs she'd phone me and say, 'Brian, do you want to come over and work on the songs so we can present them to everyone?' I'd go over to Wickham Road and sit at the piano with her, work out the chords and basic progressions and write out these bar charts so that everyone could understand them. When Kate went to Japan for promotion [or] she dis-appeared for a week or so, we'd start a track or be overdubbing when she wasn't there."

It was barely a year since they had all been scooting around London in the Morris 1000 and fighting off rampaging Scotsmen in the pubs of Putney, but the band dynamic had shifted in an almost imperceptible yet profound manner. Bush was remarkably unaffected by stardom, and never bought into the diva-like notion that it made her in any way superior to anyone else or gave her an excuse to act appallingly. She had her own personal standards of behaviour which she has maintained throughout her career, but fame brings its own inevitable distance. "All of a sudden she was cocooned in this dream state," says Brian Bath. "It was like when the KT Bush Band wound down, there was this separation. It was most peculiar. There was a difference in some way. All of a sudden you were a different kind of working partner: she's the boss, you're not. But we used to still have a laugh at the farm when we were recording these demos for *Lionheart*."

She badly wanted her own band to play on *Lionheart*, partly for her own artistic reasons, and partly as a repayment for all their hard work and loyalty. Andrew Powell, however, who was again producing, saw no need to depart from the template that had proved so successful last time. "Andrew was very keen to use the same band, and I can't blame him, it had worked very well," says Jon Kelly. "Kate was more experimental. In between the albums she'd been playing the songs with her own musicians." It boiled down to a fundamental difference in the aspirations for the new record. The company wanted another *The Kick Inside*, whereas Bush really wanted the next album to be a reaction against her first. In the end, neither quite got what they desired.

The Kick Inside had been an astonishing success on its own terms: unique, unusual songs played sympathetically by an excellent group of musicians and a remarkable singer and performer. It sounded like nothing else and there are many fans today for whom it still remains her finest hour, her most accessible and timeless piece of work.

But she held a very different view. Within a matter of months of finishing the record and even before it was released, she indicated a less than satisfied attitude towards it, not so much in terms of the songs but in terms of the execution. "It could have been so much better, there were so many more things I could have done," she lamented as early as February 1978.[6] She was troubled by that odd sensation many musicians feel when they first start recording, the shock of hearing ideas you have held in your head for so long take on a solid, robust form. There is an almost inevitable sense of dislocation and disappointment. She came to regard herself as a mere participant in her debut rather than its architect: they were her songs, it was her voice, but it was not her vision that she heard coming back at her when it was all over.

It was 1978, and although Bush would never be a punk by either sound or sensibility, she expressed admiration for The Stranglers and The Sex Pistols, admiring their aesthetic if not entirely loving their music, eulogising the way they "laid it on" the listener.[7] She yearned for her own music to have a bit more bite and punch. More guts. She dismissed *The Kick Inside* as "airy fairy . . . I'm not pleased with being associated with such soft, romantic vibes. I guess I want to get basically heavier in the sound sense."[8] That masculine, 'hunting' instinct again.

Using her own band would be a significant step towards realising this musical vision. Those who played on the initial demos recall they were often quite radically different from the versions of the same songs that ended up on *Lionheart*. "They were pretty noisy," says Brian Bath. "I think 'Wow' was pretty close to the finished record. 'Hammer Horror' was a bit of a mush but there were good bits in it. The one about the poison, 'Coffee Homeground', we had a great version of that, it was a really good effort. The tunes were all over place! It was great, we all used to join in on backing vocals."

Jon Kelly, who was again engineering, was also impressed. "I didn't get to hear them until many, many years later," he recalls. "I had a friend who had some demos from those rehearsals and they were very good." "Musically they were fantastic," adds Charlie Morgan. "A lot of the times the demos we did with Kate were pretty experimental. We'd really throw a lot of ideas in. It's hard to be diplomatic about it; all I can say is that we trod new ground."

They had fun, too. When they recorded the demo for 'Hammer Horror' at the farm, Bush insisted that she needed to be genuinely frightened in order to 'get into the role'. Paddy had the idea of "blacking the studio out and having all these strange things going on outside," says Bath. "She started singing and Paddy threw some matches past the windows, we made some [ghost] noises, and she went 'Ahhhhhhhhhhh'! She actually lost her voice, she couldn't sing any more. She came back a couple of days later to sing it again." By now, her band understood – and indeed were rather devoted to – her eccentricities. "She'd always have a very descriptive or illustrative version of how a song should be," says Bath. "She'd say, 'I want it to be mysterious sounding' or something like that."

Pretending to be a ghoul in a blacked-out studio was not, it's safe to say, the way that Andrew Powell preferred to work. However, to his credit he listened to her ideas and agreed to at least give them a try, but he had little real enthusiasm for the idea of using her group. "Kate really wanted her band very strongly, and I thought the easiest way to resolve something is to try both sides, which is basically what happened," he says.

He visited Wickham Farm shortly before they were due to set off for France and listened to the band do their thing. "Oh, I was so nervous, I'd never been so nervous in my life," says Bath. "Kate's dad gave me a couple of pills to calm me down. We'd worked so hard at it, doing the demos, building the studio, installing the tape machines and learning how to work it all. I felt kind of responsible, because I'd organised things. You could tell [Powell] wasn't really into it, but I suppose it was agreed, or Kate insisted, that we should be there, so we were flown out there to Nice, up in the mountains. Huge villa, brilliant place. Really hot."

It was a slice of luxury compared to AIR, propped as it was atop a sparkling mountain range rather than grimy Oxford Circus. The studio was set in a vast whitewashed villa which housed not only the recording facilities but also the stylish residential quarters on the lower floor. There were two cascading swimming pools, video games, pool tables.

The setting was idyllic, the recording process less so. The uneasy truce about which musicians to use was never built to last. Bush's band recorded eight tracks during the first couple of weeks, but it was clear that some issues were unresolved and eventually had to be confronted. It would be too dramatic to see it as a power struggle over control of the album, but it was significant, particularly as this time Bush was credited as assistant producer, reflecting her desire to be more in charge of the overall direction of the record. "She wanted to have more input and it [became] a little bit more conflicted," says Kelly. "I don't remember it being confrontational at the time, but I'm sure it led to some tension."

Powell felt he had some legitimate musical concerns. The group lacked studio experience at this level, and what they sometimes regarded as the producer deliberately making their lives difficult may just as easily have been attributable to their struggle to adapt quickly enough to the laborious, piecemeal nature of making an album. "I would say it took the KT

Bush Band a little longer to get their stuff together," admits Charlie Morgan. "But we did get results. I think musically we were up to scratch, but our speed was maybe slightly slower." There seemed to be constant obstacles. The arrangements they had worked on so assiduously at the farm changed markedly in the Alps; Powell would fiddle with the amp settings as they were playing; he would question their tuning. At one point he asked Paddy to 'track' (to exactly replicate the improvised part he had previously played) his playing of the Strumento de Porco on 'Kashka From Baghdad', which Paddy regarded as deliberately asking him to attempt the obviously impossible.

There were no rows or great fallings out, but neither did there appear to be any great affection or even respect between the two camps. "They started pulling all the things we were doing apart," says Bath. "There were various meetings. We were in there for days and it just didn't seem to get any better. I remember playing a guitar line with three notes in it, and [Powell] said, twice, 'The note in the middle is out of tune.' I pretended to turn the string around, but I didn't actually do anything, then I played it again and he said, 'Yeah, that's better, yes.' It was exactly the same! So there were all these kind of mind games going on, really."

Powell's explanation is simple. "Some of the tracks they did worked out rather well, others just didn't work, frankly, so we redid them with the other guys," he says. "My job and responsibility was to make sure that whatever personal things were involved, the songs were raised to their best possible level." Charlie Morgan, however, refutes the suggestion that the band weren't up to the job. "I think the problem was that Andrew Powell had to relinquish a certain amount of control, because it was a club that had already been formed and he wasn't a member of it, whereas with his session boys it was a club that he had created."

Stuck in the middle, Bush was left in a ticklish situation. Hilary Walker, at the time head of EMI's international division but soon to leave the company to become Bush's PA, flew over and it was agreed that the musicians who played on *The Kick Inside* would come and complete the album, while Bush's group would beat a retreat. She was essentially cornered into sacking her band, including her boyfriend, who had been playing bass. "It was a tricky conversation," concedes Powell. "Del made it more tricky from my point of view – and hers. It wasn't something that was specifically raised, I certainly wasn't going to raise it, but it probably did make it a little bit more difficult from both sides." In the press she later attributed the band swap to a "mix up in the organisation"[9] and promptly changed the subject.

They were told they were all welcome to stay, and they all did, enjoying the warm weather, the swimming pool, the odd trip to Monaco with Pink Floyd's Rick Wright, who turned up during the proceedings with a car load of champagne and a desire to hit the casinos. Only Charlie Morgan flew home straight away, bumping into the band of replacement musicians as they arrived at Nice airport. "I left the morning that everyone else arrived," he says. "Stuart [Elliott] was coming in and I had a 10-minute chat with him before I got on the plane at Nice. I told him what the kit was like and what he might need to do with the drums. I'd been doing a lot of freelance work so I was quite thick-skinned about the whole thing, whereas the guys in the band were absolutely *devastated*. They hung around for at least a week afterwards and possibly weren't terribly productive to the making of the album. They wouldn't have been helping the other musicians at all and there would have been this very vibey thing going on."

With the new band in place, the recording continued in France over the course of July and August. Although they were old friends and everybody got on, the atmosphere was "a bit awkward" at first, according to David Paton. "It was like, 'Get out of the way, here come the big boys,' and I wasn't comfortable doing that to any musicians. What can you say? It was Andrew's call. Andrew had confidence in us and producers like to work with the same musicians all the time, he knows how he can get the best out of them. Kate was happy for us to be doing the work. I think she realised her band's limitations, and Andrew did as well. They had no studio experience, and there's nothing better than studio experience. They weren't performing live either."

Morgan, on the other hand, claims the incident "left a very bad taste in Kate's mouth", but she was forced, for the time being, to divorce her personal feelings from her professional ones. Once everything had settled down, she could at least recognise that some of the music was sounding good. "Once she'd heard, for example, what they'd done on 'Symphony In Blue' she was kind of like, 'Hmm, OK,'" says Powell. "Because it's brilliant, and it's not an easy song to play."

"I think she basically had to agree with Andrew that we could get a better result, and we shouldn't be looking at just keeping your friends happy, we have to make the best possible record," says Ian Bairnson. "I don't think she was cold about that decision, but she took advice."

As the album sessions wore on, the days slipped into a comfortable routine. They would all rise late in the morning and congregate by the pool, some of the band leaping off the roof of the villa straight into the water. Bush would often appear poolside to sunbathe, or work with a notepad and a pen, writing lyrics or other bits and pieces. They would then start recording, stopping for meals in the canteen, perhaps returning to the pool later. Relaxation often took a traditional route. "Somebody was there constantly rolling joints," says Paton. "Not everyone was doing it with Kate, I think it was only me."

It was searingly hot, and although the residential set-up was good for camaraderie it could get a trifle claustrophobic, working together all day, sleeping under the same roof and eating all their meals together; that said, the close proximity had its side benefits. "It was very nice to finish working in the studio and Kate would be lying by the pool," says Paton. "Almost naked. Topless. To come out of working in that studio environment to find a 20-year-old girl lying on the grass by your side was very refreshing!"

Though by no means an unhappy camp, making the album was a trickier proposition than *The Kick Inside*, and not just because of the problems with the band, although it did rather dent her confidence in her vision for the record. Her promotional schedule, too, had sapped some of her energy. "I did sense she was a little tired," says Jon Kelly, although fame hadn't appeared to affect her whatsoever in terms of her personal demeanour. "She would still be the first person to say, 'Do you want a cup of tea?'" says Paton. "She was so easy to work with. I've had many ego problems with other artists but not with Kate Bush." However, the scrutiny that comes with success had certainly made her much more self-conscious. One of the new songs, 'Full House', was a rather alarming insight into the psychological struggles she was encountering, a case study in paranoia and self-doubt.

Having digested her own weight in press cuttings and television coverage, much of which she felt was misleading, she worried that people thought she was contrived, that she was somehow nothing more than a record company marionette. "I think she was going through 'second album syndrome'," says Powell. "It's always phenomenally difficult, especially when your first album is successful, and it's not unusual to start questioning why people liked it and think, 'Should I try and do the same?' That way lies potential madness." Or indeed, to try and do the opposite. She dreaded being pigeon-holed. Many of her interviews around this time can be summarised by the mantra: Must Do Better! Must Try Harder! She was setting herself almost impossible targets.

"She had become a lot more self critical, I think that's true," says Powell. "Actually, it *is* true, no question. I mean, 'Wow' took *days* for the vocal. I don't know how many 24-track tapes we had her vocals on in the end, but it was several. She really pushed herself hard – to the absolute limits – physically, mentally and emotionally."

She allowed the players the freedom to come up with their own parts, to find their own way into her music, and she was full of enthusiasm and appreciation for whatever input they put into her songs. But although she was constantly encouraging when it came to her fellow musicians, she was punishingly hard on herself. On 'Wow', "It was all in tune and it was OK, there was just something missing," she mused.[10] As ever, she was searching for the kind of emotional connection that couldn't quite be described in words. In her role as assistant producer she sometimes struggled to communicate her ideas to the musicians in a language they understood. "The reaction to me explaining what I want in the studio was amusement, to a certain extent," she said. "They were all taking the piss out of me a bit."[11]

She was beginning to realise that the studio offered almost limitless alternatives; that the song was only the starting point, and that you could do things over and over again, approach the music from opposing angles, play the same note in radically different ways. This is the first confirmed sighting of Bush the studio baby, the relentless perfectionist, enraptured by the possibilities of sound, intent on chasing the music until it reveals some shard of magic, a fleeting glimpse of wonder. "On the first album she just stuck with her songs: 'I sing it like this, I play it like this', and we wrapped around her," says Ian Bairnson. "On the second one she was open to changing things. It was the seed of her starting to think in terms of studio, and the possibilities of production."

It was exciting, but also terribly frustrating given that she was working to a strict time limit, without her preferred musicians, and without complete autonomy. Though there were no fallings out, the differences between her ideas and those of Powell's were clear. "There were a few things we didn't agree on," says Powell. "I just remember thinking, 'Oh, I don't like that idea,' and she obviously didn't like what I wanted to do either, but we'd normally find a way around it. We'd try and talk about it, and we'd do it and see. She wasn't dogmatic." Once again, everything was stored away for future reference.

They returned to London in September to add strings and some other final overdubs, and for Bush to undertake another round of unrelenting promotional duties, which included being photographed by David Bailey for *Vogue*. *Lionheart* was mixed in early October, immediately after which she flew to Australia and New Zealand for a couple of weeks, chasing her tail, singing 'Hammer Horror', already pushing the new album before it was even out on a conveyor belt of press junkets. "You've got five minutes," Hilary Walker barked at hapless journalists as Bush sat rather dazed in the middle of it all. How much more productively, she thought, this time could have been spent.

Lionheart was released the following month, on November 10, launched with much fanfare at Ammersoyen Castle, a fourteenth century pile near the River Maas two hours from Amsterdam. Her parents were there, alongside Tony Myatt and anyone who mattered from EMI in the UK, Europe and Canada. Without her willingness to support it onstage, EMI America declined to release the album.

The glitz and glamour of the launch only partially obscured the fact that *Lionheart* didn't really achieve its aims. It's a good album, and it arguably contains a truer essence of Bush's creativity – the constant role-playing and changing characterisations are particularly ambitious – than *The Kick Inside*, but it did little to move her story forward, either commercially or creatively. There are some stunning moments. The only two songs to feature the original band – 'Wow' and 'Kashka From Baghdad' – are clear highlights. 'Wow' is a classic marriage of subtle verse and barnstorming chorus, with a massively powerful vocal. Lyrically it's a pitch-perfect piss-take of theatrical conceits, and contains a pleasingly risqué joke, emphasised in the video where she sings the line "busy hitting the Vaseline" while sticking out her derriere and giving it a good slap. When she released *The Whole Story* video compilation in 1986, this promo was replaced by a collage of performance images, suggesting she no longer felt comfortable with such a blatant nod and a wink. However, in an atypically candid moment in which she dropped the faux-naif persona, she did own up to the essential duality of her work. There *was* sometimes a subversive sexual subtext to her music, but it was not necessarily something she was going to shout about. "I feel if everyone understood the real things I'm saying it wouldn't be much good, it wouldn't help me," she said. "If it seems harmless on the surface, that's all right. I don't want to upset people who don't want to know."[12]

At the other end of the emotional spectrum, 'Oh England, My Lionheart', a song which she later all but disowned as embarrassing, is deeply moving, a paragon of her ability not only to conjure up the ache of a lost past, but to instil that ache with a tangible sense of time and place and string together a series of unforgettable images – "dropped from my black Spitfire to my funeral barge" – that perfectly complements the musical accompaniment. 'Hammer Horror' is a rousing drama, all guilt, possession and dark humour, while 'In The Warm Room' is delicately erotic and not a little voyeuristic. The almost fathomless depths of 'Symphony In Blue' marked a real progression in her writing, another song prodding at her own belief system, pondering the nature of God, the spiritual purpose of sex, the world and her own place in it: a stew of soul-searching sung to an impossibly beautiful soundtrack.

Much of the rest, however, is half-cocked, and some of the songs – the muddled melody of 'Full House', the rather tired mix of murder mystery and Brechtian pastiche that is 'Coffee Homeground' – are simply underwhelming. Most disappointingly for Bush, the punch isn't really there.

The album cover featured the enduring imagine of Bush in a lion bodysuit, complete with a tail and an expectant expression. Another superb Gered Mankowitz portrait – taken, inevitably, from a concept by John Carder Bush – it fuelled many an adolescent fantasy, but spoke of deeper, more private feelings of loss and longing that harked back to the emotions captured in Jay's *Cathy* photographs. "That was her idea, of being a child going up to the attic and finding a dressing up box and dressing up," says Mankowitz, who also shot the rather more conventional portrait on the back cover. "EMI loved the *Lionheart* cover and I think she loved it, too."

In blunt business terms, *Lionheart* underperformed slightly. The debut single, 'Hammer Horror' (a fine song but an odd choice, its stomping chorus belying its unorthodox structure) entered the charts at a poor 73 and only climbed to 44. 'Wow', released in March 1979, did much better, eventually reaching number 14, buoyed by the 'Tour Of Life' and its irrepressible chorus. *Lionheart* entered the album chart on November 21 at a disappointing number 36, and only reached a peak of number six. As far as EMI were concerned the record just about did its job, keeping her in the public eye, maintaining impetus and, crucially, giving her a platform on which to perform live. It was, in other words, a typically compromised second album. "It wasn't the best album in the world," says Brian Southall blithely. "That's the nature of the beast."

Although *Lionheart* was a useful reminder to EMI that Bush had no intention of being the company's cash cow, it was not what she wanted. The destiny of the album had slipped from her grasp, the last time for many years that would be the case. She never entrusted her music to a producer again. She would never be rushed into recording, or at least finishing, an album again. Everything else – promotion, press, commercial considerations, the record company, the expectations of her fans – would from now on be very much secondary considerations. Before she had the chance to put all these new resolutions into practice, however, it was time to show her audience exactly what kind of performer she was.

6

The Tour Of Life

WELCOME to the show. There's something here for everyone, from the trench-coated, trilby-hatted gangsters frugging in a manner that suggests a close acquaintance with both *Guys And Dolls* and Hanna-Barbera's *Wacky Races*, to a wartime fighter pilot – a flying jacket for a shroud and a Biggles helmet for a burial crown – dying on foreign soil, wishing only that the idealised England of his past will become his future heaven. There's a Lolitaesque seductress, winking outrageously at us from behind the piano; a ghostly apparition, up to her waist in mist and misery; a top-hatted magician's apprentice; a souk-siren singing of her "Pussy Queen" beneath a golden coronet; a murderous gunslinger, and a leather-clad refugee from *West Side Story*.

There are 13 people onstage, 17 costume changes and 24 songs scattered over three distinctly theatrical Acts. At the centre of this wild, swirling, ever-changing musical circus, living out each song as though her life depended upon it, is one woman: 5′ 3″ in her bare feet (in which she appears throughout) and calling the shots on everything from the programme design to the veggie cuisine. She is still only 20 years old.

The Bush who unveiled her 'Tour Of Life' on the stage of the Liverpool Empire on April 3, 1979 and hauled it around Europe for the next six weeks appeared to be unleashing a new, exhilarating, hugely potent weapon in her artistic armoury. She was, it seemed clear, born to do this. Until Bush returned to the stage more than three decades later with 'Before The Dawn', however, the tour more closely resembled a compelling footnote, a brief but brilliant detour down a one-way street. Because the 'Tour Of Life' turned out to be the tour of half a lifetime rather than the beginning of a regular, unfolding dialogue between Bush and her songs, it's tempting to conclude with hindsight that it was extraordinary simply by virtue of the fact that she would not repeat the experience for another 35 years. But it was extraordinary even to those who saw it with their own eyes.

★   ★   ★

After the release – and dawning disappointment – of *Lionheart* Bush began pushing aside unwanted commitments like a snowplough carving a path through a blizzard, clearing the road ahead of obstacles, determined to focus her energy on the things that really mattered to her. She was helped immeasurably in this respect by Hilary Walker. Something of a poacher turned gamekeeper, as the head of EMI's international division Walker had been instrumental throughout 1978 in breaking Bush outside of the UK; the glitzy *Lionheart* launch in Holland had been orchestrated by her. Shortly afterwards "she was invited to leave EMI by Kate to work with her, which she did very readily," says her former EMI colleague Brian Southall. "Hilary worked very closely with her, they had a very close bond, and she knew the business backwards."

At Bush's side for most of the next 30 years, Walker was never *quite* a manager. She handled much of the day-to-day heavy lifting in the manner of a PA, but contracts and financial matters were still handled by Novercia in conjunction with their trusted accountant and solicitor. Walker was primarily a buffer, someone to field the endless enquiries, say 'no' on Bush's behalf and keep unwanted distractions at bay. As such, she was not always popular. The 'Tour Of Life' set designer David Jackson recalls her "confrontational, dog-in-a-manger management style," while Brian Bath remembers moments when "she started pushing her weight around and it wasn't very comfortable." Charlie Morgan, who perhaps has a little more distance, admits, "she was pretty tough, [but] she was good." Above all she was necessary, and the final piece in the management structure.

As 1978 closed *The Kick Inside* was named the tenth best selling album of the year in Britain and 'Wuthering Heights' the eleventh best-selling single. Bush was harvesting gold and platinum discs from around the globe and had picked up armfuls of awards from the industry and music magazines. To cope with the deluge of fan mail, the Kate Bush Club was created, based in Welling and entrusted to Lisa Bradley, who still runs it today. Bush continued to make appearances on the promotional treadmill, but they were gradually becoming less frequent. Mostly it was UK radio and TV, plugging 'Wow' and the forthcoming tour, with the odd jaunt to Italy and Switzerland to perform on television.

Some interesting opportunities came her way. She was offered, and declined, roles in two horror films – one playing a vampire – and was also invited to record the main title theme for the next James Bond film, *Moonraker*, composed by John Barry and Hal David; she politely passed on the grounds that she didn't feel the song suited her, and Shirley Bassey did the honours more than capably. She did, however, return briefly to the studio in February to record 'Magician' for *The Magician Of Lublin*, Menahem Golan's so-so celluloid interpretation of Isaac Beshevis Singer's 1960 novel. Written by Maurice Jarre and Paul Webster and all but inaudible in the film, the song was a fleeting but lovely fairground waltz, reminiscent of Tom Waits' circus songs, and a much more satisfying take on queasy, slightly sinister Weimar cabaret than her own 'Coffee Homeground'.

This was all very gratifying but essentially extracurricular. Everything was leading towards playing live. The 'Tour Of Life' was intended to be a hydra-headed beast with several distinct faces: music, movement, poetry, mime, burlesque, magic and a continuous parade of eye-popping visual stimuli. Ever since she had started conversing with the media Bush had been steadily talking herself into undertaking a tour, promising something beyond the run-of-the-mill. "Bands that do nothing, that just go out and . . . play their latest album, or sing it and then just walk off, are boring," she said with disarming emphasis and scant regard for the sensibilities of regular rock fans.[1] It was another illustration of how little she was prepared to conform to the rock model. This was the age of new wave, when the no-frills ethos of punk still held sway and turning up, tuning up and singing your songs straight was *very much* what bands did. In the era immediately following the act of symbolic regicide performed on prog rock pomp, anything other than a display of unfussy, conspicuous passion was viewed with extreme suspicion by most quarters of the highly influential rock press. The escapist Technicolor fantasy world of the New Romantic movement – arguably the logical destination of punk's Be Yourself ethos – was awaiting around the corner; Bush was already far ahead of the pack in this respect, at least visually and conceptually. It would take her music a little time to catch up.

The tour had originally been scheduled to start in March but was shunted back to April as Bush struggled to ensure that the hugely ambitious undertaking would gel to her satisfaction. Although the dates were officially announced on March 3, preparations had begun in earnest immediately after Christmas 1978. In her first meeting with set designer David Jackson at EMI's offices, many of the visual aspects were thrashed out in an impromptu, open-ended brainstorming session which started with a businesslike handshake and ended up in a huddle on the floor.

"She entered the room with a coterie of management types, smart, successful, and I thought: 'heavy hitters'," says Jackson. "Because Kate is so petite I had the impression of a precocious child surrounded by heavily protective parents. We shook hands, we made eye contact, and there was a bit of light chit-chat. I don't think we even looked at the fat portfolio of stuff I brought to show her. She was totally friendly, like we'd known each other for years, and just buzzing with enthusiasm. I had a huge scratch pad and some pencils with me, the pad was too big for any of the desks in the room so we sat on the floor and scribbled and talked and scribbled. When I looked around the management types had all wandered off, so there we were like two kids on the floor with our crayons. At some point one of my scribbles reminded her of an ankh*: 'Looks like an ankh!' 'It does doesn't it? That's what it is then!' The design for the physical stage set was pretty much done right there, and I fell in love with her right there. She was gorgeous, personable and very smart. After that it was, 'Anything I can do to make you happy, Ma'am!'"

In the coming days, between January 2 and 4, she and Jackson met again at Wickham Farm to pin down the general look and feel of the set and the lighting. Like most aspects of the tour, it was a fully collaborative process, albeit one conducted within her strict guidelines. Bush would explain – not always clearly; she tended towards opaque, abstract inspiration – what she wanted and then allow her colleagues a degree of autonomy in executing her vision. She was not dictatorial, but given full artistic control for the first time her imagination tended to run riot. "Kate would just *go off* and I would jump in now and then and say, 'Yes, OK, I think that one is just within the range of possibility,'" says Jackson. "It was out of control from

---

* The Egyptian 'Key Of Life', a hieroglyphic character resembling a Cross with a loop at the top, denoting eternal life. This may have helped give the tour its name.

the moment it began. Not literally, [but] the stuff we scribbled on the carpet was out of control."

This was not atypical. For someone whose productivity is hardly the stuff of legend, the sheer pace at which Bush comes up with ideas in all aspects of her work, and the constant supply of new and occasionally outlandish concepts, has struck many of her collaborators. "She was a great person to work with, incredibly energetic and frenetic," says Gered Mankowitz. "I used to feel absolutely exhausted after every session, because she has this effect of jumping from one idea to another. You have to continually pull her back and say, 'No, this is going to be great.' If it doesn't seem right straight away she'd want to jump to another idea, and that was exhausting, trying to keep her on the rails. But the next day you'd see the film and there would just be shot after shot after shot, just wonderful."

She spent further time in January with wardrobe assistant Lisa Hayes working on ideas for costumes and visual themes. Meanwhile, she had to orchestrate both the song and dance elements of the show. After the disappointment of being sent down from the mountain, Brian Bath, Del and Paddy had been drafted back in to form the nucleus of the touring group. Vic King was now firmly off-radar, and Charlie Morgan had amicably left the band of his own accord, somewhat weary of the piecemeal nature of the work. They needed a new drummer and, to recreate accurately the sound on the records, they also brought in a piano player, a keyboard player and another guitarist.

Ben Barson, the brother of Madness's Mike Barson, joined on synthesiser. London-born session musician Alan Murphy came in on lead guitar on the recommendation of drummer Preston Heyman, who had played on Bryan Ferry's 1978 album *The Bride Stripped Bare* and knew Murphy from gigs and studio sessions around London. Northern Irishman Kevin 'Eggs' McAlea, a pub rock veteran and a seasoned session player, played piano and saxophone.*

"We needed extra musicians, so the group just got bigger," says Brian Bath, who was de facto bandleader. "Preston showed up and he was great, a really loud drummer: when he hit the cymbal Kate used to blink, she couldn't help it! I remember Dave Gilmour's younger brother coming along, but then Alan Murphy turned up and I thought, 'My God, this

---

* McAlea later wrote the English lyrics for Nena's 1984 number one '99 Red Balloons'.

guy's good, and so positive,' so we started working on guitar parts. Kevin came along, got on the piano and said, 'Can you play that bit again, Kate?', and he copied straight away what she played, note for note. He was so brilliant, never made a mistake." Bush revealed that a major part of the attraction with McAlea was the fact that she had "never met anyone else who plays the piano – or *can* play it if he wants to – so like me. [He] was an incredible find."[2] So much so that he was the sole musician from 'Tour Of Life' who would be invited to return for 'Before The Dawn'.

The idea was to play all 23 songs from the first two albums – in the end only 'Oh, To Be In Love' wasn't performed – along with new material. There would be no idiosyncratic renditions of 'Honky Tonk Women' or 'Nutbush City Limits'. Accustomed to getting her music played exactly as she wanted it, Bush drilled the band over and over again until there was no margin for error. She had not long returned from her appearance on *Saturday Night Live* in New York, where she had briskly informed house drummer Billy Cobham, a jazz-fusion legend who had recently worked with Miles Davis, that his playing on 'Them Heavy People' was all wrong: "No, no, no, no, no," she chided, "You don't do it like *that*. . . ."

The band rehearsed for a full three months, much of that period spent simply trying to come to terms with the structures of the songs, negotiating and logging their many unexpected twists and turns. "It took us so long to learn them because they were so complicated, I just worked at it day and night," says Bath.

It's safe to say that Bush was working even harder. Throughout most of January and February she spent her mornings at contemporary dance centre The Place in Euston, central London, putting together routines and rehearsing for the show. Anthony Van Laast had been hired by director Keith MacMillan for the 'Hammer Horror' video, and she subsequently invited him to help her choreograph the entire tour. Van Laast went on to work on a number of high profile productions, including *Chess*, *My Fair Lady* and Abba's *Mamma Mia!* movie, and is now a knight of the realm. At the time, rather more humbly, he was a member of the London Contemporary Dance Theatre, and when not touring he would often teach evening classes at the school attached to the company. It was from these classes that he recruited Stewart Avon Arnold and Gary Hurst, two young, black dancers who would become Bush's principal partners onstage, in videos and in studios over the next decade and more. There was perhaps a degree of gentle provocation in her decision to choose – at a time when racial divisions in the UK were still pronounced – to dance with two black men. "She does think about cultures a lot – black culture, Irish culture, Aboriginal culture," says Avon Arnold. "She's very aware of colour and creed."

Whereas Bush was now confident enough in her musical vision to call all the shots, when it came to her dancing she still felt more like a student and was therefore willing to take direction from Van Laast, despite the fact that it was his first major job. "It was six-to-eight weeks of five days-a-week work and rehearsal," says Avon Arnold. "Kate was telling Anthony what she wanted, but sometimes we'd all work together on a movement, and Anthony would basically stage it and direct it, because she was in it. Other times he'd completely put the steps together himself. It would vary from song to song. He might say to her, 'Look, on this song it's better that you don't get up from the piano', or whatever. She was still very young then, and she hadn't had a lot of experience in stagecraft, so it needed Anthony."

"I can't emphasise the word 'collaboration' enough," Van Laast later said. "The choreographer is usually very much the master, but part of Kate's fascination is her idiosyncratic way of moving, and you can't take that away."[3] A daily routine emerged. Gruelling mornings at The Place and cold, misty afternoons spent with the band at Wood Wharf studios down by the waterfront in Greenwich, on the other side of the city though handily located for Welling and her flat in Wickham Road, where she would return late in the afternoon and continue working on her dancing – often with her partners in tow – until the early hours. It was a punishing schedule. To make matters worse a BBC film crew, headed by the laconic reporter Bernard Clark, dropped in periodically to record the historic proceedings for a *Nationwide* special. Del Palmer recalled, "She was getting up in the morning, going dancing, coming back, rehearsing with the band, going home, in a meeting 'til three in the morning, then getting up, going dancing . . ."[4]

While the artists were all knuckling under, the nuts and bolts of the set were put together in a hair-raising six weeks under the supervision of tour manager Richard Ames. It was high concept but low tech. There were no hydraulics – the ramp, which rose up vertically on 'Strange Phenomena', was made out of aluminium and hand-operated – and nothing was computerised. The rear projections were executed manually in real-time each night. It was built like an old fashioned theatre set, which is precisely what it was. Looking at the stage from the auditorium Bush's fans would see a large circular screen, intended to represent an egg, at the back of the stage, onto which slides and film images – clouds, a desertscape, waves – could be projected, and into which a circular flap was cut at the bottom through which Bush could enter and exit. From this concealed doorway the central ramp sloped down to the front of the stage, with the band tucked away on either side. It did indeed give the structure a vaguely ankh-like shape, though it was hardly obvious. A huge three-dimensional egg, upholstered in red satin like an Easter chocolate box, made sporadic appearances onstage: one of its primary purposes was to allow Bush to conduct her many costume changes out of sight inside it, without constantly running back and forth from the stage.

Most of the set, including the large back projection screen – which in reality more closely resembled a ribbed kite than an egg – shared key characteristics with *The Kick Inside* sleeve concept and the themes of many of those songs. The egg motif symbolised the womb, the beginning of life, but ultimately Bush had more ideas than could easily be accommodated within the available space, time and budget, and the result was a set design sufficiently fluid to act as backdrop to a series of short musical skits but lacking a clear visual identity. In the end, much of the show's momentum and sense of drama was generated by the costume changes, the innovative lighting from both the back and the front, and above all the dramatic energy which Bush and her dancers invested in the songs.

In early March the production moved to The Who's sound stage at Shepperton Film Studios, where huge mirrors were installed at the back of the room so everyone onstage could see what was going on and how they were projecting themselves. This was the scene of the coming together of two very different cultures: dance, still a marginal, rather esoteric pursuit, and popular music. "It was the first time, I think, that the musicians saw the dance, and vice versa," says Stewart Avon Arnold. "There was one point where Del was like, 'What are they *doing*? Where have they got their *hands*?' He didn't realise it was 'art'! Kate wasn't doing anything that was new in terms of pure dance, but in terms of applying it to rock it was very new." Palmer remembered that he spent most of the time at Shepperton "with my back to those mirrors because it was too freaky. . . . I remember looking over at Brian and going, 'What the hell is going on?'"⁵

It was a febrile atmosphere. This large group of young, highly creative but relatively inexperienced people worked very hard to make Bush's vision come alive, and their efforts resulted in equal measures of innovation and frustration. At all times, Bush was forced to negotiate the conflicts between creative control and financial and practical realities. Often, many of her more outrageous ideas were by necessity compromised. Having dreamed up dozens of concepts for the content of the rear projections, the crew shot thousands of feet of film footage of pool balls and wave machines and rotating six-shooters, nine-tenths of which were never used. "In fact, we totally ran out of time," says Jackson. "When we got to first rehearsal we were using footage she'd never seen, the film was still wet from the lab. What you're looking at [onstage] often is not the idea but the *solution* to the idea. If we'd had the Rolling Stones' budget at that point we could have got really silly. We thought we were being quite restrained!"

At other times, necessity proved the mother of invention. Towering sound engineer Gordon 'Gunji' Patterson devised the head microphone as a solution to the question of how Bush could sing and dance at the same time. The tiny microphone was attached to a wire headset which left both her hands free for dancing and expressive movement (although she didn't use it all the time; often she sang into a hefty canary-yellow hand-held mike). It was a genuinely pioneering innovation but fraught with problems, most of which involved getting it to sit correctly in front of her mouth so it picked up her voice clearly.

It was all terribly exciting, conducted in a warm, familial environment. Given the stakes and the scale of the production it was an amazingly organic, home-grown enterprise from top to bottom. Jay and his wife Judy were cooking the food, unwrapping little parcels of vegetarian fare as though servicing some over-subscribed family picnic. Bush's mother and father often popped in, and of course Paddy was playing a central role as musician and occasional dramatic foil. And, loyal to a fault, she had delivered on her implied promise to the KT Bush Band after the disappointment of *Lionheart*. Del and Brian were present and correct, at the heart of the music.

The 'Tour Of Life' was sold out by mid-March, assisted by the progress of 'Wow', which was climbing the charts to an eventual high of number 14. Between March 18 and March 29 the cast and crew moved to the Rainbow Theatre in Finsbury Park, north London, for full technical, musical and, finally, dress rehearsals. Right until the last minute at the Rainbow final additions were being made, suggestions tried and discarded. The content of the show was shrouded in secrecy, with all memos marked as highly confidential. The BBC film crew was usually left filming closed doors; behind them, strange things were occurring, some in the realm of *Spinal Tap*. The wagon-on-wheels which allowed Bush to be spun around by the dancers while still playing piano arrived back-to-front: with the glue still sticky, the decking was prised off the frame and stuck back on the opposite side, the wheels turned over, and the whole thing repainted. Afterwards, one of the running tour jokes became, *pace* Bush's much-loved *Fawlty Towers*, 'Whatever you do, don't mention the piano wagon!'

Simon Drake was a relatively late arrival. A former record plugger at Decca, back when he was plain Simon Alexander, and an old friend of Bush's ex-boyfriend Steve Blacknell, Drake came on board to provide mime, illusion and magic, adding an impish, more theatrical flavour to the proceedings. In common with almost every other element of the show, however, there was insufficient time to incorporate all his ideas. "There was a lot that Simon wanted to do that never got done," says Jackson. "He arrived too late to integrate. It was great to have him involved, if he'd have turned up a month earlier it would have been terrific."

By nature a perfectionist, Bush kept a watchful eye on the integrity of each element of the show. Right down to the last detail, every aspect of the production had her direct creative input and required her approval. The artist Nick Price, a friend of Jay's, was commissioned to design the tour programme, a beautifully realised full colour booklet with postcards, writing paper and an application to join the fan club. The cover image was a stylised painting of Bush's face, full frontal, with the hair as multi-coloured clouds; when you looked through her eyes you could see night skies, studded with twinkling stars. "She was very particular about what she wanted," says Price. "But she didn't nit-pick after I'd done it, which was very nice." Inside, heightening the aroma of greasepaint, the musicians, artists and dancers were showcased simply as The Cast.

The total cost was reputedly between £200,000 and £250,000. To the best of Bob Mercer's recollection, EMI was not involved in any aspect of the financing. "Normally, I would have been asked for a tour subsidy, and in her instance I would have given it," he says. "It may have been that there was nobody in her camp that thought to come to me and say, 'Look, this is going to cost £10,000 a night, can you help us?' In which case I would have done, but as the head of EMI I wasn't really in the habit of going around to my acts and saying, 'Are you making money on your tour? Do you need any help?' I was a pretty generous MD, but I wasn't that generous!"

Jay, who was handling many of the financial aspects of the tour, such as paying wages and dealing with insurance, recalled that EMI eventually stumped up some "token support funds".[6] However, in the days before Live Nation, tour sponsorship from commercial brands and '360 Degree' deals with record companies that encompass all areas of an artist's earning potential, Bush was effectively financing the concerts direct from her own pocket. Hard and risky enough if you're simply transporting a four-piece band around the country for a month, but a different proposition when there's an entire set to build, months of rehearsal time in a number of vast studio spaces to pay for, and a 13-piece 'cast' and an overall crew of 40 to employ and take on the road throughout Europe. It was a show with arena-production values deliberately booked into more intimate theatres, which meant it would always be a struggle to make the sums add up. The price of creative autonomy was that the buck stopped with her. "The battles were endless," says Jackson. "I tried and tried to get a bigger budget and a bigger lighting system, which would have meant more trucks, more people, more time and lots more money. It became clear to me at the Rainbow that my intense efforts to get a bigger budget were starting to upset Kate, potentially putting her off her stroke, so I shut up."

Cast and crew were exhausted before they even started, but charged with excitement. As they were picked up outside Hammersmith Odeon by the tour bus on April 2 everyone felt like they were embarking on the mother of all school trips. Following a low-key run-through that night at Poole Arts Centre in Dorset, the tour officially opened in Liverpool on April 3, 1979. The first live performance from the biggest – not to mention the oddest, the most divisive – pop star of the past 12 months brought an enormous amount of media and audience interest. It was a true event in the British pop world, an occasion to be observed microscopically. With every date sold out and more being added as the tour rolled on, opening night came with layers of conflicting emotions: excitement, nerves, anticipation, dread and expectation from all sides. Hilary Walker admitted tersely beforehand that it "means a lot".[7] Bush was not afraid of her audience, nor was she performing for the approval of the media. Instead, the pressure she felt was the need to meet her own almost impossibly exacting demands. As much as her fans and the press needed to see her sing, dance and play piano with their own eyes before they would truly believe in her gifts, she too seemed to need to convince herself that she really was capable of being the kind of artist she wanted to be. This was her chance to illustrate exactly what she could do, that she was not a record company puppet, that she was not contrived. "It has simply taken all this time to stage things the way I want to," she said in the run up to the tour. "And to match up to the standards I have set myself. It's a culmination of two years planning and six months solid rehearsal."[8]

As the BBC's Bernard Clark noted, hanging around the Empire foyer like an extravagantly moustachioed portent of doom, awaiting either a hoedown or a wake, "even parts of the audience were nervous."[9] EMI's Brian Southall was there to "fly the flag" for the company on opening night and "buy dinner, nut rissoles or whatever." He recalls that Bush "was incredibly nervous. Terribly, *terribly* nervous, I remember that, but the show was just extraordinary. We didn't quite know what we were letting ourselves in for, this extraordinary presentation of her music."

★ ★ ★

To the amplified keening of whale song the band began playing 'Moving'. The gauze curtain hanging in front of the stage was swept away, revealing a henna-haired Bush in a sea-green leotard, swishing dreamily as though beneath the waves, lost in an underwater waltz. The beauty and power of her voice was instantly apparent, as was her magnetism: it was immediately clear she was blessed with the performer's ultimate gift, that of innate watchability. "I'd never felt anything like it," Del Palmer recalled of the atmosphere. "It was electric. It almost made me stop dead, it was overwhelming."[10] Next came 'The Saxophone Song', with Bush on piano and Kevin McAlea playing the eponymous horn, after which a thudding amplified heartbeat announced 'Room For The Life', for which Bush emerged from the huge egg which had rolled on to the stage.

The first major production number of the show was 'Them Heavy People', for which Stewart Avon Arnold and Gary Hurst joined Bush. It was *Guys And Dolls* as directed by Bob Fosse: trenchcoats, trilbies, shoulder-shaking cartoon menace. There was more than a little Humphrey Bogart in there, too. "We both loved the lighting in *Casablanca*, we talked about that a lot," says Jackson. "She tended to think cinematically, rather than theatrically."

The routine was great fun, a tremendous rendition of one of her most ebullient songs, but the choice of costumes and choreography neatly encapsulated the wider difficulty of representing the depth of meaning of many of Bush's songs in a visually comprehensible, empathetic way. Onstage, the routine for 'Them Heavy People' pivoted upon the conceit of interpreting the word 'heavy' to mean noir-style 'hoods' rather than – as the song intended – serious, weighty teachers. Somewhere down the line the purity of the song's message was in danger of being scrambled.

"I can remember trying to figure out what the [hell] she was talking about," says Jackson. "At the start she wanted 'egg' images, and babies, the big red satin lined egg we built was supposed to be the womb and she was supposed to arrive onstage inside of it, but then choreography and costume had to translate the line 'them heavy people' and wound up with MI5, or the Mafia. The *point* – her point, I think – is that we're born and sometime later somebody, some inspired guru – Gurdjieff in her case, at the time – rolls us the ball of knowledge and we either catch it or unknowingly pat it back. Did it have to do with childbirth or enlightenment, or both? Nobody knew. And how the [hell] are you supposed to present a concept like that live onstage? Did anybody in the audience have the slightest idea what that song was about? I doubt it. One in one hundred. But it didn't matter cause it was Kate!"

The mixed messages mattered not a jot in terms of the audience's enjoyment, nor did they in any way detract from the richness of the spectacle, but for someone as keen on preserving emotional resonance as Bush, the yawning gap between the song's initial intent and its visual expression must have been apparent, and may have later led her to the conclusion that it was easier to be true to her overall artistic vision via the more malleable medium of film and video than onstage.

There followed a tender 'The Man With The Child In His Eyes', just voice and piano, and then a new composition, 'Egypt', which Bush – dressed in a glittering, flowing Arabian skirt – sung from beneath a simple golden crown. It was a terrific version of the song, markedly different and unquestionably superior to the one that later appeared on *Never For Ever*.

Driven by Preston Heyman's taut bongos, this 'Egypt' was snappy and lean, fast and fiery, like some distant cousin of Nina Simone's 'Funkier Than A Mosquito's Tweeter'.

Simon Drake appeared plucking a series of metal balls from thin air on 'L'Amour Looks Something Like You', and then made an unforgettable appearance as a fiddling dervish on 'Violin', another unrecorded song that ended Act One. This abandoned declaration of musical freedom demanded a suitably untethered performance and Bush delivered, leaping around the stage as though tip-toeing over electrified stepping stones; it's not a great song but it's notable, containing the first hints of the deeper, darker, more visceral vocal style she would develop on parts of *Never For Ever* and particularly on *The Dreaming*. While she was singing, Paddy and a stage hand donned huge, floppy violin costumes and flanked Bush onstage in a final, full scale fruition of the 'duelling basses' idea that first saw the light of day at his show at his Whitechapel Gallery back in 1976. As their long bows tipped back and forth, they looked both comic and eerie, resembling something from *The Day Of The Triffids*, another of Bush's favourite novels.

Act Two began with Jay fiercely declaiming his poetry, entering into a dramatic call and response with his sister on the line "two in one coffin". Vegas this was not. She then sang 'The Kick Inside' and 'In The Warm Room' at the piano, a neat erotic one-two, both dripping with heightened sensuality, before launching into 'Full House'. For 'Strange Phenomena' the sloping ramp at the centre of the stage reared up, its underbelly sending a barrage of pink fluorescent lights out towards the audience while Bush donned a top hat and tails against an astral backdrop, like a feline magician-cum-ringmaster intent on realigning the planets as Avon Arnold and Hurst floated around her looking like extras from *Blake's 7*.

The extended guitar solo at end of the song bridged the gap between yet another costume change, as Bush and Anthony Van Laast prepared to reprise their thrilling video routine for 'Hammer Horror'. This was the only song in the set not played or sung live. Instead, Bush and Van Laast danced to a newly recorded version of the track (this was deemed necessary to circumnavigate Musicians' Union regulations, and also to give the audience something with at least the whiff of live ambience) in order to allow her to perform a routine of which she was very proud; clad in black, the hooded Van Laast leapt out to shadow Bush on the choruses, a stark embodiment of both sexual need and a guilty conscience. Very physical, very powerful, very *Flowers*.

This routine – along with Jay's poetry – took the humble pop show into the realms of contemporary performance art, but most of the other dance elements in the 'Tour Of Life' were very cleverly and consciously choreographed to give the impression that more was happening than was actually the case. "The movements we were doing through Anthony were very simple," says Stewart Avon Arnold. "If you look at it as bare movement without the costume and the sets, it's very simple – Step Ball Change, kick a leg, stand behind Kate – but at that time in the rock world very few of her audience had seen dance. She was very good. She had been trained, she had worked with Lindsay Kemp and done ballet and was doing classes before we met her, but it wasn't until later on that Kate started *really* exploring movement: 'Rubberband Girl' is very different to what she was doing on, say, 'Don't Push Your Foot On The Heartbrake'."

Although Bush had by no means reached the standard of a professional dancer, this simplicity wasn't primarily down to her lack of ability. "It's incredible how far she's got," said Van Laast at the time. "I wouldn't have thought it was possible."[11] Rather, it was a matter of practicality. It is impossible to dance full tilt and simultaneously sing live for even ten minutes, never mind for two hours, and early on she had organised her priorities. "It's not a dance show," she said. "It's a music show that's being illustrated with movement."[12] Yet it was another compromise, a further example of the limiting nature of live performance and another head on collision with the problem of how best to present her music to the public. Robin Kovac, her old dance teacher, was unconvinced that all the routines – 'Wuthering Heights', particularly – translated effectively from the screen to the stage.

'Kashka From Baghdad' began with the band chanting as though shuffling slowly on some Arabic chain gang, building up momentum like a steam train puffing down the track, a highly effective and atmospheric entrée to one of her most exotic, melodically satisfying songs. It was followed by a punchy 'Don't Push Your Foot On The Heartbrake', which owed plenty to *West Side Story* and perhaps a little to *Grease*, Bush clad in black leather in a dusky city street, all flashlights and wire-mesh fences.

She had fully embraced the idea, learned from Kovac, Adam Darius and perhaps most of all from Lindsay Kemp, of presenting herself fearlessly onstage with a rather brash assurance not at all evident in her character off-stage. "When I'm onstage I'm performing, yes, and projecting, and to do those things well I have to be big and bold and full of confidence," she said. "And I am, but it's still little me inside. You can't go onstage and simper, and be timid and shy. You've got to be big and strong, and give your audience everything you've got: reveal your emotions, be romantic, transport them into another world, so they're in tune with you. That requires an awful lot of hard work, and an almost calculated force, I suppose."[13]

These controlled acts of letting go were a kind of possession, a high wire balancing act between losing one's inhibitions yet remaining absolutely in command. "She was Kate the whole time, but Kate being whoever she was being," says David Jackson. "You just suspended disbelief. They weren't always personalities – on 'Kite' she is being a *something*." It wasn't as simple as someone playing a part. It was more mercurial than that, an almost inexplicable alchemy, a subtle blending of her core traits and her dramatic alter egos. Adopting a series of roles onstage wasn't hiding; it simply allowed her to be bigger, brighter, deeper – *more*. Forgetting for a moment the physical effort involved, it was an intensely draining mental process to undergo each night.

There was another break before Act Three, which began with a beautiful, understated performance of 'Wow', featuring Bush in the same elegant long dress she had worn in the video, flanked by the two male dancers, naked from the waist up, twirling gracefully in their flowing white skirts. Her voice was stunning throughout these shows, but something about this song allowed it to truly cut through: clear, forceful and hugely expressive. 'Coffee Homeground' was played as a dark pantomime, Simon Drake reappearing as Hugo the Mad Poisoner, with more than a touch of Sweeney Todd in the mix, trying to entice Bush into a barrel marked 'Pork'.

An appropriately gentle strain of Jay's poetry – urging us "down the bluebell path" – ushered in 'In Search Of Peter Pan', with Drake as a Puckish Pan figure darting elfishly around the stage. 'Symphony In Blue' and 'Feel It' followed, the later performed solo at the piano in a teasing caricature of eroticism, all fluttering eyelashes, darting tongue and moistened lips. For all the flash and grab of the theatrical spectacle, in the end the show really was all about her extraordinary face. One minute she was

Douglas Fairbanks, the next Lillian Gish, the next Lolita.

For 'Kite' she was transformed in blue, winged and ready to take flight. Wind effects whistled through the theatre as the dancers twirled umbrellas in a clear homage to *Singin' In The Rain*. The song's reggae inflections were adapted into a circus-like arrangement, with an extended outro that allowed Simon Drake to mime battling his way across the stage in the teeth of a gale.

'James And The Cold Gun' marked the climax to the main body of the show. Bush strutted around the stage in a black, figure-hugging space-cowboy suit as the rear projection screen filled with a classic death valley movie vista, bathed in a glorious orange sunset, a pre-echo of an image Bush would use again on the same stage in 2014, albeit in a very different show and in a very different context. The Wild West theme was a hang-over from her pub performances of the same song in 1977, where she had dressed up as a cowgirl. During the song's long climax, where the meaty beat dropped to a sluggish, proggy half-pace, Bush picked up a rifle and, with some relish, gunned down the two dancers and finally Paddy as he swaggered menacingly down the ramp, scarlet ribbon shooting out of the muzzle. It was a wonderful set piece, and highly eroticised, a riveting dramatic enactment of female sexual power. Never mind the bodies piled up onstage – Bush killed everyone in the room.

There had been some good-natured debate about how to stage the final shoot-out. "Kate and Paddy wanted to use liquid movie blood squirting everywhere, like *Monty Python*, when she shoots," says Jackson. "But the set was painted white and that stuff stains. We even tested it at rehearsal, and the ramp had a pinkish hue for the rest of the tour. They compromised with red silk until the last night when of course we had to have 'real' blood." On the final night of the tour, instead of Bush facing off against just Paddy and the dancers, the entire stage crew dressed up as cowboys and Indians and by the time the scene finished Bush was knee deep in 'corpses' and red liquid.

For a first encore she performed a fragile rendition of 'Oh England, My Lionheart', the set inspired by old war films like *A Matter Of Life And Death* and *Reach For The Sky*. Dressed in an old, oversized flying jacket and air helmet, she sung her exquisite lament for the lost land of youth as her dying comrades lay around the stage. The coat belonged to David Jackson and, according to him, "she was naked underneath it. Somebody found that out and offered me £1,000 for [it] but I turned him down. He was so besotted that he wanted to buy the coat. I was so besotted myself that I wouldn't sell it to him!" His mother eventually threw it out, much to his dismay.

Afterwards, Bush left the stage and returned for the inevitable final encore of 'Wuthering Heights', played straight and true, the choreography following the template of the video, the stage swathed in mist and cloud. And then she departed for the final time, backing up the stage, waving as the cheers rang out and the curtain closed, underlining that this was pure theatre rather than a standard rock experience. Indeed, she had spoken not one word throughout, a fact picked up by many critics and fans as evidence of an aloof and impersonal onstage persona, and perhaps just a little pretentious. "I saw our show as not just people onstage playing music but as a complete experience," she explained. "A lot of people would say, Poooah! but for me that's what it was, like a play. That's why I didn't speak: 'For our next song . . .' and all that. You are a performer, you are projecting and exaggerating things and if you break the illusion you break the whole of the concept."[14]

Those who wanted to see her open up, to let her guard down and invite the audience to share her insecurities and uncertainties were inevitably disappointed. Bush never lost control onstage, nor did she veer off-message or allow the events happening in that room – right *here*, right *now* – to overtake her or divert her from the show's preordained course. It was a rigidly planned and executed exercise, but there was plenty of emotion on display, built into the songs and the performances. Anyone who saw her backing up the ramp at the end of 'Wuthering Heights', at first waving rather formally as she collected the gifts thrown at her over the footlights from the audience, then becoming more animated, her smile widening, her gestures becoming less studied, and finally reaching the top of the ramp and leaping up and down like an over-excited child, bubbling with glee and gratitude, couldn't fail to be convinced – and rather moved – that for Bush the 'Tour Of Life' was an intensely visceral experience. There was nothing cool or detached about it. It was emotional connection without speech, *a la* Lindsay Kemp, and all the more powerful for it. A few breathless hollers of 'How ya doin', Liverpool!' would not have added to the experience.

★ ★ ★

Backstage there was champagne, flowers and much laughter, a palpable sense of relief and excitement that they had pulled off a clear triumph on opening night. From Liverpool, the tour rolled out across the UK and mainland Europe throughout April and the first half of May. Because of its intricate nature, the details changed little from night to night and city to city. She might throw in the name of the place she was visiting – 'Oh Oxford, my Lionheart . . .' – but that was about it. The set list was curtailed in Stockholm, Copenhagen, Hamburg and Amsterdam because she was suffering from 'flu. In Holland, for example, she dropped 'Violin', 'In The Warm Room', 'Full House', 'Kite', and 'Oh England, My Lionheart' from the concert, shaving about 25 minutes from its length, which may have actually been a blessing: playing virtually every song she had recorded to date made for a very long night. Parts of the German and Swedish performances were recorded for TV broadcast and reveal a little vocal grittiness, but hardly anything notable. "She was faultless," says David Jackson. "I don't remember her ever fluffing a line or hitting a bum note on the piano."

The audiences tended to agree, acclaiming most of the shows with lengthy ovations. The critics were generally persuaded as well. Many of the reviews were euphoric, uniting the tabloids, the broadsheets and the music inkies in gushing praise. "Full of poise and in complete control of her vocal dexterity . . . it was the ultimate rock'n'roll extravaganza," ran *Record Mirror*'s review of the opening night in Liverpool.

Sounds caught the show in Birmingham the next night and concluded, "It's so finely realised that it's beyond rational criticism because she's created her very own universe on a stage . . . Rock turkeys the world over have forever played around with stage concepts, but apart from a smoke machine here and a thunderflash there it's all come to naught. Kate Bush, however, has put her dreams into actual flesh." *Melody Maker* reviewed the same show and simply deemed it "The most magnificent spectacle I've ever encountered in the world of rock."

There were many more eulogies along similar lines in the local press as the tour wound through the north of England and Scotland. When it landed in London for five straight nights at the Palladium, the superlatives went into overdrive. "A dazzling testimony to a remarkable talent," said the *Daily Telegraph*. "Bush lines up all the old stereotypes, mows them down and hammers them into their coffins with a show that is – quite literally – stunning," raved the *Daily Mail*. "What an ambitious adventure it is for a singer on her first concert tour – and how mediocre does she make most of her pop contemporaries seem."

"Her performance was risky, teetering often on the brink of the perilously overblown, but a nerveless triumph of energy, imagination, music and theatre . . . I was bushwhacked," said *Melody Maker*, back for another taste. Only the *NME* were unmoved, dismissing Bush as "condescending" but – with the kind of proud and rather wonderful perversity that defines the rock press – praising the magician.

Unsurprisingly, it was not a tour characterised by off-stage hi-jinks. Indeed, it began with a truly tragic epilogue during the preview show at Poole Arts Centre. After the concert, while scouring the venue to make sure nothing had been left behind, lighting engineer Bill Duffield was killed in a freak accident.

"Evidently Bill had taken it on himself to go back into the already darkened building to perform this completely redundant ritual we used to call 'idiot check'," remembers David Jackson. "You run around the theatre one last time to make sure nothing got left behind. The brand spanking new Poole Arts Centre had spiffy seating that could be retracted to the walls to change the shape and use of the space but before it would retract the staircase landings had to be taken out, basically creating a 6ft × 4ft cavity over a [huge] drop – in the dark. Bill ran up the stairs and landed on a landing that wasn't there. Probably didn't even touch the sides. There should have been flashing lights, there should have been guard rails, there should have been beeping warning things, there should have been all sorts of safety stuff. But there wasn't."

Duffield fell 17 feet onto hard concrete. He survived for a week on a life support machine, but there was little hope. He had only been involved in the tour for a matter of days, drafted in during final rehearsals to assist the over-extended Jackson on lighting duties, but such was the nature of the 'Tour Of Life' party that he was already one of the gang. He was just 21. The band were already back at the hotel when they got the news, and Bush was absolutely shattered. "It was terrible for her," says Brian Bath. "Something had happened to her little baby. Kate knew everyone by name, right down to the cleaner, she was so like that, she'd speak to everyone. I suppose it's something you wouldn't forget, but we just carried through it. We got into the mood of the show and the [tour] just kept rolling."

The option of cancelling the entire tour was discussed but the decision was made to carry on – at such short notice, what else could they do? – and organise a suitable tribute to Duffield. His death cast a heavy pall over the proceedings for several days, although it also strengthened the existing familial bond, the feeling of everyone pulling together for one another. The mood lifted as the shows gathered momentum and reactions continued to be ecstatic. Birthdays were celebrated with gifts; elaborate in-jokes and old war stories were shared. "It's one of those things you don't appreciate until you look back in hindsight," says Stewart Avon Arnold. " 'Well, *that* was amazing, new, exciting!' We earned good money, always stayed in five-star hotels. At the time you take it for granted."

Bush was an amiable, if often distant presence. It was an energy-sapping tour for everyone, but especially for her, and she was not often seen in the hotel bar after the show. "We were all exhausted, so tired," says Brian Bath. "There might be a party in the TBA room, the spare room, and we might pile in there for a noisy get-together. Kate might make an appearance, [usually] it was just the band with the roadies."

"If we had a day off we slept," recalls David Jackson. "There might be some get-togethers in hotel bars, but there were no big party scenes or anything like that. There was one night I remember in Edinburgh when we thought, 'What do rock'n'roll bands do when they're on tour? They wreck hotel rooms!' The party was in some room and I went up and as I walked towards the door the carpet beneath my feet squelched, the whole thing was wet. I knocked on the door and stepped out of the way and this bucket of water came flying out, and then Kate came out soaking wet, covered in little white feathers from a burst pillow. She had these little feathers on her eyelashes and she looked at me and went, 'Wow! Amazing!', and trotted off down the corridor. I never did go in the room."

This was the notorious water-bottle-and-pillow-fight fracas at the five-star Caledonian Hotel in Edinburgh, following the April 13 show at the Usher Hall, later reported in *Sounds* as 'Kate Bush (Not) In Wild Orgy Of Hotel Destruction Shock'. EMI footed the bill for damage, estimated at around £1,000, but that was about as rock'n'roll as it got. An after-show party on April 20 at the Dial 9 Club in Chelsea to mark the end of the initial run of UK dates was notable for its lack of excess: no "pie fights, drink fights, fist fights" grumbled *Record Mirror*, reporting that the entire Bush clan huddled together in the gloom.

Extra UK dates were added a fortnight into the tour, with three additional London concerts arranged at the Hammersmith Odeon to finish, one of which was advertised as a benefit for Bill Duffield's family. It was held on May 12, after Bush returned from 10 shows in western Europe, and featured Peter Gabriel and Steve Harley, for whom Duffield had also worked. They joined in on 'Them Heavy People' and sang 'The Woman With The Child In Her Eyes' [*sic*], while Bush and Gabriel duetted on Gabriel's 'I Don't Remember' and added backing vocals when Harley sang his own big hit, 'Make Me Smile (Come Up And See Me)'. The pair joined Bush on a closing – spirited, if rather ramshackle – rendition of The Beatles' 'Let It Be', where she broke the no-speaking spell by announcing, 'This song is for Bill. I want you all to give a big cheer for him, OK?' The crowd duly obliged. All the money raised was donated to a fund for Duffield's family.

The following night, the second of the three Odeon shows was professionally filmed for later release. It was a case of second time lucky. The Manchester Apollo show on April 10 had been recorded by Granada for their *On The Road* programme, but the results were never broadcast. The lighting used in the 'Tour Of Life' was deliberately subtle, mostly using deep, saturated colours, a theatrical ethos at odds with the flashy pyrotechnics of the standard rock'n'roll stage show but appropriate to the nuances of Bush's music. It was designed with the naked eye of the live audience in mind, but such muted hues made it devilishly hard to capture the show on film without adding vast amounts of extra, ultra-intense lighting, which would have made the stage look like an over-bright television studio.

At Manchester, the Granada film unit turned up without any prior consultation with the stage crew, and the results were awful. "Their cameras were so insensitive and the stage lighting was so dark and blue, you couldn't see anything," says John Henshall, who worked with director Keith MacMillan's production company KeefCo and was director of photography on many of Bush's early videos. According to Henshall, Bush's 'people' threatened Granada with an injunction in order to prevent them transmitting the results. "Keith sent me a pneumatic tape of the Manchester recording and it was useless," he says. "I told Keith, 'It's fucking dire!', and Keith said, 'Yeah, they've stopped them using it, they want us to reshoot it at Hammersmith Odeon.'"

MacMillan, Henshall and the KeefCo team scoped out the show twice before the Odeon taping, but the lighting problems were never quite overcome. What worked onstage never really translated to screen and the film footage is a little murky, lacking punch and dynamics. Some ground was recaptured in post-production through double imaging and posterisation and reinserting most of the rear projections which had been washed out on the night by the added film lights, but the video, released in 1981 as *Live At Hammersmith Odeon* and featuring 12 songs from the show, was never felt to be a truly satisfactory souvenir of an extraordinary step forward in the evolution of the way in which popular music could be represented onstage. There was also a little local difficulty and residual resentment over the credits for the film, which read: 'Conceived, written, produced and choreographed by Kate Bush, with the assistance of . . .'

"Everything was done by Kate Bush," laughs John Henshall. "Did you not notice? I know that a lot of people were pissed off with that. It was like, 'Oh yeah, darling? You should bloody try it!' I think a few people were annoyed by that and I'm not surprised. By that time she was definitely The Star." Publicly acknowledging the roles of others in her endeavours was a courtesy Bush rarely overlooked. The ungenerous accreditation on the film was the result of an over-zealous assertion of her desire – as a young woman in a notoriously male-dominated industry, and following the compromises of *The Kick Inside* and *Lionheart* – to have, and to be *seen* to have, full creative autonomy for the first time. The credits ended with 'Produced for the stage by Kate Bush Visuals'.

"The whole thing is a little bit diminishing of other people's contributions, when I don't think Kate needed anyone to be diminished at all," says Jackson. "Lisa Hayes wasn't just the 'costume design consultant', she was running back and forth like a thing on a string, saying to Kate, 'What about this, what about *this*?' until Kate had what she wanted. Then she built them all, then she toured them all and maintained them and dressed Kate every night. And she gets 'consultant', on the same page as choreography 'consultant' Anthony Van Laast – a serious, respected choreographer. That insults him a little bit. Of course Kate's name is the biggest, but come on! It just seemed a little ungrateful. I'm sure that wasn't much to do with her at all, I'm sure it was management and marketing and all that." She subsequently learned to assert her authority with a lighter touch.

★ ★ ★

It should have been the beginning of something truly wonderful. Audiences had grown accustomed to the preposterous bombast of a typical rock or progressive rock concert – which was all about beating fans into submission through volume and the vastness of the spectacle rather than exploring the intricacies of an integrated performance – but no one had taken the humble pop show into quite such daring and epic theatrical territory. David Bowie could certainly lay claim to some key innovations in this field, particularly on his 1974 *Diamond Dogs* tour, which shared several characteristics with the 'Tour Of Life' and set a precedent for theatrical presentation of rock. Restricted to North America and filmed only for a seldom-seen BBC documentary directed by Alan Yentob entitled *Cracked Actor*, Bush would not have seen the show with her own eyes – but had she done so she would have observed Bowie as the 'character' Halloween Jack, 'acting' out his songs on a stage that featured all manner of gantries and props, and never stopping to acknowledge the audience or his band of hired guns that was located well to the rear of the action. "I think Bowie will always be looked upon as a landmark in pop theatre, and I think Kate was the next mark after that," said Anthony Van Laast. "It broke a lot of barriers."[15]

With the 'Tour Of Life', Bush rejected the orthodoxy of a rock'n'roll show while at the same time suggesting a template for its future: theatrical, dance-based, creating an aesthetic beyond the immediate context of the songs and the music. She even performed to playback, an entirely unheard of conceit at the time but nowadays almost the norm for a show with significant visual stimuli; the head-mike, too, is now virtually ubiquitous. It was groundbreaking on all levels. Within a few years Bowie's 'Serious Moonlight' and 'Glass Spider' tours continued the thread, later joined by Prince's 'Lovesexy' tour, Madonna's 'Blond Ambition' tour, Roger Waters' staging of Pink Floyd's *The Wall* and U2's 'Zooropa' extravaganza, each one a true event in which the theatrical spectacle (although none of these acts went as far as adopting an aloof onstage character to be maintained throughout) was arguably as important as the music.

The ability of these acts to harness the enormous technological advances made in the Eighties and beyond eventually made the 'Tour Of Life' look rather quaint and old fashioned by comparison, particularly given its relatively small scale and the fact that it didn't transfer onto the screen quite as well as it might have. But make no mistake: all the elements marking the tour out as a hugely significant step forward in the evolution of live performance were evident.

"I do smile when I hear the current generation of show designers talk of 'convergence' – the supposed blending of projection and video and special effects and moving lights into one cohesive thing – as if they'd just thought of it," says David Jackson. "We had moving lights, eight of them, they were called follow spots. We had scenic projection and multimedia and song and dance and all the bells and whistles in 1979. Convergence, phooey! These new guys have computers doing everything for them, we had to drive by the seat of our pants."

So, yes, it should have been the beginning of something wonderful. Instead, the next time we saw Kate Bush in any meaningful sense as a live performer she was 56 years old. There was talk after the final Hammersmith Odeon show of taking the tour to America, and much excited discussion among the cast and crew about all the things they could do 'next time' given a longer period of preparation and a bigger budget. Everyone involved felt they had prised open the door leading to a brave new world of possibilities for Bush and her music. Yet it took 35 years for 'next time' to arrive. "I thought we were going to go around the world," says Brian Bath. "[But] it just fizzled into doing bits and bobs for TV shows and then doing songs for a new album. It was such a shame, really. The Americans would have loved it, but it never materialised." As Del Palmer drolly observed, "We went into the studio and never came out again."[16]

What are we to make of her absence from the stage between 1979 and 2014? How to make sense of it? Many time in interviews during that period Bush spoke of her intention to tour again, and there is no reason to doubt that each time she was being at least partially sincere. Prior to 'Before The Dawn', she came closest to making it happen in the early Nineties, following the release of *The Sensual World*. She and Del had gone to see Prince on his 'Nude Tour', during his long residency at Wembley Arena, stretching between June and August 1990. She was there not just to see the show – though she was a fan and he was becoming a clear influence on her music – but also to case Wembley as a potential venue for her own concerts. The early versions of the songs for her next record, *The Red Shoes*, were travelling in a direction that seemed to suit a live band, and at the Kate Bush Fan Convention at Hammersmith Palais at the end of that year she went as far as to announce to the 1,000 people present that in

1991 she was going to play some shows. The room, predictably, erupted. But, perhaps inevitably, she got wrapped up in the recording process – and encountered some choppy water in her personal life – and the plans faded away, replaced by the idea of doing a film, *The Line, The Cross And The Curve.*

Instead, an occasional series of brief, tantalising cameos provided meagre sustenance. Later in 1979 she performed three songs, one of which was 'Blow Away (For Bill)', a new composition dedicated to Bill Duffield, at the Royal Albert Hall on November 18 to celebrate 75 years of the London Symphony Orchestra. In July 1982 she stepped into David Bowie's shoes at the last minute to perform 'The Wedding List' at a concert at the Dominion Theatre for the Prince's Trust with a band that included Pete Townshend, Phil Collins and Midge Ure. She wore big boots, a peach tutu and a flimsy satin halterneck, on which the strap snapped while she was singing. She finished the song grinning sheepishly, her left hand pinning her plummeting blouse to her breast. Ure later recalled it fondly as one of the highlights of his life; Townshend simply acknowledged the "power of prayer".

There was, relatively speaking, a rash of live activity following the release of *Hounds Of Love.* Between April 4 and April 6, 1986, she performed 'Breathing' live each night at the Shaftesbury Theatre for a Comic Relief fundraiser. Sung solo at the piano, it was a truly extraordinary and emotionally charged reimagining of one of her finest songs, proving beyond all doubt that there is scope within her music for great change, for various versions, different paths: listen to this marvellous song take on another life and you can't help be filled with sadness that she hasn't explored at least some of them; it's a rather sobering reminder of the countless moments of potential brilliance we have never been permitted to witness.

There were three further live appearances in 1987. Two consecutive nights in late March with David Gilmour and his band at the Amnesty International benefit The Secret Policeman's Third Ball, where she performed 'Let It Be' and a thrillingly rough and ready version of 'Running Up That Hill'. The scene onstage was the Eighties in micro: blue neon signs flashing 'PIZZA', huge overcoats, shoulder pads, rolled up suit jackets – and *everybody* was having a bad hair day, not least Bush, who looked distinctly puffy and uncomfortable. Gilmour proved a reassuring presence, flashing her several sweet smiles during the performance. Later the same year she made a last minute, unannounced appearance during Peter Gabriel's June concert at Earls Court, descending from the top of a staircase to sing her part in 'Don't Give Up', the only time she has ever done so live. The thunderous ovation prompted by her unexpected arrival onstage spoke more eloquently about the genuine love and warmth with which she is regarded than a thousand words ever could. It was also an acknowledgement that, eight years after the 'Tour Of Life', a sighting of Bush onstage, however fleeting, had already become an event to treasure.

The same roar of surprise and delight greeted her equally unexpected appearance with David Gilmour in 2002 at the Royal Festival Hall. She sang the part of the 'Evil Doctor' on Pink Floyd's 'Comfortably Numb', perched somewhat self-consciously at the right of the stage, dressed all in black with her hair worn straight and long. She sounded a little tentative and only broke into a smile as the song ended, whereupon she waved at the crowd, hugged Gilmour, kissed the grateful piano player and made a swift, probably rather relieved exit.

These were pleasing reminders of her presence and her ability as a live performer, and it was always a treat to hear her voice ringing out, but it's an insubstantial legacy for the years when Bush was at her most vibrantly creative and commercial. The euphoria that surrounded 'Before The Dawn' cannot obscure the extent to which the world has missed out on enjoying Bush as a live performer. What might have been a semi regular occurrence became a once in a generation event, confined to a mere 46 performances, bunched at opposite ends of her career and in relatively confined geographical locations. It's certainly hard to think of another artist of comparable stature who has taken such a prolonged leave of absence from the stage while still producing a – more or less – steady stream of records. Her non-appearance onstage was not an accident. "Nothing happened for 30 years, so that's a very, very active decision that was made there," says Tony Wadsworth. For almost her entire career, Bush has been in the privileged position where she can pursue almost any creative whim that interests her. Given her tenacity and her dedication to her vision, if she had truly wanted to play live more often she would have done so. She consciously chose not to – but why?

Many of those who know Bush well plead a simple case of cause and effect, convinced that the experience of organising and then performing the 'Tour Of Life' was so unbelievably draining that, for so long it out-weighed any desire she may have had to repeat the experience. "I think it was just too hard," says Bob Mercer. "I think she liked it but the equation didn't work, it was too exhausting. I've seen that happen to other people but nothing like as severely as it did to her. These are not conversations I recall ever having with her, it was just I could see it. I went to a lot of the shows in Britain and in Europe, and particularly in Europe I could see at the end of the show that she was *completely* wiped. She danced and she sang and did the whole number, and it wiped her out."

Brian Bath tends to agree. "When she finished 'James And The Cold Gun', the last number [before the encores], I'd see her walking up the ramp in the middle and she was *finished*," he says. "Absolutely finished, sweat pouring off of her. Then she'd have to change costume, catch her breath, and come out to sing the big number, 'Wuthering Heights'. I don't know how she did it. She used to just collapse, really, at the end of the show, and I'd have to carry her back a few times. It was not . . . it wasn't really good, you know." Some of Bush's comments tended to back this up. "The idea is so unattractive when I think about what the tour took out of me," she said in 1989. "I haven't wanted to commit myself since."[17]

The tragedy of Bill Duffield's death is often mooted as another conclusive factor. "She did discuss playing live, and she said she never wanted to embrace that experience ever again," says Haydn Bendall, an engineer and friend who worked with her over four albums. "She never said, 'I'm not touring because of the accident', but she said, 'This poor guy died and it was a terrible experience' and one was left to make one's own conclusions. She felt absolutely awful about that." But while Duffield's accident was a horrendous piece of ill fortune that undoubtedly deeply affected her, it is unlikely to have been a tipping point. Other friends insist that the experience of touring was, on balance, a joyous and rewarding one. "She absolutely loved the tour, really she enjoyed it so much," says Jon Kelly, who mixed the *On Stage* EP, recorded at Hammersmith Odeon, and then co-produced *Never For Ever* with Bush. "All her dance and her theatre and her music came together in one place. The audience reaction was phenomenal, people loved it. It's not as if the tour was a disaster or things had gone wrong, it was the complete reverse. It was so pioneering."

Success came at a clear price, however. Afterwards she described herself as "a drained battery, very physically tired and also a bit depressed."[18] Most worryingly of all, she struggled to write. The sheer cost involved, meanwhile, was prohibitive and left her with a bloody nose and empty pockets. "It certainly wasn't [a] financial success," she said. "Much more a loss thing than making money . . . With 40 people to look after it was astronomical."[19]

In the immediate aftermath of 'Tour Of Life' it was glaringly apparent that any future tour would involve an enormous commitment of time, money and energy. Not only that, but it would have to be a truly spectacular event, something that not only combined her love of dance, theatre and music but also moved her story forward from the 1979 shows and incorporated the great strides being made in technology. "It did pose the problem: follow that," says Brian Southall. When she announced her intentions to play concerts in 1991 there were rumours that she had contacted the Jim Henson Company with a view to inviting them to work with her on a new stage show; Bush, of course, was a lifelong *Muppets* fan. She also wanted to embrace film and video. "I cannot help but feel it is very important to give people something visually special," she has said. "I don't think, by any means, that the tour which we did some years ago was perfect, there were a lot of things that were experimental, and we didn't know if they were going to work, but I think we did explore new territory, visually speaking, and the reaction was so positive. And I do feel that, when eventually I get the time and money to do another show, I hope we will continue working along those lines of combining music with dance and with theatre and it would be even better and much more interesting than the last time. I think that is a very untouched area in rock music, and it has great potential."[20]

Someone with Bush's streak of perfectionism and extraordinarily creative ambition could not hope to combine the conception, planning, rehearsing and performing of a major stage show in conjunction with writing and recording in the studio. "I need five months to prepare a show and build up the strength for it, and in those five months I can't be writing," she said;[21] the thought, she admitted, was "daunting . . . it scares me a bit."[22] When it came to making hard choices regarding further significant investments of her own time and money, in the Eighties and Nineties she opted to make films and videos, and to build and install her own 48-track studio at Wickham Farm. "At some point she must have sat down and thought, 'Do I really want to put myself through that again, because if I do it again I've got to make it bigger and better, and it's only me,'" said Del Palmer. "'It's not like there's a band, it's just me. I'm responsible for the whole thing.'"[23] Then came motherhood, and a whole other set of priorities emerged.

More generally, the mechanics of touring have never appealed; it is no surprise that 'Before The Dawn' was an old-fashioned theatrical residency at a venue close to her home, rather than the traditional travelling circus of the rock world. Bush has a deep seated fear of flying which, though never quite phobic (she has flown to America and elsewhere several times), nonetheless has been an active ingredient in her decision not to perform on a global stage. She certainly dislikes intensely the grind of sustained travel, having endured a promotional whirlwind throughout 1978 and much of 1979, and no other aspect of the music industry so relentlessly drives the machinery of stardom and the distancing effects of fame as touring; the lifestyle and inbuilt stress that comes with it – airports, hotel rooms, press calls, bulletproof itineraries, swift getaways, a phalanx of PAs and advisors, precious little solitude – sits entirely at odds with how she chooses to live her life.

Of course, touring and playing live are not the same thing, and her reluctance to embrace the latter more frequently is the greater puzzle. Anyone who saw her sing 'Wuthering Heights' in 1979 or 'Top Of The City' in 2014 would be left in no doubt how much unadulterated joy Bush derives from the physical act of singing, but the pay-off has not been sufficient for her to embrace the experience more often. On a fundamental level, she was not brought up in an environment where singing in public was the norm, and she has had to steel herself to perform in even the most informal of public situations. She is also immensely self-critical. Although most objective observers would agree that she acquitted herself spectacularly on the 'Tour Of Life', she was pursued by a feeling that she was not as good as she could have been. "Kate said to me one time that she had somehow lost confidence in performing, which I could never work out because she was such a staggering success on that tour," said Del Palmer.[24]

Some of those present during the making of Bush's 1993 film *The Line, The Cross And The Curve* recall her acute unease at performing on set. Bush approached 'Moments Of Pleasure' several different ways, and on one occasion she tried singing it solo at the piano. It did not escape the attention of the cast and crew that her legs were visibly trembling throughout the entire rendition. Even playing live in front of no more than 40 people, all of whom she was accustomed to working with on a daily basis, appeared intolerably nerve-wracking. For most of her career, she has found it incredibly difficult, and perhaps not terribly interesting, to perform 'straight', as herself. "If I can be the character in the song, then suddenly there's all this strength and energy in me which perhaps I wouldn't normally have," she said. "Whereas if it was just me, I don't think I could walk on the stage with confidence. It's very hard for me to be *me* on a stage."[25] It's notable that even the brief cameos she made in the time between 'Tour Of Life' and 'Before The Dawn' were in the company of close friends whom she knows well and trusts implicitly: David Gilmour, Peter Gabriel, Midge Ure. When she did finally return in 2014 it was at a time when her son had grown old enough to provide advice and considerable creative and moral support. All of them offered empathy, protection, cover.

But it cut much deeper than simple nerves. At its core, Bush's reluctance to perform live for 35 years was an active aesthetic choice. Perhaps the least *innovative* aspect of the 'Tour Of Life' was the music. On the sidelines and in shadow throughout, a pit orchestra in all but name, the band's virtually invisible profile was another deliberate concession to the theatrical bent of the show. Professional and highly polished rather than spectacular, the superb musicians gave Bush exactly what she needed – a largely unobtrusive, completely solid platform from which she could project her voice and her performances with total confidence, although it proved impossible for backing vocalists Glenys Groves and Liz Pearson to recreate Bush's superb, stacked vocal harmonies. However, the tour did throw open the vital question: just what do you *do* with your songs when you play them live? As little as possible, seemed to be the answer.

"I saw one of the last shows," says Ian Bairnson. "She basically made everyone in the band learn exactly what was on the records. Alan Murphy did all my solos pretty much note for note, and it worked. I think it was the right thing to do." She has never been one for improvising or, heaven forbid, flying by the seat of her pants when it came to public exposure. The increased chance of something going wrong – though, of course, it might just as easily go gloriously *right* – clearly unnerves her. "The worst thing is not being prepared," she said. "I have to know, before I go onstage, exactly what I am going to do."[26] The studio is the place where her imagination takes flight. Onstage, she wanted to be locked in tight.

This may have been the decisive realisation when it came to her long term plans. In some deeply ingrained sense playing live seemed to rub against the entire purpose of her music, which at its best is an attempt to dematerialise, to liquefy the physical self until all that's left is pure sensation and feeling; to achieve some degree of personal and very private transcendence. From as far back as her early years at St Joseph's Bush displayed a clear reluctance to let any light fall upon her working process; even *talking* about it seemed like it might somehow break the spell. Even today, in the studio she tends to sing her vocal parts entirely alone. In playing live – an environment with defined parameters where self-consciousness and an over-awareness of one's surroundings can easily take hold of a performer as sensitive as Bush – she may have felt she was somehow obstructing rather than aiding her connection to her music. Perhaps it is no surprise that it took time, experience and a more relaxed attitude to reach a more amenable accommodation with performing.

★　★　★

On the 'Tour Of Life' Bush had showed she could do it. Why rush to do it again? "People said I couldn't gig," she said, "And I proved them wrong."[27]

Perhaps the primary purpose of the 'Tour Of Life' was simply to force people to take her work seriously, to allow her subsequent records to be given a fair hearing. The experience certainly seemed to clarify something fundamental regarding her future path. *Director's Cut* notwithstanding, for which the motivations turned out be complex and, ultimately, oddly progressive, she does not have the nostalgia gene when it comes to her music and has displayed little enthusiasm for anything that hints at retrospection: reissues, Best Ofs, box-sets and 'deluxe' remasters, all recycled product that is highly profitable for both artist and label, have been thin on the ground. Playing live seems to fall into the same category: yesterday's news. "I can't possibly think of old songs of mine because they're past now," she said shortly after the tour ended. "And quite honestly I don't like them anymore."[28] Playing those songs over and over again would only stunt her creativity as a writer, she concluded, not feed it. Her music does not evolve that way. Unlike Dylan, who seeks to write a new page onstage each night, or perhaps just tear up an old one and throw it away, by the time Bush went onstage the story was already finished and she was desperate to dream up a fresh one. Similarly, 'Before The Dawn' featured only two songs she had sung live before, and nothing that had been performed on 'Tour Of Life'. Its primary purpose was to stage two conceptual suites rather than revisit the 'hits'.

After the 'Tour Of Life' she went into an almost immediate re-invention: 'I'm not going to do it that way, I'm going to do it *this* way.' She embarked on the tour just at the moment when she had become powerful enough to begin moving away from the notion of her albums being aural documents of what had occurred in a room between a handful of musicians performing more or less live; that kind of interaction interested her less and less. Instead, she was fully smitten with the possibilities of stretching reality in the studio, of exploring what could be *constructed* rather than merely *captured*. "We went back into the studio," said Del Palmer, "And she discovered that she could say a lot more there."[29]

And yet despite all these attempts to explain it logically, and despite the profoundly joyful surprise of 'Before The Dawn', her reticence to perform live for 35 years remains the great *lack* in Bush's career. It is not simply a conundrum, or a disappointment; it is a decision that has shaped her music and the way she was been perceived to a profound degree. In her personal life Bush is no more of a recluse than dozens of other pop stars, but her unwillingness to play live has made her seem so. Her refusal for so long to embrace one of the record industry's articles of faith set her out as a truly independent spirit but, less positively, it also fed the myth of a woman who was somehow detached and otherworldly.

More importantly, it has meant that her audience has been denied direct and sustained access to one of music's most innovative artists, while she has denied herself the traditional indulgence of reinventing her music anew as the years progress and her perspective changes. One of the key derivatives of performing live is to pull together the disparate strands of an artist's work in an easily digestible form, to shuffle the pack and provide new narrative threads, but her prolonged stage absence ensured that many of her finest albums – among them *Never For Ever, The Dreaming* and *The Sensual World* – remain unexplored. They remain strangely fixed in time, as, in a sense, are many of the various representations of Bush herself, embalmed and perfectly preserved. Perhaps that's why she has continued to hold such a strong fascination. Each album reinforces her status as a unique artist floating entirely out of time. "She is still producing music, but it's not *today*'s music," observes Stewart Avon Arnold. There is undeniably something rather lovely about this.

And yet. And yet. "It's a tragedy she didn't go back out touring [sooner], an absolute tragedy," says Jon Kelly. "A huge loss to the world, like a star dying early." It is indeed impossible, looking and listening back to the 'Tour Of Life', or hearing her sing 'Breathing' alone at the piano, not to feel a sharp pang of regret at the enormity of what we may have missed; in a sense, 'Before The Dawn' only served to make the loss even more keenly felt. Who would not have loved to hear a live version of 'Night Of The Swallow' from 1986, or 'This Woman's Work' remodelled in 1994?

But it's a dangerous game, idealising the unknown. Her decision to shun the stage during some of the peak years of her career shouldn't necessarily be viewed entirely as a negative. Unequivocally, a Bush who was touring the world every three or four years would not have been able to record the body of work she has. "If she was the kind of person who would be happy to tour and go on TV shows then you could say [the album] might have sold better, but would it actually have been the same piece of work in the first place?" says Tony Wadsworth. "If you become an artist who has to slog around the world there is an argument that that activity starts to have a negative effect on the art itself."

The question never went away, and Bush never ruled it out, but for decades the odds on her returning to the stage seemed absurdly long. As the years passed, and Bush's profile faded into near invisibility, it seemed ridiculous to imagine that she would have any desire to fly the coop for any length of time, or expose herself to the physical rigours, intense media scrutiny and knee-knocking terror of live performance. And though her fans would have happily paid through the nose just to watch her sing for 45 minutes on an old pub piano, the simplicity of this would have never satisfied her. "I would feel that that was such a cop-out," she once said. "I don't think I'd be able to feel that I had any effort or sense of challenge left in me. I don't really feel that happy doing something, in a way, unless I've really pushed myself to the limit . . . otherwise it doesn't feel like you've put enough effort into it."[30]

We now know that it never quite slipped off her to-do list. "There have been lots of times we've talked about this," said Del in 2007. "We've gone through the whole thing of doing a massive spectacular production, to have her doing it on her own, and we just go round and round and round . . . I still have my fingers crossed. You can never say never."[31]

In the end, it came down to timing. When Bush became a mother in 1998, there seemed even less imperative than ever for her to inflict the intense upheaval of playing live upon herself. And so, for a long spell, it proved. Yet in the end it was motherhood that brought her back. Her son was, it seems, the one person who could persuade her to do what for 35 years no one else could.

7

Breathing

THE quality of Bush's first two records and the vast stockpile she had amassed of songs in a similar style suggest that she could have gone on making albums like *The Kick Inside* and *Lionheart* indefinitely. That idea, however, held no appeal. These were works on which she essentially felt she only shared authorship; almost as though the words were hers but the pictures belonged to somebody else. "I don't really think that *Lionheart* expressed the true phase I was in at the time, whereas all the others have," she later reflected. "[It] could have been a lot better."[1]

The first two albums are collections of – often exceptional – group performances, the sound in the room rendered more or less faithfully. She longed to move away from this method of aural documentary and develop a more stylistically adventurous approach. Over the course of a three-year period of almost continuous recording, resulting in a final, conclusive creative breakthrough, she began to see and hear her music in dramatically altered ways, while gradually wresting control of the technology that would finally allow her albums to keep pace with her vision. *Never For Ever* edged towards a more experimental sonic palette, flirting with the idea of using the studio as an instrument; *The Dreaming* completed the transformation. She was no longer simply pointing a camera towards her subject. Now, she was becoming an auteur.

Following a short period of post-tour decompression, by August she was peering back through the lens. Bush entered Abbey Road's Studio Three with Jon Kelly to mix the tapes from the Hammersmith Odeon show and select four tracks – 'Them Heavy People' as the lead, backed with 'Don't Push Your Foot On The Heartbrake', 'James And The Cold Gun' and 'L'Amour Looks Something Like You' – for the *On Stage* EP, released on September 3. But that was old news. Already, she had her eyes fixed on the horizon. "I haven't really begun yet," she said during the mixing sessions for the EP. "I've begun on one level, but that's all gone now so you begin again . . ."[2]

You begin again. She was as good as her word. From Abbey Road, the sessions spilled almost seamlessly into AIR studios and she found herself starting work on a new album with a new set of rules and goals. Most significantly, her relationship with Andrew Powell had, amicably, run its course. "I think she just wanted to move on," says Powell. "She wanted to be in control, really, of the whole shooting match, pretty much like the live show."

Yet this was to be a relatively benign, perhaps even tentative autocracy. *Never For Ever* is a fascinating record, divided as it is almost exactly down the middle, torn between capturing where Bush had been and where she was heading. The musicians, production set-up, studios, song choices and even the chronology of the record captured this dichotomy precisely. *Never For Ever* mixes players from her own live band with those who had performed on her first two albums and features old songs alongside some stunning, pioneering new compositions; the sessions even started at the end of one decade and spilled over into a new one. It was, in all senses, a record created on a cusp.

Alan Murphy and Brian Bath shared duties on guitar; Del Palmer played the majority of the bass (Bush had also asked David Paton to contribute but he was pre-booked on another album session) and Preston Heyman most of the drums. Ian Bairnson popped in to add vocals. Paddy was there, as ever, strumming, plucking and crooning, alongside newcomer Max Middleton, the highly regarded keyboard player who had been in the Jeff Beck Group and on the landmark *Blow By Blow* album. He arrived as something of a sceptic. "I'd thought 'Wuthering Heights' was a bit gimmicky and thought, 'She won't last long,'" he says. "But the more I worked with her and listened to her lyrics, the more I thought she was very clever and wrote lovely melodies. I got more and more impressed, every track was so different and had something [special] about it. That combination of talent and being a lovely person is rare, but [that's] not to say she's not eccentric."

Middleton had been recommended by Jon Kelly who, as a kindred spirit and a trusted pair of hands technically, had been retained by Bush as co-producer. "She had control then, she could pick and choose, and lucky for me she asked me to work for her," says Kelly. "The past didn't haunt her or anything, but I remember her saying, 'Now we – she would always say 'we' rather than 'me' – have control of what we do'. We played them for days, some of these songs, but under no pressure. We just played them for the joy of playing and seeing where they developed. I just remember it being such a creative time."

Nonetheless – or perhaps understandably – the album took some time to find its feet. Bush was creatively spent after the tour and she initially struggled to compose. At AIR she started off with the songs that were already written. On 'Violin' she wanted to capture some of the residual energy from the tour and bring it into the room, stripping the sound down to two electric guitars, bass and drums, with Kevin Burke's fiddle weaving in and out of the arrangement. It featured one of her most extraordinarily *gone* vocals, and while in the studio she lived out every word. "When she sang it it was like she was performing it onstage," says Middleton. "In the sound box she didn't just stand there and sing, it was 200 per cent effort every time, really like a performance. I was very impressed with the way she went about doing those things."

'Egypt' travelled from stage to studio less successfully, losing a little of its snap en route. An opaque, opiatic erotic reverie in which the "Land of the Pharaohs" takes on the characteristics of the female body, the complex time signature tied everyone in knots. "It was in 9/8, or 11/9 or something, and nobody could play it," says Brian Bath. "*Nobody!*" The methodology at AIR was much the same as on her previous records. Bush would play the song to the band and then everyone would follow her. Even a track like 'Egypt', serpentine as a sidewinder, was recorded live in the room with any additions – Bush's vocals, Middleton's mini-moog – overdubbed afterwards. Without Andrew Powell calling the shots, and with an artist as self-critical and insistent on emotional veracity as Bush, such an approach tended to be highly labour intensive.

"She would do lots and lots of takes and I could never understand why, that was a little difficult for me," says Middleton. "It sounded good in the end, but normally with other musicians we'd do it again because it was too fast or slow or you're playing the wrong chord – something very definite – but she was looking for something a little bit nebulous that was hard to pinpoint: the atmosphere or the feeling of the song. She always knew what she wanted, but she'd just say, 'Let's do it again,' and you'd think, 'I wonder why?' We didn't talk about the content of the songs, I don't think she was into dissecting music too much, I think she wanted it to come together naturally. She wasn't doing it again out of sheer belligerence, she was looking for something."

'Blow Away (For Bill)' was a whimsical but unengaging tribute to Bill Duffield, a creaky conceit about rock stars congregating in some backstage holding area twixt life and death. Aside from Buddy Holly the musicians she mentioned were all recently deceased: Marc Bolan died in 1977, Keith Moon and Sandy Denny in 1978, Sid Vicious in early 1979, while the inclusion of Minnie Riperton dates the writing of the song to no earlier than July 12, 1979, the day Riperton died, and no later than November 18, 1979, when Bush performed it live at the Albert Hall during the concert for the LSO. Riperton is an unusual inclusion in a song otherwise dedicated to rock legends, but Bush may have felt a particular affinity with a woman whose songs – particularly the huge 1975 hit, 'Lovin' You' – were also notable, and often derided, for the extraordinary high pitch of the vocal.

'Blow Away (For Bill)' was a banal song, the weakest on the record. 'The Wedding List', by contrast, was the standout track of the early session. Another mini-movie, another four-minute psychodrama, it told the story of a bride whose husband was murdered just after their wedding – "You've made a wake out of our honeymoon" – and who then wreaked vengeance on his killer. Loosely inspired by Truffaut's 1968 movie *The Bride Wore Black*, in which a grieving widow embarks on a killing spree, hunting down the five men she blames for her husband's death, the song was loaded with highly charged imagery. Like the stage version of 'James And The Cold Gun' it made explicit the link between guns – a recurring Bush fascination, objects she describes as "fantastic, beautiful"[3] when detached from their deadly purpose – and sex, mixing the language of violence with the language of lust. In the song, hunter and hunted "come together" in the same room, and when the drama is played out she rolls him over "the butt of my gun."

It's a fabulous song with a lovely dramatic pause, a little sigh, where Paddy's harmonica wail drops in, and from the punning title on down it's filled with an irresistible black humour which spilled over into the recording. "She wanted me to sing with her at the end so we went in and I was in hysterics, I just could not stop," says Bath. "In the end she said, 'Brian, you've *got* to stop laughing, we've got to do this now.' I had to really pull myself together. She had the most incredible sense of humour. We used to be in hysterics, rolling on the floor, we were having such a good time."

Completed studio mixes of these songs – minus orchestral overdubs – were ready by late autumn, and they formed the backbone of a 45-minute Christmas television special Bush recorded for the BBC. *Kate* featured 'Violin', 'The Wedding List', 'Egypt', as well as the 'Ran Tan Waltz' – a relative throwaway which, musically, sounds like a dry run for 'Army Dreamers'; the 3/4 time signature is the same and the instrumentation very similar – and 'December Will Be Magic Again', a sweetly evocative seasonal song released as a Christmas single in 1980, with a fine original picture sleeve by Nick Price.

The television special was an odd construct. Clearly intended to mark a progression from the tour, it's likely that, embroiled as she was in the early stages of *Never For Ever*, Bush was never quite able to give it the time and devotion it required. Stewart Avon Arnold, again paired with Gary Hurst as one of Bush's dance partners, can't remember a single thing about making it. *Kate* ended up as more of a scrawled footnote to the 'Tour Of Life' than a next chapter.

Broadcast on December 28, the show featured revised versions of 'Them Heavy People', 'The Man With The Child In His Eyes', 'Symphony In Blue' and 'Don't Push Your Foot On The Heartbrake', as well as the new material. A mixture of pre-filmed sequences, dramatic in-studio setpieces and a handful of straight, at-the-piano musical perform-ances, some of the footage, admittedly, was marvellous. 'The Wedding List' was a highlight, a crazed Bush in bridal white gunning down cheroot-smoking double-dealer Paddy.

Much of the rest, however, ended up looking cheap and rather silly. The routine for 'Egypt' almost begged to be mercilessly parodied: it's the Turkish Delight advert with a social conscience, a future French & Saunders routine in the making. Bush, in a billowing pink number with a black band across her face, drifted in front of a rather over-literal backdrop of stock film showing pyramids and camels, intercut with grittier scenes of poverty and squalor, awkwardly underscoring the distance between illu-sion and reality. 'Them Heavy People' was a diluted version of the tour routine, while the choreography for 'Ran Tan Waltz' was plain bizarre.

Still, it's worth watching for two unforgettable, never-to-be-repeated moments. Bush sang 'Another Day', Roy Harper's beautiful song of domestic fracture, as a moving duet with Peter Gabriel (heralded, inevitably, as the "Angel Gabriel"), who later reappeared to perform an equally stunning solo version of his own 'Here Comes The Flood', which rather stole the show. Again, Bush said nothing to the audience throughout. This time, however, the suspension of disbelief was a little harder to hold.

★ ★ ★

The new decade brought a new perspective, a new studio, and some landmark new compositions. "EMI had asked us to record four songs, I think, before Christmas," says Kelly. "Then we agreed between us that she should write some more, because these four songs were still from the early Kate Bush Songbook. So she went off and wrote some new songs. I can remember going to her flat just after Christmas and she played me 'Babooshka'."

'Babooshka' was loosely inspired by the folk song 'Sovay', in which a young woman dresses up as a highwayman and robs her lover in order to find out whether he will hand over the gold love ring she gave to him. Even threatened with his life he refuses to part with it, and Sovay thus feels certain of his devotion. In Bush's song, the conclusion is less upbeat. An older woman tests her husband's faith by tempting him with scented letters and finally dressing up as a younger version of herself to meet him in the flesh, "incognito", and he succumbs. The title, borrowing and misspelling the Russian word for grandmother, also brought to mind Matryoshka dolls, or Russian dolls, often incorrectly known as 'Babushka dolls'. Bush claims the title came to her out of the ether, but the notion of an older figure hiding a series of other, younger figures within herself seems peculiarly apt for these ruminations on age, trust and sexual identity.

There are in existence two early demo versions of one of Bush's best known singles, dating from late 1979. The first and earliest features 'Babooshka' in its raw infancy, just her piano and voice with a single harmony vocal overdubbed on the title phrase. It's a wonderful two minutes of music, beginning with a great bluesy flourish, the piano reminiscent of the opening passage of Bob Dylan's 'Ballad Of A Thin Man', and even a jarring bum note on the keyboard can't dull its obvious ebullience. On a later demo she had added – significantly, for rhythm was becoming an essential part of her writing process – a simple electronic drum pattern, while the song's signature keyboard motif was now present.

The vocal harmonies became more complex, and the listener can hear what she's trying to do with the song and where it's heading. It's a fascinating insight into how advanced these songs were before they even arrived in the studio, a vital link between how they began and what they would later become.

Jon Kelly recognised a hit single from the very start. "It had such a rising chorus and such an impact," he says. "She had that little piano riff right from the beginning, that little motif, so it had all these ingredients. I thought it was great and would be a single, which of course damned it! It had a little bit of a stigma attached to it throughout the recording. Kate had realised that it was going towards being a single and was thinking, 'Oh God! Promotion, release, press, charts, *Top Of The Pops*,' and thinking that's not where she wanted to go. She wanted to go towards making proper albums."

Despite the fact that it was finished before it came anywhere near the studio, it was not necessarily an easy song to capture as the album sessions moved into EMI's famous Studio Two at Abbey Road in January 1980. "When we did things like 'Babooshka' we were in there for *days*," says Brian Bath. "We played 'Babooshka' for three days non-stop and I think there were about 12 bass players, they were just coming and going: 'It's not working out, we'll get someone else.'"

Bath is exaggerating for effect, but the second part of the *Never For Ever* sessions marked the beginning of Bush's habit of 'casting' for parts, selecting musicians solely for specific tracks, picking and choosing according to a song's needs and the strength and style of each player. As the notion of having a studio band began to evaporate, even Del wasn't immune. On two tracks, 'Babooshka' and 'Breathing', the rhythm section of John Giblin – a highly regarded session man with a distinctive fretless bass sound who had been recommended by both David Paton and Peter Gabriel – and Bush's old friend Stuart Elliott was preferred to Del and Preston Heyman. Bush felt the songs needed a different approach, a lighter touch. Egos were sometimes bruised, albeit temporarily.

"I remember this voice coming over from the control room: 'Brian, could you come into the control room a moment?'" Bath recalls. "I got there and she said, 'Brian, it's not really working out, maybe you should sit this one out.' 'Oh, OK then.' Then all of a sudden the intercom goes and Preston is asked to sit out, too. Preston said, 'I've never been taken off a session in my life!' There were a lot of shocks all round. When we were doing 'Babooshka' Del was taken off. I couldn't believe it. He was a bit . . . Del swears a lot. That's what he's like, Del. He's so funny, so straight with it. He does speak his mind!" Despite such unflinching decisions, Abbey Road was a bustling, happy, highly creative environment. Friends and family, including Roy Harper, Peter Gabriel and Keith MacMillan, dropped in most evenings to listen, watch and hang out, and Bush would scamper around making everyone cups of tea.

As the sessions progressed, she became more and more alive to the possibilities offered through new technology. In particular, she fell head over heels for the Fairlight Computer Music Instrument (CMI), a digital sampling synthesiser designed by two Australians, Peter Vogel and Kim Ryrie, in 1979. It was a bulky, clunky brute of a thing, a mainframe computer with an eight-inch floppy disc drive whirring away noisily, a green-screen monitor and a touch-sensitive keyboard attached. By today's standards the sounds were astonishingly lo-fi and crunchy and the set-up a little crude, but musically it was a glimpse of the future, the first stirrings of the digital age we now all inhabit.

The Fairlight enabled musicians to sample short sounds and play them back at different frequencies, either direct from the keyboard or by programming a sequence of notes. You could record anything – a cough, a broken twig – or use some of the machine's library of preset samples – a cello, a violin, or the infamous Orch5, a fragment of Stravinsky's *Firebird*, which became perhaps the most over-used sound in early days of digital samples – and hear the whole synthesiser 'become' that sound. It was musical animation. A given today, a revolution 30 years ago.

There were only three Fairlights in the UK at the time. Peter Gabriel had formed a company with a relative, Steve Payne, called Syco Systems which was involved in importing electronic instruments to Britain; he, almost inevitably, had his own machine. Syco owned the other two, one of which they loaned to Richard Burgess and John Walters of electronic group Landscape (best known for their 1981 hit 'Einstein A Go-Go') on the understanding that they would demonstrate the Fairlight to potentially interested parties on Syco's behalf.

Bush learned about the instrument through Gabriel and, immediately intrigued, requested a demonstration. In the end Walters and Burgess loaded the ungainly instrument into the back of Burgess' old BMW and brought it – shaken but still working – into Abbey Road on four separate occasions, whereupon the ensemble set about adding a variety of textures to the existing tracks. On 'Army Dreamers' they sampled Jay cocking several guns and rifles from his weapons arsenal and then played the results back on the Fairlight keyboard, adding a menacing percussive snap to the song. Much time was spent sampling voices on 'Delius (Song Of Summer)': the breathy 'usss' is a sample on the Fairlight, as is the opening and closing doors on 'All We Ever Look For'. It was a wholly democratic adventure. Everyone took turns.

"What I liked was her and Jon Kelly's willingness to try anything and go down blind alleys without any limitations," recalls Richard Burgess. "At the same time she was decisive and helpful with directions." Burgess, a drummer by trade who moved successfully into production, would tend to play the more rhythmic parts; synth whizz Duncan MacKay handled most of the string and clarinet parts on the keyboard, while Bush added her own contributions. The Fairlight was not, says Burgess, particularly "player or user friendly", so it was a case of trial, error and enormously enjoyable experimentation.

"We spent a lot of time in the studio control room with Kate and Jon Kelly trying it out on pretty well every track," says John Walters. "We created a huge mess in Abbey Road Studio Two, smashing glasses and sampling them, recording and saving the best-sounding noises as digital files in the Fairlight's memory. We then played them back over 'Babooshka' from the keyboard. Listen to the very end: that's Richard playing a slow 'arpeggio' of smashing glass from the Fairlight keyboard. The whole experience was inspiring." The canteen staff at Abbey Road were apparently less impressed by the wanton destruction of their crockery, and had to be mollified with individual boxes of Belgian chocolate.

Once Bush grasped what the Fairlight could do she was keen to try it on all sorts of things in all manner of ways, but many of her ideas didn't make the final mix. Because of the technical limitations of this new machine, several of the sounds on the album that might at first appear to be samples – Hare Krishna chants, countryside noises, random spoken voices – were actually 'flown in' by Kelly using a tape recorder, which at the time gave a much better sound quality.

"I think Kate would have liked to use it for a lot more things," says Walters. "She responded instinctively to all the sonic and cultural implications of the Fairlight, she was naturally ahead of her time and, of course, went on to do much more with it as the instrument developed. She made the most of it for her own idiosyncratic music."

For someone who had struggled on her first two records to articulate her feelings through sound, discovering the Fairlight was like stumbling into an Aladdin's Cave of sonic possibilities, opening a door into a new world. It mapped out her future and changed irrevocably the way she thought about her music, offering the ability to "layer sounds as she layers ideas."[4] It dovetailed with her desire to use cutting edge technology to access deeply atavistic feelings; to "apply the future to nostalgia", as she put it.[5] Where before she was tied to the piano and had to manipulate her voice in order to try to communicate the full richness of the world of each of her songs, now she could add anything – strings, waterfalls, sunbursts – during the writing process itself. It was a massive expansion of her musical palette, giving her the ability to immediately conjure up images and characters within her music. "As soon as I saw it I knew I had to have one, and it was going to become a very important part of my work," she said. "What attracts me to the Fairlight is its ability to create very human, animal, emotional sounds that don't actually sound like a machine. I think in a way that's what I've been waiting for."[6]

Not everyone was quite so enamoured of this new toy and the techniques it offered. Kelly, an endlessly relaxed and patient foil, admits it threw him a little. "I was brought up so old school," he says. "I was so precious, everything had to be recorded with the best mike in the best room, I wasn't as open minded as Kate." Some of the musicians were a little bemused, too. "She had recorded this penny whistle which Paddy could play and then played it on the keyboard, and I thought it was a bit of a strange circle," says Max Middleton. "Why not just play the penny whistle?!"

Ian Bairnson came in to sing on 'Delius (Song Of Summer)', a beautiful if strikingly odd tribute to the English composer Frederick Delius. The song had been inspired by Ken Russell's film *Song Of Summer* made for the BBC's *Omnibus* series, which the young Bush watched at East Wickham Farm when it was first broadcast in 1968. As a young man Delius had caught syphilis and, when he eventually became wheelchair bound in later life, a devoted fan named Eric Fenby became his amanuensis, writing down his compositions as the enfeebled master dictated them to him (hence the song's closing line, "In B, Fenby"). This oddly touching, mutually dependent partnership captured Bush's imagination and she wrote a lovely hiccupping song about it. Two points are of note: she was just ten when she watched the *Omnibus* show, which shows a certain degree of intellectual precocity; and what a capacity she has for preserving the tingle of recalled inspiration – more than a decade after the television viewing, her childhood feelings were still wholly accessible to her as an adult writer. Bush later met the aged Fenby on *The Russell Harty Show*, where he made polite if rather bewildering noises about 'Delius (Song Of Summer)' and opined that "art is pure emotion", an epigram which could have come straight from Bush's lips.

Bairnson loved the song but noted that "the technology was going quite wild at the time. I don't think she'd be upset if I said that at one point she was confused on *Never For Ever*. In Abbey Road there were four or five multi-track machines all loaded up and she had God knows how many tracks, she kept overdubbing things on it. It's that thing about having too much choice. There were synths around, the Fairlight, it was all happening." From Bush's point of view, however, not enough was happening. To her regret, the Fairlight arrived a little too late to transform *Never For Ever*, but it gave her a clear vision of where she needed to go next.

They were gruelling sessions. She was a nocturnal creature by nature and the days often stretched long into the night and through to the morning; sometimes she was working 20 hours at a time. Much of the post-studio socialising would occur at Paddy's flat at Bush HQ on Wickham Road, where the likes of Roy Harper might drop in to unwind into the early hours; she would often creep upstairs while everyone else was still chatting to grab a little rest, but she was a poor sleeper and struggled to switch off. In the studio, "she smoked [dope] but it didn't seem to affect her," according to Max Middleton. "Creativity comes from knowledge, not from being stoned. All her knowledge comes from her family, from reading. I think it just relaxed her, that's probably the most you can say."

The album's obvious masterpiece, its "little symphony"[7] was 'Breathing', the first time in Bush's career that the experimental truly connected with the emotional. It was a powerful fusion. The lyric was sung from the perspective of a foetus in the womb breathing in not only its mother's nicotine but also radiation "after the blast". The unborn child had lived in a previous incarnation and is therefore aware of how beautiful the world once was; this time it doesn't want to come out into this ruined, post-apocalyptic version of it. It was a complex, intensely beautiful song, full of love, terror and foreboding. Bush described it as a warning, "a message from the future."[8] 'Breathing' was also the song on which her voice finally broke through to a different level, climaxing in a raw howl of pain and suffering. It was a tantalising preview of the vocal riches to come on the next two records, and a metaphorical blowing away of all the TV mimics and their squeaky imitations.

Capturing and communicating the song's many emotional nuances in five minutes did not come easy. "We did 'Breathing' and I must have played the same guitar bit 200 times," says Brian Bath. "They must have got through spools of tape. I don't know [what she was looking for], just trying to get it better." Each time they played it Max Middleton insisted on adding a persistent discordant note which set everyone's teeth on edge – 'You OK, Max?' 'Yeah, fine' – until gradually the musicians began to notice that it actually *worked*. "The song had changed, there was this extra thing happening in it," says Bath.

This is precisely what Bush wanted. She demanded that the band push beyond simply mastering the technical aspects of the song until they connected with its human resonance, to play with their hearts rather than their heads. "The session men had their lines . . . but at first there was no emotion, and that track was demanding so much emotion," she said. "It wasn't until they actually played with feeling that the whole thing took off. When we went and listened, I wanted to cry."[9] 'Breathing' underscores not only the intensity of the sessions at Abbey Road, but also Bush's established hierarchy of priorities in the studio. Her relentless work ethic and stubborn pursuit of an ideal is all about finding the moment of transcendence, of getting as close as possible to the sound in her head and that precious moment of mystery, magic and emotional truth. She is a perfectionist only in terms of protecting the purity of her vision, rather than wanting to smooth all the rough edges of her music into something technically perfect. Kelly recalls how she "loved a happy accident. I think that's a massive strength. She was completely open minded about what was happening."

That's why – still – it takes so long and is so hard.

★ ★ ★

The anti-nuclear content of 'Breathing' and the message of 'Army Dreamers', a deceptively spry little waltz lamenting the high and enduring personal price of war on generations of society's young and undervalued – would-be fathers, MPs and rock stars who didn't even survive their teens – were greeted by reviewers as examples of a new-found political strain in Bush's writing. As she pointed out several times, however, these were songs in which the initial spark was intensely personal rather than polemical. "It's only because the political motivations move me emotionally – if they hadn't it wouldn't have gotten to me," she said. "It went through the emotional centre, when I thought, 'Ah, Ow!' And that made me write."[10]

These two songs did, however, illustrate an opening up and out in her writing. Her reluctance or inability to grapple with social issues and live in The Real World had certainly not gone unnoticed at the time of her initial impact. In the aftermath of punk, scribes in the weekly rock press in particular expected any 'serious' artist to have a socio-political agenda and to be engaged with what was happening around them. It was a time when anger and the desire for change were the prevailing sources of artistic impetus in music, and Bush's positivity was viewed with great suspicion and often real contempt. When Danny Baker interviewed her for *NME* in October 1979 during the early stages of the *Never For Ever* sessions, he was briskly dismissive of her spacey hippie-chickisms and "creative energy" chat. She appeared to him to be little more than a polite, pampered rich girl who wrote about the most indulgent, frivolous things, someone for whom working in Woolworths constituted a 'real' job. She didn't watch the news or read the papers, she seemed disengaged and uninformed about the wider world. The gist of his recounted experience was: 'Fine, fine, but nothing this girl is saying – or singing about – *really* matters.'

It would be overly convenient to imagine that Baker's implied criticisms gave Bush pause for thought, but within a year she had released 'Army Dreamers' and 'Breathing' and was discussing her 'protest songs' on the BBC's current affairs show *Nationwide*, while the more socially aware compositions on *The Dreaming* were just around the corner. None of these, however, were remotely comparable to explicitly political songs like The Beat's 'Stand Down, Margaret' or Elvis Costello's 'Pills And Soap', nor were they the beginning of a flood of issue-led material. She has certainly never been keen to pin her colours to the mast. An appearance at a benefit concert for Amnesty International and a televised appeal in 1990 for the same organisation, in which she looked like she was auditioning for a job reading the *Nine O'Clock News*, spoke of the broadly compassionate world-view already apparent from her songs, but nothing more defined.

As the Eighties rolled on, and the Falklands War and Miners' Strike and the grip of Thatcherism rumbled all around her, Bush remained – rather wonderfully, in retrospect – miles above the scuffle and fray. "I've been tucked away in the studio during the riots,"[11] she said at the height of Britain's inner city race violence of 1981, a line that acts as a neat summation of her general position regarding music and the wider world. When an interviewer from *Hot Press* tried to goad her into being indiscreet about Margaret Thatcher in 1985 she was not forthcoming. She fudged the issue; she was not a "political thinker". Nor would she define herself as a feminist. "When you hear 'feminist' you go 'Ummgh!'" she said. "You get all these terrible images, like women with hairy legs and big muscles. I mean, you just think of butch lesbians."[12]

If this all made her sound detached and even rather ill-informed within the highly politicised context of the times, it proved to be nothing but beneficial to the music, which soared above and beyond such considerations. The great pay-off was the complete absence in her songs of knee jerk sloganeering, hectoring, proselytizing and cause-hopping from one album to the next. Embracing any creed or cause was too limiting. She was a metaphysical poet in a roomful of hollering three-chord revolutionaries, and she has remained so. Bush's lack of engagement, particularly in early interviews, could be more than a little wearing, but her gifts are intuitive. She has never sought to hone them to present a watertight argument or world-view, so they remain dazzling, infuriating, sometimes contradictory abstractions. Rather than taking on the taint of day-to-day surface life, her music is about the politics of the heart. There's an enormous amount of trust in her songs, which is rare; they are unguarded and unposturing, which is even rarer. It's one of the reasons she has steadily retreated from the press. The utter sincerity and openness with which she discussed her art when she started out was almost painful, and made her an easy target. Raised in a nurturing environment, she was ill-prepared for being ridiculed for her creative ideas and the way in which she was prepared to share them. The realisation kicked in around the time she was making her third album that she was presenting her work to the world, rather than herself.

"We would have conversations about it, it [became] more of a frustrating thing for her, the press," says Jon Kelly. "I remember on *Never For Ever* she came in one day and had decided that there were two Kate Bushes. She'd managed to separate herself. I often use it as an example to artists now: it's good if you try not to confuse the artist who you present to the public and the one you take home. People confuse the strangeness of her songs with the way she lives her life, [but] in person she's very down to earth, girl next door."

As if to prove Kelly's point, during the album sessions she took a break to appear in a demure, high-collared dress – very *Abigail's Party* – on the *Delia Smith Cookery Course* television show, discussing her vegetarian tastes. In the peaceful, verdant surroundings of East Wickham Farm she chatted happily to the doyenne of British cuisine and introduced a series of non-meat dishes prepared by Jay's wife Judy, showing off her fruit salad, brown rice, yoghurt with honey and a Waldorf salad – even finding room to reference a *Fawlty Towers* gag, quipping "that one's got waldorfs in it!" – before concluding, "I really do think there's a lot in vegetables!" It's not easy to reconcile this woman with the one who had just made a video for 'Babooshka' in which she portrayed a sword-wielding nymphet with very little left to the imagination, or the one who sings "the more I think about sex the better it gets." The confusion was too much for some. For the tabloids, which by 1979 had already given up trying to understand what Bush was doing creatively, it was all about 'raunchy Kate', the 'sexpot'. That remained their agenda until she became less visible, whereupon she became a 'troubled recluse', pop's resident weirdo. Within a black-and-white world where the grasp of culture is forever governed by the lowest common denominator, Bush would always be trapped somewhere between Miss Whiplash and Miss Havisham.

Even the music papers were far from immune. *Record Mirror*'s review of the opening night of the 'Tour Of Life' lingered over her "unabashed obsession with sex" and "soft focus porn". In hindsight she felt the experience of the 'Tour Of Life' had been invasive, and it had a profoundly significant affect on her subsequent view of her own femininity. "By the end of the tour, I felt a terrific need to retreat as a person," she said. "I felt that my sexuality, which in a way I hadn't really had a chance to explore myself yet, was being given to the world in a way which I found impersonal."[13] She must, of course, take at least some responsibility for this. As the

'Babooshka' video clearly conveyed, her work offered her the chance to *be* the things she sometimes felt, the things, in truth, that most of us privately feel at one time or another, but the fact that she portrayed these feelings in her music so vividly, so publicly – and yes, so sexually – with no apparent inhibitions, caused considerable confusion over the years. The manner in which her public expressions have encouraged assumptions about her private nature as a woman has clearly been an active factor in her decision to make herself less and less publicly available.

Much of the time in 1980 she was simply the young, unaffected person evident in the Delia Smith clip, smoking a pack of cigarettes a day, usually alternating between Benson & Hedges and John Player Specials, living not on yoghurt and fruit but mostly on chocolate, tea, toast and chips, and spending almost all of her time either writing and recording or watching television and movies with her boyfriend in her relatively humble flat in Lewisham. She was *almost* a normal person, but it wasn't quite that simple. Normal people weren't offered the part of the Wicked Witch in *Wurzel Gummidge*, or had a driver at their beck and call, despite being able to drive herself. Bush had certain expectations about what she would and wouldn't do which came as an inevitable consequence of fame, but at the same time she was still taking her laundry round to her mother's house. She was never comfortable when asked to pull the levers on the star machine and genuinely took fright at industry parties, which she described as "unhealthy, disgusting".[14]

Her old friend David Paton recalls bumping into her at Abbey Road on November 12, 1981, during a party marking the studio's 50th anniversary, which she attended alongside luminaries such as Paul McCartney and Sting. Paton was recording in Studio Three at the time. "There was a lot of people giving her a lot of attention and she wanted to escape from it all, so she said to me: 'Have you still got Studio Three? Can we go up there, I just need a break?'" he says. "I took her up there and we spoke for about half an hour about lots of things, her relationship with Del and stuff, until two or three people discovered we were sitting in Studio Three and before you know it there are more people in there than at the party! She didn't like it. She didn't like it at all. She liked one-to-ones or being on her own a lot of the time."

Lyrically the songs from the *Never For Ever* sessions were notable less for their political content than for Bush's continued determination to reject and subvert conventional gender roles. Attuned to her own 'masculinity' as an artist, time and again she deployed the kind of twists more often found in old folk songs, where a blue-buttoned cabin-boy turns out to be a lusty young maiden already four months gone. 'The Wedding List' renounced the traditional image of the blushing bride by turning her into a vengeful killer, aroused by her own blood lust, while in 'Babooshka' Bush sided – surprisingly – with the unfaithful husband, on the grounds that it's the jealous wife whose "boredom breeds suspicion"[15] and whose initial lack of trust kills the relationship.

'Ran Tan Waltz', which eventually turned up as the B-side to 'Babooshka', was another tale where the traditional roles were switched. Loosely derived from the old folk song, 'Oh Dear, Rue The Day', and bawdily comic in tone, it told of a young husband left at home holding the baby while his wife is out drinking and philandering, forlornly predicting that she'll return only when she "picks on a dick that's too big for her pride."* Again, the sympathy falls on the male.

Most daring of all was 'The Infant Kiss', a beautiful song rather sorrowfully examining sexual feelings from an adult towards a child; where one might expect the adult in such a scenario to be portrayed as male, in 'The Infant Kiss' it was a woman who became attracted to a schoolboy. This being Kate Bush, however it wasn't quite that simple. The song was inspired by the 1961 film *The Innocents*, itself a take on Henry James' novel *The Turn Of The Screw*, in which Deborah Kerr plays a governess who believes the ghost of her predecessor's dead lover is trying to possess the bodies of the children she is looking after. There is a scene in the film where she kisses the boy on the lips, and in the song, too, the child's body is inhabited by a demonic older male – he becomes, in effect, the child with the man in his eyes. It's a fearless, complex song, venturing into uncharted ground for a female pop singer, and the music perfectly captures the mood. Using only piano, guitar, strings and voice, Bush builds the tension and momentum as the woman's feelings tumble and torment. As ever, no judgement, no blame. And how often she sings of love and sexual desire as a form of possession, a taboo, a terrifying and unwanted ghost-demon stealing into our heart and bones.

★　★　★

---

* A ran tan – and its derivative 'ran-dan' – means to go on a debauch or spree.

The *Never For Ever* sessions ended in June, with the album release held back until September 8 to avoid competing with two other major EMI records, Paul McCartney's *McCartney II* and the Rolling Stones' *Emotional Rescue*. Bush promoted the record with some gusto. She made personal appearances by car and train at record shops around the UK (in Manchester she kissed each and every fan, amounting to over 600, presumably few of whom have washed since) and embarked upon brief hit-and-run missions to Europe, where she performed dazzling new routines to 'Army Dreamers' and 'Babooshka' on television. In the UK there were several major print interviews and a fascinating appearance on Paul Gambaccini's Radio One show, where over two evenings she played some of her favourite music, including the Bothy Band, Delius, Bert Lloyd, Allegri's *Miserere*, Frank Zappa, Captain Beefheart, Kate & Anna McGarrigle, Steely Dan, Alan Stivell and Rolf Harris. Very little of it could be called pop music.

The hard work in and out of the studio paid off. *Never For Ever* went straight to number one, making Bush the first British female solo artist ever to have a number one album in the UK charts. Review coverage was extensive though decidedly mixed, and even the praise was sometimes grudging. Julie Burchill in *The Face* conceded that "at last I have to admire Kate Bush" (Bush was surely overcome with gratitude), while *Record Mirror* went as far as to opine that "by no stretch of the imagination could one describe Bush and her music as inspiring. *Never For Ever*, in fact, is as depressing an album as one might find all year."[16] She still confounded critical consensus, inspiring extreme reactions on either side of the fence.

A pair of singles roved ahead, forming a particularly irresistible advance party. The first was 'Breathing', a deliberately bold choice which reached number 16 in the UK charts, while the second release, the more obviously commercial 'Babooshka', climbed to number five over the summer of 1980, her biggest hit since 'Wuthering Heights'. A third, 'Army Dreamers', released in September, also entered the Top 20.

The title of the album was a tantalising nod to one of the great 'lost' Bush songs. "We did record 'Never For Ever' for *Lionheart*, and I thought it was a killer song but it never appeared," says Andrew Powell. "Fantastic vocal, really good song. She wasn't quite happy with something . . . so we eventually agreed we wouldn't use it and we'd save it for the next album. In the end all that got saved was the title, which must have been a mystery to some people." The beautiful 'Warm And Soothing', played on the piano as a simple run through in order to acclimatise herself when she first entered Abbey Road, was another wonderful song relegated to B-side status. It was almost as though she now found this kind of thing too easy, too conventional, and therefore viewed it with suspicion. Occasionally one wondered whether she was tossing away some of her most affecting material. "I think her best stuff, the ultimate thing with Kate, is her singing and playing the piano," says Ian Bairnson. "It's stunning, it just goes straight to you. It's there from the first note. It's really about her and the piano and the rest of us could all go take a hike!"

The cover art, meanwhile, was a remarkably frank piece of creative expressionism, a stunning coloured pencil drawing by Nick Price depicting Bush with her hands folded behind her head as a stream of alternately angelic creatures (rainbow butterflies, swans) and demonic beasts (strange fantasy creations with bats' heads and snakes' bodies) pour out from under her raised skirt. "She was quite particular about what she wanted," says Price. "The idea of all these light and dark characters coming out from under her skirt, that was the run of it, the light and dark balancing each other out. In fact, the image was taken from a photograph that John had taken of her in that position. I remember when she mentioned that it was all coming out from under her skirt I asked her to repeat that: 'From under your *skirt*?' She just said, 'Yeeeeah!' There was a [sexual] aspect to it, but I'm not quite sure what it meant." She told Kelly that that was where *all* her songs came from.

She quickly recognised, before the paint was even dry, that *Never For Ever* was an incomplete metamorphosis, a partial revolution. It was a "new step",[17] the beginning of her embracing a more contemporary sound and adding adventurous layers of instrumentation to her songs, but it was an album in which the possibilities were only unveiled as the sessions wore on and the ultimate prize remained beyond her grasp. "I couldn't take the last and decisive step then, because I lacked courage and specialised knowledge," she said. "You need an enormous amount of strength to control your own musical work."[18] Control was the next step. Controlled chaos.

8

Into The Dreaming

AT the end of September 1980 Bush and Palmer went to see Stevie Wonder perform during his week-long run of concerts at Wembley Arena. He played for over three hours and, inspired by the sheer energy of Wonder's performance and by meeting him backstage, she returned home and wrote much of 'Sat In Your Lap' the following day. It marked the symbolic end of what was becoming a pattern of sorts: complete immersion in a project, then deflation. She described the period immediately after finishing *Never For Ever* as "sort of terrible introverted depression. The anti-climax after all that work really set in in a bad way, and that can be very damaging to an artist. I could sit down at the piano and want to write, and nothing would happen."[1]

It was a salutary lesson that there was, after all, more to life than work, but it was a lesson she wasn't quite ready to take on board. She had moved almost immediately from the 'Tour Of Life' into the making of the album and the batteries were drained. She took a short break, saw her friends and spent time with her family – and then proceeded to throw herself back into her music, with even greater conviction and an increasing obsession for attaining perfection.

Shortly after the release of *Never For Ever* Bush bought a property on Court Road in Eltham, south London, a large, detached Victorian house set back from the road, hidden behind imposing entrance gates and surrounded by trees. Located just across the road from the rather opulent greenery of Royal Blackheath Golf Club, it was hardly a flashy locale: low-key, suburban, calm, sober and middle class, tucked out of the way and still within easy striking distance of East Wickham Farm. It became another Bush base camp, a hub for all three siblings. Paddy moved in next door, while Jay frequently used the property. It was 44 Wickham Road on a grander scale, offering security in numbers.

It also gave her music more room. She installed an eight-track demo studio in the house and throughout the rest of 1980 and into early 1981, between promotional appearances, she dedicated herself to writing, trying to orientate her new sound using a combination of piano, Yamaha CS-80 and electronic Linn drums. She had developed ideas for 'The Dreaming' and 'Houdini' during the latter stages of *Never For Ever*, but, significantly, this was to be the first of her albums where no pre-1978 songs would be included or indeed even considered. The record's starting point (indeed, arguably *the* point) was rhythm and texture – the song itself was only the first footfall in a long, arduous climb. On *Never For Ever* she had again been troubled by the difficulty of adding a kick, a real rhythmic thrust to songs written on the piano – the stripped down rock band approach of a song like 'Violin' was too conventional, too *solid*, too grounded. For many of the new songs she reversed the compositional process, starting with the beat and then afterwards painting in the chords, melodies and words. "I felt as if my writing needed some kind of shock," she said.[2]

She remained infatuated with the possibilities of the Fairlight, and was determined to use its varied sound palette on almost all the songs on the next album. At first she hired one from Syco Systems before finally investing heavily in buying her own instrument towards the end of making *The Dreaming*, recognising it as an indispensable addition to her arsenal. Although she was towards the head of the pack, Bush was far from alone in embracing new possibilities. It's near impossible to overstate the manner in which technology was influencing music at this time. In the early Eighties a growing obsession with the *sound* rather than the song made for some arresting, strange and highly innovative pop music. Listen back to records made during that era by everyone from Public Image Ltd, Killing Joke and Buggles to Duran Duran, Spandau Ballet and Eurythmics and you will hear some sonically extreme, rhythmically interesting and downright odd pop records. Pared down duos such as Soft Cell and Yazoo became intrigued by the idea of juxtaposing the clinical sound of cutting edge technology with the exposed nerve ends of raw human emotion, of combining a machine-like chilliness with a warm, human presence. Bush had the same idea; she simply insisted on taking it to the furthest extremes.

Stevie Wonder apparently cleared her writer's block. 'Sat In Your Lap' appeared almost without her trying, a fitting arrival for a song partly concerned with the slippery nature of knowledge and creativity. A flood of new material followed. She quickly came up with 20 songs for the album, writing in her home studio more or less spontaneously, coming up with a new song or a strong idea for a song almost every night. "I sat down at the piano, got a rhythm and just literally wrote the songs!" she recalled. "The words probably weren't there, but the idea was there and all the tunes were there."[3] It was to prove the only part of the album process that happened quickly. Once she moved into the studio, all "the speed and spontaneity seemed to evaporate."[4]

First, she had to decide upon the practicalities: Who? Where? How? She had concluded that she no longer wanted to work with her friend Jon Kelly, deciding with a typically firm resolve that it was time to sever all ties with the old order and finally strike out on her own. "She phoned me up and said how much she'd loved the album but she was going to try something different on this next one," says Kelly. "I can't remember what the words were but she said it beautifully. She went on to do *The Dreaming* and called me up to have a listen as soon as it was finished."

From there, she toyed with hiring a big name producer. Tony Visconti had worked with David Bowie on most of his landmark records of the Seventies and also his most recent, 1980's *Scary Monsters (And Super Creeps)*; according to Visconti's admittedly rather vague recollection, he and Bush affected a somewhat strange but agreeable meeting to discuss working together. "During the making of *Lodger* [released in May, 1979] I was listening to *Lionheart* in my Montreux hotel room," he recalls. "I was so moved by the album I wrote her a fan letter on hotel stationery, which she received and read. About a year or so later I received a phone call from her asking me to meet up with her to discuss working on her new album. Before we met I made a very specific astrological chart for her. I had been a dabbler for a decade by then. I gave it to her over lunch in a restaurant near her studio in the West End, and we spoke a lot about Bowie and Aikido, her family's preferred martial art.

"After lunch we were driven to the studio and she played a track or two for me. Honestly, I can't remember a note. She was bent over, leaning on the back of a chair in front of the console. I was sitting behind her on the couch, and all I can remember is the Bush bum swaying in my face. I'm sure I loved the music, too, and I told her I'd like to work with her. Afterwards we had two phone conversations. In the first she told me how accurate and amazing the astrological chart was – she used the word 'amazing' a lot.

In the second phone call she said, 'I've decided to produce the album myself. But, Tony, if there was a producer I'd work with it would be you!' It was the sweetest rejection I've ever had.'

It is still possible to hear Bowie and Visconti's influence on *The Dreaming*. The thrilling "I must admit . . ." section of 'Sat In Your Lap', in particular, is an astonishingly precise imitation of *Lodger*-period Bowie, a fine example of the style of singing he calls his 'histrionics'. There are echoes, too, of the burbling Afro-beat of 'African Night Flight', while the song's unconventional rhythm shares similarities with 'Golden Brown' by another of her favourite bands, The Stranglers, although this time Bush's song came first.

It was to be another pioneering artist, however, who exerted a major influence on the record. The sleeve credits on *Never For Ever* were significant. Bush had thanked Roy Harper for 'holding on to the poet in his music' and Peter Gabriel for 'opening the windows'. These artists, alongside Pink Floyd, who had just released *The Wall*, which she loved, had become her peers, exemplars of artistic excellence, intelligence, integrity and experimentation, though their detractors would just as quickly call them precious, pretentious, portentous and about as relevant as Copernicus. This was a line of criticism Bush, too, constantly courted.

Harper had been recording his *Universal Soldier* album in Abbey Road while she was making *Never For Ever* and he had come in to Studio Two to add backing vocals to 'Breathing'; Bush happily returned the favour, singing a duet on his track 'You (The Game Part II)'. It was the beginning of a lifelong and continuing friendship. Gabriel, meanwhile, was not only a personal friend, but his career path had provided Bush with the outline of a yellow brick road which she occasionally followed. The connection began at the Bill Duffield benefit and had been solidified through making the *Kate* Christmas special and subsequently popping into each other's sessions. "He came in a few times when we were doing *Never For Ever*, listened to some stuff and was very quiet," says Jon Kelly. "They were very similar. They were kindred spirits in the way they were experimental with their work and groundbreaking, not following the normal route."

Some of those who worked closely with both artists at this time suggest that Bush was rather calculated in her befriending of Gabriel. "At the time she just wanted to *be* Peter Gabriel as far as I could work out – the female

Peter Gabriel," says producer Hugh Padgham, who engineered parts of *The Dreaming*. "That's from me observing. When I worked with her on *The Dreaming* she was always trying to do things but she didn't realise that it wasn't as easy to be Peter Gabriel as she might have thought."

"Kate, I think, had made a point of making Peter her friend," adds Steve Lillywhite, Gabriel's producer at the time. "I'm sure she was influenced a lot by Peter, and subsequently she went on and made art her career. That's all you can ever hope for."

Although Bush has several times displayed an uncanny knack of narrowing in on artists she admires and is far from reticent about approaching them to work with her, it's unlikely to have been *quite* as calculated as it seems – after all, it was the tragedy of Duffield's death that had initially brought them together. It's certainly true, however, that in Gabriel she saw an artist whose sense of experimentation, use of new technology and ability to tackle non-traditional lyrical themes, all marshalled within a broad pop sensibility, matched her ambitions for her own music. "The only person I've met who is really into the same kind of approach to playing as I [have] is Peter," she said. "He's going for emotional content of the music and lyrics, and he changes his voice."[5]

It was only a matter of time before they recorded with one another. During the *Never For Ever* sessions Bush was invited into the Townhouse studios to sing on Gabriel's third album, often known as 'melt' due its distinctive cover image, adding atmospheric backing vocals to 'I Don't Remember', 'No Self Control' and, most significantly, 'Games Without Frontiers', on which she was something of a last minute addition. "We had someone else sing the 'Jeux Sans Frontieres' line on 'Games Without Frontiers', and we realised that their accent wasn't so great," recalls Lillywhite, who refuses to name the singer who was replaced. "So Peter decided to ask Kate down. It was fantastic, [she was] this wonderful sort of hippie chick. She had that song, 'Wow', and I remember her saying "wow" all the time and I thought, 'Well, that's why she wrote that song, because that's what she says!' I just remember sitting around smoking joints with her and having a good time. It was easy, really, no more than half an hour in the studio."

'Games Without Frontiers' became Gabriel's biggest solo hit to date, released in February 1980 and rising to number four in March. Around the same time, EMI asked Bush and Kelly if they could hear some of the new

Never For Ever material, and they travelled to the A&R department at Manchester Square – Bush was keen not to let the company suits into her domain – to play four songs, including 'Babooshka', 'Breathing' and 'Army Dreamers', all lined up as potential singles. "They were happy," Kelly recalls. "And as they were making idle chat at the end, one of them said, 'Have you heard that new Peter Gabriel song?', and someone else said, 'Yeah, that woman, I can't understand what the hell she's singing!' Kate looked at me and we both struggled not to laugh. Poor bloke. Didn't know it was her. I wonder how he felt when he found out."

A little later they tried to write a song together called 'Ibiza', but it was not completed to their satisfaction. It's difficult to imagine such a private, personal composer as Bush being a natural co-writer, but the process of befriending, observing and recording with Gabriel fed directly into her aspirations for her next album. She had been impressed by the Town-house's Solid State Logic (SSL) 4000 B console, a new development which integrated a studio computer system with an in-line audio console. "We had this SSL B desk, a prototype, with a lot of quirks to it," says Nick Launay, an in-house engineer at the Townhouse. "It was very strange, it had compressors and gates on every channel, which had never been done before."

More significantly, she had been blown away by the drums on Gabriel's album. Although played by Jerry Marotta and Phil Collins, the sound was primarily the creation of Hugh Padgham, another house engineer at the Virgin-owned facility who is widely credited with creating the famous 'gated' drum effect at the Townhouse's 'stone room' studio during his work with Steve Lillywhite. In simple terms, the drums are heavily com-pressed and then their natural reverb brutally cut-off using a 'noise gate' on the recording console, so that, in Padgham's words, "when [the drummer] stopped playing it sucked the big sound of the room into nothing."[6] It can be heard to full effect on Phil Collins' 'In The Air Tonight'.

This mixture of thunderous rhythm cannoning off the stone walls fol-lowed by an almost immediate, uneasy silence was the sound Bush craved. "Seeing Peter work in the Townhouse studio. . . . was the nearest thing I'd heard to real guts for a long, long time," she said. "[It] was so exciting because the drums had so much power."[7] Tired of "a lazy acceptance of a drum kit",[8] she wanted something tribal, huge, with none of the concilia-tory splash and sizzle of cymbal or hi-hat. This was to be the driving force behind her new music, onto which she could build structure and add detail.

Thus it was Padgham to whom Bush turned for the first sessions, and it was to the Townhouse that they decamped in May 1981. Most of the album's backing tracks were recorded here over a period of three months using a small core of musicians, often just Preston Heyman or Stuart Elliott on drums and Del or Jimmy Bain, a former member of Rainbow turned session player, on bass. Bush played piano and Fairlight on almost every song. Brian Bath, Ian Bairnson and Alan Murphy played guitar, but most of what they added was never used; in the end, unusually, seven of the ten songs featured no guitar at all. The supreme – and supremely different – bass stylists Danny Thompson and Eberhard Weber later popped up on a track apiece. David Gilmour added backing vocals. Far more so than *Never For Ever*, it was to be an album defined by painterly overdubs, adding layers and layers of light and shade rather than relying on full-blown band performances.

It was not an auspicious start. Hugh Padgham is perhaps unique among humankind in that he doesn't have terribly fond memories of working with Bush; the sessions lasted no more than three weeks before they parted company. "I couldn't bear it after a bit, actually," he says. "She didn't really have any idea of the sonics, and didn't understand why, if you put 150 layers of things all together, you couldn't hear all of them. The whole thing with Gabriel is that everything had much more space around it. She would take 100 things and want them all to work together, and it didn't. She didn't really want to listen. As far as I was concerned, when we were doing those sessions it sounded shit. It pissed me off, actually."

Bush, on the other hand, ever polite, recalled Padgham's contributions as "positive" and "productive".[9] They worked together long enough to get a complete mix of 'Sat In Your Lap', which Bush hastily released as a stand-alone single on June 21, eager to preview her new sound. It was a song as complex lyrically as it was rhythmically, musing on the nature of enlightenment, cutting to the heart of her quest for spiritual advancement: is knowledge innate, instinctive and sexual (something literally "sat in your lap"), or can it only be gained through a lifetime of searching and striving ("The longest journey across the desert"), and even then possibly not at all? Heart or head; body or brain; nature or nurture; to look within or without? The single reached number 11, her last commercial success for some time, although its tribal statement was rather diluted by the impact of Adam & The Ants double-drum driven hits earlier the same year, 'Stand And Deliver' and 'Prince Charming', as well as the emergence of Bow Wow Wow and their highly stylised adoption of Burundi ritual music.

Padgham and Bush collaborated on two further songs, 'Leave It Open' and 'Get Out Of My House', but the engineer was busy and his enthusiasm for the project was, clearly, not engaged. Pencilled in to work on new albums by The Police, Phil Collins and Genesis, he was essentially engineering *The Dreaming* in his spare time and was happy to hand it over. "I had so much work going on at the time that I couldn't really be bothered with it, it was just a pain in the arse," he says. "I was doing it on my weekends off, and I think she wanted more attention, which was fair enough. I don't remember every really having an argument with her – maybe a little one – but nothing major. The only other thing I can remember is that she used to say a helluva lot of, 'Skin up, Hugh!' I certainly didn't lose any sleep when I passed the thing on."

He suggested to Bush that his friend Paul Hardiman take over, but he was otherwise engaged, so Padgham's assistant engineer Nick Launay held the reins; the pair met and clicked both personally and creatively. Launay had just finished producing Public Image Ltd's *Flowers Of Romance* album at the Townhouse, another album showcasing the famed studio drum sound to fearsome effect, and another album of unbounded sonic experimentation. Bush listened and liked. She had always admired the Sex Pistols (she has since established a long-running mutual appreciation society with John Lydon), and for Launay the connection was not as strange as it might first have appeared. "She'd go out and play stuff on the piano and she was so, *so* brilliant," he says. "The way she played didn't sound like rock'n'roll at all. It sounded like classical music, but it didn't come over as prog rock, which I didn't like. I came from the punk rock thing, and to me she was punk rock. She was doing stuff that was going against the grain."

Launay was only 20, and she still just 22, and it "really was like the kids are in control – it was great!" he says. "There wasn't a record producer, there was basically her, the musicians that she chose, and me. That was it. Making that record had no rules. We could try everything that came to mind, which worked well for me because I didn't really know what I was doing. I was hyper and imaginative, had all these ideas going round my head, and I think the combination was magical. We were both kind of in the same place: 'I wonder what *this* does?'"

For the musicians, recording the backing tracks for the songs was a process somewhat akin to assembling furniture when the instructions are in Aramaic and written in disappearing ink. A typical session on a song such as 'Suspended In Gaffa' could be a long, strange affair. Bush would first play the song on the piano and the drummer and bass player would drop in and try to follow. Then the questions would start. The drummer might ask, 'You know the second time we go to the fifth section, something strange happens there and I end up on the wrong beat.' Where most musicians deal in conventional verse, chorus, bridge structures, Bush's songs – though not always lacking choruses – were often split into several distinct sections, sometimes in different time signatures. The musicians would be constantly writing down where the changes fell and frantically matching them to the lyrics. Bush would play the song again and everyone would concentrate intensely, trying to find a way of playing such a choppy piece of music as seamlessly as Bush seemed able to sitting at the piano. Often the entire ensemble collapsed into exasperated hysterics.

"I did a lot of editing together of different takes and it got very confusing at times," says Launay. "Eventually you'd get there but it would be really complicated. I don't think she had any realisation of how complex her songs were – to her they were very simple. She would explain things to the different musicians who came down, not in terms of notes, but in terms of the feeling she wanted to get across."

She sat in the control room, watching intently as they played parts over and over again, trying to capture what she wanted. For much of the album Bush, as producer, was fighting the creeping suspicion that many of the musicians were looking at her and thinking, 'God, does she *really* know what she's doing?' Some of them were indeed having doubts along those lines. Hers was neither a conventional nor terribly 'musical' way of working, and it was hard work for the session players, even those who had played with her for several years. "I did a lot of the routining for the songs on that album, but I just stepped aside in the end, I think I walked away," says Brian Bath. "I felt a bit superfluous to what was going on. After five hours of playing the same bit you think, 'What do I do? Am I going anywhere, is anything happening?' Some of the stuff was just overdone. *The Dreaming*, to me, was just a massive noise, I couldn't really listen to it."

Other loyal servants agreed that too much choice might just as well have been no choice at all. "She was thinking more in terms of production and using unusual sounds," says Ian Bairnson, who appeared on 'Sat In Your Lap' and 'Leave It Open'. "That's what people did when the technology thing went off like a bomb: 'They'll never guess what *this* is!' There was Midi stuff, drum machines, Fairlights, and if you've got the money there it is. She had all these tools to play with and in some ways it was too much."

The fact that she was not quite in mastery of the technology was both thrilling and time consuming. Once the basic tracks were laid down it was a question of digging away at the songs and letting her imagination loose on the machines, exploring the freedom that allowed her and Launay to indulge every single idea she had, often chasing their tails and ending up back where they started. Bush's stated desire was for the music to be "experimental and quite cinematic",[10] and Launay felt that his job was to capture the essence of the films playing over and over again in her mind.

"We were always sat in front of this desk, just me and her, and at the end of the desk there were two huge bars of Cadbury's milk chocolate and this huge bag of weed," he recalls. "I think it helped make her imagination real. On 'Houdini', the lyrics to that were all very clear and when you're working on those songs you're *there*. It's like working on a film, it's extraordinary. I saw *Sweeney Todd* recently and that film made me think of Kate Bush: Olde Worlde London and England, a lot of superstition, gruesome tales, and tales of love. Musically you could tell she was in this world. The way she would communicate was very much like an excited kid: 'How do we make those characters and the feelings they have into the music?' 'Can we do this, can we do that?'"

On a cover of Donovan's 'Lord Of The Reedy River', one of the first things she and Launay recorded, specifically intended for the B-side to 'Sat In Your Lap', she wanted to sound like she was floating down a river as she sang, like some doomed heroine trapped in a pre-Raphaelite painting, so she descended to the disused swimming pool in the basement of the Townhouse in order that her voice could be recorded reflecting off the water.

To create the spacey metallic background sound on 'The Dreaming' she plugged a guitar and a piano into a harmoniser which was set an octave higher and connected to a reverb plate fed back into the harmoniser, resulting in the note going up and up and up in octaves until it went so high you couldn't hear it. This effect was used on several songs. "It was an approach of: plug things in, play a few notes, see what it does, work out how you can manipulate the instrument you're playing to work with those effects, and you end up with something unusual and different," says Launay. For the drums they miked up 12-foot long strips of corrugated iron to make them sound like cannons firing from across a valley.

Partly inspired by Bush's trip to Australia as a child (she 'met' a kangaroo and Paddy 'met' an emu, she recalled, both referenced in the song) and again in late 1978, 'The Dreaming' focused on the plight of Australian Aboriginals, their land exploited for ore to make plutonium and their people abandoned to the ravages of alcohol ("Devils in a bottle"), although her assertion in an interview that there were only "about two thousand aborigines left"[11] suggested a certain lack of factual rigour. The song was built on the bones of a hard rhythmic tattoo, and marked her first collaboration with the Australian singer, painter and TV personality Rolf Harris, who in 2014 was convicted of a string of indecent assaults against underage girls and sentenced to almost six years in prison. Bush had loved Harris' 'Sun Arise' since she was a youngster and still cites it today as a seminal piece of 'world music'. The song was a key inspiration for 'The Dreaming', prompting her to write a part for didjeridu on Fairlight and invite Harris into the studio to play it. She was hoping to have a blow herself, but was denied. "I went up [to the studio] the day the didjeridu arrived, and she wasn't allowed to play the thing, which was deeply upsetting for her," says Brian Southall, by now director of corporate PR at EMI. "Women aren't allowed to play didjeridu, it's Aboriginal law, and she wanted to emancipate the didjeridu for all women around the world, God bless her! It was great fun." Harris taught Paddy how to play it instead.

At one point Robert Palmer, working next door, came in to say hello and throw a few kind words her way. "Every time somebody made a compliment about her music she would look like a deer caught in the headlights," says Launay. "She'd literally say, 'Wow!' and blush. I don't think she was aware of her talent. She is a genius, but it's a kind of innocent genius."

★ ★ ★

Because she was using a commercial studio owned by Virgin Records, Bush was at the mercy of their schedules. The Townhouse had other bookings and Launay was needed elsewhere, so the sessions moved to Abbey Road for several weeks in July and August, where she worked with house engineer Haydn Bendall, whom she first met when he was working on Roy Harper's *Universal Soldier*. They recorded 'Pull Out The Pin' and 'Night Of The Swallow' during the sessions, which Bendall recalls as being "fragmented, difficult, very long hours. Everyone worked very hard."

At one point during the recording of 'Night Of The Swallow' the musicians utilised all three Abbey Road studios at once: as Stuart Elliott played drums in Studio Three, the sound was fed through speakers into Studio One, where the ambience echoing through the cavernous hall was also taped, while the results were simultaneously recorded on the console in Studio Two. Afterwards she flew to Dublin and spent a day in Windmill Lane, working all night to record members of traditional Irish band Planxty (a long-cherished favourite of Jay and Paddy) and The Chieftains playing Bill Whelan's exquisite arrangement for the song. And then straight back to the studio in London.

Perhaps unsurprisingly there followed a kind of crisis where Bush felt she was becoming lost in the woods of her own imagination, and struggled to locate the trail of breadcrumbs leading back to her initial inspiration. "I seemed to be losing sight of my direction, I wasn't really sure what to do next," she said.[12] As the sole arbiter of the album's progress, the responsibility sometimes weighed heavily but "she [was] very stoical about that," says Bendall. "She doesn't give up and she's extremely tenacious." A spontaneous visit to Loch Ness on the sleeper seemed to clear her mind, and she returned after a spot of monster-hunting with renewed focus. In the period leading up to Christmas 1981 she worked at home, concentrating on the songs, changing lyrics, creating backing vocals, making sure this wasn't simply going to be an exercise in style over substance.

The final, interminable sessions were completed with engineer Paul Hardiman, now available, beginning at Odyssey Studios in the autumn of 1981 and completed at Advision Studios on Gosfield Street (hence the 'Gosfield Goers' credited on 'The Dreaming') between January and May 1982. Hardiman had pre-punk experience with groups such as Yes, ELP, Slade and Fleetwood Mac, but he had also worked recently with experimental punk band Wire on their first three albums, *Pink Flag*, *Chairs Missing* and *154*. He was an innovative, somewhat eccentric presence with a highly attuned sense of the ridiculous, and his patience and understanding were a vital part of getting the album finished. "I understood the long haul," says Hardiman. "As Kate is a snail-paced perfectionist, you [knew you] were in for the long run, which was OK." Bush and Palmer both had a great deal of affection for him.

Although perhaps three quarters of what can be heard on the album had already been completed, these long sessions provided the all important top line: finalising lyrics, adding instrumentation, textures, new players, miking up a car door for the opening 'Bang!' on 'The Dreaming', stripping away, adding, subtracting.

In particular, she worked relentlessly on the vocals. Still lazily stereotyped as 'hee-hee' high and squeaky, Bush felt the way she had previously used her voice lent her music an association of sweetness and light that undermined much of her more serious lyrical intent. She wanted, she said, to give her voice "some balls".[13] Having recorded guide vocals at the Townhouse and Abbey Road, she now re-recorded the master vocals in sections, a highly intricate process considering that many of the songs utilised five or six completely different voices which required not only a different physical approach from her as a singer, but also different textures and production techniques. "It took weeks to do the vocals," she said. "Especially because we were having to find the right effects and ambience for each voice."[14]

Finding the precise timbre to communicate the emotions of the lyrics was an imperative. For 'Houdini' she did all the things singers aren't supposed to do – drank a pint of milk, ate two bars of chocolate – to build up mucus in her throat and make her voice match the "spit and gravel in the thought."[15] A similarly exact marriage of vocal sound and song subject can be heard on the sobbing chorus of 'All The Love'; in the desperate roar of "I love life!" on 'Pull Out The Pin'; in the soaring tension of 'Night Of The Swallow' and the primal scream of 'Get Out Of My House.' Deeper, stronger, abandoned yet supremely controlled, it is the range and shifting textures of her voice, amid all the surrounding techno-fuss, that is the album's greatest triumph. It was almost like hearing a girl becoming a woman.

Advision became a hermetically sealed environment, running to it own strange yet inevitable sense of time and logic. "Every night we ate take-away food, watched the evening news and returned to the dingy little treasure trove to dig for jewels," Bush recalled.[16] Del later talked about "coming up"[17] from the windowless basement studio as though they were on a submarine. "Musicians were not around most of the time," says Hardiman. "After their particular overdub was finished that was it until next time. The only constant was Del. One came with the other."

During these long final sessions the fabric of reality started to warp and fray. The last two months coincided with the Falklands War, and they would surface occasionally to be greeted with a downward spiral of grim news. Del would look over at Hardiman and tell him they were both going to be called up for action. Towards the end Bush "was exhausted, and on nothing but a grape diet," says Hardiman. She would work a minimum of 15-hour days at the studio then go home and listen to rough takes of the day's work to establish what she needed to do tomorrow, and even during meal breaks at the studio she would be tinkering with the Fairlight in the control room. It was all consuming, leaving room for nothing else. "When I come out of the studio", she said, "I feel like a Martian."[18]

The sessions became "hours of crippling tedium with occasional bursts of extreme excitement,"[19] and they resorted to unusual methods to keep spirits afloat. Hardiman created the character 'My Dad', which involved wearing a bald ginger wig he had bought in Wall's Carnival Stores on Caversham Road in Reading. At moments of crisis, 'My Dad' would arrive and don a pair of polystyrene cups with the bottoms removed (or, as Hardiman calls them, 'sound enhancing ear attachments') which, when fitted over the wig, helped delineate the sound. "In times of ear fatigue these helped enormously," says Hardiman, adding. "I am not making this up. They added focus to the session."

Another unlikely source of inspiration for 'My Dad' was the Star Turn On 45 Pints series of records, a Geordie pub singer spoof of the Stars On 45 medleys that were all the rage at the time. The closing minutes of 'Get Out Of My House', where Bush and Hardiman take on the role of 'Eeyore' and begin braying like donkeys was, says Hardiman "based on the 'You Are The Sunshine Of My Life' segment of Star Turn Pints On 45, in itself a parody of the Stars On 45 single 'Stars On Stevie', a gallop through the hits of Stevie Wonder which was a hit in February 1982. "It was obviously 'My Dad' singing the part of Eeyore," says Hardiman. "Thinking back, Eeyore was an early version of the lead vocal sound we refined for some of *Hounds Of Love*." From tiny acorns, indeed.

In other words, it was a long, strange, thoroughly exhausting trip. "The hardest thing I've ever done," according to Bush at the time, "Even harder than touring. It was worrying, very frightening."[20] Even mixing took months. She had decided on a digital mix using Advision's console, but "we had a lot of problems. . . . editing was the main one, it was so time consuming."[21]

The Dreaming was finally completed on May 21, 1982, cut by Ian Cooper at the Townhouse on June 4 and released on September 13, 1982, almost exactly two years to the day after *Never For Ever*. It's a bewitching album, Bush's first truly unified record in intent if not always in sound, a shedding of several skins and a punishing process of reinvention. The lyrics return again and again to conflict and claustrophobia, destruction and flight, battling inhibitions and barriers. "It was about how terribly cruel people could be, what we do to ourselves, what amount of loneliness we expose ourselves to," she said of the album. "It was a searching, questioning album and the music did tear you from one point to the next."[22] The troubling 'Leave It Open' – another "hee haw" moment, another gun song – encapsulated the album's bleak message: "Harm is in us."

The Dreaming did not sound like the work of a happy person; indeed, it seemed to be the consequence of a woman intent on making herself suffer unnecessarily for her art, who mistrusted her natural optimism and her outwardly straightforward life. "I've always felt . . . that in order to write something, you know, that has meaning . . . that you should be unhappy, that you should be in some kind of torment," she said.[23] There was a definite whiff of the determinedly tortured about *The Dreaming*. Even a relatively lightweight track like 'There Goes A Tenner', a comedy crime caper narrated in Bush's soft, sing-song cockney, had a murky subtext. The Ealingesque story of amateur robbers plotting their 'big job' but being stricken with paranoia when the time comes to execute their plans, it requires only a small interpretive leap to hear it as a subconscious comment on Bush's own feelings of fear and insecurity as she sets about producing her own record. Beyond a quest for spiritual knowledge, the opening roll of 'Sat In Your Lap' also speaks of creative frustration, veering rapidly from pleasure at the incremental gains she has made ("My goal is moving near") to a gloomy realisation of how far she remains from achieving fulfilment ("Then it disappears").

'Get Out Of My House', inspired by reading Stephen King's novel, *The*

Shining, about a building that is possessed, brings the inanimate to life and in doing so lends a shocking solidity to Bush's hidden anger, giving full voice to a woman who has been intruded upon and has had her privacy and sanctuary violated. It works as an indirect comment on the invasive nature of fame, and remains one of the most effective and disturbing examples of Bush dramatising her Id, giving living expression to her darkest fears and latent instincts. Then again, many people simply laughed when they heard it.

Every song was in some way extraordinary. 'All The Love' opens with the casually brilliant, almost quintessential Bush line, "The first time that I died . . ." and laments the difficulty of expressing love and letting others in. It ends with a heartbreaking litany of warm, familiar voices saying 'goodbye' on the telephone – these are the voices of Bush's friends and family, taken from real phone messages – while the singer hides behind her answering machine, contemplating "all the love we should have given."

On 'Pull Out The Pin' – *musique concrete* meets Jimmy Bryant in the Asian jungle – Bush proved yet again that she is truly a poet of the senses, vividly capturing the darker forces that animate humanity and the stark terror of warfare in a song about Vietnamese soldiers who can literally sniff out their American opponents because they reek of the west: sweat, cologne, tobacco and "Yankee hash." You can almost feel the heat and taste the humid stench spilling from the speakers as the song scythes through the undergrowth. "I think that the essence of all art is sensuality," she said,[24] and she has spent her working life proving it. Moving. Breathing. Humming. Dreaming. Feeling: the sensual world.

Several songs touched on broadly political themes – land rights, terrorism – but the album always returned to the predicament of the individual. The tongue-twisting 'Suspended In Gaffa' was another quest for personal fulfilment, speaking intriguingly of the girl lurking in the mirror "between you and me", a vivid image of self-doubt and alienation.

Three tracks in particular plotted a path towards the sounds and techniques she would explore further on *Hounds Of Love*. 'Night Of The Swallow' is full of foreboding and shadows, an exquisite match of light and dark, and the deliriously beautiful mix of Baroque balladry and traditional Irish instrumentation is something she would return to several times in the future. Inspired by Paddy's deep interest and her own background, Bush was well ahead of the game in incorporating Celtic textures into her music. The likes of the Waterboys and Elvis Costello wouldn't follow suit until several years later.

The combination on 'All The Love' of crisp technology and the very pure, human sound of a choral voice pre-empted a similar juxtaposition on 'Hello Earth', while 'Get Out Of My House' was the one song on *The Dreaming* where Bush really got *hold* of a propulsive rhythm by the scruff of the neck and rode it over simple chord changes. In contrast to the choppy, see-sawing rhythms elsewhere on the album, where the groove is rarely sustained for longer than a minute, this track in particular pointed towards her next bold move. Indeed, her original idea of creating a pounding rhythmic record was only partially realised. Paul Hardiman points out that, pre-CD, "sequencing Side A and Side B was hugely important." Musically, *The Dreaming* starts with brisk brio but slows to something close to a lament, the closing clatter of 'Get Out Of My House' notwithstanding.

The trio of songs at the centre of Side B formed the album's deep emotional heart. The last of these, 'Houdini', was another spectacular song of the supernatural, based on the true tale of Bess, the wife and assistant of renowned escapologist and illusionist Harry Houdini, attempting to communicate with her husband following his death in 1926. Houdini was a committed debunker of spiritualist frauds and séance-scamming hucksters, so he and Bess had devised a code – 'Rosabelle, believe', recounted in the song – to ensure she knew that it really was him. In January 1929, the *Detroit News* reported that Bess had succeeded in contacting Houdini via a séance, but she later came to believe that their code had been betrayed and it was a trick. This barely credible tale of loss, love, sorrow and supernaturalism could hardly *not* have appealed to Bush, and she battled with the song throughout the album sessions. In the end it still required comprehensive footnotes to explain itself, but the power and feeling in the music – Is love really stronger than death? Perhaps there are some things we can never escape from? – was unmistakeable. The sepia-tinted album cover, shot by Jay and credited to his studio, Kindlight, was also inspired by the song. Bush portrays Bess hiding a tiny gold key in her mouth to slip to her husband as she kisses him before his show, in order to facilitate his escape.

On *The Dreaming* Bush pulled off her own feat of escapology, slipping loose from the chains of her past. It is a remarkable document in which she at times achieves her long desired feat of *becoming* the music, as though all we are hearing are not drums, or bass lines, or guitars, but different parts of Bush herself fragmenting into sound, an aural depiction of all her varied (and, in this case, largely negative) emotions. Hugely exciting, but by no means an easy listen. There is a barely contained hysteria in the music that isn't merely attributable to the dark matter of the songs, but also comes from the vast amount of information, a sense of sonic overload. For all her desire to build space around her songs there is a – compelling – claustrophobia hanging over the proceedings. It is not, as many critics have claimed, over produced; it is simply overloaded. "The trouble with that album is, I think, that in a lot of ways she was using everything she recorded," said Del Palmer. "Over the years she learned to know what can work and what won't, and be a bit more discerning."[25]

It's a relatively straightforward process to listen to *The Dreaming* today and, working backwards, hear how it slots into the great continuum of Bush's music. At the time, however, it was a truly radical departure. Listen to 'Blow Away' and 'Get Out Of My House' back-to-back and you get some idea of the strides she made in under two years. She wanted it to be an album that took time to sink in, for the beauty and intricate detail of the songs to emerge slowly. She saw it as a "long lasting album. My favourite records are the ones that grow on you, that you play lots of times and hear something different."[26] That process took more time than she may have thought. To the casual listener, *The Dreaming* sometimes sounded less like a collection of songs than a series of experiments.

Much of the press reaction was positive, if often baffled, awarding Bush a critical kudos she had previously lacked. Colin Irwin's review in *Melody Maker* was perhaps the most thoughtful, capturing the mixture of awe and confusion many felt about the record. 'Mind boggling,' he wrote. 'Always an artist of extremes, Bush has allowed her highly theatrical imagination to run riot, indulging all her musical fantasies, following her rampant instincts, and layering this album with an astonishing array of shrieks and shudders. Initially it is bewildering and not a little preposterous, but try to hang on through the twisted overkill and the histrionic fits and there's much reward, if only in the sense of danger she constantly courts.'

Within EMI the mood was far less sympathetic or forgiving. You could see their point. There was a hint of petulance about *The Dreaming*, a bit of, 'Look, I *told* you I was an artist' about its determination to go to extremes.

There was no 'Babooshka', no 'Wow', nothing even close in terms of commercial accessibility. It was dense and demanding, with no easy entry point. Not only did the single feature Rolf Harris on didjeridu and Percy Edwards pretending to be a sheep, but the album ended with a cacophony of braying donkeys. "I think it got to the point of the nearest album we ever returned to the artist," says Brian Southall. "There is a clause in all contracts that gives the record company the right to refuse, or return, or object. From conversations I had, that was the closest EMI got to returning an album in my time."

Bob Mercer had left his position in 1980 to become an executive at EMI Films, depriving Bush of a key ally within the company. Luckily she found another in David Munns, a former product manager who had left EMI UK in 1979 to work for EMI-Canada, but returned in 1982 as head of A&R and marketing for EMI UK, a position with a far-reaching remit. According to Southall, it was Munns who effectively made the unilateral decision to accept, if not actively support, *The Dreaming*. "Without question he was very powerful," says Southall. "If he got behind something he had the authority to make it work. He was always an advocate of Kate's and made an enormous difference to her career, because there was a danger of her falling off the radar."

His loyalty to Bush was unequivocal and very useful. From a commercial point of view EMI had every reason to be concerned. Radio play for any of *The Dreaming* material was sadly lacking, with EMI undertaking an almost apologetic attitude to their campaign. Bush's personal profile, however, remained high. She undertook a sizeable amount of press for the record, partly because she believed in it and partly because she knew it needed her backing, and was still willing to turn up on children's television programmes and lukewarm talk shows, even consenting to a Radio One roadshow appearance, the Holy Grail of banality, but to little material effect. *The Dreaming* debuted at number three in the album charts but fell swiftly, selling only some 60,000 copies compared to *The Kick Inside*'s million plus, a steep and significant commercial decline between albums one and four. Following the success of 'Sat In Your Lap', released a year previously, the UK singles from the record also flopped dramatically. 'The Dreaming' limped to 48, receiving largely negative reviews and struggling to secure airplay, while the expensive video, co-directed by Bush, was all but ignored. It was, in truth, a supremely odd and bloody-minded choice of lead single, turning Bush's calling card, her remarkable voice, into a nasal Australian twang and containing, by conventional standards, no clear hook. The follow-up, 'There Goes A Tenner', disappeared into the brine without leaving even a ripple. "It's questionable that EMI ever sold the amount of Kate Bush records that they could have done and should have done," says Bob Mercer. "But that was because of her, not because of EMI."

Had it been a question of simple number-crunching Bush may have begun to find life a little more difficult but Munns, to his credit, could see the bigger picture. This was not so much a decline in fortunes as an indication of what an anomaly 'Wuthering Heights' had been in the first place. As Brian Southall points out, "If you're dealing with Duran Duran you're talking about commercial records, [and] you can go back and say we need a couple of hits on this. You can't argue that with Kate because it wasn't part of her make up to start with. You can't go back and say there's no 3½ minute pop single on here. She'd say, 'I know. I didn't write one.'"

She was an artist, not a pop star. Sometimes the two concepts would meet in the middle, more often they wouldn't. Munns accepted this as fact. "This is my favourite artist in the world," he said. "But for someone like her it's sometimes a lonely road and that can be difficult for people to understand. Make a record that's a bit obscure and some people in the company may start to say things to the artist that aren't sensible. Well, EMI and Kate just lost the plot for a while."[27]

With *The Dreaming* the genie was well and truly out of the bottle. Bush had staked her claim, marked her territory. If she was a little bruised and disappointed by reactions to the record, it didn't alter her opinion of the work. She had revelled in the freedom. Although at times undoubtedly she had missed the steadying influence of Jon Kelly, she declared *The Dreaming* to be her favourite album by far, the first occasion where she had come close to hearing her own ambitions reflected back at her. It was the record where she delivered on the promises she had made to herself while making *Never For Ever*, the moment where she absolutely *disappeared* into the limitless possibilities of the studio, and the music.

Everything she had went into it. It had cost her a fortune, way beyond the advance she received, took her a year of almost solid recording, hopping around studios and between engineers, and it had pushed her to the point of mental and physical exhaustion. The record company hated it and it killed her as a singles artists for four years. It was the album that nearly sank the ship, her "she's gone mad"[28] record, but the experience simply made her more convinced and determined than ever about the need to conduct her career in her own way. It was a decisive moment. Hereafter, all attempts at identifying signs of the performer Bush had been on the 'Tour Of Life' and the albums that preceded it are akin to staring at another country. *The Dreaming* was a definitive act of secession from all that had gone before.

9

A Deal With God

"WHEN she got into the studio to do music she was like a Yogi," observes Stewart Avon Arnold. "She was completely lost to the world." Bush had travelled deep within herself while making *The Dreaming*, emerging to find herself cut adrift from a life that needed some urgent attention. The studio had become an inclement micro-climate, a hostile, self-contained ecosystem fuelled by smoke, chocolate, fast food – she was "lasting three months on Chinese takeaways during the last part of the album,"[1] she said – and far too little sleep, a place where she cultivated an absolute fixation with what she was doing to the detriment of almost everything else. The only reason she was able to maintain a relationship with Del, presumably, is because he was right there beside her in the eye of the storm.

In early June 1982, as soon as the album was mastered, she had gone to Jamaica for a break but failed to unwind. "It was a real culture shock," she said. "I went from this dingy little London studio with no windows to absolute paradise. I could barely stand it. Even the sound of the birds was deafening."[2] She returned to immediately undertake heavy promotion. Having conceived, rehearsed, performed, co-directed and shot the extremely complex video for 'The Dreaming', she was back on the band-wagon again, making personal appearances in Glasgow, Newcastle and Birmingham, miming to 'Suspended In Gaffa' and 'The Dreaming' on French, German and Italian TV. When she finally jumped off the treadmill in early November she disappeared from public view almost completely. Houdini strikes again.

During the next two-and-a-half years Bush registered only the faintest readings on the radar. Band Aid and Live Aid, the most visible and cultur-ally significant music events of the decade, occurred in late 1984 and July

1985 respectively and found room for every star, megastar, has-been, once-was and might-be in the global rock and pop firmament; nevertheless, both occasions passed off without even the merest whiff of Bush's involvement. She wasn't invited to participate, although she claims that, had she been asked to perform at Wembley Stadium, "I would have said yes, I'm sure."[3] Perhaps. The fact that she didn't even have to consider whether or not to sing in front of a live audience of 82,000 and a television audience of 400m viewers only goes to show how far from shore her ship had sailed.*

During her prolonged absence there were mischievous media rumours of nervous breakdowns, plastic surgery – "were those pin-tucks around those pixie ears?" asked *Sounds*, presumably safe in the knowledge that the answer was 'no' – and colossal weight gain, backed up by photographs of her "ballooned" to "18 stone". The reality was less dramatic. At 5′ 3″ and a little over seven stone, any additional weight was always going to be hard to hide; after months of largely sedentary work and poor eating habits Bush did, indeed, occasionally appear a little heavier, with more than a hint of an extra chin and rounded cheeks.

There was similarly loose tittle-tattle about her attending drug rehabilitation clinics in either France or the Caribbean; the lyrics to parts of *Hounds Of Love* – "poppies heavy with seed . . . take me deeper and deeper"; "cutting out little lines"; "spitting snow"; "speeding" – were later cited as evidence that she had developed a serious habit. Hard drug addiction was the stock rumour in the Eighties when a pop star had the audacity to take longer than a year between albums: Elvis Costello endured similar treatment in 1985 when, according to press reports, he was either a junkie or an alcoholic. He was neither, and nor was Bush. Not one of the scores of sources interviewed during the research for this book has ever seen her consume a Class A drug, and she has never been much of a drinker. In the snowbound Seventies and Eighties, where cocaine use was routine and

---

* She did, however, participate in Ferry Aid in 1987, one of less memorable of the Eighties' obsession with charity singles, singing on a new version of 'Let It Be' released in aid of the victims of the Zeebrugge ferry disaster. Organised by *The Sun* and featuring an array of D-list celebrities, among which Bush and Paul McCartney, and also Mark Knopfler, stood out like a royal cortege strolling along Blackpool promenade, she agreed to do it but banished all press photographers from her presence and reportedly had the studio cleared while she recorded her vocal.

"She could turn it on immediately the cameras started rolling. Of all the people I've ever worked with, visually her and Iggy Pop were the most aware." - Paul Henry. Transforming herself in 1980 to become 'Babooshka'. (REX FEATURES)

Off duty: just prior to recording a relaxed interview
for *Personal Call* at Radio One, 1979. (BBC)

On duty: in a clearly chilly Switzerland recording
her contribution to the *Abba Snow Time Special*,
broadcast in the UK on Christmas Day, 1979. (BBC)

Recording 'Sing Children Sing' for UNICEF with, among others, Joe Brown, Pete Townshend and Phil Lynott.
Paddy is on the far right. November 1979.

"There's a cast of people in there. That's what so amazing about her." – Ian Bairnson. Bush performing highly theatrical routines for, left, 'Army Dreamers', and right, 'December Will Be Magic Again'. ABOVE LEFT: (ADRIAN BOOT/LFI). ABOVE RIGHT: (BBC)

"I came from the punk rock thing, and to me she was punk rock. She was doing stuff that was going against the grain." – Nick Launay. In the late Seventies, Bush's unlikely admirers included John Lydon, Phil Lynott and Ian Dury, pictured here chatting with her at the Capital Music Awards, March 3, 1980. (CHRIS SKARBON/REX FEATURES)

"She mentions karma a lot, and reincarnation, and witchcraft and paganism and Buddhism. We always end up in these conversations about life in general and spiritual life in particular." – Stewart Avon Arnold. Bush casts her spell performing 'Wuthering Heights' on *Top Of The Pops*, 1978. (BBC)

"Not innocent, our Kate, but very sweet. You don't write those songs if you're innocent!" – Jon Kelly. Performing a sultry new routine for 'Babooshka' on Germany's *Rock-Pop*, September 2, 1980. (PETER MAZEL: LFI)

"Half Irish, Bush connects with a harder, more mythical England, a pre-Christian Celtic land, a deep, green dream of a country." (CLIVE ARROWSMITH)

"From conversations I had, that was the closest EMI got to returning an album to the artist in my time there." – Brian Southall. Bush promoting her pioneering but doggedly uncommercial album, *The Dreaming*, in 1982. (PETER STILL/REDFERNS)

"She came in one day and had decided that there were two Kate Bushes. She'd managed to separate herself." – Jon Kelly (NEAL PRESTON/CORBIS)

"She was bitten by the charity bug which, post-Live Aid, infiltrated much of popular culture." Promoting the Comic Relief book with Lenny Henry and a pair of *Spitting Image* puppets at Claude Gill book shop on Oxford Street, October 23, 1986. (DAVID CRUMP/DAILY MAIL/REX FEATURES)

"You knew you were involved in something really special. I felt *Hounds Of Love* was something special then and I still do. It was very exciting." – Haydn Bendall. Bush affects to enjoy the launch of her masterpiece at the London Planetarium, September 9, 1985. (EUGENE ADEBARI/LFI)

"It was all a bit hush-hush and keep-it-careful." – Brian Bath. Bush and Del Palmer finally appear together in public at the *Hounds Of Love* launch, seven years after the beginning of their relationship. (BRENDAN BEIRNE/REX FEATURES)

A rare stage appearance during Bush's 35-year break from live performance, singing 'Running Up That Hill' at an Amnesty International benefit, 1987. (MAURO CARRARO/REX FEATURES)

"She's very down to earth, apart from the fact that every man in the room falls in love with her." – Daniel Lanois

rife, her predilection for the occasional joint seemed almost quaint. Tea (up to 20 cups a day), chocolate and cigarettes have been her most enduring vices, but work has always been her addiction. It took her six months to recover from the experience of making *The Dreaming*. "I was just a complete wreck, physically and mentally," she said. "I'd wake up in the morning and find I couldn't move . . . eventually I went to see my Pa."[4]

Dr Bush diagnosed stress and nervous fatigue and prescribed a rest cure. Body and mind needed her attention. She did as she was instructed, reconnected with her family and friends, many of whom she hadn't seen in over a year, went to the movies, bought a VW Golf and began to drive herself, spent quality time with Del and her cats, caught up with her music listening, mostly classical, went for walks, and generally pottered about doing small, important things. Gardening and cooking became therapeutic pursuits. She stocked up on fresh fruit and vegetables and instead of takeaways she prepared at least one healthy meal a day. Even this simple task gave her life a domestic focus, a sense of calm routine.

During this period she implemented three major life changes, later recalled as some of her "best decisions".[5] One was to move out of London to the countryside; another was to take up serious dance instruction again and to overhaul her diet; and the third was to build her own studio, this time to professional specifications. As these changes took shape, life and music began to roll in tandem once again, creating a happy, healthy, almost idyllic context within which she set about creating her greatest work: *Hounds Of Love*.

★ ★ ★

Bush and Palmer moved into a seventeenth-century farmhouse in the Kent countryside in 1983, not far from Sevenoaks and within easy commute of Wickham Farm and central London. She described her new home in typically romantic terms. "One day we suddenly stumbled across it and a back door had been left open so we were able to go inside," said Bush. "I'm sure there's a kind of force, a magnetic energy saying, 'Come in, we're meant for each other.'"[6]

London had become a negative influence. She spoke of the "air of doom" hanging over 1981 and 1982,[7] and although she turned the sometimes oppressive energy of a big city into a positive creative force on *The*

Dreaming, she sought a fresher, cleaner source this time around. "The stimulus of the countryside is fantastic," she said. "I sit at my piano and watch skies moving and trees blowing and that's far more exciting than buildings and roads and millions of people."[8] In 1983 she spent a "summer out of the house, something I didn't do for several years,"[9] and began to appreciate simple pleasures. "She bought the cottage down in Kent, and suddenly you'd ring up and she'd be gardening," recalls Brian Southall.

Slowly, she relaxed back into a rounded life, searching for a balance she had struggled to maintain since 1978. The changes coincided with a new resolve concerning her involvement with Del. While still firmly holding to the opinion that "I don't feel our relationship is anything to do with anyone other than us,"[10] she no longer actively sought to keep it secret. On one extremely rare occasion during this period she lifted her head above the parapet, during a radio phone-in on July 29, 1983, the eve of her twenty-fifth birthday. She was asked by the typically brash, brass-necked DJ why 'we never hear any dirty gossip about you and fellas, Kate?' "Well it's probably 'cause I've got a very nice fella," she replied with a laugh. "His name's Del. . . . Del from Kent."[11]

It was hardly on a par with Richard Burton and Elizabeth Taylor breaking cover on some paparazzi-plagued Roman strada, but in the carefully calibrated world of Bush's personal life it marked a quantum leap. When she launched *Hounds Of Love* at the London Planetarium in September 1985 she arrived hand-in-hand with Del, the first time they had ever appeared in public as a couple, and she opened up tentatively in interviews, revealing how she would cook an evening meal and they would watch trashy Saturday evening game shows or films taped off the television, or how he gifted her an antique pocketwatch for her birthday. Del, in turn, would talk touchingly about the fact that there were "two Kates: there is the girl at home I love and there is Kate the star. I must admit I sometimes wonder what she sees in me. . . ."[12]

For those who could scarcely imagine the woman in the 'Babooshka' video or singing 'Get Out Of My House' as a happily domesticated creature, tending to her man and her marigolds, she was keen to (over) emphasise their status as "Mr and Mrs Boring! At home Del and I just potter about, being ordinary. We give cuddles and we have rows, all that. Del and I argue a great deal – over songs – but we consider it healthy. Who wins? Normally, I do. I'm not the shy, retiring, fragile butterfly creature I sometimes read about. My relationship with Del is very stable. We work together, we live together, it works so well for us. That can be a very intense set-up, but I wouldn't have it any other way. It's all very close and direct."[13]

Bush kept the house in Eltham as her London base, but she spent less and less time there. When she was in residence she was often to be found in her private dance studio, a large room suffused with natural light, fitted out with an elegant wooden floor and a mirrored wall for choreography. Taking up dance again was highly significant. After the 'Tour Of Life' she had stopped dancing to any disciplined degree, simply lacking the time. She would call up her dancers for videos or television appearances and they would hastily assemble a routine (on one memorable occasion, choreography for the 'There Goes A Tenner' video was thrashed out in the goods van of a train travelling between London and Manchester) but she missed the regular interaction, that discipline of taking classes with a tutor. *Learning* rather than simply *doing* always opened up something within Bush and her music. "Not only did I feel I needed to be fit again," she said, "but I really wanted the stimulus and inspiration that comes from true teachers."[14]

Her closest dance partner, Stewart Avon Arnold, was unavailable, busy with his own projects, and so she started taking private classes in London with Dyane Gray-Cullert, a Detroit born African-American with an impressive CV in many respected European dance companies. Like Robin Kovac, Gray-Cullert's background was in Martha Graham technique and contemporary dance, although she also taught Bush ballet, something that led directly to the choreography for the 'Running Up That Hill' video.

Significantly, when she returned to sustained dance instruction her writing seemed to gain an extra dimension and her songs positively took flight. She had unearthed the sound and textures she wanted on *The Dreaming* but it was a subterranean album, dark and inward. It had been a necessary step, a purging of sorts and a powerful platform for further progression, as well as a triumph on its own terms, with a certain kind of twisted beauty, but the music – and its creator – had in the process lost some of its vivacity and spring. Bush has always found inspiration in the grotesque, the weird and unsettling, but out and out *bleakness* doesn't suit her. Synaesthetically speaking, *The Dreaming* was an album of gloomy browns, deep dark reds, blacks and blinding whites, full of soil and sand and dust. *Hounds Of Love*, on the other hand, was to be decked out in greens, light blues, dusky purples and silvers. It was to be the bright mirror image of its shadowed predecessor, where the window to the natural world is wide open. "After the demanding lands that my last set of songs took me to, I had to think again about where to go," she said. "Maybe somewhere a little sunnier."[15]

The experience of finding a symbiosis of her creative pursuits and her home environment took her back to some of her happiest times. "For me it's like 1976," she wrote to her fan club in the summer of 1983. "It was a particularly special year, when things were full of adventure. I was dancing every day, and singing and writing all night. I feel in many ways that '76 and this year are linked together, for me."[16]

The move to the countryside and return to dance helped to clear away much of the cloud-cover hovering over her music. The final breath of fresh air was a return to making music at East Wickham Farm. She was painfully aware that the degree of autonomy she was afforded by EMI came at a shockingly high price: £90 per hour, to be precise, the going rate for hiring Abbey Road. Given the frequent round-the-clock sessions for *The Dreaming*, this meant the outlay routinely weighed in at well over £1,000 per day. It was a crippling overhead, while an awareness of the clock ticking also tended to make her creative muscles seize up.

Once again taking a lead from Peter Gabriel, who had recently built his own studio, pre-Real World, at his home in Ashcombe House, near Bath, Bush invested heavily in fitting a professional 48-track studio in the barn at the farm, in the spot where she used to poke away at the old church organ after school and later bashed through the songs for *Lionheart* with the KT Bush Band. The decision had a pleasing synchronicity, another return to a solid, enduring love. She was involved in the design and conditioning, and Dr Bush played an active role, building parts himself, overseeing and advising. It wasn't quite state of the art, but it was sufficiently well appointed, featuring a Soundcraft mixing desk – later replaced with an SSL board – two Studer A80 24-track machines, plus compressors, emulators, a Fairlight and a Quantec room simulator.

Del was beginning to develop aspirations as an engineer. Aided by Paul Hardiman's generous mentoring, *The Dreaming* had marked the beginning of his move away from simply being a bass player towards becoming more involved in the technical aspects of Bush's records, an ambition he would pursue further on *Hounds Of Love*. Bush, too, had become comfortable around technology, very much au fait with the terminology and the purpose of all the gadgets, although at this stage she was rarely hands on. "She'd know how to manipulate sound if not actually do the twiddling herself," says Haydn Bendall, who engineered much of *Hounds Of Love*. "She'd come up with lots of suggestions like, 'Maybe we should compress that, maybe we should expand that, maybe we should gate that or put a pre-delay on the reverb or use a Lexicon reverb.' She knew what sounds were available, but I – or Del or somebody else – would kind of be the mechanics. And she had an incredible audio memory. She'd remember a take she did on a vocal where one particular word was great, or that on track 13 there was this great sound."

The struggles with *The Dreaming* and its poor commercial performance had forced her to reflect on her aims: yes, she concluded, I want to produce my own albums and, no, I don't really care about being famous or selling millions of records. I just want to be allowed to do the work. It did not happen without a fight. "It was felt that my producing *Hounds Of Love* wasn't such a good idea," she later recalled. "For the first time I felt I was actually meeting resistance artistically."[17] Once again David Munns was an invaluable ally who cleared her path and ensured she was left alone to deliver the finished product when she was ready. Beyond her contact with him, her relationship with EMI by this stage was cool and distant. There was a definite sense of raised stakes, that after *The Dreaming* she had to deliver something both commercially viable and artistically profound.

Completed in the autumn of 1983, her new studio became a private study, a place where she could write and create at will according to her own natural rhythms rather than the exaggerated pace of the record industry. The clock stopped ticking, the meter was no longer running. Most importantly, it was a happy and supportive place in which to work. Where Advision and Townhouse had been dark, dingy caves lacking any natural light or sense of time – places where the real world all too easily ceased to matter – the farm studio was physically and emotionally connected to the life she was singing about. Windows looked out to the grounds where she danced and dreamed as a child, while one of the recording booths was the old stable, with the flagstone floor intact. The family were always popping in and out.

"We'd be there doing a track and suddenly Jay would turn up to say hello, sit there for 15 minutes and nod," says Charlie Morgan, who returned to the fold to drum on several songs on the album. "Then Pad would come in and start talking to Kate about some mandolin part he had an idea for, and Kate would say, 'OK, let's put that down tomorrow.' And then suddenly Hannah would come in with a tray stacked high with teapots and cakes and we'd all have a cup of tea. And then Dad would come in and say, 'What're you going to eat tonight? I'll go and get a take out, what do you fancy, do you want some Indian, or a Chinese?' Someone would drive off and pick up a curry – it was all so conducive to creativity."

This was how she had always wanted to work; you can see her striving for the ideal as far back as *Lionheart*, but it was beyond her reach at that time. As soon as she had built her home base and peopled it with her most loved and trusted supporters, the relationship between her life and her work became far more harmonious. And a great gust of fresh air blew through her music.

★   ★   ★

There was to be a marked shift in the recording process this time around. Working from home with a piano, a Fairlight, a Linn drum programme and her voice, recording onto an eight-track Soundcraft desk and tape machine, Bush and Palmer worked up much of the album in the Kent countryside between the summer and autumn of 1983. These were not traditional demos, early scratchings to be referenced but ultimately discarded in favour of re-recorded versions. Instead, they were kept and built upon at East Wickham Farm for the final versions. In this way, the demos from the home studio morphed into the masters, and the initial spark of emotion and inspiration in each song could be preserved. The writing and recording processes finally dissolved into one another, a much longed for development: using the Fairlight as her primary compositional tool, Bush was now creating in sound and had ceased to distinguish between the two.

The first song to arrive was 'Running Up That Hill', composed in the summer of 1983 in her music room, looking out through the window to the valley below. The track's most instantly recognisable components – the riff, that searing Fairlight part, and the rumbling electronic drums, programmed by Del – were present from the very beginning, located right at the heart of the song.

Originally called 'A Deal With God', the song spoke passionately of Bush's impossible wish to *become* her lover, and he her, in order that they could finally know what the other felt and desired. It was a sobering comment on misfiring communication and the impossibility of men and women ever really understanding one another, and yet – in capturing the basic human need to strive for compatibility – it was not without hope nor optimism. 'Running Up That Hill' was another artful and wholly original take on gender roles and relationships, but it also worked as a wider artistic statement. The reason Bush has always so vigorously resisted being defined by her looks, her background and her sex is because she craves a 360 degree perspective as an artist. She has sung as a child, a ghost, a man, a woman, a donkey. . . . She is eternally seeking to 'swap places' because she desperately wants to cover all possible angles of available experience.

'Running Up That Hill' took her an evening to write. The component parts of her next composition, 'Hounds Of Love', were also assembled quickly, inspired by one of her favourite films, the 1957 British horror flick *Night Of The Demon*, a lip-smacking tale of a Satanic occultist unleashing a demonic yet terrifyingly ill-defined beast on those he curses. Many of the other tracks – 'And Dream Of Sheep', 'Under Ice', 'Watching You Without Me' – also came relatively easily. Contrary to the evidence suggested by the yawning gaps between her records, Bush is not necessarily a slow writer; it is capturing the nuances of texture and mood that takes so much time. "I remember Paddy saying she often writes an entire album quite quickly, but then spends ten years recording it!" says Colin Lloyd-Tucker, who sung on *The Red Shoes* and has frequently collaborated with Paddy Bush. "It used to drive him mad – 'Oh for God's sake, Kate!' I don't think she has ever struggled with the songwriting process, it's a natural thing for her."

The alternative version of 'Hounds Of Love' featured on the *This Woman's Work* box set offers a tantalising glimpse into her writing process. The significant elements are already present – the scything string figure (performed here on Fairlight, later replaced with cello), the deep, irresistible drum rhythm – yet the song is clearly in its infancy: the lyrics are sketchy and the melody isn't yet fully formed, but it's almost there. Between this version and the finished article, however, lay over a year's intensive work; God, for Bush perhaps more than any other artist, lies buried deep among the details, in some strange pagan future where earth and EQ meet. Making a record is not a quest to achieve technical perfection; it's far more mysterious and explorative than that. "It's about selection rather than musicianship," says Youth, the former Killing Joke bass player who appeared on the album. "She's after the currency of ideas reflected in the music rather than academic virtuosity."

"It's experimental, but within that I don't think she's diverted or goes off on tangents," says Haydn Bendall of her recording process. "Maybe she doesn't know exactly what notes, or exactly what sounds or harmonies or melodic structures or dynamics she wants to use, but I believe she has an extremely clear impression of the atmosphere she wants to create. How she achieves that involves the experimentation, but she has an incredible, innate sense of what works for a song. [On *Hounds Of Love*] we were using Fairlight and Linn drums a lot, and they'd come out with these funny little sounds which you might think weren't very interesting, and she'd say, 'Isn't that wonderful, isn't that great?' She'd *make* it great, and in a way that's the mark of a genius, to make something fabulous out of a simple idea. She'll just have a little kernel of an idea that would develop into a huge blossom."

'Running Up That Hill' was the gateway to the new record, and most of the rest of the material was written and in reasonable shape by the end of 1983. Aside from the 12 songs on the album, during the sessions she recorded 'Burning Bridge', 'Under The Ivy', 'Not This Time', as well as versions of the traditional tunes 'My Lagan Love' and 'The Handsome Cabin Boy'. There may have been several more that have never surfaced. "From what I remember I think we recorded at least twice as many tracks as ended up on the album," says Charlie Morgan. "There was quite a rate of attrition, I know there's a bunch of stuff I played on that never made it."

There was no shortage of quality material, but Bush had a very clear idea of what she wanted. As soon as she had written the breathtakingly beautiful ballad 'And Dream Of Sheep' and its companion piece 'Under Ice', she envisioned a record split into two distinct sides, one of strong individual 'up' songs and one of darker, interwoven pieces recounting the cinematic tale of a girl cast adrift in the sea at night following some kind of catastrophe, awaiting rescue, slipping in and out of consciousness, trapped between a waking nightmare and dreams that are even worse.

She had been toying with the idea of writing an extended suite of music for some time, intrigued by the possibilities. "One of the first ideas I had [for the album] was to try a concept," she said. "It was really the concept side that came first. I was a bit worried that it wouldn't work, so until I'd written, say, four or five songs, I wouldn't really know if it was going to be successful. I thought it was wise to just use one side of the album, so there would be half an hour to play with rather than going for an hour's worth. And the other side, I thought it would be nice to balance with five or six completely different songs, not linked in any way, that were perhaps more positive and up-tempo, so there was a nice balance between the two sides."[18]

Stretching across seven songs on the record's second side, 'The Ninth Wave'* was inspired by a lifelong attraction to the dark, deadly romance of water. She loved old black and white war movies, letting the countless images of soldiers being jettisoned from bombers into the sea below play on her imagination, while one of her favourite pieces of art – which she owns – is the *Hogsmill Ophelia*, a macabre, modernist satire on Millais' more famous *Ophelia* featuring the disturbing image of a cracked doll drowned in sewage overspill. As early as 1978 in a teen magazine she had described her "strangest dream": "I'm sitting on this raft in the middle of a gigantic ocean. There's no land in sight – just limitless water – yet I have no fear and no desire to be rescued. Just a feeling of complete peace." These stimuli, and no doubt many more, had been percolating for some time and fed subconsciously into the songs, though the final effect was far from peaceful.

As a coherent narrative, 'The Ninth Wave' can withstand only the gentlest of examinations. The girl in the water is visited in real time by events around her, but also by memories, future projections, hallucinations and possible past lives; like most extended conceptual works of popular music, to make sense it requires rather a lot of caveats along the lines of 'and then she fell asleep and dreamed about witches . . .' Bush's own explanation, given during a lengthy analysis on Radio One's *Classic Albums* in 1991, can be encapsulated as follows: the story starts with the girl bobbing in the sea, fighting off sleep and sensory deprivation ('And Dream Of Sheep') with only the emergency light on her lifejacket illuminating the pitch darkness; she falls into restive sleep ('Under Ice') and

* The title, taken from a passage of Lord Alfred Tennyson's 1869 poem *The Coming of Arthur*, was applied retrospectively. The poem did not directly influence Bush's work.

endures jagged, discordant, vivid dreams of being trapped under ice. Her subconscious then slips back in time, passing through the voices of her childhood, both scolding and gentle, returning eventually to a bygone age of female persecution ('Waking The Witch'), her predicament in the water recalling the historic barbarity of witch-ducking, where guilt was determined by whether the woman sank or floated.

The girl's imagination then drifts back to the present day, and she visualises her own home ('Watching You Without Me'), her loved ones "watching the clock", waiting for her return as she gazes unseen at her own life like Scrooge in *A Christmas Carol*, invisible, cut off and powerless to communicate. "You can't hear me," whisper the backing vocals, in the album's saddest, most bereft moment. The vigorous 'Jig Of Life' turns the mood of the narrative around, pounding along like a dose of spiritual CPR, letting in some hope. It's another visitation, this time from the girl's future self, an old lady begging her younger incarnation to "let me live", showing her the riches that await: her two future children, her long, vigorous life. This is the place "where the crossroads meet", where her destiny is decided.

On the magnificent, deeply moving 'Hello Earth' the camera – for this suite, notwithstanding its later adaptation for the stage, is essentially a cinematic conceit – pans away from the water and travels up into the sky, from where Bush gazes down on the scene and contemplates our planet, underscoring our individual insignificance in the face of the enormity of earth, and earth's insignificance in the face of the universe, and through it all the terrible power of nature, storms gathering, the wind whipping, the sea a "murderer of calm". Finally, 'The Morning Fog' details a new morning and an act of emotional rescue, the vaporous haze a benevolent force sweeping in from the waves and bringing the girl back to land, back into her life, thankfully alive and filled with reaffirmed love.

It need hardly be stated that, on record, 'The Ninth Wave' works much better as an allegory than a literal story-in-sound. We do not learn, for example, how the girl is rescued – there is no conventional conclusion to the narrative, little in the way of mechanics, only a profoundly satisfying emotional afterglow. Beyond the confines of its rather skittish storyline, 'The Ninth Wave' is a psychological travelogue through a supremely dark night of the soul, documenting a tiny figure adrift in a sea of powerful blackness. It's a distillation of 25 years' worth of Bush's fascinations, nightmares and recurring obsessions: the sea, witchcraft, death, the supernatural, the dangerous power of the senses, feelings of exclusion, the thin line between reality and fantasy – if, indeed, there is any line at all, for don't we all exist most completely and vividly within our own minds?

"I can't be left to my imagination" is the key line, for above all 'The Ninth Wave' is a panicky swim through the murky waters of the human psyche. Bush creates a stark dramatic scenario – being lost at night at sea – to suggest that what lies within our heads and hearts is more terrifying than anything the world can throw our way; and yet therein also lies our most precious and creative resources. Even at her most elemental, the transformative power of our inner senses takes paramount place in her work. A veritable gift to the armchair psychologist and amateur analyst, it's tempting to hear 'The Ninth Wave' as a highly stylised, oblique dramatisation of much of the difficulties Bush had undergone in 1981 and 1982 before emerging happier in 1983, moving out of isolation and back into the world. Tempting, but no doubt overly simplistic. Whatever the underlying motivation, capturing on tape its highly complex eddies and flows was by far the most demanding part of the recording process.

★ ★ ★

Bush played the new tracks to Paul Hardiman on October 6, 1983, on his first visit to the newly constructed farm studio. Hardiman, who had been working with The The and Lloyd Cole & The Commotions since *The Dreaming*, engineered the first stages of the album and was immediately impressed by how much progress had already been made. "The first time I heard 'Running Up That Hill' it wasn't a demo, it was a working start," he says. "We carried on working on Kate and Del's original. Del had programmed the Linn drum part, the basis of which we kept. I know we spent time working on the Fairlight melody/hook but the idea was there and also I think the pad, the wind/train sound, was there plus guide vocals."

Sessions began in earnest at Wickham Farm on November 4, starting with the transfer of the home studio eight-track recordings to the farm's two 24-track masters. Between November 7 and December 6 they worked on the backing tracks. Stuart Elliott came in to add drums, either working 'with' the existing Linn drum – on 'Running Up That Hill' he overdubbed a snare part, for example – or replacing it but closely following the programmed pattern.

An acute awareness and understanding of rhythm drove the entire record, particularly the first side. "It was obvious to me that Kate had finally found a groove," says Hardiman. "On 'Running' we worked a lot on the Fairlight part which, incredibly, reminded me of the synth line in [Seventies disco-funk classic] 'Atmosphere Strut' by Cloud One. I [was] *very* happy to push the groove." *Hounds Of Love* was indeed the album where Bush, finally, successfully married rhythm to melody. The songs had "a constancy of rhythm [that] perhaps wasn't always there in previous albums," she allowed. "When I was initially coming up with the songs . . . I would actually get Del to manifest in the rhythm box the pattern that I wanted. As a bass player I think he has a very natural understanding of rhythms and working with drums, and he could also get the patterns that I could hear in my head and that I wanted. It's . . . through him that we started off with the rhythmic basis that was then built upon."[19]

Her piano was becoming less of a central feature, but when it was showcased – 'And Dream Of Sheep', 'Hello Earth', 'Under The Ivy' – it had a rich, resonant texture, deep and sad, very much in tune with Bush's maturing voice. Replacing the upright Bechstein of her home studio with a Grotrian-Steinweg grand for recording, she wanted "a live sound, reminiscent of Erik Satie, Chopin: the empty ballroom after the party when everyone has gone home."[20]

After Christmas rough mixes were assembled with provisional lead vocals and backing vocals, in order to take the album sessions over to Ireland. Following the success of 'Night Of The Swallow' Bush envisaged more Irish instrumentation on the new album. Planxty keyboardist Bill Whelan travelled to the studio to hear the tracks and they agreed she would travel to Dublin in the spring of 1984 for extended sessions at Windmill Lane, where bouzouki, pipes, fiddles and whistles were added to 'And Dream Of Sheep' and 'Hello Earth'. She was typically exact and demanding: Donal Lunny later recalled how Bush asked him to play the single whistle note at the end of 'And Dream Of Sleep' over and over again for three hours, searching for just the right 'bend' in the note. The main item on the agenda was 'Jig Of Life', based on a Greek tune Paddy – ever the musical archaeologist – had unearthed. Bush only finished writing the song in Whelan's house in Dublin the day before the session, and it was recorded over the next few days with the cream of Ireland's traditional musicians – Lunny, Liam O'Flynn, John Sheahan – jamming for hours, spinning the track into a delirium. "They started playing along with it and just reduced both of us to gibbering wrecks," Del recalled. "It was such a magic moment."[21]

Ireland was also where Bush finished the lyrics, tightening, adding lines and verses. She tends to write words in bursts, whole chunks arriving fully formed, but often the most time consuming part is plugging the small gaps in the fabric of the lyric, maintaining the initial mood. Appropriately enough for songs that were mostly composed looking out at the Kent countryside, the words were completed within reach of the salt and spray of the Irish sea, holed up with Del. You can hear it, too: *Hounds Of Love* is an album positively *propelled* by nature, soaked to its bones with a "tremendous stimulus from the outside."[22] This elemental rush isn't present only in the words, with their countless references to big skies, rain, sun, clouds, white horses, ice, forming storms, wind and waves (there was, as Bush pointed out, "a *lot* of weather on this album"[23]), but also in the sound. The songs are swept along by a primal force, at times almost bestial in its power; a thrilling, thudding, irresistible pulse runs through the heart of the record.

As well as fascinated by our inner nature, *Hounds Of Love* – like *Aerial* – is smitten by Mother Nature, bursting with the rhythm of life; it was no accident that the two albums came together to form the spine of 'Before The Dawn'. On the other hand, it is also a truly modern record, a layered and artificial construct, using the best of Eighties technology and further removed from the standard 'band in a room' format than ever before. Often it was just Bush and Palmer working on sounds, with Hardiman and later Haydn Bendall coming in and out of the sessions. Into this tight-knit hub musicians arrived as and when required, according to what would "be good, karmatically," as Del rather grandly put it.[24] The Medici String Quartet became a sextet through the power of overdub on the session for 'Cloudbusting'; John Williams added a beautiful guitar part – bright, shimmering dew drops of sound, like a bud bursting into a flower – to 'The Morning Fog'; the Richard Hickox Singers filled the black holes in 'Hello Earth', their eerie voices slipping across the surface of the song like clouds scudding across the face of the moon.* She sent tapes of relevant tracks to

---

* The choral section of 'Hello Earth' is taken from a Georgian folk song called 'Zinzkaro', which Bush heard performed by the Vocal Ensemble Gordela on the soundtrack of Werner Herzog's 1979 German vampire film *Nosferatu The Vampyre*, one of her more esoteric borrowings.

her favourite electric guitarist, Alan Murphy, who came in and made a particularly effective contribution to 'Waking The Witch', and also added explosive counterpoints on 'Running Up That Hill'.

Much fuss was made in 1984 over Prince's hit single 'When Doves Cry', a dance record without a bass line. *Hounds Of Love* was in some ways even more groundbreaking; many of the songs have neither bass nor guitar. The pounding title track is built on the highly unconventional bones of two drum kits, cello, vocals and a snatch of dialogue – 'It's in the trees! It's coming!' – recreated from *Night Of The Demon*, a suitably stark setting for the definitive expression of one of Bush's most consistent themes: the fear of being trapped by love, ripped to shreds by passion. Here, love is a prowling source of terror and the singer its quivering quarry, while the music is perfectly in sync with the subject matter. The rhythm track pounds like a heartbeat in the throes of panic-stricken ecstasy, while the scything strings add a manic, compulsive element to the chase. And after three minutes of enthralling will-she-won't-she comes the magnificent climax: "I need la-la-la-la-la LOVE!" After all the hide-and-seeking with Del, it's hard not to hear this as a very personal declaration. It remains one of her most moving, magnificently realised songs.

The bass, when it *was* featured, was democratically deployed, spread between Del, Eberhard Weber – "There's God and then there's Eberhard"[25], according to Del – Danny Thompson and Youth. The latter, called in to play on 'The Big Sky', was particularly struck by Bush's working methods. "Every individual musician would come down and play their parts separately: drums, and guitars, and bass," he says. "It gives it a slightly futuristic atmosphere. It doesn't have that natural dynamic arrangement and progression that you have with musicians playing together – it's quite linear, quite flat, quite modern, in the way that a lot of people do today all the time. Then it was quite unusual, it was only people like Kraftwerk and Can who were doing stuff that was that linear. She's a visionary, and she has a very clear idea of how she'd like to direct the scene at any time. She commands a great respect in the room and everybody is clearly looking at her to lead, and she's very able to do that. She let me do what I liked, she gave me some direction, then she said, 'Thanks very much, off you go'. Then she sort of chopped it up and arranged it in the Fairlight. I learned a lot from that, how to put a record together. Pete Waterman actually worked in a very similar way!"

★ ★ ★

Following Bush's return from a month in Ireland, sessions continued with Paul Hardiman at East Wickham Farm between April 15 and May 24. Hardiman was booked to begin work on another project, so Haydn Bendall came in during the summer of 1984, working full weeks and half weeks over a period of six months. He recalls a fundamental difference in mood between these sessions and the ones he had engineered at Abbey Road for *The Dreaming*.

"We had lovely times," he says. "You walked through the garden into the kitchen, and all the family's business and conversations took place around this huge kitchen table. Paddy was always around, always involved, and the two dogs – Bonnie and Clyde, the hounds of love! There were pigeons and doves all over the place, and her dad smoking his pipe and her mum making sandwiches – it *was* idyllic. We spent a lot of the summer months there and I have very fond memories of that time together, but it was hard work as well. We weren't just floating around, it was really hard, concentrated work, because when Kate works she's incredibly focused. Nobody looks at the clock, and you find yourself doing the same thing for hours and hours and hours, but it was fun and exciting because you knew you were involved in something really special. I felt *Hounds Of Love* was something special then and I still do. Whenever I hear any one of those tracks I get a thrill."

The tingling sensation that the music they were making was imbued with some kind of deep magic touched most of those working on the record. "It's like a very old, almost Druidic thing," says Youth of the album. "It has a mystical, Bardic quality, part of our Ancient British tradition. It's not overt, it's hidden, and I love that. That element synergised with cutting edge technology and a genius writer and you get a classic album. It was a great honour to work with her."

The sessions were peppered with countless memorable moments. Bush wanted to add another layer of rhythm to 'Jig Of Life', and handed Charlie Morgan an array of Irish percussive instruments – the lambeg, the bodhran – and asked him to fill all 24-tracks with his clacking, beating and booming. "Each verse a bit more of me came in, until we ended up with an entire

24-track of me playing different drums," says Morgan. "I came back from that thinking, 'What have I *done* today?' Just on cloud nine from being thrown the gauntlet and saying, 'OK, we're going to do something completely different here.' I think Stuart [Elliott] and I did some of our best stuff we ever did with Kate, because there were no rules or barriers. It was pure creativity."

Ensuring the vocals were right was, again, hugely time consuming. When the farm studio was built Bush had deliberately chosen not to install a glass window between the live room and the control room, instead relying on microphones for two-way communication. This was primarily to make her feel less self-conscious when she sang. She admitted to still needing to get "psyched up" to record vocals with the requisite emotional clout, and also to getting a "little drunk"[26], which may have been a euphemism. "There was quite a lot of the 'exotics' going around," says Youth. "She's quite hippy-dippy, dreamy and 'out there' anyway, she's a romantic for sure. She had quite a squeaky clean public persona and I was quite impressed that she was actually quite a 'head', she likes to get out of her body a bit."

Youth lent his big, leggy bass sound to 'The Big Sky', a song that became the album's unruly child. In the end, the finished version was light years away from the way the song had started. "It went through three different incarnations," says Haydn Bendall. "It's hard to know who did what, and it's hard to know what we added or took away. Kate would work on a [track] for ages and ages and ages, it might cost a lot of money and a huge amount of time, but if she didn't like it she'd scrap it but still retain faith in the song and record it in a completely different way with different people. She definitely controls it all, she's in charge."

'The Big Sky' encapsulated the twin forces that drove *Hounds Of Love*, diving headlong into the elements as well as building up a huge, rolling wave of rhythm. It's an almost perfect pop song, as simple or as complex as you wish it to be, combining a beguiling childlike innocence, the aural equivalent of a big, bright crayon drawing* with an undercurrent of doom, hinting at an impending biblical flood ("Build me an Ark"). As Stewart

---

* On the 12-inch Bush gently mocks the song's hippyish vibe by arranging an impromptu 'That Cloud Looks Like . . .' competition mid-song, featuring friends and family and a parade of very Pythonesque silly voices.

Avon Arnold has noted, Bush has a fascination with the End Times. Here she suggests that, come Armageddon, the fools and the dreamers will be the ones who escape.

From its very inception, 'Cloudbusting' was blessed with a synchronicity that Bush must have appreciated. The song was inspired by *A Book Of Dreams*, a memoir Bush had bought in 1976 – that pivotal year again – in Watkins occult bookshop in central London, written in 1973 by Peter Reich about his father, Wilhelm Reich, a well-known Austrian-American psychiatrist and psychoanalyst who was a colleague of Freud in the Twenties and, in later years, Einstein. Reich attracted much controversy for his unconventional techniques (he would frequently ask patients to strip to their underwear) and his belief in a 'primordial cosmic energy' called Orgone, which he described as blue in colour and which, he claimed, could be seen by the naked eye. Reich believed Orgone was the essential life force that we often incorrectly identify as God, an all-powerful cosmic energy which streams through the universe and the body, particularly present during times of sexual stimulus and orgasm.[*]

Reich also posited the existence of Deadly Orgone, a negative force that counteracted Orgone, causing, among other life-sapping effects, dry weather and desertification, a catastrophic quenching of the life flow. In response, he developed a 10-foot-tall 'cloudbuster' machine, an ungainly marriage of metal tubes and pipes placed in a large drum of water which, he claimed, when pointed at the sky could form clouds and create rain, thus increasing the flow of Orgone. He bought 160 acres in Maine and named it Orgonon, a place where he could build a laboratory and continue his work. However, his public experiments with the 'cloudbuster' and his unorthodox methods drew increasingly hostile attention from the US authorities, particularly the Food & Drug Administration, and he was finally jailed for two years in 1957 for contempt of court. He died of a heart attack a few months into his sentence, aged 60.

The genius of 'Cloudbusting' is that it doesn't even attempt to distil

---

[*] Bush's work contains many examples where the moment of creative breakthrough is portrayed as essentially orgasmic. Given that she had read the book in 1976, it's distinctly possible that 'Symphony In Blue' – with its triple threat of God, sex, and the colour blue – was partly inspired by reading about Reich's theory.

Reich's bizarre, brilliant, esoteric and in some respects highly dubious life into a five-minute song. Instead, it focuses on the profoundly touching relationship between a child and his father. Peter Reich witnessed the ransacking of his father's labs, watched the FDA take him away, and visited him in prison many times. He was 13 when Reich died, and *A Book Of Dreams* is written from the universally accessible perspective of a son celebrating the magic of a mysterious and powerful man, a man who can *make rain*, and his feelings of pride, helplessness, loss and confusion (Reich Jr. never can make up his mind about the legitimacy of Orgone and the 'cloudbuster') following his death.

Bush was haunted by *A Book Of Dreams*. She had contacted Peter Reich to explain her motives in writing 'Cloudbusting' and to express the wish that she hoped that he approved of the song; in a neat, serendipitous touch, she received his reply while they were working on the track at the farm. "When we were doing the vocal, she got a letter from Peter Reich saying he loved the idea of what she was doing," says Haydn Bendall. "Doing the vocal on that was just fabulous, the power and the passion is stunning. When Kate stands in front of the microphone and sings, it's fantastic, it takes your breath away. That's a huge privilege. We're used to effects in the studio and computer graphics in films, but when you're faced with raw talent it's still stunning. She's quite softly spoken and laughs a lot and is very joyous, but she takes on these different personae when she is singing – she's an actress as well as a singer."

It's a wonderfully balanced song, both sad and strangely ecstatic, and filled with a real understanding of a child's love for a parent; for don't we all, as children, want to believe that our parents can perform miracles and cosmic sleights of hand? It's almost impossible not to hear 'Cloudbusting' as a hymn of love and gratitude for Bush's own inspiring, kind and somewhat eccentric father, a man who always sought to open her eyes to the power of beauty and magic. By the time she gave the song its live debut in 2014, it had also become a hymn to her own son.

That her family remained her strength and joy was a truth communicated time and time again on *Hounds Of Love*. In 'And Dream Of Sheep' she slipped in one of her mother's favourite expressions, the oddly touching – and very Irish – "Come here with me now", while 'Mother Stands For Comfort' was a more complex, disturbing account of the all-encompassing nature of a maternal love that extends far beyond the bounds of moral and legal right and wrong. Elsewhere, Jay slipped into his best Irish accent to declaim poetically over the end of 'Jig Of Life', while the entire brood popped up in 'Waking The Witch', Paddy switching effortlessly from Geordie to a Yorkshire accent to implore the girl to wake up.

Perhaps mindful of the warning contained within 'All The Love' on *The Dreaming*, in which she contemplates the sorrow that comes from deep feelings left unexpressed, *Hounds Of Love* ended with 'The Morning Fog', a song pricked with glorious points of light, expressing the joy and gratitude felt by someone who has returned from far away – "I kiss the ground" – and is now determined to celebrate the things that truly matter: life, love and nature, and music. It can be read as a note to self: hold on to your happiness, sing it out, celebrate it. And indeed she does, ending the album with a promise to tell her mother, her father, her lover and her brothers "how much I love them." Simple and heartfelt, it's an extraordinary gift of a song.

Listen closely and you can hear that sentiment running through every note of the album. Joy is a fiendishly difficult emotion to capture in any art form. With *Hounds Of Love* Bush gathered up the positive forces of her childhood home, surrounded by her friends and family and her treasured collaborators, and returned to something fundamental in her music, an elemental vigour. The words are some of her best, containing her most inclusive, dramatic and beautiful thoughts; the music is a force of nature, all wind, weather, light and love; her voice is sublime, the potency she discovered on *The Dreaming* harnessed and perfectly rendered.

Familiar, less jubilant themes are also present: the difficultly of connecting, the impossibility of really knowing and loving another, the fear of surrender, the fear of *not* surrendering, the constant yearning. Several tracks are honest and imaginative examinations of human struggle, but nothing is insurmountable. *Hounds Of Love* is ultimately about maintaining hope and happiness against all the odds. 'Running Up That Hill', though not her choice of title, was a perfect analogy – life is hard, but we're getting somewhere. Though bleak and often nightmarish, similarly 'The Ninth Wave' is a story about *not* dying, not going under, but instead riding the waves and, somehow, keeping going. Every moment of darkness and doubt is balanced and leavened by a ringing affirmation, an unfakeable *joie de vivre* – she had *fun* making this record. "It was one of the most content, happy periods of my life for quite a while, in that I actually had time to breathe and work creatively," she said.[27] *Hounds Of Love* is a thrilling portrait of the artist as a truly alive, fully connected human being.

* * *

She had been gone a long time. In her absence, Marvin Gaye had died and Madonna had arrived, ushering in an age of brash, blatant sexuality that made Bush's purring eroticism seem positively demure; MTV was the new kingmaker, the compact disc had undergone its 'Big Bang' moment, and that 'gated' drum sound could be heard on records by everyone from David Bowie to Bruce Springsteen. The world had moved on apace. In their August 3, 1985 issue *NME* ran a feature placing Bush firmly in the 'Where Are They Now?' file. Yes, she *had* been gone a long time.

The response was swift. Two days after *NME* hit the shops Bush released 'Running Up That Hill' as a single and appeared on *Wogan* to sing it, her first public performance in the UK for almost three years, and in the final third of 1985 and for much of the following year she was *everywhere*, exposed to more interviews, television appearances and awards shows than at any time since the late Seventies.

'Running Up That Hill' had been called 'A Deal With God' until EMI expressed concerns that the title would damage its chances of success in staunchly Catholic territories, and probably also hinder its prospects in America, where Bush had been steadily building a profile. "We were told that if we kept this title that it wouldn't be played in any of the religious countries," she recalled. "We might get it blacked purely because it had 'God' in the title. This seemed completely ridiculous to me . . . but none-theless, although I was very unhappy about it, I felt unless I compromised I was going to be cutting my own throat."[28]

Bush hadn't had a hit record since 1981, or a Top 10 single since 1980, a lifetime in pop's accelerated chronology. She had already insisted that 'Running Up That Hill' be the first single rather than 'Cloudbusting', the company's choice, so she reluctantly consented to the title change, reasoning that "after *The Dreaming*, I couldn't be bloody minded."[29] She had learned when to pick her fights. Whereas the dust-up over 'Wuthering Heights' at the launch of her career was a defining battle she felt she simply had to win, the compromise on 'Running Up That Hill' was made from a position of strength. She could see the bigger picture, the wider victory.

She even deigned to appear on *Top Of The Pops*, her first performance on the show since the 'Wuthering Heights' debacle over seven years earlier. This time she called the shots and her band came with her.

'Running Up That Hill' was greeted with almost universal acclaim. Even *Melody Maker*, whose reviewer Helen Fitzgerald initially gave it a desperately ill-considered brush-off, re-considered and printed a glowing write-up in a future issue. It quickly peaked at number three, her biggest hit since her first single, and proved a resounding success worldwide. It remains – alongside 'Wuthering Heights' – her most widely recognised song. Its accessibility wasn't hurt by the fact that the insistent rhythmic pulse that drove the song was so effortlessly in synch with the times.

The B-side was 'Under The Ivy', a hushed, two-minute retreat into an internalised world of childhood that she had succeeded in carrying with her, recorded in an afternoon early in the album sessions. Here, she brings her past and present selves together in a lament for lost innocence, set in the farm's rose garden, where "someone is recalling a moment when . . . they were children, something they used to do . . . that they won't be able to do again."[30] It is a testament of the strength – not just of songwriting, but also of unity and form – of *Hounds Of Love* that such a magnificent song was left on the sidelines. 'The Ninth Wave' concept bustled some fine tracks into touch, but she seemed to retain a soft spot for 'Under The Ivy', performing the song live from Abbey Road in March 1986 for a special anniversary edition of the Channel 4 music show *The Tube*.

The album had been completed in June, Bush having added all the necessary atmospheric flourishes, which included whirring helicopter noises borrowed from Pink Floyd's *The Wall*, Palmer simulating a steam train to help disguise the slo-mo collapse at the conclusion of 'Cloudbusting', and her old friend Morris Pert dropping in for some percussive fun on 'The Big Sky': "Ah yes, we *do* get going, don't we!" he fondly recalls. No donkeys this time, no emus. The mix, overseen by Brian Tench, was once again suitably complex, and even mastering the record was something of a trauma. Ian Cooper, who cut all Bush's records from *The Dreaming* to *The Red Shoes*, recalls, "*Hounds Of Love* took the longest. I won't say it was a nightmare, but I remember the list of what I had to do rolling onto the floor, it was jumping around all over the place. I have a funny feeling we were still doing it when it was released. I remember asking her when it was coming out, and she said, 'It's out!' I said, 'Then why are we doing it?' and she said, 'I think we could do this and that right.'" It's tempting to surmise that nothing is ever *quite* finished to her satisfaction.

Hounds Of Love was yet another autumn baby, launched at the London Planetarium on September 9, 1985 and released a week later. Bush and Palmer attended the launch together, arriving hand in hand amid an eruption of flashbulbs as the papers finally got the shot they'd been waiting for. Inside, the entire album was played to the accompaniment of a light show in the Laserium, but the event was rather overshadowed by some of the subsequent press coverage in which Bush was bitchily portrayed – still – as some air-headed ingénue, while the gossip sheets took great delight in the fact that a well refreshed Youth had called Del a "wally".

"I got drunk at the launch of *Hounds* and made some serious indiscretions," says the bass man. "All I can say is that I was extremely jealous. I wanted to be Del! But I don't want to talk about that, really." It can certainly prove hazardous for the heartstrings recording with Bush. One musician deliberately stopped working with her for many years because he "was absolutely desperately and totally in love, just besotted with her. She and Del were together and I wasn't going to do anything to change that, and in the end I kind of absented myself. It was very tricky. I was getting emotionally involved and I lost all objectivity, so I bowed out."

Nick Launay admits that while working with Bush on *The Dreaming* he became "very confused by the whole thing. She bought me towards the end this big box of chocolates with this wonderful note in it, and wrote lovely cards saying 'Thank you for making my music come alive' and all this. It was all very lovely. I was, like, 'Wow, what does she mean by this?' But she had a boyfriend, Del Palmer, and he was there all the time, and that was obviously ongoing. She's just a very, very loving person and I think she puts this feeling of love and appreciation out there when you work with her, and you tend to get a little confused about what it all means! Some people put out an incredible energy of love, and I think she was just like that. I was really young. I was 20 but more like a 12-year-old, so it was pretty amazing just being in the room with this amazing looking person. To me it was like being with a cartoon character, almost, like a Japanese *anime* character. And the way she talked! This incredibly high voice, quite bizarre and very seductive. None of it was put on at all, she was just like that."

Daniel Lanois describes her as down to earth, "apart from the fact that every man in the room falls in love with her! If you call that down to earth. . . ." On the set of *The Line, The Cross And The Curve*, the entire crew scrambled over each other to do her bidding. It's a widespread affliction, and one not merely confined to men. "Her gentleness, you just can't help but fall in love with her," says Borimira Nedeva, who worked with Bush during her sessions with the Trio Bulgarka. "The trio adored Kate as everyone else did."

Scores of interviews with Bush over the years have ended as fawning paeans to her 'sensuality', every male journalist fancying himself as a potential suitor, eulogising everything from her dimples to her toes. Among her closest friends and collaborators, however, she inspires a deeper loyalty and sense of protectiveness, not only in deference to her artistry, but also her privacy. "People who work with her tend not to talk out of school," says the author David Mitchell, who worked with Bush on 'Before The Dawn'. Bush's natural warmth, genuineness, lack of prudishness, tactility, sincerity and artistic integrity, combined with her obvious beauty and great gifts, is a large part of the reason people love working with her to the point where they become almost devotional. She surrounds herself with musicians and technicians and creative people of all ages, stripes and experience who will go the extra mile for her because not only does she treat them with respect, but they understand more than anyone that what she does is extraordinary. "No disrespect to anyone I've worked with since, but I've not met anyone else who is in the same league," says Jon Kelly, echoing an oft-repeated mantra. "She was so different, and just the sweetest lady."

★ ★ ★

Building on the success of 'Running Up That Hill', *Hounds Of Love* went straight to number one in the UK charts, knocking Madonna's *Like A Virgin* off the top perch. Not only was the album a superb artistic statement but it was cleverly constructed, front-loaded with the most accessible songs before introducing the more demanding material that comprised 'The Ninth Wave'. *The Dreaming* had been somewhat uneasily ahead of its time and portrayed Bush in a light so far removed from how she had appeared previously that great chunks of her audience couldn't, or wouldn't, connect with it. On *Hounds Of Love*, conversely, she succeeded in looking and sounding utterly true to herself and yet also conveniently in tune with the mood music of the mid-Eighties: big hair, shoulder pads, great melodic hooks. Technology, too, had caught up with her. During her studio hibernation the Fairlight had become ubiquitous, and any number of songs were flying around the ether featuring its bright, synthetic string sound rubbing against bubbling Linn rhythms; The Blue Nile's 1984 single 'Tinseltown In The Rain', for instance, bears a striking resemblance to 'Running Up That Hill'. And let us not forget that 1985 was the year the charts succumbed to the power of love: Huey Lewis, Jennifer Rush, the afterglow of Frankie Goes To Hollywood. What better time for a cry of, 'It's in the trees, it's coming!'

The colossal success of *Hounds Of Love* had a certain inevitability about it. EMI were excited and pushed the album hard. It sold over 600,000 copies in the first nine months, ten times more than *The Dreaming*, and became the fourth best selling compact disc released in Britain, lining up behind the coffee table classics, Dire Straits' *Brothers In Arms* and *Love Over Gold* and Phil Collins' *No Jacket Required*.

The critics were also impressed. *Sounds* gave it the full five stars, declaring simply that "*Hounds Of Love* is fucking brilliant. All human life [is] contained herein. Dramatic, moving and wildly, unashamedly, beautifully romantic." *NME*, the volatile weather front charged with shaping the nation's musical temperature on a weekly basis, pronounced that Bush was, at last, cool. "Kate's a genius, the rarest solo artist this country's ever produced," wrote Jane Solanas. "She makes sceptics dance to *her* tune. The company's daughter has truly screwed the system and produced the best album of the year doing it." *Smash Hits* gave it a nine out of 10 rating and made it pick of the month; *No 1* called it "a haunting collection of musical images" and then spoiled it all by declaring it "one for Marillion fans everywhere." *Melody Maker* liked it but had an unpleasant Pavlovian reaction to 'The Ninth Wave'; anything with a 'concept' was deemed profoundly suspicious.

The last months of 1985 were almost entirely given over to dedicated promotion, not only throughout Europe but also further afield. In mid-November she visited the United States for the first time since 1978. Her stock had steadily been growing across the Atlantic since *The Dreaming*, the first of her albums since *The Kick Inside* to get a release in the US. Its oddness and originality had earned some highly favourable reviews and also considerable exposure on college radio, her designated home on the airwaves; in the States, Bush has always been considered unequivocally 'alternative'. Michael Davis characterised her in his 1982 *Creem* review as "a cross between Stevie Nicks, Joni Mitchell, Nina Hagen and [The Motels' lead singer] Martha Davis." In latter years she has often been bunched in with other 'sensitive' female musicians like Jane Siberry and Sarah McLachlan, the Lilith Fair set. In a musical landscape obsessed with categories, she was always going to have a problem finding her niche.

Nick Burton in *Record* called *The Dreaming* a "masterpiece . . . she's the only female rocker out there doing anything original (or experimental) in contemporary pop. What's pending? Stardom, one hopes." Building on these positive reactions and a subsequent foothold in the nursery slopes of the *Billboard* 200, EMI-America had finally mobilised behind Bush's career, organising the release of a five track mini-LP in June 1983 featuring 'Sat In Your Lap', 'James And The Cold Gun', 'Babooshka', 'Suspended In Gaffa' and a French vocal version of 'The Infant Kiss' called 'Un Baiser D'Enfant'. In Canada, the mini-LP included an extra track, 'Ne T'Enfuis Pas', specially aimed at the French-speaking Canadian market and recorded and mixed – alongside the new vocal for 'Un Baiser D'Enfant' – by Bush, Palmer and Paul Hardiman in a single day at the house in Eltham on October 16, 1982. A personal promotional tour was planned to coincide with the release of the mini-album, but last minute engine failure on the QE2 – one of the least hackneyed of all rock star excuses, but Bush was still not a happy flyer – put paid to her trip, and in the end she publicised it via telephone interviews.

In an amusing acknowledgement of Bush's continued stage absence, the release was supported by a 32-date college 'tour' undertaken by the *Live At Hammersmith Odeon* video, followed by the belated but highly promoted release of *Lionheart* and *Never For Ever* in January 1984. The net effect was as desired. By the time 'Running Up That Hill' was released in the US in August 1985, snazzy 12-inch and all, followed by *Hounds Of Love* a month later, Bush's profile Stateside had grown appreciably. It didn't hurt that the US reviews for the album were superb. "Bush compellingly stakes her claim as a major voice in pop music," said Pam Lambert in the *Wall Street Journal*. The *Los Angeles Times* deemed the album a "dark and dreamy masterpiece" while *Spin* called her a "genius [who] creates music that observes no boundaries of musical structure or inner expression." The *Boston Globe* declared the album "an upbeat affirmation of life and love; Bush has come a long way from her early days as a soft-rocking singer-songwriter."

For the first time, she agreed to undertake serious promotion in North

America, following up a handful of preliminary phone interviews with a visit (Concorde, naturally) to New York in November, where she taped several TV and press interviews and visited the MTV studios. She also hit the streets, signing copies of *Hounds Of Love* at Tower Records in Greenwich Village, where the queue snaked hundreds of metres around the block, and she stayed – happily, amazed by her popularity – many hours longer than arranged. There is no question that her promotional input made a palpable difference. 'Running Up That Hill', supported in the US by the film clip of her performance on the *Wogan* show (the video she made with David Garfath, with its ballet moves, low-key colouring and lack of lip-synching, was deemed by MTV to be too esoteric for US audiences; surely a backhanded compliment), climbed to number 30 on the *Billboard* chart in late November. Had she also released one of the album's outtakes, 'Not This Time', as a single rather than relegated it to the B-side of 'The Big Sky' she might even have scored a genuinely huge US hit. One of her most conventional songs, built along the lines of a standard rock ballad with a well-worn chord pattern and big, reverbed drums, 'Not This Time' seemed absolutely tailor-made for Stateside success. The thought, no doubt, didn't even occur to her.

★　★　★

Hounds Of Love had legs, stamina. In the US the album peaked just before Christmas at 30 on the *Billboard* album chart, but in Britain the record's initial success triggered a series of aftershocks that lasted long into the following year. She won three BPI nominations – Best Album, Best Single, Best Female Vocalist – and lip-synched to 'Hounds Of Love' at the ceremony in February 1986, looking suitably vampiric, her hair jet black, her eyes lined with deep purple, her lips a vicious dark red. She also performed the song on *Top Of The Pops* and, from certain angles, came almost to resemble a conventional pop star, popping up in the unlikeliest places. She sang backing vocals for Big Country and Go West (her guitarist, Alan Murphy, also played with them) and was bitten by the charity bug which, post-Live Aid, had infiltrated much of popular culture. Over three nights in April 1986 she performed 'Breathing' solo at the piano for a Comic Relief benefit at the Shaftesbury Theatre and, effortlessly flitting from the truly sublime to the patently ridiculous, duetted with comedian Rowan Atkinson – looking like a cross between Lou Reed and a prototype Jarvis

Cocker, and clearly channelling his inner Neil Diamond – on a fine slice of comic capery called 'Do Bears . . .?', in which she played the fragrant if slatternly love interest to Atkinson's smarmy loser: "He was rich and I was down on my luck," she purred. "So I charged him a fortune for a flying fu-" at which point Atkinson hastily interjects with "for crying out loud." Later in the year she turned up with other Comic Relief stars at the Claude Gill book shop in Oxford Street to launch the charity's Christmas book and she also did her bit for Sport Aid, running on Blackheath to raise funds for famine relief in Africa.

Three more singles were released from *Hounds Of Love*, each accompanied by expensive, hi-spec videos which – again, in keeping with current trends, but also reflecting Bush's move away from dance as a medium of visual expression towards film – were less pieces of performance art and more like mini-movies. The 'Cloudbusting' film, in particular, was a hugely ambitious undertaking, incorporating a Hollywood star (Donald Sutherland), a member of *Monty Python*'s creative team (Julian Doyle) and Bush acting the part of a young Peter Reich. Filmed over three intense days in September on White Horse Hill in Uffington on the Berkshire Downs, it fuelled her desire to become even more involved in filmmaking. Even on such a huge project, however, she always kept her eye on details elsewhere.

Her instinct was to lead from the front and, where possible, to oversee personally every last detail. She rushed from the set of 'Cloudbusting' to attend the pressing of the single to ensure that the correct message ['For Peeps', the nickname of Peter Reich] was cut into the run-out grooves. Bush does not have a natural flair for delegation. She favours the kind of obsessive attention to detail which has led to charges of control freakery, but which also ensures the results of her endeavours are frequently flawless.

'Cloudbusting' reached number 20 in October 1985, followed by 'Hounds Of Love', which peaked at number 18 in March 1986, and 'The Big Sky', which scraped into the Top 40 in the summer, almost a full year after the album was released.[*]

---

[*] The progress of 'The Big Sky' wasn't helped by the fact it was released only days after the Chernobyl nuclear disaster in the former Soviet Union; not everyone was gleefully looking up at the clouds, although it did rather underline the song's less obvious, less positive message of impending disaster.

Even when the *Hounds Of Love* singles dried up, Bush was still a fixture in the charts; in the autumn of 1986 she had two further hit singles. The first – and biggest – was 'Don't Give Up', a duet with Peter Gabriel, another art-rock individualist undergoing a commercial gold rush with his 'Sledgehammer' single and *So* album. Bush had recorded her part of the song back in February at Gabriel's home studio at Ashcombe House, where she would have felt fully at home amongst the rural informality. "The cattle barn was Peter's PA room, and then we had a side room for the control room, with cows peering in through the window," recalls Daniel Lanois, the Canadian who co-produced *So*. "Pretty makeshift, very West Country!"

A beautiful, burbling ballad with gospel overtones, 'Don't Give Up' is a song of battered pride, sung by a man who has lost his job and, in the process, has also lost his faith and sense of identity. Yet it also reinforces the essentially comforting idea that a bond between two people can overcome the most grievous setback. "Peter wanted it to be a conversation between a man and a woman," says Lanois. "This completely came from Peter and was there early on, so Kate was volunteered to play the role." The pair did not sing together in the studio; Gabriel had already recorded his vocals, and Bush followed his lead on her parts. The first time she reacted spontaneously to the song, feeling her way into it. Ashcombe House was a tiny space, and she sang from the control room wearing headphones, squeezed in beside Gabriel, Lanois and the engineers. Not her ideal creative environment.

There was a raw intimacy in her vocal that matched the lyric, but she felt she had "messed it up"[31] and, having been sent a cassette copy of the song with her vocals dubbed on, she returned later to sing it again. In the end, some of the doubt and fragility of her initial vocal was retained in the final version. "She was a sweetheart to work with," says Lanois. "It's a bit of a funny song to sing, because the time signature is really odd, and until you wrap your head around it it's quite complex, but she managed to pull it off nicely. If I can be blunt about it, she is just a great emotional singer, and that really came across in that performance."

'Don't Give Up' rose to number nine in the UK and entered the *Billboard* 100, an unlikely hit single for a song of its length, subject matter and unusual time signature. It has become a beloved and much-covered standard – Lady Gaga and Midway State being the most recent – and for many listeners, particularly in the US, it remains their first point of reference for Bush. The simple, highly effective video featured Bush and Gabriel in a long, loving clinch – both emotional and erotic, this was an embrace full of pain, comfort and reassurance – which fuelled further speculation that the two were, in time-honoured tabloid parlance, 'more than friends'. The same suggestion had often been made about Bush and Gilmour. Gabriel had a deserved reputation as something of a swordsman, but "there was certainly [nothing between her] and Peter at that time," says Lanois. Sinead O'Connor, one of his past romantic partners and never one for playing the diplomatic card, later said, "I've got to admire Kate Bush because Peter Gabriel tried to shag her and she wasn't having any. She's the only woman on earth who ever resisted him, including me."[32]

As 'Don't Give Up' was sliding down the charts it waved hello to Bush's new single, 'Experiment IV', which peaked at 23. It was a curiously flat song, B-grade Bush, and another tale of weird science and shadowy figures from the government. This time the plot concerned a military plan to create music that can secretly kill people, a further twist on a familiar Bush concept, the notion of a hidden evil lurking within beauty: it could be love, music, or the lure of water lulling her to fall and then ripping her to shreds. The video, featuring an array of alternative comics such as Hugh Laurie and Dawn French, was another cinematic showpiece; her performance of the song on *Wogan*, the band decked out in lab coats as Bush sang from behind a large desk, proved more compelling.

She had recorded 'Experiment IV' to accompany *The Whole Story*, a selective compilation of 12 of her singles released in November 1986 and, to date, her first and only greatest hits collection.* She re-recorded a new vocal and added a very Eighties beefed up drum sound to 'Wuthering Heights', suggesting both a lack of love for the original and a reluctance to be side-swiped by the fatal embrace of nostalgia. "It sounded dated," she said. "I think if we'd had more time I probably would have done the same with a couple of songs."[33] The seeds of a desire to do something practical

---

* It is not her only collection of previously released material. The *Single File* video and box-set of singles were released as a stop-gap between *The Dreaming* and *Hounds Of Love*, while *This Woman's Work* was a lavish compendium of her entire output plus B-sides and rarities, released in 1990.

with her creative dissatisfaction were sown here, and would eventually lead to *Director's Cut.*

Even if she thought it was "a crap idea"[34], releasing a compilation of old material was an atypically regressive and obviously commercially motivated move, followed by a video collection of similar songs, issued despite her own misgivings about the quality (she felt she was only really beginning to get to grips with the form) of much of the material

She felt she owed EMI – in particular, David Munns – some payback, and thus allowed them to cash in on her catalogue at a time when her commercial profile was at its highest. There would never be a better time, and she may have realised that if she did it now she wouldn't ever have to do it again. *The Whole Story* was released on the back of a promotional drive of almost military precision, heavily advertised in the press and on radio and television, and proved by far her most successful record. It has sold over six million copies to date, and has taken her music into households she might never have otherwise reached.

She undoubtedly worked hard for the extraordinary successes of 1985 and 1986, and in many ways allowing the release of *The Whole Story* was her final concession to playing the industry game, while pushing *Hounds Of Love* would be the last time she promoted an album with such a wide ranging, conventional campaign. The clash between the banal flippancy of a TV studio and the style and substance of her music had become increasingly pronounced, just as the disparity between the isolation of her working methods – much of the time now it was just her, Del and an engineer, squirreled away in the studio for months – and the fanfare with which she was expected to announce and promote her work made for increasingly discordant mood music. "I do get a bit scared of the exposure," she said. "Coming out of work and saying, 'Here's the new album!' It's a bit frightening how exposed you are suddenly everywhere, being on the side of a bus when it goes past. I hate that![35] I think sometimes the work speaks much better than the person does. I certainly feel mine does. I think sometimes it can go against the work; the personality can almost taint it."[36]

Promoting in America may have sealed the deal. The interview she taped in November 1985 with cable show *Night Flight* was too ghastly to be entirely typical, but it summed up the hard sell, say-this, say-that, say-it-again conveyor belt of US media promotion. Faced with an under-briefed female interviewer who insists on calling *The Dreaming* 'Dreaming' and a technical crew who keep interrupting her, Bush keeps her cool – just – but you can tell the entire charade is sapping her soul. It was clearly an excruciating experience.

Back home, she still often felt misunderstood and misrepresented. In critical terms, the progress Bush had made on *The Dreaming* was largely cemented by *Hounds Of Love*. Bush certainly had her supporters within the music press prior to 1985, but they were swimming against the tide; she was just as likely to be dismissed as irredeemably naff, someone guaranteed to add a weird and titillating novelty factor to achingly uncool pillars of the 'entertainment' establishment such as *Pebble Mill* and BBC Radio One. After *Hounds Of Love* she was generally viewed as hip, sexy and in control, but even the glowing testimonies came with a degree of age-old baggage. Her art might be dismissed or grudgingly praised, but rarely without an obligatory remark about her breasts and a derogatory dig about her dancing thrown in for good measure. Even eight years after the Mankowitz portrait, in a positive review of *Hounds Of Love*, *NME*, then a bastion of left-leaning political correctness, was still fixated with her "famous tits", while there was a condescending tone lurking in several other reviews, a kind of apologetic undertow, as though liking Bush remained a guilty pleasure.

Today there is a climate within popular culture of instant assimilation and mass consensus, and it's easy to forget how fiercely delineated the battlelines were two decades ago. It was a time of rigid side-taking, heightened class awareness, ruthless scrutiny of motives and methods. For some commentators there was still something not-quite-right about Bush, the 'girl' who had swanned her way to the top, twirling and caterwauling and getting the middle-aged TV execs all steamed up with her 'artistic' dancing. She was regarded by many as part of the Peter Gabriel, Phil Collins, Annie Lennox and Pink Floyd axis of orthodoxy, the Prince's Trust and BPI set: comfortable, privileged, somewhere 'over there', a bit of odd pop for mums and dads and girls in Laura Ashley dresses, but nothing more. "Most of her records smell of tarot cards, kitchen curtains, and lavender pillows," wrote the Stud Brothers in *Melody Maker* which, as a fundamental misreading of her art, is hard to improve upon. Yet this perception of her work as something twee and prettified served with a side order of entrance-level kookiness still lingered.

When Bush appeared on *Whistle Test* in 1985 host Richard Skinner erected an immortal monument of condescension in her honour, beginning the interview by smiling, "Now, you're a *very* determined girl. . . ." She greeted his idiotic gambit and others like it with the smirking, silent contempt it deserved, but it was little wonder she resolved to subject herself to this process with increasing infrequency, and that when she did there was a palpable change of tack. She had become a very different interviewee from the unguarded, gushing, enthusiastic young woman who emerged in 1978. Having long since recognised that the press pursued their own agenda no matter what, she duly adopted a more formal demeanour, backing away from any discussions of a more outré, hippy-dippy nature. This was business, not therapy. Any questions concerning Gurdjieff or 'communing with nature', for instance, were met with firm stonewalling. You could almost see her running through her answers in her head before she spoke. She was prepared to be there, at least, and to talk politely about her music, but no more.

"I find it very difficult to express myself in interviews," she said. "Often people have so many preconceptions that I spend most of the interview trying to defend myself from the image that was created by the media eight years ago. That is understandable to a certain extent – that's when I did most of my interviews, and I think the image was created by what the press felt the public wanted, how they interpreted me as I was then, and how I projected myself at that time. I was very young, idealistic and enthusiastic about so much then, but I felt they exaggerated these qualities. And I was – and am even more so now – a private person."[37]

★ ★ ★

Hounds Of Love was enormously significant in determining the path of Bush's future career and her subsequent media profile. It was both her best-selling blockbuster and her escape route, amassing the kind of sales and critical hosannas that allow an artist to do whatever they want, whenever they want. "They [EMI] left me alone from that point," she said. "It shut them up."[38] Had she so desired, she could have grasped the nettle of global stardom by quickly recording a follow-up album, going on tour, writing an autobiography, acting in a dubious film, and generally teaching Madonna a trick or two about how to be an emotionally and intellectually engaged female pop phenomenon. Instead, she gratefully recognised its success as an opportunity to bolt in the opposite direction. "Absolutely good luck to her because – talk about being on the front line!" she later said, gazing in Ms Ciccone's direction. "She's such an exposed person. I would find that so difficult to live with."[39]

The success of the record, combined with the fact that she now had her own private studio, was her one-way ticket out of the rat race. She never really came back, at least not fully.

Making and recording *Hounds Of Love* was not just a creative peak, but the first practical application of Bush's working ethos: her career hereafter has become a self-sufficient cottage industry conducted in real time, at home, alone or among her friends, keeping the industry and most other observers at several arms' lengths. It meant, after the ripples surrounding the album's extraordinary triumphs subsided in late 1986, that we would see much less of her. "When I come out into the world, it's only to say, 'Here's the album', so I can get on with the next one," she said.[40]

In terms of her cultural status, *Hounds Of Love* marked the birth of the Kate Bush we all now take for granted: an unimpeachable goddess, the critic's darling, iconic, influential, a national treasure. Before 1985, the jury was divided. *Hounds Of Love* eventually settled the matter once and for all. It was a high watermark of artistic and aesthetic excellence – those songs, those videos, that languidly erotic sleeve, the mastery of technology – which she has found almost impossible to better. In 1991 she called it the "most complete work I've ever done. In some ways it was the best and I was the happiest that I'd been compared to making other albums."[41] It has proved a prophetic statement. In *Aerial*, she has made at least one further album of comparable range, quality and distilled emotional impact, but she has never again sounded quite so imperious, or displayed such absolute mastery of all her numerous talents, as she did on *Hounds Of Love*.

10

"Put Your Feet Down, Child. You're All Grown Up Now"

B USH turned 30 on July 30, 1988. She spent the day volunteering as a shop assistant at Blazer's boutique in London to raise money, along-side scores of other celebrities, for an AIDS charity (which was in itself significant; the disease was soon to have a direct impact on her life and music), looking relaxed and happy as she posed for the inevitable photo op in front of the equally inevitable cake. There was no sign of the additional weight around her face and body which had been so apparent when she appeared at The Secret Policeman's Third Ball in April 1987 and was even more evident when she descended from the heavens to sing 'Don't Give Up' with Peter Gabriel at Earls Court that summer, and which brought with it tabloid rumours – cheap shots in all but name – that she was pregnant.

Nothing quite so dramatic was happening, just another recurrence of an imbalance in the work-diet-exercise dynamic. To rectify the situation, Stewart Avon Arnold was called in to put together a programme designed to get her back into shape. "Once or twice a week I'd go over to her house and give her a work out," he says. "It was very regimented, it had to be. There was no, 'Right, that's enough, you can relax now if you want to.' No, no, no! I did it as though it were a professional class. She came out totally sweating and exhausted, otherwise there's no point. It was a pure 90 minutes work out, physical training and dancing. We would sit around and have a cup of tea and a chat afterwards, that was something to look forward to."

Like the gaining and shedding of a few pounds, on the surface the changes taking place in Bush's life were almost comically fractional. She tried to cut down on her smoking and switched from Benson & Hedges to

232

the milder Silk Cut; she was spotted at the odd show, including those by Dave Gilmour's Pink Floyd, her new friend Nigel Kennedy and old collaborator Davey Spillane, all of whom would appear on the next album; she added fish to her diet, at the same time as lending her name to the Vegetarian Society's campaign to stop excessively cruel practices within the meat production industry.

There were, as ever, no great personal extravagances or jaunts to far flung sunny climes – "I'd rather stay at home,"[1] she shrugged – although she did find time for a short break in France with her family. Off duty she was usually dressed down in jeans, jumpers, boots or trainers and, as ever, chose to relax by watching films and television and, increasingly, gardening. She appeared on BBC 2's *Rough Guide To Europe* in August 1988 to select her favourite sights in London, and seemed reconciled with the city; she was once again based mostly at Court Road in Eltham.

And yet, while hardly a gravely tolling bell, her thirtieth birthday provides a useful point of reference. In the years and songs that immediately follow, a shadow slowly falls across Bush's work. Not the metaphysical phantoms, demons and ghosts that have always lurked in the psyche of her songs, to be called up and dismissed when the need arises, but something less easy to negotiate: the deeper, longer shadows of death, disenchantment, broken relationships and ageing arrive on her doorstep and – often clumsily and uncomfortably, as though she really has no choice – inveigle their way into the heart of her music.

* * *

She was already up to her hips in the next album, which for the first time involved a close collaboration with other female singers. Bush first heard the extraordinary diaphonic siren call of the Trio Bulgarka in 1985, towards the end of the *Hounds Of Love* sessions. It hit her with a physical force, demanding her attention, though it would be three years before their paths finally converged.

The Trio consisted of Yanka Rupkina, Eva Georgieva and Stoyanka Boneva, three middle-aged women who had been singing traditional Bulgarian music both together and apart for a couple of decades and had contributed to the semi-legendary compilation *Le Mystère Des Voix Bulgares*, first released by a Swiss label in 1975 and later reissued, in 1986, on Britain's hip indie imprint 4AD. Bulgarian folk had already exerted a small but appreciable influence on western popular music. In the mid- to late-Sixties, the State Radio and Television Female Vocal Choir's album, *Music Of Bulgaria, The Ensemble Of The Bulgarian Republic,* was released on the Nonesuch label and reached the likes of David Crosby and Graham Nash, soaking up the vibes a world away in the blissed-out, false idyll of Laurel Canyon. They were stunned by its otherworldly sound.

"Those women sing rings around everybody in the world," said Crosby many years later. "They make the Beach Boys sound loose. They did things that no one else has ever done. Repeatedly. And they were a huge influence on Nash and myself both. We listened to that album probably a couple of hundred times. There is no question they influenced me, strongly. I thought that was the best part singing I have ever heard in my life."[2]

Almost 20 years later, it was Paddy (but of course) who first introduced Bush to this astonishing music. She was "devastated"[3] by its emotional purity, likening their voices to those of angels, although there was nothing sweet or mellifluous about it. Singing from the throat rather than the chest, the trio employed diaphonic stylings, the lead vocalist singing the melody while the others sustained a single drone note, creating an effect much like that of a bagpipe. Punctuating the dissonant, brittle harmonies in sevenths and ninths with strange whoops, trills and yelps, the results were raw and powerful, utterly alien to western ears and yet touching the receptive listener at a profoundly deep level.

The three women had been involved in the Bulgarian State Radio and Television Female Vocal Choir and, like all its members, came from the more remote, rural regions of Bulgaria. Together they sang the preserved music of a lost world. "[Bulgaria] was under the Ottoman Empire for 500 years, and the part of the population that wasn't slaughtered went into hiding in the mountains," says Borimira Nedeva, a Bulgarian musicologist, composer and translator who, in the Eighties, was executive manager in the copyright agency of the country's state music department and worked closely with Bush on her sessions with the Trio. "They made nests of culture that couldn't be reached, and they preserved language, [identity], songs. It was absolutely isolated for 500 years, and these songs are sung in [that] old style."

The influence of Irish folk music had steadily become more pronounced in Bush's music, and in making an atavistic connection with

Bulgarian peasant music she perhaps subconsciously recognised a link with the musical heritage of her mother. "Irish (and Scottish) folk music and Bulgarian folk music have so much in common, that one wonders how it jumped through the whole of Europe," says Nedeva. "There are so many things that I just can't explain: bagpipes, tartan, the folk stories, the stamping of the feet in the dances. When I see *Riverdance* I think, this is a Bulgarian folk dance! But they have sharp differences as well, which is why a lot of people can't make the parallel. The style of singing is totally different."

After hearing the Trio, Bush resolved to use the women's voices in some capacity, but it took her nearly three years to develop the thought and also to pluck up the courage. Faced with the purest of folk sources, she worried that mere pop music was perhaps an unbecoming home for such deep reserves of raw beauty and unadorned emotion. She was concerned that the Trio would be "belittled"[4] by her music, but it wasn't as big as leap as it might have first appeared: it was simply her boldest attempt yet at unifying musical worlds.

Eventually, she phoned producer Joe Boyd. A genuine pioneer in the development of folk-rock and much else besides, Boyd had worked with everyone from Fairport Convention, Nick Drake and the Incredible String Band to John Martyn, Billy Bragg and R.E.M., and had first become involved with the Trio Bulgarka in 1986, when he visited Bulgaria to put together the all-star folk group Balkana, of which the Trio were a part. He subsequently signed them to his Hannibal label and released their album *The Forest Is Crying* in 1988.

"The phone rang in my office and my assistant looked at me funny as she pressed the hold button," recalls Boyd. "'It's Kate Bush for you,' she said. Kate told me that she had heard – from Danny Thompson, I believe – that I was the man to talk to about Bulgarian music. She said she wanted to have Bulgarian harmonies on a couple of tracks on her new album. I told her the best way to accomplish that would be to go to Sofia and work out the arrangements there. She hates to fly, but agreed to go next time I went, which was a month or so after our conversation."

In October 1988 Bush duly flew to Sofia, a giant leap out of her physical comfort zone and, even for an artist as fearless as she, a bold step into unknown musical territory. She stayed in the capital for a weekend, meeting the Trio and attempting to find some common ground between her songs and their culture. The following week all four women were back in London for several more days' intense work on three songs; within the space of a fortnight they were done, and Bush had radically altered the landscape of her new album. When it comes to her music, she often resembles a chess Grand Master: she can spend an inordinate amount of time plotting her next move, but she can certainly move fast enough when it's time to strike.

★ ★ ★

The Bulgarian sessions gave fresh impetus to a project that had been stuttering a little, struggling to find its identity. With much of 1986 given over to publicity and feeling for a new musical direction, it was early 1987 before Bush turned seriously to the new record. She was given a push from the outside. One of her most accessible, enduringly beautiful songs, 'This Woman's Work' was written in the spring of that year for the romantic comedy *She's Having A Baby*. It was a bespoke creation, commissioned by the film's American director John Hughes and designed specifically to match the scene in which an expectant father (Kevin Bacon) sits in a hospital waiting room and silently faces up to his considerable shortcomings as a husband and a man while his wife (Elizabeth McGovern) struggles to deliver a breach baby. The song was a perfect fit, and in truth the power of Bush's voice, unadorned piano and carefully crafted words gave the scene an emotional punch the rest of the movie failed to sustain or arguably even deserved.

'This Woman's Work' touches on familiar Bush concerns. Its urgings that we make the most of life and its regret at words and acts of love left unexpressed ("All the things I should've given but I didn't") echo 'All The Love', but the sense of it being almost a sequel to 'The Man With The Child In His Eyes' (time, finally, for this overgrown boy to stop being a kid) ensures that it also looks forwards, neatly teasing out some of the themes that would become central to her next two albums: growing up, breaking apart, facing adversity, female strength – above all, a putting away of childish things.

With additional orchestral overdubs, recorded much later with Michael Kamen at Abbey Road, 'This Woman's Work' appeared on *The Sensual World* over a year after it graced *She's Having A Baby*, essentially unchanged. She recalled the writing of it as "quick and easy, because the song had to be about [the scene]. It couldn't be about anything else. I think that helps tremendously. The big problem with songwriting [is] the blank page; you can start anywhere."[5]

There is some evidence that the 'blank page', and increasingly the enormity of choice that the studio afforded her, were causing some problems. She and Del had upgraded the farm studio, adding an SSL console and many new tricks and technical treats, and she felt "overwhelmed by the amount of equipment around me. It was quite stifling, and I made a conscious effort to move away from that, and treat the song as the song."[6]

In the end *The Sensual World* turned out to be a songwriter's album filtered – not always successfully – through the available technology, neither terribly elaborate in design nor particularly conceptual in its ambitions. Working primarily with her Fairlight III and the DX7 synth to form demo-masters, Bush wrote quickly but then took a break of several months while she struggled to find her direction. "I wrote a few songs but it didn't take me long to realise I wasn't happy with them," she said. "I went through a period where I couldn't write at all. I thought I'd lost it. Didn't have anything to say and I didn't want to go out . . . I went back to it bit by bit and eventually worked it through."[7]

She proposed a record of "10 short stories"[8], flitting between distinct moods and textures. Once again writing and recording dissolved into one long process. Her working methods had become even more refined since *Hounds Of Love* and the time frame was loose. Del was now her principal engineer and often they worked alone; they could go home for the day if things weren't working out, or indeed take an extended break to allow her to evaluate where they were. A friendly face such as Haydn Bendall appeared now and again to add experience and expertise, and of course the family were constantly around, providing tea, sandwiches and exotic instrumentation – this time, folks, say hi to the valiha (a Madagascan bamboo tube zither) and the tupan (a Balkan drum) – on tap.

Periodically, musicians were also invited in to add a splash of paint to the canvas. Bush called upon her usual retinue of drummers, bassists and guitar players, augmented by some exceptional craftsman in their chosen fields, such as Celtic harpist Alan Stivell, or Nigel Kennedy, the brash, somewhat contrived *enfant terrible* of modern British classical music. They each performed alone to the existing backing track, and even then usually a composite of several different takes would be used.

The sense was of a musical jigsaw being slowly and rather painfully assembled. The first track written, 'Love And Anger', was still being laboriously manipulated into shape over two years later, and even after the record's release Bush still didn't regard it as finished, nor indeed have much idea what it supposed to be about. The title song also underwent a long and troubled birth. Written with a DX7 and built on a sparse rhythm track, much of the musical texture was added during sessions at Windmill Lane in Dublin, where Irish instrumentation was also added to 'The Fog' and 'Never Be Mine', and where Davey Spillane's piped Macedonian air accentuated Bush's vaguely Eastern melody on one of her most seductive compositions.

Bush had been inspired to write 'The Sensual World' after hearing the celebrated Irish actress Siobhan McKenna read the torrential closing soliloquy from James Joyce's *Ulysses*, where the character Molly Bloom recalls – in lovely, liquid detail – her earliest sexual experience, the moment she gave herself, in body and mind, to husband-to-be Leopold Bloom. As a piece of writing it's a rolling monument to unashamed female desire, a celebration of a purely physical life-force. *Ulysses* was first published in its entirety in 1922 and Bush, believing that the novel was now out of copyright, simply lifted parts of Molly's speech and sang them over the soft, swaying backing track, astonished at how well the words fitted. Those who heard the track in this original incarnation regard it as one of her greatest pieces of work. Presumably, in style and structure this song closely mirrored the version of 'Flower Of The Mountain' eventually released on *Director's Cut*.

"Jeez, it was a stunning record," says Jimmy Murakami, director of the animated classics *The Snowman* and *When The Wind Blows* and, later, Bush's 2005 video for 'King Of The Mountain'. "Kate came to me in the late Eighties when I had a commercial studio in Dublin. She wanted me to do a video promo on this song, this beautiful music for James Joyce's lines for Molly Bloom. I went over to her house in England and she played this track and it was absolutely fantastic. It was done. She said she thought it was PD [Public Domain] but I told her I wasn't so sure, because the Joyce relative who lives in Paris [Joyce's grandson, Stephen James Joyce] owns it. She got nervous about that and she called up and found out that it was true."

The Joyce estate refused to release the words. Bush, not used to having her creativity stifled by pettifogging red tape, spent over a year trying to gain permission before accepting defeat. "Obviously, I was very disappointed," she said. "It was completely their prerogative, you know, they don't have to give their permission, but it was very difficult for me, then, to re-approach the song. In some ways I wanted to just leave it off the album, but we'd put a lot of work into it."[9] It would take over 20 years for her to finally persuade the Joyce estate to relent.

The fact that Bush was already in discussions about making a video for the song (she eventually co-directed the promo clip with the Comic Strip's Peter Richardson) indicates how far down the line she was before she had to change tack. In the end she kept the backing track and simply "re-approached the words",[10] painting a scenario where Molly, the sensualist *in excelsis*, steps out of the two-dimensional confines of the page (and out of the clutches of a male author, albeit one with a genius for female dialogue) to experience the joys of the real world.

Bush's rewrite – painstaking as it was – is remarkably effective, and preserves the giddy sexuality of the original text as well as invoking Blake's 'Jerusalem' ("my arrows of desire rewrite the speech") to provide a decidedly post-modern comment on her own struggles to complete the song. 'The Sensual World' is the ultimate hymn of affirmation. The bells at the beginning are celebratory, a marriage or a rebirth is being announced, while the recurring echo of Molly's long, languorous 'Yesssss' – which Joyce referred to as 'the female word'* – is the perfect expression of Bush's ability to be directly erotic without being either crass or coy. With its talk of "wearing a sunset" and exalting the down of a peach (in *Ulysses* Molly describes the female sexual organs as 'soft like a peach'), the track is a stunning insight into the way Bush seeks to melt into the world of the senses. Art is fine, but nothing is quite as electrifying as simply *being*. And all this in a four-minute pop song.

The mood music surrounding the new material was obviously feminine. Now in her late twenties and having recognised some of the missteps of her past, Bush felt she had finally gained "power o'er a woman's body" and began to see the album as "a strong expression of positive female energy."[11] The lyrical themes followed suit: she said frequently that the

---

* The Trio Bulgarka's forenames, Yanka, Eva and Stoyanka, also spelt YES, Bush noted happily.

album was "all about relationships." This is the very loosest of loose definitions, but true in the sense that, if *The Sensual World* has any unifying theme, it is the intrinsic human need to connect to something or someone. The album consistently comes back to our desire for contact, which brings moments of joy, warmth and ecstasy, but also loneliness, uncertainty, sadness, pain, unresolved emotions and a striving for all the things we can never have. The need to touch and hold comes, inevitably, with a corresponding awareness of the transience of everything. "The older I get, the more I feel that this is what life is about," she said. "Letting go of all these things that you get caught up in."[12]

It was a bittersweet calling card. 'The Fog' swirls between childhood recollection and a very adult dilemma, a song about having the courage to leave the nest and swim alone into deep water, taking solace in the notion that pushing out from safe ground is usually far worse in thought than reality. On the beautiful 'Never Be Mine' she examines the perennial fight between dream and fantasy: the battle between reason and instinct, what we know to be true and what we feel, "the thrill and the hurting", is a recurring motif on the record. Bush is so good at this, capturing the way in which we are entrapped as well as set free – as on the title track – by the things we can't help but want to feel. And how vividly she conjures up the association of memory, the inescapable conspiracy of the senses which ensure that "the smell of burning fields will now mean you and here."

'Heads We're Dancing' is a dark little song about the masks we all wear and also place upon the faces of others, marking the distance between who we are and who we appear to be. Inspired by a family friend who had once – unknowingly – sat next to J. Robert Oppenheimer, the creator of the atomic bomb, and been charmed by this anonymous dinner guest, it told the (highly implausible, it must be said) story of a girl who had waltzed with Hitler in 1939 and found him perfectly alluring until she discovered in the next day's newspaper that she had effectively been dancing with the devil.

On 'Reaching Out' the child not only grasps for the hand that holds, but also the hand that scolds, and also the fire that burns. Every act has a consequence. The song also touches on one of her passions – gardening. "See how the flower leans instinctively towards the light," she sings. In her mind, music and horticulture seemed to share certain core characteristics. "I've planted a flower bed; you have to be very patient," she said. "And it's a good thing for me to work with, because making an album, you have to be very patient, and this flower bed helped me tremendously, to watch how things have to fight for space. You have to get the weeds out, a little bit of water every day, every day a little something."[13]

Patience was indeed required by all parties who claimed a stake in the album. Even compared to the more leisurely pace of music-making in the mid-to-late Eighties, *The Sensual World* took its time; the diehard loyalists at the Kate Bush Club Newsletter ceased trading as a point of protest until a new album was forthcoming, but still she would not be rushed. By the summer of 1988 most of the 10 tracks had been mixed by Julian Mendelssohn. EMI badly wanted product and suggested semi-publicly that the album might be released that autumn − a presumption which angered Bush, who knew that it wasn't ready. She had become so wrapped up in the largely isolated process of recording that in the summer of 1988 she called in Kevin Killen, the Irish engineer she had worked with previously at Windmill Lane and on 'Don't Give Up', and invited him to come and hear some of the mixes. She needed a fresh pair of ears.

They agreed that the mixes were technically excellent but also concurred that the songs and performances weren't yet finished. Therefore, a full 18 months into the recording of the album, a second wave of studio work started: lifting up the bonnet and getting into the nuts and bolts of the songs, adding, taking away, changing textures and tones, generally seeing what could be improved upon. Bush recorded some new vocals; David Gilmour came in with his box of tricks and added explosive guitar to 'Love And Anger' and 'Rocket's Tail'; John Giblin added his distinctive bass parts. By far the most radical addition to the album's overall sound palette, however, was the Trio Bulgarka.

Bush had already written 'Rocket's Tail' for them, a track built almost entirely around the voice and one for which she had conducted a dummy run in her studio, with some friends providing a block of shrieks and gargles to get a sense of "vocal intensity".[14] Ahead of her October trip to Sofia she faxed through the lyrics to the song, a preview which caused understandable bafflement within traditional Bulgarian musical circles. 'Rocket's Tail' describes a couple watching a firework display from Waterloo Bridge, one wishing that they were up there in the sky, experiencing a true, dangerous connection with the world, while the other at first sees only a "stick on fire, alone on its journey", but then changes her mind and – armed with a witch's hat, a silver suit, Size 5 boots and a gunpowder pack strapped to her back – transforms herself into a human rocket, "tail on fire".

Although named in good humour in honour of one of Bush's three new kittens (the others were Torchy and Sparky), brought into the fold after the death in 1987 of her beloved Zoodle, it was really a deeply symbolic song underscoring the necessity of taking risks, of being able to transcend the constraining pressures of both self and society to live in the moment of dangerous impulse and inspiration. It was an appropriately fearless song to send to Sofia as a statement of intent. If it summed up the spirit of the risky collaboration, it also worked as a standard bearer for Bush's general artistic ethos: don't be afraid to crash the rocket.

With this suitably eccentric warning flare lighting her path Bush, accompanied by Joe Boyd, flew to Bulgaria for a weekend in October 1988. It was an eventful few days. She was invited to dinner with the Trio on the first night and watched in astonishment as Eva picked up the phone in order to take her pitch from the dial tone, before the three women began to sing in perfect unison around the kitchen table. Not for the first time, she was almost immediately moved to tears.

But there was much hard work to be done. Translator and musician Borimira Nedeva drove Bush and Boyd around the city to various rendezvous in her tiny little car – at one point it broke down and Bush had to get out and push. It was another apt metaphor for an uphill struggle. The structure of Bush's songs and their detailed backing tracks could not be changed at this late stage. Meanwhile, the Trio's harmonies – though they might have appeared raw and spontaneous – were formal and meticulously planned. Between the Trio, Nedeva, arranger Dmitir Penev and Rumyana Tzintzarska, an ethnologist from the state radio station, it was a process of trial and error to find which of these centuries old melodies might best fit Bush's new songs, a case of trying to bend history, tradition and clashing cultures to suit a shared purpose.

"They spent two days in a school room with Kate and her beat box and a tape of the tracks," says Joe Boyd. "The ethnographer would suggest a folk melody that might work with a line of Kate's song, the arranger would come up with a harmony for it and Kate would say 'yes' or 'no'. All those harmonies are arranged, not spontaneous folk harmonies. They couldn't just play a part on the piano and sing it – the women could only perform if they could fit it into their experience of Bulgarian traditional music. Otherwise, they wouldn't have been able to sing in the 'open throat' style that Kate wanted."

At the end of the weekend little had been resolved in practical terms. "We didn't have any idea how we were going to do it!" laughs Nedeva. "The conclusion was that we *were* going to do it, that was probably the only certain thing." Bush had already booked time at Angel Studios, and the next step was to move the ensemble to London for recording. Bulgaria was still a Communist country (free elections did not take place until June 1990) with all the restraints that implies, and Boyd had already encountered difficulties in previous trips travelling to the remote villages in order to access music, because they were close to the border and required a special pass; he often had to keep quiet and pretend to be asleep as they approached. Getting the Trio and their entourage back to London at such short notice required similar acts of jiggery-pokery.

"At that time it wasn't easy to arrange things for foreigners in Bulgaria," says Nedeva. "The political climate was extremely difficult but I was in a very good position because my father was a high party member, and I managed to open a lot of closed doors. There weren't any [plane] tickets, and Kate had already booked a studio in London. I had some connections and I went to the main computer and put them in the list of the passengers, which obviously led to the plane being overloaded. They didn't know how this happened and they put on a second plane. It was crazy times, there was no other way but to go around the circumstances and do what you had to do. They all went on this plane, but I didn't because I got arrested! I went three days later, which wasn't too late, fortunately. Music is my life, and I was absolutely convinced that it was a group project that was going to work and deserved to be supported, so I would risk anything."

It was another example of the extraordinary loyalty Kate Bush and her music inspires, even among those who have only just met her. In this case, it was the establishing of a close human bond between the two sides that enabled the sessions to work. The party which finally arrived in London included the three singers, arranger Penev, and an official translator – Nelli Svetkova – who was effectively there as a state chaperone to ensure the women didn't defect; no one heard her speak a word of English

243

throughout the entire trip. It was Nedeva, when she arrived, who had the task of translating not just words but also musical ideas, emotions, delicate shifts of emphasis. She felt, she said, "like a live electric wire, high voltage currents running back and forth. I had to shoot words back and forth and see how they react and try to see what's good and try to promote it. Because sometimes Kate didn't know what she wanted."

Fortunately, Bush and the Trio immediately formed a sisterly bond ("She's modest, with a very big heart," said Yanka[15]) and recognised a shared instinct for what they were doing, communicating largely through the use of smiles, hugs and sign language. "They were so emotionally on the same wavelength, there wasn't much need for words except where there was a specific thing that Kate wanted them to do," says Nedeva. Bush defined the experience as "extraordinary. They didn't speak a word of English and we didn't speak any Bulgarian, but we could communicate through music, so that absolutely transcended barriers. There were things we needed to translate but, generally, we communicated emotionally, and I just loved that. . . . They'll just come up and touch you and cuddle you, and you can go up and give them a big cuddle, and I really enjoyed that kind of communication, it felt very real and direct to me."[16]

Nonetheless, the few days of sessions at Angel Studios were long and hard, typically stretching from late morning until almost midnight. On Boyd's advice Bush placed the Trio around a single ambient microphone and, having only scratched the surface in Sofia, most of the experimenting was done in the studio, Penev suggesting arrangements of folk tunes and Bush either agreeing or hinting that they might try something else. For 'Rocket's Tail', the most complex track, Penev's prepared arrangement combining several traditional 'Shop' songs rather miraculously succeeded in fitting Bush's densely layered opus. Towards the end, however, something extraordinary occurred. Yanka, the de facto leader and a strong, glamorous, imposing presence, reacted to a translated suggestion from Bush by improvising a hair-raising polyphonic solo – *i-i-iiiiii* – which mimics the explosion and flight of the rocket, triggered by David Gilmour's solo.

It worked purely on emotion: the Trio didn't know what any of the songs were about, and the words they sang ("Darling Mando, beautiful girl") were in no way connected to Bush's lyrics, but the effect was stunning. Such a freewheeling approach to Bulgarian traditional music was very unusual, and the approach to 'Rocket's Tail' shifted the emphasis of the session. "After Yanka's solo everything else was mostly improvisations," says Nedeva. "We found out that this is a better way of working, even though it takes a lot of studio time. When you have a good leader like Yanka, and she starts singing something they don't know, they can just start singing along and they make perfect harmony. They have this feeling for each other, they are tuned to each other, it's some amazing inner feeling."

The next track, 'Deeper Understanding', was an astonishingly prescient pre-internet tale of how obsessive computer love engenders a breakdown of communities and families, leading the protagonist to an isolated state where she turns to a machine for solace and interaction. It's both desperately poignant and yet strangely touching, that amidst such a bleak and lonely existence she still craves emotional connection. "I suppose I liked the idea of deep, spiritual communication . . . coming from the last place you'd expect it to, the coldest piece of machinery," she said. "And yet I do feel there is a link. I do feel that, in some ways, computers could take us into a level of looking at ourselves that we've never seen before."[17]

This was crystal ball stuff. She had toyed with using vocoders and other synthetic special FX to vocalise the computer, but the idea of using instead the raw, human voices of the Trio was inspired, imbuing a song about emotional estrangement with a spiritual, otherworldly dimension. The lack of literal understanding between the two groups – the Trio were simply told to communicate a feeling of despair, while Bush had no idea what they were singing – works perfectly in the context of a song where humans and machines don't understand each other yet can still find an underlying connection and, improbably, salvage some comfort.

On the third song, 'Never Be Mine', the clashing styles and harmonies underscored the divergence of purpose and conflicted feelings at the heart of the lyric. However, by now the newly liberated Trio were also poking a little good-natured fun at their esteemed arranger. When Bush sings "This is what I want to be, this is where I want to be", the Bulgarians are singing "Mite, Mite, I am not going to ask you". It was a sly declaration of artistic freedom: 'Mite' was Penev's nickname. While Bush gained much from the collaboration, it was a mutually nourishing relationship – she in turn freed something in the Trio. "It had a great impact on Yanka," says Nedeva. "Before that she was more confined to the normal ways of doing things, but she took in this creative spark. I think the arranger was a bit put out that his final input maybe wasn't as much as he wanted. He expressed disappointment about that in a private conversation. He was sulking a bit!" In truth, Penev did a fine job in exceptional circumstances, and Bush had nothing but praise for all his efforts.

It was a highly charged few days, exhausting, emotionally draining and yet hugely rewarding. To compound the pressure, a BBC crew popped in to interview Bush and film her singing with the Trio – a brief piece of film which captures beautifully the bond between the four women – for the *Rhythms Of The World* series on global music, which aired in March 1989. But nobody forgot the deep, shared love of music that had brought this improbable ensemble together in the first place. During a rare break towards the end of the session, sitting around the studio in a semi-circle, the Trio instinctively broke into a series of ancient Bulgarian love songs. Everyone present – Bush, Paddy, engineer Kevin Killen – promptly burst into tears. Again.

In the end the Trio's contribution was by far the most discussed and lauded aspect of the record. It added a thrilling extra dimension, although those with a close affinity to Bulgarian music – including Nedeva and Boyd – felt that at times, particularly on 'Rocket's Tail', there may have been too much going on to convey the music at its best. "Kate got to realise her vision," says Boyd. "Personally, I like to hear those harmonies in a big, open a cappella space, so they sound a bit smaller than I'm used to when blended with a modern mix with lots of instruments. But I was pleased with the project and full of admiration for Kate's skill as a producer."

* * *

Editing and mixing continued until May 1989, including a session recording string overdubs with Michael Kamen at Abbey Road. To accommodate the CD and cassette market, a bonus track was added right at the end of the process. 'Walk Straight Down The Middle' sprung to life from an old backing track, originally intended as a B-side, which was rapidly dusted down for action. Bush wrote the lyrics and recorded the vocals and synth overdubs in a single day, using the next day for final overdubs and mixing. The track, finished in just over 24 hours, put the seal on a gruelling four year process.

The Sensual World was released on October 16, 1989, just as the leaves were turning gold, preceded by the title track as a single, which entered the charts at number 12.*

'The Sensual World' was a marvellous song but it was no 'Running Up That Hill', not the kind of track that demanded radio play and propelled the album forwards. The single, highly praised, dropped immediately down the charts, while the following pair – 'This Woman's Work' and 'Love And Anger' – barely scraped into the Top 30 and 40 respectively. The album quickly reached number two on the UK album charts and sold well, achieving Gold status (over 500,000 sales) in the US and multi-platinum status (over a million sales) in the UK, but success is about more than facts and figures; it is also about perception.

The album reviews were generally strong, though many contained a ghostly subtext of minor disappointment, a lurking sense of feeling somewhat underwhelmed which was given full vent when the later single releases attracted some highly uncomplimentary comments, as if many of these songs sounded unconvincing stripped from their context – a harsh but not unreasonable viewpoint. Bush dramatically scaled down her promotional activities. TV performances were scarce, there were no personal appearances at all and interviews were generally conducted at discreetly plush London hotels or recording studios. The media were kept at arm's length and given little access to her world, while almost every interview followed a well travelled path; guarded and measured to the point of dullness, which presumably was the point.

She held round table briefings at a hotel in Kent with 40 overseas

---

* The 12-inch had a double grooved A-side which, depending on where you placed the needle, would either play the vocal version or the instrumental. "She didn't tell the record company," recalls her mastering engineer Ian Cooper. "They pressed them all up and they were getting quite a few returns, people complaining that the vocals had disappeared. She just did it for a laugh, and it worked. Eventually, EMI had to put a sticker on it." Bush would often push EMI's patience to the limits when it came to ensuring the quality of her records at the crucial mastering stage. "She would always get EMI to do test pressings, and check them out, and if they weren't good enough they'd get rejected and remastered, and told to do a better job next time. EMI never learned their lesson that this was a woman who would check everything."

journalists, at which 15 paltry minutes were parcelled out to each party with Del hovering in the background, but eventually she relented to a brief promotional visit to US in January 1990. She had signed to Columbia in America, something which EMI's Brian Southall "never understood – she should have gone to somewhere like Geffen. Small, bespoke. [With CBS] she was just another act signed to a big record company." In the end, the switch made little material difference to her Stateside fortunes. 'Love And Anger' was a college radio hit, achieved a degree of MTV interest and reached number one on the *Billboard* Modern Rock Tracks chart, while the album peaked at 43 on the *Billboard* chart and received a Grammy nomination for Best Alternative Album. Respectable showings, but by no means a breakthrough. She had not escaped her niche as an alternative, marginal act. There's no suggestion that she ever really wanted to.

In the UK, radio exposure was muted. One of the problems of taking so long to make a record was that world moved on inexorably. Bush emerged from the studio to find a host of 'new Kate Bushes' – Sinead O'Connor, Bjork, Enya, Suzanne Vega, Jane Siberry – making 'quirky' music; Bulgarian folk had become this year's hip world music hobby horse while, at a time when the Madchester scene, house music and rave were at the vanguard and people were making highly sophisticated sounding records with the most basic of equipment, she was certainly no longer working at the cutting edge of technology. In a world where U2's unsubtle Americana shtick ruled the earth, and where Stock, Aitken & Waterman's pop factory ruled the charts, Bush was listening to Jeff Beck and John Lydon and declared herself largely "in mourning" for good new music.[18]

She was now a thirty-something member of the art-rock establishment, rather than a thrusting young pop star. She had never been one for following trends, or even being aware of them, but with *The Dreaming* and *Hounds Of Love* she had established herself as a pioneer. *The Sensual World* did little to advance that reputation. It is a fine album, with several moments of breathtaking beauty which tend to obscure some of its failings, but it lacks the imprimatur of wild, unbridled adventurousness that marks out her finest music. It smoulders at a much lower heat than the fireworks of *Hounds Of Love* and the musical colours are generally more muted, decidedly autumnal, deliberately avoiding the elemental power of her previous album. "[It] had a male energy, but I didn't want to do that on this album," she said.[19] Rhythm was far less emphasised – even on a song like 'Heads We're Dancing', which is heavily in thrall to the Prince of *Parade* and *Sign O' The Times*, the rhythm track is sparse and mechanical, in no way overpowering.

The downside of this approach was that, aside from the riotous invention of 'Rocket's Tail', there was a certain reined-in conventionality about the musical settings, a uniformity of pace, less leaps through time and space in her lyrics, and the occasional sense of someone trying to bully good-but-not-great material into shape. 'Between A Man And A Woman' expresses a fateful view of romantic relationships – "let the pendulum swing" – and holds to a course that outside interference in these matters can be destructive. Hardly an original thought, and one that makes for a remarkably dull song. 'Heads We're Dancing' is an interesting idea, but clunkily told over an unappealing melody. 'Love And Anger' sounds like a rather less successful version of 'The Big Sky', that other troublesome album track, starting small and ending in a riot of clattering rhythm.

There's a distinct lack of clarity to the production – overly compressed, the voice in particular sounding uncomfortably squeezed. Bush later came to this realisation herself, returning to four of the songs for *Director's Cut* with the intention of cracking them open and allowing them to breathe more easily. She called it her most honest, most personal album, but it frequently sounded cold and a little remote. It's not the most tactile record. Ironically, aside from the title track, another unimpeachable highlight, the sensuality of *The Sensual World* largely has to be imagined rather than felt.

★ ★ ★

With the benefit of hindsight, it's clear that something fundamental changed with Bush's sixth album. There is an audible slackening of intensity which betrayed a conscious re-ordering of her priorities. Henceforth, quality of life would take precedence. "It's not everything now," she said of her music shortly after it came out. "I think at some point it was – my work was everything because it had such a sense of importance about it. That's so stupid, so blown out of proportion, and if you're not careful that spiralling effect can make you believe what you're doing is the most important thing in the world! Ha! When it's absolutely not at all."[20]

Of course, she had blazed through her twenties in the manner of someone who very firmly *did* believe that her work was all-consuming and of primary importance in her life, even if the attention it brought her was usually entirely unwelcome. Now, she was forced by a series of tragic events into recognising that music couldn't always come first.

The period between *The Sensual World* and *The Red Shoes*, and for a spell thereafter, was by far the most challenging of her life. The first portent arrived almost immediately: on October 19, 1989, just days after the new album was released, her guitarist of ten years, Alan Murphy, died of pneumonia in Westminster City Hospital, fatally weakened by the AIDS virus. He was just 35 and, though visibly ailing, had kept the nature and seriousness of his disease largely secret. "I cried my eyes out," says Brian Bath. "I read it on the front of the *Daily Mirror*: 'Kate Bush guitarist . . .' I phoned up Paddy, it was such a shock. What a player."

As he had on Bush's previous three records, Murphy had added his guitar to *The Sensual World*, although the last ever song he played on was her cover of 'Rocket Man', recorded just after the album was finished in June 1989 for an album called *Two Rooms*, a tribute to the work of Elton John and Bernie Taupin. John was one of Bush's favourite artists from her teenage years – "When I asked to be involved in this project and was given the choice of a track it was like being asked 'Would you like to fulfil a dream?'" she said[21] – and she took due care over 'Rocket Man', giving it a lilting treatment which divided opinion (the group St Etienne, reviewing it collectively for *NME*, declared that it made them want to vomit; in 2007 the *Observer Music Monthly* voted it the best cover version of all time) but was both bold and quietly moving, somehow combining uillean pipes and a reggae beat without scaring the horses. The public vote hoisted it to number 12 in the charts when it was issued as single in late 1991 to coincide with the release of *Two Rooms*, with her unremarkable, indeed rather cloying, version of 'Candle In The Wind' on the B-side.

Bush performed 'Rocket Man' on the *Wogan* show (virtually the only TV show she regularly consented to perform on, not least because it was a favourite of her mother, Hannah) in December of that year, one of her most stunning television appearances. Looking dark and rapturous in a knee-length skirt, she revisited the theme of the video, strumming a ukulele in a subtle homage to Marilyn Monroe in *Some Like It Hot*; an electric guitar sat on a chair towards the back of the stage in silent and poignant tribute to Murphy.

She later recorded 'The Man I Love' for a 1994 album, *The Glory Of Gershwin*, a celebration of the eightieth birthday of the venerable harmonica specialist Larry Adler, produced by George Martin at Abbey Road. Her sighing, sensuous reading of the standard struck just the right note of wishful projection into a longed-for future – "Someday he'll come along . . ." – reinventing Bush for four minutes as a trembling torch singer. It was a side that some of those closest to her career had long encouraged her to show.

"I always wanted her to do an album of covers," says Bob Mercer. "She did 'Rocket Man', which was excellent, and she did a Gershwin thing, and it's fucking *wonderful*, and that's exactly what I was saying to her at the time: 'I would love you to do covers because I don't think people understand how good your voice is.' Her voice was so much a part of her writing that the two just went together; you always got the feeling that she somehow had a peculiar voice, and I wanted people to understand that she really could fucking sing, and to do that you kind of need to say, 'You've heard this song a million times, now listen to her sing it.' But we never did that. I don't think she really had any enthusiasm for it, she just went along with the conversation because it was silly old Uncle Bob sounding off. She got a bit pissed at me for going on about it, because the implication in her mind was that I didn't think her writing was quite up to par, which wasn't right at all."

Following Murphy's premature death, another grim blow followed. One of her two long-standing dance partners, Gary Hurst, also died as a result of AIDS in 1990, again at a heartbreakingly young age. With their passing came a sense of a chapter closing, underscored by the dawning of a new decade and capped by the release in October 1990 of the vast, eight-disc retrospective box-set *This Woman's Work*, which included all six of her previous albums as well as two discs of B-sides and rarities.

"I feel the box-set marks the end of an era because I'll never work with [Alan and Gary] again," she said. "And I do miss them, and it's made me think about a lot of things, and I have consciously taken a break from work since their deaths to do nothing. I've just taken six months off. I've had six months gaps between things, but always carrying this project around, and I don't know why I haven't done it before. I'm a bit obsessive about my work you see. But now I can see there's a part of me that loves not being tied into a project, that loves just to be able to go off."[22]

When she did finally begin writing material for *The Red Shoes* in the middle of 1990, she was determined to "go back to a rooted way of working"[23], returning more frequently to the piano, physically playing the song over and over, kneading it into shape. She expressed concerns about her music being "too complicated for people to take in – that they have to work too hard at it.[24] Ideally I would like the music to be an easy experience."[25] Like many artists before and since, after the first flush of wild adventure has passed through her work, Bush began to seek a greater, hopefully more profound simplicity in both her words and her music. This wasn't a commercial aspiration, more a worry that she wasn't communicating as well as she might, or really getting to grips with what was happening in her own life.

Perhaps as a result, she seemed to crave direct contact, something more spontaneous, a positive outlet for all that negative energy. She talked, intriguingly, of becoming more comfortable being "the observed" rather than the observer.[26] At the fan convention in late 1990 she announced that the new songs were leading her in a direction that suggested – "*if* circumstances allow," she hedged, "*If* things go well"[27] – that she would be playing live the following year, which was also, she hoped, when the new album would be released.

"The idea of this album was to get it recorded quickly and get out on the road with it," said Del Palmer. "It didn't work out that way, but the idea did influence the way the album was put together."[28] The initial plan to make a relatively uncomplicated record was a good one but, as Palmer suggests, it proved unsustainable.

For the first time in many years, the songs were often built upon the sound of a bass player (John Giblin) and drummer (Stuart Elliott) playing together in the same room, giving the songs a live feel. Some of that spontaneous punch is preserved on the record. The title track whipped itself up into an appealing frenzy, 'Big Stripey Lie' was engagingly odd if ultimately unconvincing, while 'Constellation Of The Heart' featured some of Bush's most labyrinthine vocal arrangements, a maze of syntax-snapping call and response trade-offs between Bush and Paddy and Colin Lloyd-Tucker.

"We were in hysterics with all that question and answer business," says

Lloyd-Tucker. "It's difficult to imagine now, but we'd never heard it until we walked into the room. She was singing us all these answer lines, and we were like, 'Hang on a minute, what was *that*?' We were literally sliding down the walls by the end of the session. Working with her is quite tough. Every syllable had to be bang in time, she's a perfectionist, which is great, it gets results. When you're working with her she's incredibly professional. She's very relaxed, but she wants to get the job done and you work hard."

At some point, however, Bush seemed unable to distinguish between what a song needed and what it could live without. 'Why Should I Love You?' tends to sum up the problems that afflict *The Red Shoes*. The demo is simple and moving, a beautiful mixture of voice, organ and rhythm. The song as it appears on the album, however, is wildly overloaded, a hellish broth featuring the attentions of Prince, the Trio Bulgarka, Lenny Henry, a trombone and a flugelhorn, all seemingly straining in different directions. It's a mess, and a shameful waste of what could have been a truly inspirational collaboration.

Bush and Prince had been edging closer for years. In many ways they were remarkably similar artists: relentlessly mythologised, very private, undeniably eccentric with a dry, quirky sense of humour, obsessed with control and displaying an inventiveness that was often misunderstood and sometimes ridiculed. After Bush turned up at one of his 1990 Wembley shows they had communicated with an eye on a collaboration, and in 1991 Bush sent him the multi-track tape of 'Why Should I Love You?' In the words of Del Palmer, it returned "from . . . Paisley Park studio covered in vocals, guitar solos and keyboards."[29] Prince's engineer, Michael Koppelman, was less diplomatic, calling his contribution "lame disco".[30] It was certainly wildly over-the-top and unrestrained, and it took Bush and Palmer a further two years to negotiate his maze of overdubs and retain some sense of the original track, eventually retaining only lead guitar, synths and chorus vocals. If it had been anyone other than Prince, you suspect, Bush would have ditched his contributions entirely.

'And So Is Love' fell foul of a similar problem. At heart a simple, brooding minor key pop song, it's dogged by a terribly mainstream, Americanised arrangement which attempts to combine the trademark blues guitar of Eric Clapton – in itself a distressingly conventional sound to hear on a Bush record – with an irritating synthetic keyboard effect. These identity crises happened all over the album, sounds and styles constantly bumping awkwardly into one another, with little attempt to find their common ground. The Trio Bulgarka, likewise, are used on three songs in a manner which largely renders their contribution a shadow of what it had been on *The Sensual World*.

She had other, more important things on her mind. The process of making *The Red Shoes* was completely overshadowed by the serious illness of her mother. After Bush had performed 'Rocket Man' on *Wogan* on December 16, 1991, the host, Terry Wogan, had sent a greeting to Hannah, and added a 'get well soon' message. She died just two months later, on February 14, 1992, succumbing to cancer aged 73. Roy Harper sang the traditional Irish song 'The Lark In The Morning' at her funeral. Everyone was crushed, especially her daughter, who said it felt "like the end of the world."[31]

"It obviously devastated her, though I don't think she let on how much," recalls Stewart Avon Arnold. Her passing not only left a gaping hole at the very heart of the Bush family, but also in the working and domestic environment of Wickham Farm, in which Hannah had been the centrifugal life force for so many years. "Suddenly she just wasn't around," says Charlie Morgan. "And she had *always* been around."

Bush's instincts would normally have told her to push on through a crisis. This time it proved impossible. "Usually I can pull myself through things like feeling low or having problems . . . but I have been at points where I just couldn't work," she said. "I couldn't possibly sing – it was beyond me, it just hurt too much. . . . I think that the biggest thing that happened on this album is that my mother died. I couldn't work for months, I couldn't go near the whole process. I had no desire to start, no desire to work at all."[32]

Somehow the album sessions eventually had to go on. Hannah's death was too cataclysmic to be digested straight away or directed into the music, but – coming on the back of a period of loss, and a certain confusion about how the record should sound – the impact can be felt throughout the album, which is both pensive, painful and unfocused. "I haven't been able to write about any of it – nevertheless the experience is there . . . being expressed through very subliminal things, like the quality of some of the performances," she said, very honestly.[33]

'Rubberband Girl' is a deceptively jaunty sounding opener, twanging away on a single note, its raw, repetitive groove betraying the fact that it was written quickly in the studio. "When we arrived to do 'The Red Shoes', the night before she'd been up doing 'Rubberband Girl'," recalls Colin Lloyd-Tucker. "It was very rough, hardly anything on it with just a guide vocal. She was still working out the lyrics – she had a verse, which she kept repeating on the rough version, and said she was going to write the words later."

The song is a brave attempt but ultimately a futile gesture. This is the album where Bush does not bounce back. In a sense, she spent her first couple of albums as little more than a girl trying on the clothes of a woman. On *The Red Shoes*, she sounds like a woman trying desperately, and in vain, to cling onto her sense of hope and innocent wonder. "When you lose your mother, you're no longer a little girl any more," she said.[34]

The songs are full of doubt, literally full of questions. Lyrically, the listener can take their pick of lines that might stand as manifestos for the way she was feeling: "We used to say, 'Ah hell we're young', but now we see that life is sad," she sings on 'And So Is Love', in a thought borrowed from Joseph Campbell, the American writer and mythologist and author of *The Masks Of God*. On 'Lily' she even consults her – real life – healer, Lily Cornford, of London's Maitreya School of Healing, about what to do, because "life has blown a great big hole through me." *The Red Shoes* describes a world defined by absences "Life is loss, isn't it?" she mused. "It's learning to cope with loss."[35]

"Just being alive it can really hurt," is the killer line from 'Moments Of Pleasure', which recalls fleeting times of past happiness while commemorating a sadly growing list of departed friends: her aunt Maureen, Alan Murphy (Smurph) and Gary Hurst (Bubba), Bill Duffield, not forgotten after all these years, and John Barratt (nicknamed 'Teddy', from the children's show *Andy Pandy*: Bush was 'Loopy Lou' and Jon Kelly 'Andy'), the assistant engineer on *Never For Ever* and *The Dreaming* who would enthusiastically join in the game of spinning round and round in the control room chair at Abbey Road.

Michael Powell is also name-checked, the renowned British film director who had worked with Hitchcock and, in 1948, made one of Bush's favourite films, *The Red Shoes*, taken from the Hans Christian Andersen fairy tale in which a ballerina cannot stop dancing. The film inspired the album's title track and was also a direct influence on Bush's own short film,

The Line, The Cross And The Curve, which she made immediately after finishing the record. She had contacted Powell not long before he died to see whether he'd be interested in working with her, which sparked a short but intense long–distance friendship. While on a visit to New York in the late spring of 1989 to discuss a different master of *The Sensual World* by Bob Ludwig for the American market, and also to talk tactics with her new record label Columbia, she had met the aged director at the Royalton Hotel during an unseasonal blizzard. Their encounter is recalled in the second verse; he was 84 and already frail, and within a year he too was dead. Although it was recorded in mid-1991 and finished long before her death, Hannah also appears in the song, dispensing one of her stock phrases, "Every old sock meets an old shoe". Prior to the album's release, Bush previewed the song on the *Aspel & Company* talk show on June 20, 1993, on what would have been Hannah's seventy-fifth birthday.

In other ways, too, *The Red Shoes* has all the ache of letting go. In Alan Murphy's absence Danny McIntosh came in to play guitar. A member of the Seventies rock band Bandit, with future Eighties pop star Jim Diamond on lead vocals, McIntosh went on to play in Grand Hotel, a band which featured Ivan Penfold, an old friend of Del and Brian Bath who had played in their pre-KT Bush Band group Conkers and whom Bush had mentored briefly as a writer, playing piano on a couple of his songs. McIntosh had had prior contact with many of those in Bush's orbit, which may have been the reason he was invited to play on the album. "[Danny] reputedly taught Alan Murphy all his stuff," says Bath. "Great player."

His arrival was noteworthy in more ways than one. It coincided with another highly significant change in Bush's life, for it was during the sessions for *The Red Shoes* and the filming that took place immediately afterwards that her 15-year romantic relationship with Del Palmer came to an amicable close. Soon after she began dating McIntosh, who remains her partner today and is the father to their son, Bertie.

The break–up was not, as you would expect, conducted publicly. She dealt with it privately, as she had done with her mother's death. Because of the close working proximity of all parties, however, her friends and colleagues were of course aware that *something* was afoot regarding her relationship with Del. But what exactly? It was a confusing time for everyone. In addition to Hannah's death, the album was proving problematic and she appeared to be bouncing between splitting up with Palmer, getting back together with him, then splitting up again. That it wasn't the happiest or most stable period of her life was obvious to those around her. Nevertheless, when she finally ended up with McIntosh it came as a surprise to many of her friends.

"I didn't see anything that I thought, 'Oh, they're going out together,'" says Stewart Avon Arnold. "We did talk a lot, me and Danny, on the set, but to me he was just a professional musician until some time later they were going out – officially."

In retrospect, Del's description of Bush playing guitar – for the first and only time on record – on 'Big Stripey Lie' appears full of portents of what was to come. "She said to the guitarist we were using [McIntosh], 'I'm really into the guitar, I'd really like to be able to play it'. And he said, 'Oh, here, play this one (a Fender Stratocaster) for a bit.' So, he showed her a few chords, and – this is no kidding – a week later she was in front of this Marshall stack in the studio giving it her all! I've never seen anything like it. She's a natural. She was playing lead guitar and no one would know it wasn't an experienced guitarist."[36]

Whatever seismic changes were occurring in private, in public Del remained very much on the scene. When *The Line, The Cross And The Curve* premiered in November 1993, Bush attended with Del and her father. When she flew to New York shortly afterwards for a short round of promotion, Del went with her. At the fan convention later in 1994, Del was there (as was Bush, briefly), helping to auction items. Despite the final parting of the ways romantically they managed to retain their close friendship and Del has remained her engineer, her most trusted voice in the studio. He later moved to Reading, near Bush's current home, and all parties seem to have reached a very civilised accommodation.

"Every time I went round to teach her classes Del would be there working in the studio and Danny would be there working in the house," says Stewart Avon Arnold. "If [Danny] wasn't playing he'd be doing housework or saying, 'Kate we've got to go and do this this afternoon.' When we'd come back in from the workout, sometimes all four of us would be sitting around drinking [tea]. It's quite bizarre, really, but then Del has been very much a part of Kate's life since she was a teenager."

It's impossible to listen to the album's closing track, 'You're The One', and not hear it as a troubled attempt to reconcile an inevitable but deeply hurtful ending. "Everything I have I bought with you," she sings. "Everything I do we did together." Perhaps tellingly, McIntosh doesn't play on the track; Jeff Beck does, as does Gary Brooker, Procol Harum's former keyboard player, a further example of the album's tendency towards celebrity cameos. It's only a shame that 'You're The One' is so stodgy, an unconventional Bush song only in the sense that it's so entirely conventional, a thudding, ponderous rock ballad with an artless, heart-on-sleeve lyric, the kind of apparently unvarnished autobiography we perhaps thought we always wanted to hear from her. When it finally arrived it was clumsy and clunky, the bald words actually getting in the way of the emotion. Banal, almost, although it is the one track where the Trio Bulgarka really shine.

The Red Shoes is the first time that clichés – both lyrical and musical – begin to appear in her writing. It's interesting how much of a struggle her quest for greater directness became. Spelling out what she was once able to suggest and imply, the net results were a significant drop in artistry. As a lyricist, Bush is by no means beyond reproach. She's most assured when showing rather than telling; she does not have an easy, natural gift for the vernacular or conversational in the way that someone like Joni Mitchell does. Even the fun, fleshy eroticism of 'Eat The Music' – in which Bush truly makes a meal of her "food of love" metaphors – is laboured and obvious, as is the similarly themed inner album artwork, in which soft fruit is sliced open and displayed, labia-like, filled with seed. In her quest for direct communication, everything becomes overstated.

Much of the music has a similar, uncomfortably forced quality to it, as though, in the phrase that Bob Dylan once used to describe his own creative travails in the Seventies, she "had to learn to do consciously what [she] used to do unconsciously." Listen hard and one can hear her physically trying to summon up the inspiration; very little appears to be coming through naturally. Struggling to adapt and shape real life into song, for once she failed to make a glorious artifice out of her art. She does not transcend.

Instead, the results were solid but a tad uninspired. In these versions at least, 'Top Of The City' and 'The Song Of Solomon' leaned perilously close to sanitised background music. Their true potential would be partially unmasked on *Director's Cut*, while the former was given a revelatory makeover in 'Before The Dawn', but for now their flatness seemed symptomatic of a wider loss of focus. The doubts in Bush's mind and music were shared by those old chums working on the record. "It was a very difficult time and I was aware of that more than anything," says Haydn Bendall. "Because of that I didn't really connect with her that much. It was a bit of a mess, to be honest. I was sort of half-booked through a third party to do some work on it. Del was there and he was engineering and needed to assert himself in a way, I think there was some personal stuff going on that I don't really want to go into [but] that I was aware of. I was kind of on the periphery a bit, I wasn't terribly involved. It was just a weird, fractious, fragmented time, and nothing really seemed to gel. I didn't really understand why I was there. I just tried to be as diplomatic as possible."

The Red Shoes marked a move from analogue to digital recording, and it all ended up sounding rather tinny, not at all deep or warm. Del oversaw the mix as Bush began dance practice in preparation for the film, and right up until the final mastering sessions she seemed uncharacteristically unsure of her own judgement. "*The Red Shoes* was one of the very first albums I did at Metropolis Mastering," recalls Ian Cooper. "After it was done she essentially said it was OK and myself and Del Palmer couldn't believe it. He said, 'I think we'd better do it again, because I can't believe she's approved it. That's a first!' So we redid it and changed it a little bit, which is the way it went out."

The Red Shoes is nowadays often dismissed as the runt of the Bush litter, but it was by no means a catastrophe. It sold well, reaching number 28 in the US, her highest ever position, although all the UK singles bar 'Rubberband Girl' struggled to make much impact, while the album suffered the ignominy of being beaten to number one by Meat Loaf. Many of the reviews, however, were positively gushing, falling into the trap of writing what they thought they were supposed to think about a new Kate Bush record, rather than what they were actually hearing. Chris Roberts' review in *Melody Maker* – "Bush in on form like the Bible is well-known. *The Red Shoes* dances so far ahead of the rest it's embarrassing" – was a memorable case of expressing a laudable sentiment at precisely the wrong time. Stephen Dalton in *Vox* was much more perceptive, concluding that the album "adds up to less than the sum of its unorthodox parts." Several reviewers echoed Colin Irwin's observation that the album displayed a "firmament of distress."[37]

The release was held back until November to accommodate the completion of the 45-minute film Bush had resolved to make. Until midway through the album process Bush was still talking about the possibility, indeed the likelihood, of doing a tour, or at least some shows. She eventually decided against it, for any of the reasons already discussed, though it's possible Hannah's death knocked any remaining enthusiasm out of her.

She decided instead to make a film featuring six songs from the album linked by a narrative thread, starring the actress Miranda Richardson, her old friend and mentor Lindsay Kemp, Stewart Avon Arnold and most of the musicians who appeared on the record. Filming began in July 1993 with a planned finishing date in mid-August, in order to get the performance segments finished and readied for video release to support the singles.*

A film in which she would sing, dance, act, write the script, direct and generally hold sway over every creative decision appeared to be an insane undertaking at this stage in her life. Throwing herself into the movie may have seemed like a necessary distraction from other, more pressing issues, but it was clear she struggled to successfully focus her concentration on the project. On reflection, it was the worst of all possible times to embark on such a challenging new endeavour.

"If I remember rightly, she wasn't feeling that great," says Colin Lloyd-Tucker. "She had headaches and things, she wasn't really herself when we were making that. There was her mother, which had a big affect, and I think maybe she bit off a little bit more than she could chew. I remember a lot of times we had to keep stopping because she wasn't feeling that great. It was a difficult thing to do, that kind of format, and she took it all on herself – no wonder she had a headache! That was hard work again, because it was that perfectionist thing and she wouldn't give up. It was a difficult period."

"Directing it exhausted her completely," recalls Stewart Avon Arnold. "The next one down from the 'Tour Of Life' is *The Line, The Cross And The Curve*, in terms of the length of time of the project. She was exhausted after that."

---

* This proved impossible, and Bush had to hastily shoot extra performance footage for the 'Rubberband Girl' video, the first single, released in early September.

After a lot of long, hard days and gruelling nights, the film was finished by early November, presented to EMI on the tenth and screened at the London Film Festival on the thirteenth, an event which sold out in ten minutes and which she attended with Del, Dr Bush and the film's producer, Margarita Doyle. Gazing up at the vast 60ft screen at the Odeon on Leicester Square, the Bush party nervously sat through the support film, Wallace and Gromit in *The Wrong Trousers*, wondering how *The Line, The Cross And The Curve* would fare by comparison. The screening – dotted with Bush fanatics – went well, and at the end she gave a brief but graceful speech following a very generous standing ovation.

It was perhaps the kindest review the film received. It toured several other city film festivals in Europe, the US and Canada through late 1993 and into early 1994 and enjoyed a brief cinematic release before coming out on video. It even received a Grammy nomination in 1995 for Best Music Video: Long Form – Bush didn't attend, being a fan of neither awards nor Los Angeles – but the critical reception ranged from lukewarm to hostile. "High on whimsy, low on content," said *Variety*, while *Q* deemed it "not so much a movie as the sort of linked sequence of promo vids that pop stars are wont to hang themselves with, given a feature length rope."

Bush herself quickly distanced herself from the film. As early as April 1994, while ostensibly promoting it, she admitted she had taken on too much. Later, she was less measured. "I shouldn't have done it. I was so tired. I'm very pleased with four minutes of it, but I'm very disappointed with the rest. I let down people like Miranda Richardson who worked so hard on it. I had the opportunity to do something really interesting and I completely blew it."[38] Later still, in 2005, she simply dismissed it as "a load of bollocks."[39]

Shortly after the premiere, Bush – again, accompanied by Palmer – flew to New York for a round of promotional appearances. Most notable was a signing session at Tower records, where she arrived in a white limousine and stayed for over three hours as the enormous queue slowly drained into the building, and an odd, rather out-of-it interview with JBTV, a small Chicago based station. Sporting big brown shades and clearly wishing herself anywhere else but here, her utter exhaustion is almost painful to behold. On her return, slowly the brakes were applied and the shutters came up. She hadn't had time to properly grieve her mother, nor absorb all the other changes she had undergone in the past few years. "I needed to stop working because there were a lot of things I wanted to look at in my life," she said. "I was exhausted on every level."[40] Bush, that most magnificently airborne of artists, had slowly lost altitude. She had run herself and her music into the ground.

11

An Architect's Dream

PRIOR to 'Before The Dawn', with its ambitious blend of film and theatre, *The Line, The Cross And The Curve* was Bush's last significant visual statement. It was the logical, if not wholly satisfactory destination of a journey that began in early 1978 on a grey, misty Salisbury Plain – a rather drab approximation of wild northern moorland – with Bush leaping through the undergrowth wearing a fiery red dress and a rather startled expression that at times looked something like embarrassment. The contrast between the first 'Wuthering Heights' video and Bush's lavish mini-film of 1993 could hardly have been more pronounced, excepting the fact that, as Brian Southall drily points out, Bush's earliest promo clip also "got an awful lot of bad publicity".

Her earliest videos can be viewed with a certain fond indulgence. Open, odd, naïve, capturing a disarming innocence that may not be quite what it seems, they are primarily filmed pieces of dramatised choreography, a diaphanous legacy of what she had learned from her mentors in mime and her teachers at the Dance Centre, caught somewhere between sensuality and acute silliness and unlike anything captured on film before or since.

They are small, idiosyncratic baby steps that later caused her to wince a little, but they are still amazingly compelling, simply because she is in them. Bush's greatest asset as a visual artist is her face, and as such it's possible to trace the genesis of her performing instinct to an early source, moving through her dancing days back to those powerfully evocative *Cathy* photographs from her pre-teens, and then presumably further back still. From a young age she clearly possessed an instinctive and intrinsic understanding of how to captivate the lens, displaying a powerful gift for being observed that has permeated every aspect of her career.

"She was fantastic, she was very visually aware, she knew what the camera was, where the boundaries were, she completely understood all that," says Paul Henry, who directed her in 'The Dreaming' and 'There Goes A Tenner'. "She could turn it on immediately the cameras started rolling. It was a privilege to work with her. Of all the people I've ever worked with, visually her and Iggy Pop were the most aware." Gered Mankowitz has photographed her on dozens of occasions, and agrees. "She has an ability to focus on and give to the camera something special about [herself] which might only last a fraction of a second, but it is there," he says. "It's a quite mysterious process that occurs between the subject and the camera, you don't question it too much or over analyse it. It's a strange, intimate process. It doesn't always work, but some people just respond fantastically, and can communicate something special. That aura only really occurs in front of the camera."

You suspect that even Bush herself has never entirely understood this alchemy, or been wholly comfortable with it. The gap between the reality of her life and the expression in her work has always proved somewhat difficult to reconcile; many have failed to make a distinction between what she is projecting and who really lies beneath, yet it's difficult to overstate the extent to which her ability to transform herself for the camera is integral to her work. Ask a stranger to contemplate Kate Bush and it's very often not a song that will spring immediately to mind, but a kaleidoscope of changing images. "I don't think I want to be up there . . . being me," she said. "I don't think I'm that interesting for people to see. I think what I want to do is to be up there actually *being* the person that's there in the song. I think that is much more interesting for people and it is much more of a challenge for me."[1]

Who is she? Even her friends were sometimes not immune to wondering. "The 'Babooshka' video was a shock," recalls Jon Kelly. "When the single came out and I saw that video of her dressed up, I was really quite shocked." It's easy to understand what he means – who *is* that half-naked scimitar-wielding temptress? Not the woman making cups of tea and sitting next to me in the studio, that's for sure – but the correlation should be clear: the track is about a woman who is split down the middle, a middle-aged wife dressing up as a young seductress to entrap her husband, and in the video Bush is serving the song faithfully, just as on the cover of *Hounds Of Love* she is also in character, embodying the suggestion in the title: herein awaits something languorous, seductive, yet also with an implied threat. It clearly does not make her, as one interviewer seemed to imply, an advocate of bestiality. And yet – even though she has always been as happy to play grotesques, or 'go ugly', or swap gender as she has been to appear alluring – in her head-on visual representations she has always walked a precarious line.

"Kate is a very assertive Leo, and Leo's tend to be quite exhibitionist in many ways," says Charlie Morgan. "Part of Kate wanted to be centre of attention, but there was a certain reserve about her as well; part of her is this incredibly reclusive, creative artistic type. Again, a dichotomy, a battle within herself. There's no doubt that when she did those videos she was very out front and wanted people to see them and appreciate them, and yet in terms of her private life and public image, she really wants to keep them separate, which is very hard to do."

Regardless of the risk of people misunderstanding the line that separates public performance and the private person, film and video was always likely to prove irresistible to Bush. A woman who has frequently found cinema a direct source of inspiration in her writing, who often approached composition in a highly visual way and is acutely aware of the importance of projecting a compelling image, she was bound to recognise the medium as an outlet for many of the ideas – dance, cinema, role-playing – that form an integral part of her music.

Its illusory nature and the freedom it allowed also appealed to someone who was never comfortable in the gladiatorial environment of the live arena, where the battle commences and we see whatever we see. In concert, once the bell rings it cannot be unrung; with video, conversely, she discovered a medium for her performance talents in which she could control the picture all the way down the line. "Perhaps that's where she transferred the impulse to play live, and put it into that expression," says Jon Kelly. Certainly, following the 'Tour Of Life' she actively stepped up the ambition and scale of her videos, moving away from straight perform-ance to something more ambitious and allusive.

★ ★ ★

The story of Bush's progression as a visual artist is partly that of astutely selecting highly influential collaborators and mentors. Thanks to EMI she started out in the hands of Keith MacMillan, alongside David Mallet one of the key figures of early music video, but as she began to spread her wings she craved not only greater freedom but greater knowledge and craft, aligning herself to recognised film-makers such as Terry Gilliam, Nic Roeg, Michael Powell and Jimmy Murakami. She instinctively leaned towards the auteur.

The beginnings, however, were not so auspicious. Shot by Rockflix in a day on a budget not much bigger than a petty cash float, the original 'Wuthering Heights' video was the clip that launched a thousand parodies, mother's milk to mimics like Faith Brown. It was swiftly withdrawn by EMI, who commissioned MacMillan to shoot another video for the song in the more hospitable environs of Ewart's Studio A in Wandsworth. The film was hastily assembled even as the single was climbing the charts, and within a matter of days was being shown on *Top Of The Pops*. These were the Dodge City days of smash and grab film-making.

"We did 'Wuthering Heights' through the middle of the night," says its editor, Brian Wiseman. "We got halfway through it, decided we didn't like what we were doing, and started over. We got an idea from some Canadian movie Keith had seen, did it on video and went down a load of generations to get that [swirling] effect. She didn't have any input on that at all, I don't think. That was Keith's idea, and the same with 'The Man With The Child In His Eyes'."

"The great thing about music videos [then], and especially with Keith MacMillan, was that you could do what the hell you wanted," adds John Henshall, who worked as director of photography on several early Bush videos. "There were no rules. I remember with 'The Man With The Child In His Eyes', we used the heaviest fog filter, which was unbelievably revolutionary. We started her looking down in that foetal position, and then we opened the exposure to burn her out, and then just took the exposure down again so she appeared out of it. It was shown on *Top Of The Pops* and there was this complete change of mood and image with this weird girl singing this weird song. It was unbelievable."

There's no doubt that those early videos, somewhat dated though they appear today, made an immeasurable contribution – for good or ill – to creating Bush's public image, even if they did lean a little heavily on the dry ice, a simplistic *meme* of the times for any female artist deemed a little 'quirky' and mystical. In some ways, MacMillan was to Bush's early videos what Andrew Powell was to her early records: an experienced, empathetic, occasionally inspired figure with very strong ideas who liked ultimately to call the shots, although she was always in charge of the choreography. She learned a lot from him, and his contacts. For the rather risqué 'Hammer Horror' video he introduced her to Anthony Van Laast, which proved to be the start of a highly productive relationship.

"Keith understood that she was a sensitive artist and totally different to the other people, so it was very much a partnership," says Henshall. "It wasn't just a Keith thing, but I think she had phenomenal guidance on those early ones. He was good to work with, he would definitely take ideas, and I think he was a major influence on Kate, who was a little 18-year-old, just a normal girl, no edge at all. She wasn't grand in any way, shape or form. She was a bit . . . not *vacant*, but a lot of 'Yeah, wow'."

Paul Henry, for one, was never fooled by Bush's oft-mentioned 'cosmic, amazing' shtick. "She could be quite vague at times once the camera was cut, [but] I think that might be just very clever, actually, because it's so obvious that she is very bright and is pretty shrewd about how to get what she wants," he says. "That rather beguiling look that she'd have occasionally, as if she didn't really know what was going on, was all just part of an invitation to put in your thoughts about something."

As if to prove the point, following the tour and the making of *Never For Ever* she sought the kind of control over her visual output that she had gained over her records. After that solo, eye-popping interpretation of 'Babooshka' in the studio, her focus began to move away from presenting herself as a dancer or a mover who chipped in with storyline and choreography ideas but ceded control of the final product to the director and editor. She started edging towards something more obviously dramatic, using outdoor locations, stronger narratives and larger casts.

"My God, the expense was nothing," recalls Brian Bath. "We used to go to the forest out in [Windsor], Black Park, where all the Hammer Horror stuff was shot. We did 'Army Dreamers' there, and 'Breathing', where they all come out of the water at the end. Del wouldn't do it: 'Ah no, I ain't doing that!' We had scuba suits on underneath these overalls, it was February and it was freezing. Paddy says, 'Don't worry, I'll get you if you float away.' I always said I'd sit in a tree upside down if they asked me."

Bush loved 'Breathing' and particularly 'Army Dreamers', a snappy, powerful, stylish summation of the song's personalised anti-war themes, declaring that "I got everything I wanted to say across."[2] However, it marked the end of her relationship with MacMillan. The director could be a tricky customer, as could Bush in her own way, and she was about to disappear over the horizon of her own imagination and into *The Dreaming*. "Ever since 'Breathing' I've wanted to make videos like little films," she said.[3] She had her own agenda to pursue.

"[Keith] had quite good ideas but she wanted much more creative control," says Brian Wiseman. "She wasn't getting that kind of freedom from Keith. She did 'Army Dreamers' with him and then they fell out. I'd stopped working with Keith, but she had a relationship with me and asked if I would effectively direct with her [on 'Sat In Your Lap']. It was her ideas and me making sure that it worked."

'Sat In Your Lap', an exercise in highly kinetic abstract impressionism, with roller-skating bulls thrown in for good measure, is hardly coherent but it is eminently watchable. The other videos for *The Dreaming* singles revealed someone still struggling to master the art of matching music to visual expression. Bush sought the same absolute creative control she had had on the album but did not yet have the technical expertise to pull it off, and so was forced to hire directors to do her will. It was not always a comfortable fit. Wiseman, who also directed 'Suspended In Gaffa', admits "she was a very nice lady, there was never any arguments or anything, but as a piece of video it wasn't hugely interesting." Actually it *was* interesting. Filmed in a set of a barn, the dusk punctuated by shafts of sunlight, and featuring her mother in a brief cameo, it conjured up a very distinct sense of Wickham Farm. But it is doggedly uncommercial.

'The Dreaming', the opening single from the album and therefore a relatively important piece of film in terms of promoting the record, was based around a highly stylised piece of slow choreographed movement, presented with cinematic values. Ewart's sound stage was transformed into a vast, desolate stretch of Australian outback, with a 10kW light rigged up as the sun, topped off with lasers borrowed from The Who. It was an ambitious and very expensive undertaking, and yet many of the visual effects were obscured by clouds of red cement dust ("I think people probably died because of the video," jokes John Henshall. "For years the dust was all over Ewart's lights, everywhere, we were breathing that stuff") while the action, full of vivid visual stimulus, was rendered inaccessible because of the way it was shot.

Bush had initially approached Terry Marcel, the director of the cult 1980 swords and sorcery movie *Hawk The Slayer*, to direct the video; Marcel wasn't interested but suggested his friend, Paul Henry, instead. "I was pretty excited about the idea of working with her," says Henry. "She knew exactly what she wanted, and in a way that made it quite difficult. She wanted it based around dance routines, so whilst I shot a lot of close ups, mid-shots and so on, when it came to the edit she basically insisted that it was pretty much kept as a wide shot, which worked for her, but I think it was compromised from my point of view. For me it was very unfortunate, because she was entering a phase where artistically she was expressing herself, but commercially it was no good. The record company didn't like it *at all*. Martin Wyn Griffith [EMI's Head of Production at the time] called me and said, 'This is one of the worst films I've ever seen. I can't believe you've spent all this money and made this terrible film.'"

The song was far from innately commercial in the first place, but the video hardly helped its fortunes as it stalled at number 48. John Henshall also worked on the film and is equally damning about the experience. "That was a bit of a shambles. A lot went into it, but she was lost. I don't think [Paul] controlled it, you know, but she needed a guiding hand and she didn't get it. She thought she knew."

On the next video, 'There Goes A Tenner', Henry was under strict instructions from EMI to draw in the reins. Before they began, he told Bush that it had to be made much more in the manner of a conventional video. We need to shoot this in the standard way, he told her: cover it in a wide shot, then go in for two-shot, mid-shot and close up, so we have the ability to cut it conventionally and it will have a better chance of being shown on television which, presumably, was the point of the exercise.

"I don't think she liked that," he says. "So after that one she employed everyone that I had employed on 'There Goes A Tenner' – except me! She had my art director, my set dressers, my cameraman, wardrobe people, everyone but me, because she didn't like the fact that I tried to be more in control of it. Most creative people want complete control. On one hand it was a gift to be able to work with her, on the other hand she was heading in a direction that wasn't going to be commercially successful. Both the films I made didn't get a huge amount of exposure."

Indeed, that's an understatement. 'There Goes A Tenner' is the least successful single of Bush's career, played and seen virtually nowhere, primarily due to the song – the video is perfectly fine. As ever, there were no great scenes, no fallings out; neither Henry nor Wiseman have a bad word to say about Bush personally and, you suspect, would have leapt at the chance to have worked with her again. For her part, she remained resolute in her belief that she had to follow her vision, resolving to do it better next time. Which is what she did.

★ ★ ★

By the mid-Eighties Terry Gilliam had forged a reputation as a cinematic innovator. A confirmed fan, occasionally Bush would ring Gilliam's office in Neals Yard in Covent Garden to rave about his work, particularly *Time Bandits*, and suggest that he direct her videos. Eventually she came into the office and the two met. Gilliam was struggling with the edit of *Brazil*, so he suggested that Bush instead used his cameraman, David Garfath, for her next promo, 'Running Up That Hill'. She tried to tempt Gilliam again with 'Cloudbusting', and this time he recommended another member of his creative team, Julian Doyle.

Much of Bush's creative world spins out from a very tight-knit cluster of central spokes: Abbey Road, Pink Floyd, Peter Gabriel. She has been very conscious and astute in her choice of collaborators and working environments, and these trusted hubs have served her well. A constant throughout her career has been her ability to surround herself with supremely talented people. She has lofty ambitions for her art and is far from shy or retiring when it comes to approaching those she admires, and her ability to zone in on quality people and use their resources – not in a cynical way – has had a positive impact on her work. Her attitude has always been: if you're going to have somebody else contribute, get the best. So if she needed a choral group, she would get singers overseen by Richard Hickox, one of the great English conductors. If she required a classical guitarist, she would get John Williams. This tendency has been even more pronounced in terms of her videos. "Kate was so respected by people and they were so fascinated by her that they would do it," says David Garfath. "And she's got that thing: no harm in asking."

Terry Gilliam became another spoke in the wheel. It's little wonder she made a bee line for the *Monty Python* animator, who at the time was at the early stages of a consistently intriguing and visually enchanting career as a film director. *Time Bandits*, his fantastical grown-up kid's adventure – or perhaps it's an very adult fable with a child-like veneer – about a young boy taken on a series of time travelling adventures by six dwarves, was very much her kind of thing. Bush had loved *Monty Python* since her schooldays and *Time Bandits* was one of her favourite films. Gilliam's vision chimed with the vividly unusual way in which she saw the world.

Although she was disappointed not to be working with him directly, Gilliam became a close friend and he gave her the benefit of his advice on things like story boards, while her collaborations with his colleagues made groundbreaking forward strides in terms of her own visual work.* Perhaps she felt she had less to prove; certainly her ideas were stronger and more focused; and the music she was working with was considerably more accessible.

David Garfath recalls a woman who was typically unaffected and pleasant in person, always open and willing to hear ideas, and yet absolutely resolute about what she wanted. "When I first went to her house in Eltham and she opened the door, I remember thinking, 'Is that Kate or not?'" he says. "Just for a split-second moment, because she was so relaxed in her dress sense, and so friendly. 'Come in and have a cup of tea', it was a natural warmth. We sat and talked over ideas. I thought of this ballet dance troupe I'd heard of somewhere in west Africa, which sounded fascinating, and doing it outside at sunset, but it wasn't right for her. I came up with something else, and once again that didn't click, and I thought, 'Hmmm, I don't know that this is going to work.' But I gave it one more shot, I came up with other ideas and went to her and she picked up on it and we pushed it forward together. She has very strong ideas about which way it should go and how it should develop. I enjoyed it very much indeed, it was a very good experience. She pushes people to try and make something [special] of it."

'Running Up That Hill' was always intended to be a beautifully filmed piece of pure classical dance. Bush had been studying hard with Dyane Gray-Cullert, and in the absence of Stewart Avon Arnold – who was, to his eternal regret, busy with other commitments – she was partnered in the film by Michael Hervieu, a young dancer who had passed an audition to win the role. The Japanese *hakama* costumes and the recurring miming of

---

* She also quickly returned the favour, recording a short, shimmering, symphonic version of 'Brazil' for Gilliam's film.

the firing of an arrow nod to the family interest in Kyudo. Out of long discussions between Bush and Garfath came the idea of placing photographic cut-outs of the faces of Bush and Hervieu onto an army of invading dancers to convey the song's core idea of the difficulty in resisting our given gender and identity.

It was all too much for MTV, who used a clip of her performing the song on *Wogan* instead, but it was a beautiful and rather haunting piece of film. Bush, as usual, put her all into it. "She would go on and on in her performance until she felt it was right," says Garfath. "She loved dance, and she was very professional about it, and very anxious to get it right. She was still dancing at midnight when we would have started at six in the morning. It was fantastic. I can't remember anyone having a bad word. People really loved her, they warmed to her. When we finished some of us went off to have a drink together. We went to a bar somewhere in London and she didn't want to be recognised. When she used to order a cab she would use a pseudonym, but I should think that's quite normal."

The director, who had worked on films such as *The Empire Strikes Back*, *Superman II* and *Another Country*, was also impressed by the amount of autonomy Bush exercised. There was no one from the record company looming over the proceedings, and she always seemed to get what she required. "I remember one night we needed to go past midnight, where it suddenly gets much more expensive because of crew and everything, and my producer said we didn't have it in the budget," says Garfath. "Kate just picked the phone up, spoke to someone, and said, 'Yeah, no problem.' A wonderful freedom."

'Running Up That Hill' was intended as a fond farewell to dance, at least as far as her video appearances were concerned. That proved premature, but she was already fixated on film, and had been talking seriously about developing 'The Ninth Wave' concept from *Hounds Of Love* into a mini-movie. It "*was* a film," she said, "that's how I thought of it"[4], and indeed, when she discussed her songs it was clear how vivid and real they appeared to her. 'The Ninth Wave' movie never happened, disappointingly, as it had a much stronger dramatic thread than the film she eventually did make, but the ambition to turn it into a visual centrepiece stayed with her.

In many ways her next promo video was a small, self-contained film in its own right. She made 'Cloudbusting' with Julian Doyle, who had edited

Monty Python's Life Of Brian and had been a second unit director on *Time Bandits* and *Brazil*, and who went on to become a feature director. Bush's ideas for the video originated from some preliminary drawings she had made, most memorably a picture of the sun displayed as a huge face coming over the horizon. The shoot was the scene of perhaps her biggest coup, recruiting the renowned Canadian actor Donald Sutherland – star of *Don't Look Now*, another of her favourite films, directed by another of her favourite directors, Nic Roeg – to play the role of Wilhelm Reich.

Originally, they had talked about the possibility of hiring the British actor and former Doctor Who Patrick Troughton to the play the father, but then Sutherland's name cropped up. Bush had a contact for the actor through Barry Richardson, a stylist who had worked on Pink Floyd's *The Wall* and who was part of the crew on the film Sutherland was currently making in Kings Lynn, the disastrous American Revolutionary War movie *Revolution*. When she asked Sutherland's agent if he might be available the answer was a simple 'no', so she tried a less formal tack, using Richardson as an intermediary.

Sutherland agreed to meet for dinner and quickly accepted the part; aside from the fact he was charmed by Bush, he may well have been looking for a little light relief. He later confessed he was having a miserable time on *Revolution*, where he was surrounded by intense method actors, including Al Pacino, who would completely ignore him off-set because he was playing an English sergeant in the film and they were all fighting for the freedom of the colonies.

EMI's Brian Southall maintains that Sutherland "was in it in order to attract the American market. She was a great fan of his, but there was also, 'It's gonna be good for America'. From our point of view, it wouldn't do any harm." There was certainly an awareness that cracking MTV might provide a short cut to success in the US; pop videos had become increasingly homogenised, and it was felt that the cinematic qualities of 'Cloudbusting' might stop viewers flipping between channels and force them to pay attention. MTV, however, ultimately shied away from it precisely *because* it was so different. "In the end, it made no bloody difference," says Southall. "They don't get this stuff." 'Cloudbusting' eventually played in cinemas in support of the Michael J. Fox teen vehicle *Back To The Future*. There was some discussion about adding a statement at the end of the film revealing that Reich was sentenced to two years for contempt of court and had died in jail, but Bush decided that such a bald announcement had no place in a pop promo.'

The video was filmed over three days at the White Horse Hill, near Uffington on the Berkshire Downs, at a cost of a little over £100,000. The sky stayed blue and the clouds, arguably the true stars of the piece, were bought from Oxford Scientific and added in post-production. Bush cast herself as the son, Peter Reich, who was a pre-pubescent boy in the period the video describes. The crew were sceptical that she could pull it off, and they had every right to be. Decked out in dungarees, the addition of a short, spiky wig admittedly lent her a certain boyish quality while making her head seem bigger and thus helping her appear younger; while Sutherland – already a towering 6 ft 4 – stood on a box in order to make the petite Bush seem even smaller. Even after all that effort, however, she remained a highly unconvincing male.

The schedule was impossibly tight. Sutherland was only there thanks to a brief spell of shore leave and had to be surrendered back to *Revolution* within the agreed time span. As a consequence, he was filming right up until the moment of his departure: the shot of him getting into the car as the sun starts to sink behind the hills captures his actual exit from the 'Cloudbusting' set. Every available moment with the star was grabbed with both hands, and by the end of the third day he was exhausted, beginning to lose focus and jokingly wondering aloud what exactly he had let himself in for, slumming it on the set of a pop video. His presence was tangible evidence not only of Bush's tenacity, but also the genuine esteem in which she was held beyond the confines of the pop world. Few other artists would have managed to get him to play ball.

Everyone loved Sutherland. He brought a real gravitas to the project, and he not only made a perfectly sympathetic and convincing Reich, he was very generous with Bush. "He was really professional, really patient, and an incredible help to me," she said. "I mean, whenever we were acting, he *was* my father. I just had to react to him like child. He made it very easy."[5]

Sutherland's strength as an actor pulled these feelings out of Bush. There is a lovely scene in the video when they both look down at the approaching car. Bush backs into him, turns around and they embrace. When they broke apart Bush was crying real tears. The openness of Sutherland's performance brought her emotions to the surface, to the point where she was living the moments described in the screenplay. In common with the best of her music, it wasn't so much acting as *being*.

If she was learning simply from her proximity to a masterful actor, she was also picking up technical tips from the crew, who would talk constantly to her, gently and informally tutoring her in the art of filming, explaining what they were doing and the best means of getting certain results. It seemed to have the desired effect. Buoyed by the experience of working with such a stellar group, she immediately began directing her own videos, beginning with 'Hounds Of Love' and 'The Big Sky' in 1985 and 1986, followed by all the subsequent videos for *The Sensual World* and *The Red Shoes*, as well as 'Experiment IV' and 'Rocket Man'. In many of them she used her friends from the world of alternative comedy – Hugh Laurie, Dawn French and Tim McInnerny – whom she had met through Comic Relief functions and her Amnesty International fundraisers and via mutual acquaintances; Robbie Coltrane had even appeared on *Hounds Of Love*. She co-directed 'The Sensual World' with *The Comic Strip Presents'* . . . actor, writer and director Peter Richardson, which led to her being invited to play the role of bride Angela Watkins in the Comic Strip's rather deranged 1990 film, *Les Dogs*, also featuring McInnerny and her future co-star in *The Line, The Cross And The Curve*, Miranda Richardson. Another member of this set, the actor, director and writer Stephen Fry, would end up working with her on *50 Words For Snow*. More spokes, more contacts.

It would be easy to put rather arch inverted commas around the description of Bush as a director, and it's true she did get help from many of her right hand men, experienced cameramen, editors and cinematographers such as Roger Pratt, Brian Hurley and Julian Doyle. But watching 'Hounds Of Love', 'Experiment IV', 'The Sensual World' and 'This Woman's Work' a clear unity of style to Bush's direction emerges: the videos are heavily stylised, dramatic and rather stagey.* When not conjuring a Hitchcockian sense of menace ('Hounds Of Love' is partly a homage to *The 39 Steps*) and casting long shadows, she favours deep, warm browns, greens and purples. She's excellent at switching atmosphere

---

* Watch 'The Big Sky' video, on the other hand, and weep for the fact that she has never played the song live.

by changing the backdrop – the weather, the season, the time of day. That elemental touch again.

She is a classicist. Her love of Thirties and Forties noir and caper comedy is clear in the clothing and the crisp lines of many of her videos, and she is fond of the somewhat operatic grand gesture: there's lots of clenched fists, enveloping hugs and long stares into the mid-distance. It's not always subtle, it's perhaps a tad indulgent, and it does often border on pastiche, but it is undeniably accomplished in places. At home Bush had a room full of films by favourite directors like Michael Powell and Alfred Hitchcock, often video-taped from the television. Her passion for cinema bequeathed a certain amount of technical knowledge, as well as a genuine thrill at being behind the camera.

While directing and performing these songs, she was edging towards something bigger, more ambitious. Ever since 'The Ninth Wave' she had yearned to make an extended piece of film combined with her music. She gradually conceived *The Line, The Cross And The Curve*. "She started to talk about this project about a year before it happened," recalls Stewart Avon Arnold. "She said she wanted to put together this story, like a mini-film. She talked about different elements of it when I was coming down there to teach her private classes at Eltham, the house next to [Paddy]. She'd bounce any ideas off me, and then it came up and she asked me to help her with the choreography, because there were quite a few other dancers. I helped her put it together, although obviously all the ideas were coming from her. There were some great people in it. She wanted to get some mature dancers, so I recommended Christopher Bannerman and Bob Smith, who were Michael and Gabriel, the angels, and she used Lindsay Kemp, of course. The number that she did with the Madagascan musicians ['Eat The Music'], they were all dancers that were auditioned at the Pineapple, I helped put that together."

For the lead dramatic parts she recruited the fine actress Miranda Richardson, who had a sparkling CV and had worked with her in *Les Dogs*, to play the Irish dancer, and Lindsay Kemp as her tour guide through the mirror world, a show of gratitude for all he had taught her. Her band all participated, her 'healer' Lily showed up, Paddy was there, Peter Richardson had a cameo.

None of it, alas, amounted to very much. The plot was essentially an extended and confused re-telling of the lyrics of the album's title track, which was in itself inspired by Powell's film, in turn inspired by a Danish fairy tale. It opens with Bush and Stewart Avon Arnold dancing while her band perform 'Rubberband Girl': a good, straight pop video. The routine ends with her flailing in a straightjacket (a nice poke at all those "she's mad" naysayers) and after a bit of lame tomfoolery with a wind machine Bush's character – who is never named – expresses her dissatisfaction with her dancing. There is a blackout, the band leave, and Bush sings 'And So Is Love' amid some dread symbolism involving candles and dead birds. Richardson's character then arrives, requesting from Bush the mysterious symbols – the line, the cross and the curve – in order for her to "get back home." She gives Bush her possessed red shoes in return and Bush sets off into a mirror world, beckoned across fire by Lindsay Kemp. She must then try and get the symbols back, avenge the evil Richardson, while also joining the dots between songs as diverse as 'Lily' and 'Eat The Music'.*

There are some fine and memorable moments. The scene of Bush twirling like a musical box ballerina in a snowstorm to 'Moments Of Pleasure' is sublime; 'And So Is Love' is very powerful, while the story climaxes in a slow-motion cat-fight between Bush and Richardson which is quietly gripping. It can be fun spotting the many references to her favourite films – *Night Of The Demon, The Gold Rush, The Red Shoes, The Wizard Of Oz* – and there is plenty of evidence that Bush's creative pulse was still ticking over at a steady rate. Although often tired and distracted, she was still capable of coming up with inspired ideas and was constantly willing to try new things. She certainly kept the cast and crew on their toes. During the filming of 'Rubberband Girl', she arrived at first light one morning and asked someone to find her a trampoline. Nobody was ever quite sure what she would come up with next.

There is some magic in the film. It's not the complete catastrophe that it has sometimes been painted, not least by its director, but both Bush's ambitions and external expectations were far too high, and she suffered because of it. As anything remotely resembling a 'film' *The Line, The Cross And The Curve* simply fails. It doesn't hang together, falling foul of the curse of the over-extended pop promo, and the script and storyline were

---

* Some scenes in this section of the Madagascan dancers with watermelons had to be re-shot for the US, because they were deemed racially provocative.

badly malnourished. "I didn't have time to develop the story," she said. "I took on a bit too much."[6]

Although some interesting concepts are hinted at, nothing is pursued or resolved as the narrative cannons groggily between one song and the next. Some familiar Bush themes emerge: escaping the constraints of mind and body to achieve transcendence; spirituality, more than a dash of witchcraft and the supernatural; the power of music and dance and the dizzy compulsion of creativity, something scarily intense that takes hold and doesn't let go. Perhaps *The Line, The Cross And The Curve* should really be read as a confirmation of what Bush had recently been saying in the press: music isn't everything. I'm unlacing these red shoes and taking a break from all that stuff.

One insurmountable problem with the film is the fact that the acting – specifically, Bush's acting – is below par. She has occasionally displayed a measured gift for comedy during past appearances on *The Kenny Everett Show* or singing with Rowan Atkinson at The Secret Policeman's Third Ball; in another *Comic Strip Presents . . .* film, *GLC*, she produced the wildly kitsch theme song 'Ken' – "Who's a funky sex machine?" – in praise of Ken Livingstone. She is obviously able to project a variety of emotions and feelings superbly through her music, and has a magnificently expressive face, but acting with dialogue was another matter. She never wanted to be an actor, she said, she had no real passion for it. When she has dipped her toe into the water – *Les Dogs*, 'Cloudbusting' – it was because it was fun and brought her into contact with people she liked and could learn from. She seemed to recognise her limitations. "If I was to make [another] film I wouldn't want to be in it so much," she admitted.[7]

She was frequently offered parts, in films, musicals, plays and TV shows, but almost always turned them down. Nic Roeg asked Bush to take the lead role in *Castaway*, which would have required her to spend most of her screen time naked on a beach with Oliver Reed. Although she admired Roeg, she turned the opportunity down, not on the grounds that she objected to the nudity, but rather that spending months in a confined space with the notoriously debauched Reed didn't appeal.* The role was eventually played by Amanda Donohoe.

If Bush had planned to seriously pursue acting, she may have needed a

---

* She did, however, contribute 'Be Kind To My Mistakes' to the film's soundtrack.

substantial amount of assistance. As director on *The Line, The Cross And The Curve*, not only was she dealing with numerous technical headaches – filming the bird and the lacing of the shoes both posed problems – but she was then coming out from behind the camera and attempting to give a convincing performance.

The odds were stacked against her. As someone lacking meaningful directorial experience, it would have been difficult enough simply being in overall creative control of a film; trying to act at the same time (and doing so in the knowledge that she was not a naturally gifted acting performer) made it an almost impossible conjuring trick. Perhaps in a straight pop video, where Bush the Actor was not required to convincingly convey dialogue, and Bush the Director needn't worry overly about maintaining a narrative thread, the equation seemed more plausible. But this was intended to be so much more than a mere pop video. One scene in particular underscored the problem. Before 'Eat The Music', Bush and Miranda Richardson perform a scene where they change positions, sizing each other up. Richardson is – typically – sure-footed, but Bush is all at sea, over-acting and over-emphasising. Her performance jars, but it needn't have been an insurmountable glitch. The presence of a director to suggest that she take things down a notch or two would have done the trick.

The film fell short in post-production, too, with a final cut that the editor Julian Rodd struggled in vain to convince Bush could be improved upon, and a poorly judged sound mix that bowed more to the flashy techniques of a pop promo than the requirements of film-making. The scene with Lindsay Kemp in the storm failed to pack the desired dramatic punch partly because his voice was coming from the back of the mix rather than the centre, lending an odd detachment to the scene.

The Line, The Cross And The Curve was a ridiculously tall order simply because she was trying to do so much, so quickly, at such a difficult time. It's hard to think of any artist who could pull off singing, dancing, writing and directing in their debut film. Nevertheless, for someone with her cinematic knowledge, her love of the form, her talent and desire for perfectionism, to achieve little more than the typically overblown Eighties and Nineties 'concept' video – inflated, badly acted, rambling, wracked with faux-profundity, everything coated with that shallow glossy sheen – was a bitter disappointment.

There was some *Schadenfreude* in the reviews, a sense that the experience had knocked Bush's high falutin' artistic pretensions down a peg or two. It's a terrific shame, and a sign of how off-kilter she was at the time, that when it came to the realisation of a long-held ambition for once this most fastidious and careful of artists rushed into it woefully ill-prepared. She would not make the same mistake twice.

* * *

Almost exactly 12 years later, Bush was heavily involved in the creation and execution of her next video, 'King Of The Mountain', producing storyboards and holding lengthy meetings with Jimmy Murakami, whom she had contacted about 'The Sensual World' almost 20 years before and had finally got around to working with. For the first time in two decades, however, she did not direct. Tracing the journey of Elvis's jumpsuit, from lonely wardrobe back to the arms of its owner, hiding out in the mountains, it was another mini-movie, somewhere between *The Snowman*, the *Harry Potter* films and *Citizen Kane*. She brought her innate quality of presence to the screen, but, with Bush approaching 50, it was more muted now, less frenetic.

This may well prove to be a positive. No matter how eccentric or occasionally misconceived the final product, her visual gifts had always been central to her work, and certainly a key part of her being regarded as an icon. There was something rather fitting, however, about the passing of time taking her further away from an implicitly visual representation of her work. It was as though she was reminding her audience that at heart she is a writer, not a performer. Strip away everything about Bush, leave only the voice and the piano, and you would still have a vast world of imagination, colour and characters into which to dive. Her songs are already like little films; they have depth and texture, they construct an aural landscape which conjures up clear images, they have shape and proportion, often they have narrative, they carry mood changes, emotions and strong atmosphere. It's all there.

"When people listen to your record, that's an audial experience; you don't necessarily want to see things," she has said. "Like when you write a song: the person singing the song is a character. Although it might be you vocally, it's not yourself you are singing about, but that character. It's someone who is in a situation, so you treat it like a film. That's how I see songs. They are just like a little story: you are in a situation, you are this character. This is what happens. End. That's what human beings want desperately. We all love being read stories, and none of us get it anymore."[8]

Since she began in 1978 deconstructing and rebuilding herself almost on a song-by-song basis, Bush has rarely been less than magnetic to watch on screen, but the misfiring *The Line, The Cross And The Curve* and, in 2011, the ungainly video for 'Deeper Understanding', were reminders that doing justice to these already visually audacious songs could be harder than it seemed; it's a miracle, indeed, that she has pulled it off so successfully so many times. Her videos are a sweet, sexy, silly, sublime accompaniment to the music, but without her anchoring presence at the forefront they became increasingly marginal and inessential. With her next record, Bush would prove once again that she could tell stories, take on roles, act them out and weave a dense, intoxicating spell simply through the deployment of her words, voice and vaulting imagination. But first, there was to be a break in transmission. Necessary repairs.

12

How To Be Invisible

WHILE Nick Hornby was compiling lists of his top five Elvis Costello songs in *High Fidelity*, Kate Bush was busy ranking her preferred songbirds. On July 4, 1996, the English songwriter Don Black, the man responsible for the lyrics of countless standards in the fields of pop, film and musical theatre, appeared on Radio Two and mentioned a recent meeting with Bush. "I asked Kate if she had a favourite singer and she said her favourite is the blackbird and her second favourite is the thrush," he said. "Well, I told you she was different."[1]

What was intended as a breezy showbiz anecdote turned out to be something close to a profound premonition of the substance of her next album, as yet only a distant satellite orbiting far above the planet of sound. Bush had recently purchased a 160-year-old listed building, a former mill house at Theale, near Reading, about 40 miles west of London, situated on a small, natural islet by the Sheffield Mill Weir on the Kennet and Avon canal. Unlived in for over a decade, the 14-roomed house cost £750,000 and Bush spent an even larger sum modifying it to her needs. In time, she dismantled the studio at Wickham Farm and installed it in a building in the six-acre garden, which also included a guest cottage, the remains of the old water mill, and her own dance studio by the water. "She asked me about the floor and so I went to have a look at it while she was doing it, and it's a really lovely little studio right by the lock," says Stewart Avon Arnold. "She did it properly: harlequin floor, sprung floor, ballet bars and mirrors."

In the upside-down world of celebrity culture, of course, this move to the country was later portrayed as a gloomy exile into a world of melancholy and paranoia. But if it was a further retreat from the spotlight, it was also a return to the most fundamental touchstone of her creativity –

solitude, privacy, the sense of time stretching out like an ocean, a certain kind of direct connection with the elements around her – which had always animated her best music. By ruthlessly protecting her personal space, Bush slowly rediscovered a familiar alchemy, putting the magic of the everyday world back into her music.

"With her you're getting the pure expression of someone living a home life," says Tony Wadsworth, CEO of EMI between 1998 and 2008, the man who supported Bush for seven years – without hearing a note of new music – as she endeavoured to restore the essential balance between her work and her family. "Because what *Aerial* is, as a piece of work, is someone obviously speaking about a very private and domesticated life. It's massively personal. And it wouldn't surprise you to know that a *lot* of birds fly into her garden!" *The Red Shoes* struggled to get off the ground; *Aerial* literally means 'of the air'. Those songbirds proved to be significant co-writers.

★ ★ ★

The idea, widely perpetuated upon the release of *Aerial* in 2005, that Bush signed off on *The Red Shoes* and its companion film and immediately disappeared down a foxhole – "vanished from view" as the *Times* and many others put it – only to emerge 12 years later is convenient to the mythology but not quite true. Like a train whose engine has cut out, her momentum carried her a little way forwards before she came to a halt in a secluded siding.

She embarked on a series of promotional interviews to mark the limited cinematic release of *The Line, The Cross And The Curve* in April 1994 (the video went on general sale in October; the world shrugged); her cover of 'The Man I Love' was released as a single and briefly entered the charts in July; in September, she donated two pieces of artwork to War Child for a celebrity charity auction, entitled 'Someone Lost At Sea Hoping Someone In A Plane Will Find Them' ('The Ninth Wave', it seemed, was the concept that just kept on giving) and 'Someone In A Plane Hoping To Find Someone Lost At Sea', each consisting of a black surface containing a tiny, twinkling red light. And there was a rather perfunctory performance on *Top Of The Pops* in November 1994, her first on the show for over eight years and her last to date, to promote the release of the final single from *The Red Shoes*, 'And So Is Love', as it limped to number 26. All in all, by her standards we actually saw and heard quite a lot from Bush in 1994.

More intriguingly, the same year she accepted a commission to write several brief pieces of music to accompany the $30m US TV ad campaign for the launch of Coca-Cola's new fruit drink Fruitopia (the Cocteau Twins' Liz Fraser was the voice in the UK; this, clearly, was to be *the* soft drink of choice for fans of enigmatic female singers the world over). It seemed an incongruous move. Bush had consistently turned down advances of this nature, although she had appeared in one Japanese television advert in 1978, singing 'Them Heavy People' and intoning the tag line – 'We have many varieties of mood within us; it's up to you to choose' – with a comical lack of enthusiasm, all for the glory of Seiko watches.

Ever since, her unwillingness to bow to commercial pressure and use her music to promote a solely commercial purpose had been resolute. The motivation for her changing tack wasn't clear but was probably varied: far from the commercial ingénue she sometimes appears, certainly the financial rewards would have been extremely significant; perhaps she liked the tone of the ads, which were relatively innovative and visually stimulating and over which she was given complete artistic control. She may also have recognised an opportunity to cast the net of her music a little wider, while also finding a home for all the melodic waifs and rhythmic strays that had never quite found a home in her 'proper' songs; and indeed, the snippets, averaging around 30 seconds each and entitled 'Solstice', 'Some People', 'Nice', 'Skin', 'Soul', 'What If', 'Thirsty', 'Person' and 'Fighting Fruit', were uniformly fascinating, each one hinting at a longer piece, several reminiscent of the kind of odd, rhythmic, electronic pop music she was making around the time of *The Dreaming*.*

A little later her friend and regular collaborator Donal Lunny curated a compilation called *Common Ground*, featuring contemporary artists singing Irish songs. Recording her contribution in 1995, Bush sang 'Mná Na h-Éireann' ('Women Of Ireland'), a well known piece with vaguely

---

* She reasserted her natural distance from the grubby compromises of commerce a few years later, in 1999, when she was asked to write a song for the Disney film *Dinosaur*. At first Disney asked Bush to rewrite the words, which she refused to do, before telling her they now wanted it to be entirely instrumental. The director, Eric Leighton, said that "the rest of the score was instrumental, and hearing a voice singing seemed to confuse and unsettle the [test] audience."[*USA Today*] She quietly withdrew.

nationalist leanings based on the words of the eighteenth century poet Peadar O Doirnin. It was a lush performance, her voice backed by harp and strings, and sung – bravely, and rather well – in Gaelic. "I'm sure Ma gave me a helping hand!" she said.[2]

These were, however, soft footfalls in a forest of gathering silence; slowly, she wandered out of public view. It should have come as no great surprise. The experience of making and facing up to *The Red Shoes* had constituted a natural full stop. She had been writing and recording – and occasionally performing – since the age of 18 with barely a gap in between, and despite the seemingly modest output – one tour, a few videos, seven records over two decades – each successive album seemed to take more and more out of her.

"I remember talking to her when she had just put *The Red Shoes* out," says Bob Mercer. "I was living in Nashville, and I said, 'What are you going to do now?' She said, 'I'm going to take a rest for a while, this writing and recording and mixing and putting it out and promoting it just exhausts me.' I said, 'Fuck me, Kate, you do it every five fucking years, for Christ's sake!' But she spends a long time and she is meticulous, and it shows, it really does. You're talking about obsessive behaviour. She is obsessive, those kind of people are, and it tends to impinge on their lives, and not just their artistic lives."

The impact of the relative critical and artistic failure of *The Red Shoes* and *The Line, The Cross And The Curve* shouldn't be underestimated. She had certainly had her fair share of bad reviews and naysayers in the past, and she had also frequently felt that she hadn't quite achieved what she had intended on a record, but rarely had the two coincided quite so conclusively. Critics began comparing her unfavourably to Bjork and even Tori Amos, complaining – with some justification – that her eccentricities were now more interesting than the music. It touched a nerve. Everything Bush does has the imprint of quality and integrity (her voice, her music and her lyrics all are given a huge investment of time and care), but when the muse is misfiring sometimes the whole seems to be considerably less than the sum of its parts.

More worryingly, she felt decidedly lukewarm about one of her own albums for the first time since 1978. Even before it came out she was almost apologetic, explaining it was "the best I could do at the time."[3] She stood by most of the songs but later felt that, at 55 minutes, *The Red Shoes* was at least ten minutes too long, falling foul of the modern temptation to fill an entire CD with music rather than using only what is up to par.

Also, there was rather a lot of negative feedback about the album and film coming from her most loyal fan base, through fanzines and – increasingly – the internet. She and Jay and Paddy, always amenable and available to trusted sources, subsequently backed away a little from direct contact; the 1994 fan convention was to be the last Bush attended. She may have a strong centre of self-belief, but she is hyper-sensitive to perceptions of her. "I was actually viewed in quite a negative light at that point . . . it dissipated my energy severely and threw me into a state of severe exhaustion," she said later. "You just get worn down."[4]

She was negotiating a fairly complicated confluence of major life changes: some practical, some planned, some unexpected, some challenging, some sad and some immensely joyful. Re-reading the few significant interviews she conducted upon the release of *The Red Shoes*, it's clear with hindsight that she was saying some significant goodbyes. "I am at a point . . . where there's a few things I'd like to be doing with my life," she said, speaking in drizzly Cricklewood during the dubbing sessions for *The Line, The Cross And The Curve*. "I'd like to catch up. Over the next few years I'd like to take some time off. . . . It's silly that I haven't taken more breaks. I've spent a long time in the city and I love being by the sea, and I'm starting to pine for it. I'd like to put energy into stuff like that . . . I haven't wasted any of my life yet, but I'm a bit fed up of being stuck in a studio."[5]

For many, the rhythm of the jobbing musician simply *becomes* their life, often with consequential diminishing returns. Bush was determined not to let that happen. Her mention of the ocean evoked memories of her childhood holidays in Birchington-on-Sea; when she later talked about a new love of visiting museums, it brought to mind her *annus mirabilis* of 1976, when she was soaking up knowledge and inspiration from all quarters. At 35, there was a sense of someone taking stock and realising there were several significant tears in the fabric of her existence, a certain loss of direction. There is a clear desire to get back to the stabilising nexus of family, and home – or perhaps more accurately, since the death of her mother and her parting with Del, to establish her own domestic nest.

It's very easy to get hysterical about what happened to Bush in the years between 1994 and 2005. As she became less and less visible, the tabloid press needed little encouragement to peddle the by now standard dark rumours of nervous breakdowns, binge eating, a woman in perpetual retreat in some overgrown gilded cage, lost behind high gates and shuttered windows in her "vampire castle".[6] They even ran a story that she had officially changed her name on the voters' register to Catherine Earnshaw.

If not quite plumbing the depths of this Gothic nightmare, it's clear that it was a very difficult period. Although she had taken some time off during the making of *The Red Shoes*, she hadn't really addressed the death of her mother – "I hadn't grieved properly"[7] – and was also adjusting to the end of a 15-year relationship, and the beginning of another with Danny McIntosh. After her split from Del she moved to a flat in south London overlooking the Thames – the proximity to water seemed to have an increasing allure – before moving with McIntosh into the renovated house in Theale, which eventually became their primary base; Court Road was kept on but was increasingly not used, and was eventually sold for £900,000 in 2002. Shortly afterwards she bought a £2.5m cliff-top house on the South Hams peninsula in Devon, with a boathouse and private beach.

Through 1994 and 1995 there were periods of isolation, exhaustion and something resembling a black dog scratching at the door. "I slept, I spent a lot of time sleeping," she said. "I used to enjoy bad television, like really bad quiz programmes or really bad sitcoms. . . . I needed to be in a position where there were no demands . . . I was very quiet. I was just trying to recuperate."[8]

The subtext is clear. However, this dark night of the soul was relatively brief. And far from being a recluse, she was still around if you knew where to look: at David Gilmour's fiftieth birthday party at Fulham Town Hall; in theatre land, at the *Lion King* and the musical *Maddie*; in Julie's, a discreetly high-end restaurant in Holland Park, where she could be seen relaxing with, among others, Robert De Niro and Bob Geldof after a Van Morrison concert. Attending the People's Banquet in 1997, held at the Banqueting Hall in Whitehall to celebrate the Queen's Golden wedding anniversary, she shared a table with John Major, whom she had first met six years earlier when, as Prime Minister, he invited her and Joe Boyd to Downing Street as an acknowledgment of their work promoting Bulgarian music. In 1996 she spent some time at the Royal College of Art, working on a bronze sculpture inspired by Billie Holiday. Entitled

'Strange Fruit', it was donated to another War Child auction and suggested fairly conclusively that her future did not lie in visual art.

She did not advertise her whereabouts, but neither was she hiding under lock and key. She also began to compose again. Instead of treating writing as a job or a compulsion – pushing and pushing until something came – she reversed the process; when an idea arrived, and the time was appropriate, she would address it. In 1996 she wrote and recorded the demo version of 'King Of The Mountain' – indeed, some of the finished track and much of the final vocal dates back to that time. A song about fame, isolation and possible redemption, it was inspired by the notion that Elvis Presley, a modern day Citizen Kane, was still alive, watching from the mountain top, ready to "rise again".[*]

A year later she wrote 'Sunset' – a hymn to her favourite crooner, the blackbird – and 'An Architect's Dream', a sweet, drifting sigh of a song that pulls together the work of a street painter with the meeting of two lovers, both parties engaged in their own acts of precarious creation. The beginnings are inauspicious enough – a "kiss", a "smudge" – but look "what it becomes."

The knowledge that she was pregnant when she wrote those words invests them with an extra level of significance. Bush was finally looking forward to the prospect of motherhood at the age of 39. She had been asked about children almost from the moment she had first become famous, and throughout her twenties had always said she could not conceive of having both a family and a career. She had stuck to this mantra for many years, but her maternal instinct was strong and her position had changed with the passing of time and the turn of events.

In an interview in early 1994, an admirably fearless writer from the US magazine *Details*, using a transatlantic phone line for cover, pressed her on her desire for children and the impact of her mother's death and got an unexpectedly straight answer: "I would like to have kids, yeah," said Bush. "It's certainly loss that heightens the realisation that life is short . . ." In fact, she had wanted to have children for some time, and her pregnancy was a source of profound joy.

Her son Albert, known to all as Bertie, was born in July 1998. Naturally,

---

[*] A similar theme runs through some of the songs on Prefab Sprout's 1990 album, *Jordan: The Comeback*.

her creative pursuits once again took a back seat during this period, though for very different reasons. Although she and McIntosh were "completely shattered much of the time"[9], she found herself entirely consumed with love for her child. "I didn't want anything to interfere with that process," she said. "I wanted to give as much time as I possibly could to my son. I love being with him, he's a lovely little boy and he won't be little for very long.[10] The idea was that he would come first, and then the record would come next."[11]

"When she became a mother she turned into her own mother," says Charlie Morgan. "She had a good role model, [and] she became her mum: 'This is what I'm doing right now. I've been the singer songwriter and I'm going to be a mum for a while, until Bertie is old enough to understand. I have this human being that I need to protect.' Kate's songs were her babies, definitely, and when they turned out to be less than she expected she was always very disappointed. I think the mothering instinct took over. All things considered, it is the ultimate creative act!"

Tony Wadsworth made it one of his first objectives to make contact with Bush and establish a bond on a purely personal level. It was apparent to him that making a new record was not of primary importance. "It was pretty clear that her priority was her family, specifically this new baby, who was just a few months old," he says. "One of the . . . nice things about paying visits to her place was meeting her and her partner and watching the baby grow."

It was hardly surprising that Bush did not announce the birth with an interview – he was not a new album, after all, he was a human being – a *Hello!* photo spread or indeed any kind of public declaration. However, it is a testament to both her vice-like mastery of privacy and the fierce loyalty she inspires that news of her pregnancy, the birth and the subsequent existence of Bertie was kept firmly within her circle of friends and associates for almost two years. She could have counted on discretion from within the medical profession, but there were others in her orbit who simply wouldn't have known who she was, such was the discrepancy between Bush the Pop Goddess and the way she presented herself on a daily basis. "A lot of people I mix with are the mothers of Bertie's friends," she later said. "I don't even know if some of them know who I am."[12] This, no doubt, she regarded as progress.

Of course, those whom Bush wanted to know about Bertie were well aware. Her family, naturally, and close friends like Michael Kamen and Peter Gabriel, as well as people like Tony Wadsworth and artists she barely knew in the industry like Jean Michel Jarre, who had recently contacted her about a collaboration. Though she insisted there was no great denial or cover up, she managed to enforce a remarkable and rather fearsome feat of prolonged and collective omerta. She felt it was simply nobody else's business.

It was left to Peter Gabriel in an online interview in 2000 to unintentionally spill the beans. In response to a question about his old friend and collaborator, he answered: 'Kate Bush has become a mother. I have not been to see her for about six months but I think she is working on her music now.' When the news broke that Bush had a two-year-old child there was a predictable flurry of press interest. The *Mirror* and *Mail On Sunday* each ran typically immoderate articles in mid-July, the latter under the headline THE SECRET SON OF KATE BUSH, exhausting the whole lexicon of pejorative clichés: 'Miss Haversham' [*sic*], 'forlorn and derelict', 'reclusive', 'lonely and isolated', 'a web of secrecy', 'perfect hiding place', 'turning her back on showbusiness.'

She had already grown properly sick of the press. In many ways, the tabloid's perception of Bush has never moved far beyond that initial first impression cultivated in early 1978. They have never understood her, and what the tabloids don't understand (which is plenty) they simplify and mock. She was caricatured as either the screeching sexpot or, later, the dotty recluse. The music was an irrelevance.

What had once been an irritant was by now something far more intrusive. By 1990 she had taken to recording interviews on her own tape recorder, while Colin Lloyd-Tucker recalls "sitting in the kitchen in Eltham, and there was a picture of her in the paper at some opening. I said, 'Oh, there's a really nice picture of you in the paper,' and she didn't even want to look at it. She said, 'Oh, I'm avoiding all that kind of stuff.' She'd had enough of all of that." During a visit with Del to see the Ben Elton play *Silly Cow* at the Theatre Royal in February 1991 she was photographed taking great exception to the intrusions of photographer Robin Kennedy, and had to be calmed down by Del as she aimed a boot at the snapper's rear end. Afterwards the cameraman said: 'I didn't think that anyone so small would be able to kick so hard.' More fool him. She had, after all, once convincingly pretended to be a donkey.

In 1993 she endured a highly combative *Sunday Times* interview with celebrity journalist Chrissie Iley, who found her polite but obvious hostility – her "assassin's smile" – and her refusal to answer even the most straightforward question – what kind of doctor is your father, for instance – deeply infuriating, and you could see her point. Bush often experienced her most testing interviews with women; an early interrogator likened her to Lady Macbeth. They fancied that they could see something cold and steely lurking beneath her immaculate exterior that men – too busy rhapsodising about her dimples and tiny stature – tended to overlook.

Iley subsequently wrote what amounted to a sincerely felt hatchet job. The articles about Bush's son and her lifestyle went even deeper. Shortly after they appeared, she sent a message to her fan club:

Hello everyone,

Here is a press statement I have issued and I wanted you to see it. . . .

"A number of inaccurate comments have been made about me in recent articles which I am taking further. I just want everyone to know I am very happy and proud to have such a beautiful son, Bertie – he is absolutely gorgeous. Far from being secretive, I am just trying to be a good protective mother and give him as normal a childhood as possible whilst preserving his privacy – surely everyone can understand that. I am having great fun being a Mum as well as working on a new album."

I hope you will understand how invaluable it has been to me to have a very fulfilling and normal start to motherhood and I felt unable to tell you about Bertie previously for reasons already explained. He is the most beautiful thing I have ever seen. He is my joy and I'm very happy and very busy being a Mum. I am finding time to write for the new album and very pleased so far.

Thanks again for your lovely letters and kind wishes. I hope you will be happy for me.

Lots of love, Kate XX

Indeed it would seem she went out of her way to ensure that her son was given every chance to enjoy normal, uninhibited social interaction. "I was at Paddy's fiftieth birthday party [in December 2002] and she had her little boy then," says Colin Lloyd-Tucker. "She was in good form, she was in good spirits – very much a *mum*, that's the main difference I noticed.

Suddenly there's a little chap running around, so we had a good mums and dads kind of chat. She looked well and seemed happy, talking about going to garden fetes and school starting and all that." At Terry Gilliam's sixtieth birthday party, in November 2000, she bumped into many old friends, and introduced them to an energetic Bertie. Little wonder, they might have pondered, that she was now writing songs that took the humble washing machine as their starting point.

★ ★ ★

The fuss had all but blown over by the time Bush broke cover at the Q awards on October 29, 2001 to receive the Classic Songwriter award.* She had been out of the public eye long enough for her attendance to cause quite a stir. She looked happy and healthy, smartly dressed in a black trouser suit, and her obvious joy at being a mother ran though her brief acceptance speech and her subsequent conversations, almost to the point of parody. For all that Bush was keen to keep her son out of the public eye, like most new mothers she was certainly not averse to making him a conversation piece. She revealed Bertie had won an inflatable hammer at a local fair, was into Bob The Builder and Elvis Presley, and that she had finally given up smoking.

The event was a timely reminder of the solid foundations that supported the rickety infrastructure of rumour and hysteria, and how much she had been missed. It was an opportunity for her to witness the direct appreciation of a diverse group of contemporaries – ranging from Cher to John Lydon, Elvis Costello and Liam Gallagher – who had no truck with cobbled together mythology; they simply recognised her strength and her artistry. She greeted the rapturous applause with an orgasmic squeak – 'Oooh, I've just come!' – strategically intended to puncture any notions of her as some precious, fragile, doe-eyed creature.

"I remember talking to her about it beforehand and she'd obviously thought about it really seriously because she'd not been out in public for ages," recalls Tony Wadsworth. "The fact that she turned up in an audience of her peers – if there are such things – and got the best reception of anybody throughout the event, that to me was something that was

---

* She later turned down a Brits Lifetime Achievement award, in 2006, partly because she wouldn't perform live at the televised event.

completely undistorted by the legend. Here was a roomful of musicians and producers and people in the industry who know that a lot of this imagery can sometimes be artifice and can be distorted, [and] what they were doing that day was applauding her incredible talent that has sustained. And she was knocked out by it. It was interesting seeing her chin-wagging with John Lydon. You never fail to be surprised by Kate – they knew each other, these two very uncompromising artists."

She told the audience at the Park Lane Hotel that she was working on her new record – and she was, although it was by necessity a part-time process. The way Bush had always worked, the intensity with which she approached her music and the hours, days and years she put in simply couldn't continue if she was to be the mother she wanted to be. In the past, music was ultimate act of creation. When the act of creation took on a human face – "I look at him, know I gave birth to him, and I know magic does exist,"[13] she said – music was bound to take a back seat.

"I think she was obsessed with the music [in the past]," says Haydn Bendall. "We were younger then. Now she has Albert. I'd never insult her by saying she has a better perspective now, but maybe she has a different perspective." Or, as Bob Mercer puts it, rather more succinctly: "She never chose to have hoards of nannies. She's not fucking Madonna, she does it all herself. She's just a *ferocious* mother. It's wonderful to watch it all happen."

As such, she wrote and recorded in short bursts in stolen moments. She would put down the music on her Kurtzweil 250 keyboard or her piano, perhaps adding a drum loop or a click track and then a guide vocal. The set up may have changed – they were no longer at Wickham Farm, they were no longer an item, and they no longer worked 16 hour days – but Del remained her foil in the studio, turning up most mornings and getting down to work. "He's the only one who can say [things about her music] without damning her, without putting her down, and that comes from decades of experience," says Charlie Morgan. "He's just like an old friend, y'know," she said. "Working with Del, there's a very relaxed feeling."[14]

Danny McIntosh was naturally present, picking up musicians and dropping them off, popping in and out. He played all the guitars, which were more prominent than on any Bush record since the first two and became a prime component of the album's sound, adding flamenco stylings to 'Sunset', a reggae rhythm on 'King Of The Mountain', and a real crunch to 'Aerial'. His atmospheric, interlocking parts on 'How To Be Invisible', meanwhile, were a highlight, immeasurably enhancing one of her best new songs.

McIntosh had some technical input, wrestling with the digital convertors when everyone else had given up, but, as ever, it was mainly Bush and Del working on the nuts and bolts of the songs. "We didn't see much of Dan," says Peter Erskine, the American drummer who played on several tracks. "John [Giblin] at one point explained a couple of things one night as he was driving me back to the hotel, because I was a little bit puzzled. I wasn't quite getting the dynamic, that was all, but it wasn't my business."

Towards the end of 2000 Bush had made sufficient progress to begin inviting outside musicians into the studio to add parts to the songs; Erskine was one of the first. Primarily a jazz drummer who had played with John Martyn and Joni Mitchell, Erskine had been spotted by Bush on a BBC documentary about English composer Mark Anthony Turnage. Typically, she picked up the phone and made direct contact, and shortly afterwards Erskine was flown to England.

"There was a bit of secrecy attached to everything, in terms of where the drums would be delivered – there was a protocol that they wanted observed," he says. "The cases should be labelled in a specific manner so it would not be apparent to anyone handling those along the way where they were going or what the project was. They had a car service that would pick me up [from my hotel] and drop me off a specific spot and then I'd get through the security gates, but there was nothing disproportionate. They're all very well-balanced, an incredible amount of normality. That security apparatus is to maintain some normalcy."

Erskine was there for three days and played, by his estimation, on seven or eight tracks, although he only appears on three: 'An Architect's Dream', 'Prologue' and 'Nocturn.' It was a leisurely process – "they just work at a different pace" – which encouraged experimentation. It was a very much more organic process than Bush's most recent albums. Erskine even recalls that at first he, Giblin and Bush performed together as a kind of ad hoc jazz trio. "Kate was playing piano," he says. "Like, 'here's a new song I'm working on.'"

Later, he added his contributions to previously recorded backing tracks. On 'King Of The Mountain' he "came up with a wacky idea. I put on a beat like the Weather Report track, 'Nubian Sundance', this double tempo, free-syncopated, aggressive drumbeat. It's not the easiest thing to play, and then I added a half-time Ringo style beat as a counter point. When Del mixed it I said it sounded like [US drummer and member of Presley's TCB Band] Ron Tutt with Elvis, and she gave me a startled look: 'Of course, that's what the song is about! Elvis!' " Erskine hadn't picked up on the lyrics nor Bush's idiosyncratic Elvis impersonation. "I had no idea," he laughs. "Her tune conveyed this subliminally to me! I'm sure at some point they realised that the drum part I put on was an absolute mess, but the nice thing was that they indulged the idea."

This working process was mirrored throughout the sessions. Musicians would be invited to improvise on a variety of tracks. If it worked, great; if not, no harm done. Someone else would get a shot. Steve Sanger, an old friend of McIntosh's from his session days, came up from Dorset on several occasions to play drums, bells, shaker and percussion. He added a more conventional pattern to 'King Of The Mountain' and Bush also asked him to play along to the rhythm of birdsong on 'Aerial', the title track.

The idea had slowly evolved to make *Aerial* a double album with two distinct sides, a little like *Hounds Of Love* but on a larger scale (in a premeditated gag, in interviews Bush would refer to it as 'Great Danes Of Love' or 'Irish Wolfhounds Of Love'). The first side would be a collection of seven individual songs, while the second would be a connected, conceptual piece tracing the arc of an entire day through nine interlinked pieces of music, from the afternoon through sunset and night to the following dawn, all soundtracked by the trill of her favourite band: the birds. "It's almost as if they're vocalising light," she said. "And I love the idea that it's a language we don't understand."[15] In Kaluli culture in Papua New Guinea, Bush may or may not have been aware, bird song is believed to be communication from the dead.

"She explained that when this particular birdsong starts that's when I start playing," says Sanger. "I did it on an electronic kit, just playing the bass drum. That was a different day! Great food, great fun. It was me and Del the engineer and Kate, and Danny was popping in and out."

These sessions were punctuated with long periods where very little happened, but when she was working things often coalesced quite quickly, particularly towards the end of the project. Much of the musical decoration for 'Bertie', for example, came together in little more than an afternoon. Susanna Pell and Richard Campbell, head-hunted after a performance of

St Matthew Passion at the Festival Hall, came to the studio to play gamba – a renaissance period viol, and distant cousin of the guitar – alongside classical guitarist Eligio Quinteira.

"My memory was that she had laid down the basic track, I think the day before, which was her vocals and the dulcimer she was accompanying herself on," says Campbell. "We were overdubbing onto that, playing from the notation that [arranger Bill Dunne] had provided. Eligio did his guitar overdub after we did the gamba track, so he stayed a little bit longer. It was reasonably close to chamber music. We were playing to what we heard through the cans, which gave it a kind of natural freedom."

'Bertie' was a madrigal of devotion to her son, a song that vaulted the barrier between heartfelt and mawkish, though only a churl could fail to be touched by its artless candour and sheer heartbursting expression of love. Just when you thought Bush has exhausted her rapture, she found deeper reserves: "You bring me so much joy," she sings, "And then you bring me – more joy!" It's a shamelessly sentimental song, basking in the eternal sunshine of an idealised childhood, though its subject may not care to have it sung back at him now that he's a teenager. The visiting musicians were able to get a first hand glimpse of the song's inspiration. "Bertie himself bounced in at one stage, so we met the person who the song was about, which was nice," says Campbell.

She had preserved the atmosphere of familial informality that had permeated Wickham Farm, except now she was the mother figure. Accordionist Chris Hall had been recommended by Joe Boyd after Bush mentioned she wanted the sound of Cajun accordion on 'How To Be Invisible'. In the end the instrument proved too rich for the song, almost overpowering it, and instead Hall played two-note accordion which – with the aid of advanced sonar equipment – can just about be heard on the final track. "I was there for a couple of hours," he recalls. "Had a chat, drank some tea and ate pizza, met her family, played with the kid, did some recording and went away. Not [mystical] at all!"

Everyone who worked on the album was struck by all the things people are usually struck by when they first work with her: her cheerful informality, her genuineness, her distinct lack of ceremony. "I turned up, came in through the gates, parked the car, got the gamba out and walked into the studio," says Campbell. "Up came this person who said, 'I'm Kate, I'm making the tea,' and I confess that I initially thought it was another Kate.

And then I suddenly realised, that is Kate *Bush*." They ended up trading lines on that perennial middle-class lament: the difficulty of getting a good builder.

And then there was the endless stream of tea, without which no session could run smoothly. "She was *always* offering tea," says Peter Erskine. "The running joke at the session was that Del or John [Giblin] would say, like a British actor's voice in a movie, 'Ah, you're a fine woman, Kate.' That was the motto, I remember." Says Susanna Pell, "We arrived and went straight to the studio and within minutes this woman arrived and said, 'D'you want a cup of tea?' And that was her. She bumbled off and made a cup of tea. She was just incredibly nice. Very unassuming, she knew what she wanted and had a clear vision but in the nicest possible way. When it was all over she sent us a personal cheque with a very nice note attached, thanking us. It was just a very, very nice experience."

Although she sometimes wondered if it would ever be finished, over a period of three or four years Bush began to edge closer to the end of the album. Friends such as Lol Creme and Gary Brooker popped in to add vocals and keyboards, and in October 2003 she went to Abbey Road to record orchestral overdubs with Michael Kamen, who sadly died of a heart attack shortly afterwards, aged 55. "The last time I spoke to her was soon after Michael died and we spoke to each other because we were both very sad about it," recalls Haydn Bendall. "She adored him and so did I."

Throughout this period, Tony Wadsworth kept in regular contact. After Bob Mercer and David Munns, it was clear Bush had found another 'music man', someone prepared to give her the time and space to create without making demands or waving the small print of the company contract in her face. There is a fine story about Bush one day telling Wadsworth that she was finally going to show him her latest creation, and then taking some cakes out of the oven and plonking them in front of him. It's an apocryphal tale, sadly, but it is true that he travelled to see her a few times every year for several years, and not once did Bush play him so much as a note of music.

"Even though it was never stated explicitly, it was pretty clear that I wasn't going to hear anything until it was finished," he says. "It was simply starting a relationship of trust. That was the main product of those meetings over the years. I'd like to think that she eventually developed a trust, and I developed an understanding of what her concerns her and what was important to her when it came to dealing with a record label. When it comes to the nitty-gritty of, 'OK, we've got an album that we have to put into this *machine*' which is a corporate record label and can go many different ways, I think an artist likes to feel that there's somebody pretty senior in the organisation that's looking out for them at crucial times, because it can get impersonal. [But] I thought there might be a distinct possibility that I might get fired before anything came!"

Rumours about the album and projected release dates, alternately woefully misinformed and optimistic, had been doing the rounds since 1997. In late 2004 Bush finally announced that recording had finished and the record would be ready for release sometime in 2005. If she had been worried, as she claimed, that people might have forgotten her, she needn't have been: the news sent the papers, magazines and the internet into an overdrive of anticipation. Some time afterwards, Wadsworth and David Munns, Bush's old champion who had recently returned to the company from Polygram, were summoned to the studio to hear the finished album. There was no one else present. She handed each of them a track-listing, set up the machines herself, said, 'It's a bit long,' and then sat down behind them as they listened, like a spectre at the feast, no doubt ultra-sensitive to every twitch, cough and shuffle. It was the first time anyone outside of herself, Del and Danny had heard the complete record.

"She was definitely nervous," says Wadsworth. "We sat there and listened . . . and were stunned. I suppose the first time certain things really stood out for me: I don't think I'd heard the human voice singing with birds before; I thought, 'My God, still she is doing things that are incredibly original, and yet seemed absolutely right and natural.' That was striking. Her voice is always striking, because it's so powerful and emotional. You came out after listening to the two albums back to back and just thought this was an amazing piece of work."

They talked about how it should be released, with some debate about whether it should be a double album or two single albums staggered over a six- to 12-month period. In the end Bush thought it was fairer to her fans and better value to release it as a double, not to mention the fact that now the music was finally finished she wanted to get it all out. She was not a big fan of the miniaturised CD format. She preferred the glory days of vinyl, and wanted *Aerial* to be a meaningful, unified piece of work physically as well as musically. "There were more discussions about work in progress when it came to the artwork than there was about the music, interestingly," says Wadsworth. "She would show me something and say, 'What do you think about that? Do you think that works?'"

Some aspects of the sleeve art were clearly autobiographical – photographs of Bertie and his drawings – and some deeply impenetrable but no less private: pictures of a large red-brick house and a garden, the washing flapping in the breeze; a reproduction of James Southall's painting 'Fishermen'; a simple portrait of a figure that resembled Bush as a young girl; several birds and a reproduction of a photograph featured on the cover of June 2000 edition of *National Geographic*, called 'Indus bird-mask'. As with the music, there were codes within the artwork so personal they will never be cracked. "She did discuss what she wanted to put across," says Wadsworth. "It was . . . pretty personal stuff, there were a few conversations about that."

The title and cover were also carefully conceived, a combination of visual puns – at first the image looked like some desolate rock formation, but was actually a soundwave of birdsong – and layered wordplay: *Aerial* suggests flight and height, but it's also an antennae, a tool for sending and receiving. "And as I pointed out to her, it's also a washing powder that Mrs Bartolozzi might want to use," says Wadsworth. "That might be the key."

★ ★ ★

In August 2005, a November 7 release date was announced for *Aerial*, preceded by a single, 'King Of The Mountain', on October 24. There had been some talk between Bush and EMI of making 'How To Be Invisible' – a far more persuasive, characterful song with which to announce a return after 12 years – the first single, but in the end 'King Of The Mountain' "jumped out", according to Wadsworth. I'm not sure how much jumping it does. The song was not one of the album's highlights, with a curiously uncommitted vocal and a rather flat structure. It was nevertheless widely hailed as a welcome comeback, if not one of her most arresting songs, and reached number four in a singles market that was by now all but moribund.

Reviews of the album when it arrived ranged from the ecstatic to the muted to the confused. Many were written after only one or two supervised listens, an almost impossible undertaking. *Aerial* is a dense, complex piece of work, split into two distinct discs: *A Sea Of Honey* and *A Sky Of Honey*. Far more than any interview, it provided eloquent answers to all those awkward questions that had arisen over the past decade. In many ways it completed the story that *The Red Shoes* started. We knew why she had to go away; now we had a fair idea of what she had been doing.

Aerial pulled off the trick that lies at the heart of much of Bush's finest music: that of being evocative of her day-to-day life and innermost feelings without being personally revealing. Singing of her physical environment, her son and her lover, there was a deep sense of joy, tinged with the loss that time brings. Mimicking the journey of the sun on the suite of songs on *A Sky Of Honey*, the feeling was of someone travelling through a period of darkness into sunlight.

The stand-outs were the two unadorned piano and vocal songs. 'A Coral Room' was a desperately moving track about lost cities, lost times, about all those lives and places that were once here but had now gone; it mourned the death of her mother in the most poetic way imaginable, using her little brown milk jug as the central image. Performed without a safety net – no strings, no backing vocals – it was impossible not to be transported back to Bush's earliest songs, written in 44 Wickham Road at a time of relative innocence. There was even an explicit reminder of one, 'Atlantis', where she had sung of a blue city "covered in coral and coral", adorning treasure chests and ancient scrolls from the Caribbean. But 'A Coral Room' showed how far she had come, both musically and emotionally. It was oblique and impressionistic but utterly true, and it cut far deeper than the more formal pitch of 'Moments Of Pleasure', which covered similar ground in much more awkward shoes. She had once again perfected the craft of saying without telling.

Most reviews also latched upon the other stark piano ballad. 'Mrs Bartolozzi' seemed to finally reconcile the interests of Bush the housewife and mother with Bush the impenetrable artist. A song combining earthy domesticity and magic realism, it depicted a woman falling into a reverie, both erotic and disturbing, while watching the clothes in the washing machine spinning around and around, the trousers and blouses intermingling among the soap and suds. She imagines herself in the sea with her lover, fish swimming between her legs, but there is also a taint in the song, the idea of the clothes, with their distinctive smells and stains, being the most tangible memory of a person who is no longer there. It is another dark song of the senses, and deeply, stubbornly unreadable, even if the final lines of "Slooshy sloshy, get that dirty shirty clean" veered perilously close to self-parody.

If some songs were opaque, 'Bertie' was courageously direct and truly unabashed, not just lyrically but also in summing up the clear distinction Bush makes between her work and her life. She poured her love for her son into her song, the album artwork featured pictures of him, she admitted she could "talk about [him] all day,"[16] and yet she remained fiercely protective of his privacy. The message was clear. Bertie is not shielded away, he is the central part of my life and therefore part of my work, but he is not up for grabs. Musically, it was a rare and pleasurable opportunity to hear her singing with acoustic stringed instruments providing a tugging *obligato*.

In the beautiful, effortlessly slinky 'An Architect's Dream' she sang of the artist's "best mistake", another important strand of her creative ethos. "She likes a happy accident," says Colin Lloyd-Tucker. "Anyone who is genuinely creative will take that on board. On 'The Red Shoes', she said 'Just put a harmony on there, whatever comes into your head, let's see what happens.' Me and Paddy both went into the same harmony, which was actually the wrong note, and she said, 'That's fantastic, leave it like that.' It wasn't the note we were trying for, but she heard that it fitted. She picks up on things like that, she's very good at spotting them."

Not everything worked. Rolf Harris sounded like he was having a minor seizure on 'The Painter's Link', while parts of the first disc were hit and miss. Aside from the 'King Of The Mountain', 'Joanni' struggled to engage, while 'π' was a rather listless piece of synthetic background music on which Bush at least proved that – if not quite singing the phone book – she could at least sing the handset, reciting the numbers as though each were some lost holy scroll. Her father had harboured a love for mathematics, so this most seemingly oblique of songs may well have hidden a very personal message to a "sweet and gentle sensitive man / With an obsessive nature and deep fascination for numbers."

Her interest in numerology was nothing new. Long attracted to the 'Strange Phenomena' of coincidence and synchronicity, astrology and the paranormal, she had been struck in her teens by the fact that she and Emily Brontë shared a birthday, while David Paton also recalls conversations about such matters back in the Seventies. "Her boyfriend's name was Del

Palmer, mine was David Paton," he recalls. "She said, 'You've got the same initials, but did you know you've got the same birthday?* She was always interested in things to do with numbers or anything slightly unusual."

'How To Be Invisible' was a more playful immersion in a supernatural world, another ghostly tale rolled out over a wonderfully elastic, spooky rhythm. Bush was the witch with her "eye of Braille" and her "hem of anorak", every breath of wind and falling leaf a potential unseen force flitting through the world. And is there a better summation of her music than the image of a million doors, each one leading to a million more?

The second disc, *A Sky Of Honey*, began with her piano accompanying cooing birdsong, a sound that runs like a thread through the whole disc, as the music works its way up and up, further into the air, peaking on the last few minutes of 'Nocturn', where Bush finally lets fly vocally as she takes a moonlit swim. Despite the Balearic feel of the music, she is singing of the Atlantic, the sea directly below her Devon home. This feels like a shared private moment of release. The final song, the title track, sustains the mood of energy and rebirth. It ends, fittingly, with laughter.

Aerial was a terribly generous record. "My work is very, very personal and intimately connected to my everyday life," she said, and she was as good as her word.[17] Musically, after the kitchen-sink overload of *The Red Shoes* there was a blessed sense of light and space; a marked reduction in backing vocals, and far less technological fuss. The use of rhythm as a songwriting tool was largely absent, too. This time the textures were more traditional; piano and guitar, natural drums, while her voice had deepened and matured. *Aerial* came through deep and clear, befitting a deeper, clearer life. It was an exorcism of excess, the touchstones of her musical, domestic and imaginative life boiled down to their essence.

Everywhere there was a sense of distillation, a masterly grasp of what was necessary and what was extraneous. It was also imbued with a real sense of an external life – of travelling beyond her own mind and into the wider world, to Italy and Spain, or just to the beach – that few of her previous records had possessed. Indeed, very little of it resembled anything Bush had done before, yet she was back in tune with something elemental, a pastoral sensuality, that lay at the heart of her work. *Aerial* is all sun, sea

* This is not quite true: Paton was born on October 29, Palmer on November 3.

and sky. The pulse rate is slower than *Hounds Of Love*, but there are certain similarities of intent. 'Prologue' even sounded a little like a slowed down 'Watching You Without Me'.

Unsurprisingly, much of the critical emphasis was weighted away from the content of these complex songs and placed very firmly upon Bush's prolonged absence. That, sadly but perhaps understandably, was the real story. After a recording silence of 12 years, it was little wonder that everybody wanted some time with her. Predictably, she was even less enamoured of the promotional process than ever before.

"Most artists, regardless of how they're disposed to that whole palaver, will just take a deep fucking swallow and suck it up," says Bob Mercer. "She's not one of them. Since Bertie it's even more [horrible]. She doesn't really see beyond going into the studio and making music, she really doesn't stretch beyond that. Whatever the record company want to do doesn't really engage her. I don't think anyone at EMI is driving up to Reading and saying, 'Kate, you gotta get off your ass and do things here.' And if anyone came to me to suggest doing that I'd advise them against it!"

She was highly selective in her choice of interviews, but the fact that the public and her fan base didn't actually *see* her once during the entire release window of *Aerial* was, even for Bush, extreme. There were a few carefully chosen print interviews in the UK, Europe and North America, a little radio and a video for 'King Of The Mountain', but no personal appearances or television spots. Tony Wadsworth was philosophical, and entirely unsurprised, by her unwillingness to undertake a lot of promotion.

"I've always taken the view that one of the aspects of dealing with music as a business is that with a real artist you've got to take the full package – and that includes things that they're going to do and things that they're *not* going to do," he says. "If one of the things they will do is make an artistic statement that is excellent and lasting, I'd rather they did that than go on a Saturday morning TV show. It's like pushing water up a hill – why do that with people who you know are not going to do it? You can bang your head against a brick wall forever. With Kate, you accepted what you got."

Most of the promotional interviews she did consent to were conducted from her house in Theale, and several indulged in a breathless roll call of the banal details of life *chez* Bush: pizza, cheese flan, crusty bread, cream cakes, tea, messy kitchens, jeans, floaty tops, children's DVDs scattered around, the fact that she went shopping and took her son to school. There were those who suspected an element of contrivance in all this, that in showing herself to be apart from the realm of groomed, over-managed, macrobiotic celebrity culture she was very consciously declaring herself a member of The Real World. If so, it was a good act. Apart from the fact that she behaved the same way when there were no journalists present, it tallied precisely with the way she has lived her life for the past 30 years and more.

Home, of course, was where she was most comfortable and, crucially, where she would attract the least attention. Aside from her natural reticence for publicity, there was a suggestion that, at 47, having had a baby and rarely able to keep up with her dancing, she was insecure about her body image and consequently reluctant to present herself to the public. Jimmy Murakami directed the video for 'King Of The Mountain' and recalls that "she was always worried that she'd put on weight. I thought she looked fabulous, but she kept bringing up her weight. I told her she looked lovely. I mean you can't go back to your teenage days, and to me she still looked very good. She'd been away a long time, and we had a cameraman that she wanted who came all the way from America – it was very expensive, first class! He did the shoot, but it didn't really require anybody that top notch."

Stewart Avon Arnold, on the other hand, doubts that her looks have ever played a significant part in deciding whether or not to appear in public more often. "She doesn't haven't to worry about looking like Posh Spice or Jordan and having face lifts and arse lifts and God knows what," he says. "She's very natural, Kate, very much an earth woman. As long as she looked presentable, but not to extremes."

The video itself, shot in London on September 15 and 16, 2005, was created using live animation techniques rather than a 3D computer because, says Murakami, Bush felt "computers don't have that human quality." She was closely involved in crafting the story, which depicted Elvis's trademark rhinestone jump-suit returning to the King while a shadowy Bush weaved around the millionaire's mansion. Like Presley in '56, she was largely shot from the waist up. "I did a series of storyboards and sent it to her, and she'd make her corrections and I'd redo it, and we worked on it quite a bit," says Murakami. "We had long chats over the phone and emails. She was very, very strong about it."

It was a good video, both funny and poignant, but the pop promo was yesterday's medium. Bush returned to an industry where her natural milieu was old hat. She understood the ramifications of the digitalisation of music, and invested a lot of time and effort into ensuring that the digital files of *Aerial* were of the best possible quality, but where once she had been at the cutting edge of new innovations, nowadays she was at the back of the queue and was suspicious of its influence. She said "music is suffering greatly from the overuse of computers, and taking away the human element."[18] At a time when multi-media platforms were finding new ways to bring the imagination to life, Bush, one of the few artists really capable of capitalising on the advances made in this regard, refused to click on the mouse.

Aerial was received with the greatest respect and affection, it reached number two and went platinum in the UK and very quickly sold more than a million copies outside of north America, but it rapidly slipped out of sight. Arguably, it was not properly assimilated or appreciated by either the critical mass or a wider audience until *A Sky Of Honey* formed the centrepiece of 'Before The Dawn' almost a decade after it was released. Partly, this is attributable to the nature of the work. Elliptical, layered, entirely ill-suited to the vogue for short, sharp sound experiences, it's not a record you would happily play on an iPhone, or that fits the shuffle function on an mp3 player. It takes time and space to digest. But it also betrays the fact that *Aerial* was born into a new world of limitless options. We have become accustomed to the idea of musicians, of all ages, using blogs, podcasts, SMS and YouTube to sell their music and reach their audience, and it's hard to think of any artist less suited to this relentlessly *present* and self publicising age than Bush.

At a time when music was in the process of becoming more of a disposable commodity than ever before, and its perceived value negligible, Bush sought to retain its preciousness by stepping outside of the spotlight and allowing the work to speak for itself. The downside is that the lack of a visual presence in 2005 made it much harder for *Aerial* to exert any widespread cultural significance. It felt as though she had returned to a large but defined niche, well away from the mainstream. She probably felt most comfortable there. "I don't think she was sitting there thinking, 'Oh my God, why didn't *Aerial* sell X million?'" says Bob Mercer. Its reputation, however, has only grown with time and exposure.

The new album certainly put her back on the tabloid radar, with all the discomfort that implied. In December 2006 there was a widely reported kerfuffle with British Waterways over repairs to her weir, which had collapsed due to heavy rains and for which she was at first deemed liable. The wider issue was that the proximity of her house to the water – and hence the public – caused a few run-ins, with more than one canal-based internet message board ringing to tales of a small, irate lady standing on the tow path shouting "This is private property!"

Those who were surprised at her apparent openness in bringing the media to her doorstep for the interviews for *Aerial* overlooked two things. Bush has never had a problem *inviting* people into her house; she has always been a very open and hospitable host: it's uninvited guests, physical and psychological prowlers, with whom she has a big problem. Privacy was also the meat of the matter in May 2007 when it was reported that local residents in Devon objected to the security cameras around her seaside property, and also resented the fact that Bush – reacting to an extension in the UK's 'right to roam' laws – wanted to divert two public footpaths that provided views into her house on the Devon coast and, it emerged, occasionally brought trespassers into the grounds of her house. "I'm afraid the coast path and the beach were there long before Kate Bush," said a local councillor. "And I'm fairly confident they'll still be in the same place with the same unhindered access long after she's gone." Bush agreed to scale down her security presence and the matter was settled amicably.

Although she was sometimes infuriated by the intrusion of helicopters buzzing over her head to photograph her house, she could also play the rock star trump card when she wanted. "We took a helicopter that she paid for all the way from Hammersmith to her summer house in Devon, just for a meeting for a day," recalls Jimmy Murakami. "She fixed lunch and everything, [then] we went back that evening – that must have cost a few quid. She has a helicopter pad at her second house. No one seems to complain."

More productively, more new music arrived relatively quickly. 'How To Be Invisible' was an incantatory song with a hint of Philip Pullman in its supernatural spell, so it was fitting that the celebrated author of the *His Dark Materials* trilogy was a friend of Bush's. When she was asked to contribute the closing theme to the film adaptation of *The Golden Compass*, the first book of the trilogy, she jumped at the chance. Her friendship not-withstanding, it's easy to see why the story of the coming of age of young Lyra Belacqua appealed to Bush, scattered as it is with spirits and demons, nascent sexuality, matters of religion and dark philosophy.

She put the whole thing together in a blink of an eye. "She got the call a month before it was needed – and delivered," says Tony Wadsworth. "I said, 'Look, see, you *can* do it. Just focus!' I think it might have been something she had been working on for a while and realised it was appropriate for the work, but she really wanted to do it. She said, 'I work well to deadlines.' I said, 'Now you tell me!'" She recorded the track at Abbey Road and enlisted Oxford's Magdalen College School boys' choir on background vocals; it didn't hurt that Bertie was among their ranks. She popped in to give them a quick pep talk beforehand and promised to pay for them all to see the film when it came out.

'Lyra' emerged late in 2007 and was a rather limp affair, far from her finest hour, and even its quick execution proved a false alarm. Two years had already elapsed since *Aerial*, and it would be a further three and a half years before the world heard from Bush again. During that time the wider landscape of the industry changed markedly, and Bush was directly affected. David Munns and Tony Wadsworth left EMI in 2008 when the company was taken over by the private equity firm Terra Firma, overseen by chairman Guy Hands. Profitability at the company had never been more highly valued, while true artistry had arguably lost its premium. "The attitude at EMI was always 'Whatever you want,' and that was an attitude I put in there," says Bob Mercer. "If I made any contribution to her career at all – and I did, there's no question about that – it was to let her march to her own beat."

"The fact that EMI have indulged her and let her get on with it is to their credit," says Brian Southall. "She must have breached her contract a dozen times. No-one's bothered, what are you going to about it? She owns her own product."

But the tide was turning. Both the wider changes in the industry and the lack of a benevolent father figure within EMI were not incidental to Bush and her future music. Entirely creatively self-sufficient, she could record her music at will, with or without the help of EMI. Her unwillingness to hand over her music to people she didn't know or particularly trust had become an issue, and one she would set about rectifying.

It was yet another reason why there appeared to be no sense of her being harried by the ticking of the clock. With age, real life displayed an increasing tendency to get in the way. In the summer of 2008 she turned 50, just after Bertie turned 10; Dr Bush had recently passed away, cremated at Eltham Crematorium. It was a time of deep sadness, of catching up with old friends and reflecting on the past and what was to come. Paddy and Jay were there, naturally, still as close as ever to their sister but much less involved nowadays in the day-to-day aspects of her life and career. Afterwards they all returned to the farm, where Bush's nephew Owen, Jay's son, now lives and works as a blacksmith and bladesmith. They sat around the kitchen table, just like the old days. It looked so small, suddenly. They used to think it was huge.

As the first decade of a new millennium drew to a close, inevitably some question marks lingered over her impetus and desire to create. Would we hear more music from Bush? The demands of being a mother simply could not account for the appearance of just one record in the space of 16 years; there seemed to be other factors at play. However, in 2009 news emerged that she was working on material (featuring, among the usual suspects, Danny Thompson) and had also permitted Rolf Harris to release the version of 'She Moved Through The Fair' they had relatively recently recorded as a duet. The cogs were still in motion, although anyone drumming their fingers hoping for a quick turnaround would have been forgiven for resigning themselves to a dose of familiar frustrations. Brian Bath recalls speaking to Del Palmer on the telephone in the spring of 2009. "He said, 'I can't talk, Kate's just putting this Fender Rhodes part on'," says Bath. "I phoned him back a couple of days later and said, 'How's it going?' He said, 'We're just putting this Fender Rhodes part on. . . .'" Bath laughs ruefully. "Still doing it, two days later!"

Who could have foreseen that one of the most intensely productive periods of her career lay just around the corner?

13

"Up She Comes, Up She Rises"

WORKING office hours in her home studio at Theale and swearing the few musicians involved to secrecy – says soul singer Mica Paris, enlisted on backing vocals, "I remember her saying to me, 'Don't tell anyone about it, Mica! Don't let anyone know I'm making an album!'" – Bush was already undertaking a project unlike any other she had attempted before. It was an intense, very personal endeavour that began as nothing more ambitious than addressing some of the disappointments of the past which had been niggling her; but it ended up taking on a wider significance, heralding a burst of accelerated creativity not seen since the earliest stages of her recording career. If anyone had suggested in 2010 that during the following year Bush would release not one but two new records they would have been tempting outright mockery. Yet that is what happened. Even she seemed astonished.

The initial impetus seemed to contradict almost everything we might have thought we knew about her creative philosophy: the urge to take a chisel to the painstakingly carved sculpture of her studio work and reshape it was something she had always resisted. The only precedent was a very old one, her 1986 reworking of 'Wuthering Heights', on which she added new drums and a new vocal. Few would claim that it had improved on the original.

A similar but much more ambitious act of revisionism took place throughout 2009 and 2010. For some time, it transpired, Bush had felt "a long, lingering dissatisfaction" that *The Sensual World* and *The Red Shoes* contained "some interesting songs that hadn't had the chance to speak properly . . . On my earlier work I was trying so hard, trying, *trying*, and sometimes that can come across. I wanted to have a more laidback approach, not trying to rush through."[1] She formulated a plan to revisit songs from these two records, stripping out the clutter and the tyrannical fads of Eighties and Nineties overproduction, adding more organic textures and new vocals, extending them, reshaping the floor plan, and generally making them sound the way she now wanted them to.

It was a surprise on a number of levels. Bush has frequently admitted that she feels all of her music ends up falling short of her expectations – so why focus on these two records in particular? Indeed, rather than her more recent work we might have expected her to revisit her earliest albums, where she hadn't been in control of the production process, on which she disliked her singing style, and wherein the results often felt to her like a compromised, overly polite version of the sound she heard in her head.

Then again, these were the two albums that were arguably most beholden to the production trends of the time, and had perhaps aged least well out of those from her catalogue. She had also recently regained ownership of them – alongside *The Dreaming* and *Hounds Of Love* – from EMI. She talked now about the harsh, "edgy" quality of *The Red Shoes*, in particular, which had been recorded on digital equipment and specifically designed for CD. She wanted to soften that abrasive sound, find the depth and space in the songs, let them breathe. It was clear that she needed – rather than merely wanted – to scratch an itch that had been bothering her for a long time and had become more persistent. She couldn't progress creatively until she had dealt with it; it had to confronted and overcome. "It's more a nagging voice than an itch," she quibbled, before mimicking it: "'Aren't you going to go back and sort them out? Get on with it then and hurry up!' Now I can move on."[2]

For those who felt that titling the album *Director's Cut* implied a lack of control over the original albums that seemed entirely at odds with the absolute authority she had over her work, she remarked, slightly gnomically, that "You only have control over what you can do at the time. In hindsight, I think it's quite common for artists to look back and think, 'Oh, I could have done this', or 'I could have done that'. That was really something I wanted to play around with."[3]

She claims that she "didn't really take a great deal of time choosing the list of songs, I just kind of wrote down the first things that came into my head",[4] which may or may not have been the case; it is surely no accident that almost two-thirds of the songs selected came from the weaker album, *The Red Shoes*. What is certainly clear is that something she had envisaged

"She has an ability to focus on and give to the camera something special about herself which might only last a fraction of a second. It's quite a mysterious process." – Gered Mankowitz. Diving into *The Sensual World*, 1989 (TS/KEYSTONE USA/REX FEATURES)

"She succeeded in looking and sounding both utterly true to herself and yet also conveniently in tune with the mood music of the mid-Eighties: big hair and great melodic hooks." (Tom Sheehan/LFI)

"If Bush had planned to seriously pursue acting, she may have needed a substantial amount of assistance."
Appearing as Angela Watkins in the Comic Strip's 1990 film, *Les Dogs*.

It was a weird, fractious, fragmented time, and nothing seemed
.." – Haydn Bendall. Bush puts on a brave face amidst the upheaval
of making *The Red Shoes* and *The Line, The Cross And The Curve*.

(TS/KEYSTONE USA / REX FEATURES)

Bush lashes out at an intrusive photographer as
Del Palmer plays peacemaker, February, 1991.

"She ain't daft. People shouldn't be fooled by the mystical, hippie stuff. This girl is very, very tough." – Brian Southall. A wary Bush scans the landscape for enemy fire. (KEVIN CUMMINS/GETTY IMAGES)

"Much of Bush's creative world spins out from a very tight-knit cluster of central spokes."
Prime examples include (clockwise from top left) Terry Gilliam, Midge Ure, David Gilmour,
the man who first brought her to the attention of EMI, and Peter Gabriel.

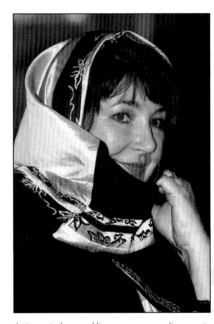

"She turned up in an audience of her peers and got the best reception of anybody throughout the event; that was something completely undistorted by 'the legend', and she was knocked out by it." – Tony Wadsworth. Bush briefly re-enters public life at the Q Awards, October 29, 2001.
(RICHARD YOUNG/REX FEATURES)

An increasingly rare public appearance, attending a music industry reception at Buckingham Palace, March 1, 2005.
(FIONA HANSON/TIM GRAHAM PICTURE LIBRARY/GETTY IMAGES)

"Now I've got something really special to put on top of the Christmas tree." Bush collects her CBE from the Queen at Windsor Castle, April 10, 2013. (©PA ARCHIVE/PA)

"What a lovely afternoon…" Bush, mannequin, puppet master and band drift into 'A Sky Of Honey' during Act II of 'Before The Dawn'. (GAVIN BUSH/REX FEATURES)

"She looked both entirely ordinary and utterly remarkable: powerful, fierce, radiant, a benevolent Gothic goddess." (GAVIN BUSH/REX FEATURES)

Bertie McIntosh as the artist in 'Before The Dawn'. (GAVIN BUSH/REX FEATURES)

"One of the most extraordinary pieces of imaginative theatre ever staged by a popular musician."
Bush performs 'The Ninth Wave' during 'Before The Dawn'.

(Gavin Bush/Rex Features)

would be a relatively quick, straightforward enterprise ended up taking a lot longer and being far more demanding than she had first imagined.

The first task was transferring the original digital recordings to analogue tape. Bush now enjoyed the best of both worlds in the studio, using vintage gear and old valve amps alongside Pro-Tools. It was a very modern ethos, harnessing the depth, warmth and tactility of analogue to the convenience afforded by new technology.

She took out all the original drum parts played by Stuart Elliott and Charlie Morgan, all the lead vocals and much of the backing vocals. Sometimes that was all the removal work required on a track; on other songs, Bush also stripped away keyboard parts, bass lines, guitars, pipes and Michael Kamen's string arrangements. Suddenly there was a lot more space in the attic.

So what now?

Absolutely integral to the project was the involvement of Steve Gadd, the celebrated American session drummer who has worked with everyone from Paul Simon and Paul McCartney to Chet Baker and the Manhattan Jazz Quintet. He was renowned as a real musician's drummer whose playing was full of feel and nuance. "I've been a fan of his work for a long time, and his interpretation of music is quite extraordinary," she said. "He has a great subtlety in his approach, and he's someone who isn't afraid to leave stuff out."[5] This less-is-more quality was significant, not only for *Director's Cut* but also for what followed.

A 67-year-old New Yorker based in Phoenix, Arizona, Gadd received a call from a Bush associate in 2009, after which the two made direct contact. "She explained that these were albums she'd done a long time ago and she wanted to revisit them," he says. "I thought that was very interesting. She didn't want me to go back and listen to the originals, she wanted me to start with how she had stripped them down. I heard as far as she had gotten to the point where she wanted to put drums on. She wanted me to treat them as new songs. She had a definite way she wanted to do it. She wanted fresh ears, and not to compare it to what was going on before."

Gadd flew to England for an initial session and thereafter returned a handful of times, working on the songs for five days or a week on each visit. "It was just about letting the music take me for a ride, with her sort of being the pilot," he says. "We tried different things. Sometimes I'd do a pass and there were a few things she really liked and some things that didn't work, so we meticulously choreographed the thing as we went along – picking sounds and feels that were good. She's a great artist, she's got great ears. The closer you get the more it all makes sense."

As usual, Bush was working with a skeleton crew in the studio, often just herself and Del Palmer. "I feel very relaxed with Del," she said. "In some ways, in the nicest possible way, it's almost like he's not there."[6] As a rule no two outside musicians on the record would play together; each came in to the studio independently. "It was just me, her and the track," says Gadd. "No group – just me, Kate and the engineer. I really got to know her and love her as we worked together." The two of them enjoyed a genuine chemistry. According to Bush, his playing breathed new life into the tracks. His was by far the most extensive musical contribution, but there were others: Danny Thompson and John Giblin added new bass lines; Danny McIntosh contributed a variety of guitar parts, most radically on 'Never Be Mine' and 'Rubberband Girl'. There were a number of new backing vocals and choral arrangements. She asked Paul Hardiman to get involved but it proved impossible. "Kate got in contact with me to start working together again, mixing *Director's Cut*," says Hardiman. "Unfortunately my wife was ill and I had to decline."

Often these were not radical reinterpretations but vibrant acts of sonic restoration. There were small but significant shifts in pitch, melody and lyrics; previously buried details were unearthed, polished and brought forward. The floor plan of many songs stayed more or less the same while Bush moved the furniture around. Tracks such as 'Never Be Mine' and 'Song Of Solomon' opened up in a way that recalled the spacey, slightly jazzy pastoral mood music of Talk Talk's *Spirit Of Eden*. There was a new-found sense of space, with the rhythm playing a far more significant role thanks to a big, dubby bass, brought forward in the mix and packing a real punch, and Gadd's rolling drums.

It was at the point where Bush began recording new lead vocals that the project almost became unstuck. "It felt very strange when I first started to re-sing them," she said.[7] Her voice had deepened with age. It was perhaps less versatile but came with greater depth and warmth, and she found it difficult, both technically and emotionally, to re-enter these song worlds. Indeed, it became such a trial that at one point she considered setting the entire album aside. After a time she realised that what was required was not a faithful rehash of former glories, but yet another act of inhabitation in a career full of them. In opting – finally – to look back she chose (or was forced, it seems) not to simply disinter but to reincarnate: to breathe new life into the skeletons of her old songs.

She realised that if she lowered the key she could find a way in. "That was the key," she said. "The key was the key!"[8] Dropping the pitch allowed Bush to approach the tracks as newly written songs, and to sing as the woman she was now rather than perform an impersonation of the singer – and person – she was 20 years ago. This became not just a technical switch, but an emotional entry point. The entire process was perhaps the closest Bush had come since 1979 to the mechanics of preparing for a live show; indeed, it may well have been the process of reconfiguring her back catalogue for *Director's Cut* that lead her on a path, albeit indirectly, to 'Before The Dawn'.

'Never Be Mine', 'The Red Shoes', 'Lily' and 'Song Of Solomon' dropped a semi-tone. 'Rubberband Girl' a tone; 'This Woman's Work' two. Yet she could still rattle the chandeliers when she needed to. After *Aerial*'s generally more restrained vocals, *Director's Cut* lets much of the old Bush weirdness back in. The power, versatility and mystery of her voice remained a wonder to behold. 'The Red Shoes', made-over into a big, ravey slice of electro-folk, bounces along to her joyous "whoop-whoops!" On 'Lily' she casts out her demons with thrilling fury, harking back to the unhinged days of 'Violin'. At moments like these, *Director's Cut* reclaimed Bush's birthright as our most truly abandoned singer.

" 'Lily' was so powerful," says Mica Paris, who sang backing vocals on the new version, arriving at Theale for a day's intensive work early in 2010. "What a track! When I heard it I looked at her and said, 'My God, that's a killer.' It was already recorded and I just came and added my vocals to it. She sat there showing me where she wanted things, but she was very open to suggestion as well, which is a fantastic trait. A real sharing energy. It was a long day of recording. She's hands on, she does everything herself. I was so impressed with that. She knows her way around a studio like you wouldn't believe. She's so relaxed about it but she knows exactly what she wants – and often it's very unusual, the things she asks for. Where she hears things. She'd say, 'Mica, I want some vocals in that part there', and it was really unusual. Then you'd hear the way she put it together and you think, Wow, she was right."

On 'Rubberband Girl', Bush's haphazard new vocal sounded throwaway in the best, most liberated sense. Bush-does-the-Rolling Stones, the entire track is a hugely generous throwback to her pre-fame days singing 'Honky Tonk Women' in the Rose of Lee in Lewisham, an act of abandon suggesting a newfound (or perhaps regained) sense of playfulness and spontaneity in her work. Somewhat predictably, given its rough edges, she agonised over whether to include it on the album: "It is my least favourite track," she said shortly after it was released. "I had considered taking it off, to be honest. It's just a silly pop song, really."[9] It has a live, garage band feel, although Steve Gadd draws a big red line through any romantic notion of him, Bush, Thompson, McIntosh and harmonica player Brendan Power blasting away together in the studio. "It was just me on my own playing along to what was there," he says. "It was just her communicating exactly the way she wanted it to sound. Maybe she was telling me she wanted it to sound a little bit freer and liver. At times she encouraged me to really stretch, in a way that was like we were just jamming and she wanted me to be really free."

'Rubberband Girl' was one of three old songs re-recorded entirely from scratch. The others were two much-loved piano ballads which offered Bush a path towards the vast, open-ended landscapes which would come to characterise the new music already taking shape in her head. Perhaps no song exemplified her burgeoning interest in a more loose-limbed approach to storytelling and song structure than the new version of 'Moments Of Pleasure', now remodelled with just voice, piano and the hums of what sounds like a Red Army choir but is actually Waynflete Chamber Choir. "I wasn't really quite sure how 'Moments Of Pleasure' was going to come together, so I just sat down and tried to play it again," she said. "I hadn't played it for about 20 years. I immediately wanted to get a sense of the fact that it was more of a narrative now than the original version; getting rid of the chorus sections somehow made it more of a narrative than a straightforward song."[10]

Discarding the original's lush string arrangement accentuated the wintery lyric, and it became a song of loss so intimate you could now *hear* the snowfall. Bush curbed the cast list of the departed at the end, apparently because her piano track ended up being just a fraction too short and something (or someone) had to give.

She performed a similarly bold tightrope walk on 'This Woman's Work'. Almost doubling its length to over six minutes, she transformed one of her most beloved, universally accessible ballads into something ambient and glacial, the huge reverb-heavy notes decaying into silence. In attempting to neither replace nor compete with the original, Bush fashioned something entirely new, unsettling, moving, and quietly spectacular. Yet neither of these tracks made complete sense until we heard *50 Words For Snow* six months later, at which point the idea that they were as much a part of the creative process for that record as for *Director's Cut* became truly apparent. Only then did they start to sound like genuinely new creations.

The new 'This Woman's Work' omits the line about there being "a lot of life in you yet". There are several other lyrical readjustments on the album, some of them equally key. On 'And So Is Love' she changed the dominant line from – "and now we see that life is sad" – to "life is sweet" because "I thought it was so bloody depressing! I thought I couldn't just leave it in such a downer".[11] Age brings changes in perspective, but such 180-degree revisionism was bound to feel alienating to many diehards.

The most significant lyrical rejig was Bush's realisation of her original intention for 'The Sensual World': to put her music to James Joyce's words. In the spring of 2010 she had approached the Joyce estate again seeking permission to use Molly Bloom's soliloquy. This time they said yes. Why? "Dunno, I don't really care, to be honest," she said, happily – and perhaps disingenuously. "To be allowed to do what I originally wanted is a great feeling."[12] The fact that under EU law copyright expires 70 years after the author's death may not have been insignificant. *Ulysses* would fall out of copyright in 2012. The Joyce Estate may have sensed a final opportunity to make some money from Molly.

For Bush, the opportunity to reset the title track of *The Sensual World* was one of the highlights of the entire project, almost a reason in itself for doing it; this is, lest we forget, a woman who hangs on tight to her original vision and doesn't take compromise easily. It's a story with a happy ending aside from one fact, which is that the revised 'Flower Of The Mountain' falls rather short of the expectations raised by its longstanding semi-mythical status. What should be momentous ends up feeling somewhat detached and static. She sounds startlingly close in an oddly conceived mix, and while her low, sensuous vocal certainly evokes a middle-aged woman looking back to her early sexual awakening (she performs a particularly ecstatic, purring pirouette on the word "perfume"), compared to the audaciously post-modern original the track ultimately proves flat and underwhelming.

It was evidence, if any were needed, that time-travel is not without its pitfalls. There were other questionable, underwhelming or borderline redundant reimaginings: 'And So Is Love' hardly sounded less ponderous in its new incarnation, while 'Top Of The City' kicked out its legs in search of some Broadway pizzazz ("Ooowaa!") but didn't quite cut the mustard until it was let loose onstage in 2014. 'Deeper Understanding' was another track that attracted considerable debate, and not just because it was selected as a single, released on April 5 to herald the coming record.

A song of obsessive computer love which was eerily prescient in 1989, it made a certain literal sense to re-examine it again from the vantage point of our age of technology. Yet as Bush quaintly sang about picking up a phone and pressing "execute", the song sounded positively antediluvian rebooted in 2011. Surely she can afford Wi-Fi? The Auto-tuned chorus, featuring Bertie as the distorted, dehumanised voice of the computer, succeeds only in making clumsily explicit what the original elegantly implied, although a considerable amount of thought had gone into the changes she made. She was very clear about the effect she was after: rather than the stack of vocals on the original, now she wanted a single voice, a "solo benevolent spirit coming through the computer"[13]. Technological advances enabled her to do it, but the results struggle to convince. Conceptually all over the place, strangely mixed and oddly unresolved, it's a song of two parts which ultimately settles for being entertainingly unhinged, Bush spitting a mouthful of digital feathers before imitating a malfunctioning PC.

As the dust started settling on *Director's Cut* it was hard to know quite what to make of it all. It still is. Sacrilege? A daring act of iconoclasm? Hit-and-miss? Genuinely misguided? Perhaps a little of all of those. One possible point of entry is to imagine for a moment that Bush had recently staged an intimate, one-off live show and recorded it for posterity. Restricting the set list to songs from her previous two records, she played for around an hour, sometimes subtly tinkering with the material, sometimes radically revamping it.

In the end her return to live performance didn't quite happen that way, of course, but if it had the resulting album might have sounded a lot like *Director's Cut*. For if the record proved perhaps a tad anti-climactic for those who had waited six years for new material, it at least kick-started a process which involved Bush reappraising and embellishing her old songs, and which illuminated a viable path back to the stage. It was the first time since her tour in 1979 that Bush had made a sustained effort to reinterpret and recontextualise her back catalogue. Not a tour of life, perhaps, but a significant act of reimagining nonetheless – unusual, unexpected, a little bit strange. If nothing else, *Director's Cut* retains interest and value for these reasons alone. Hearing her grappling with her legacy was sufficiently rare to prove compelling. She may well have come to the same conclusion.

But ultimately it is likely to be chalked up as an enjoyable curio rather than a classic. Bush said she wanted it to be regarded as an entirely new piece of work. It doesn't wholly succeed on those terms. It's at times bold, fascinating, brave, occasionally raving mad, and it's undoubtedly wonderful to hear her cultivating her past with energy and innovation. However, it can only be deemed truly essential on the handful of occasions where she takes her songs somewhere so far from their origins that comparisons are rendered wholly worthless. Significantly, it was in these songs that she began clearing space for what was to come. From the husks of the past, she immediately started ploughing a path into the future.

★　★　★

The buzz began, as it always seems to these days, on Twitter. Rumours of a new Kate Bush record began circulating in the second week of January 2011, followed by a statement from her old friend David Munns on January 20 concerning reissues of the four albums Bush now controlled (an event which turned out to be so low-key as to almost not register on the radar). It wasn't until March 10 that news of *Director's Cut* broke officially, signalling a flurry of blogs, tweets, columns, think pieces and web forum comment.

That the basic details were delivered via leading PR firm Murray Chalmers (who handle publicity for, amongst others, Lily Allen, Noel Gallagher, Radiohead, Coldplay, Kylie Minogue and The Stone Roses) hinted at a change in Bush's core habits. By the second decade of the new millennium she had realised that the music industry had altered irrevocably and for ever. *Aerial* appeared when the extent of the change was still in some doubt; *Director's Cut* came after the flood.

The music was completed some months before the album eventually came out on May 16, 2011. As well as working on the mixing, pressing and packaging, offering her customary focus to every detail, Bush spent a lot of time rearranging the infrastructure which enabled her to release and spread the word about her music without having to rely on outside parties, or allowing the changes sweeping through the record industry to start dictating their terms to her.

The most prominent change was the decision not to continue her 35-year relationship as a recording artist for EMI. Instead, she created her own label, Fish People; EMI would still distribute her albums, but everything else would be looked after in-house. She claimed the move was necessary to give her even more creative freedom, which on the face of it seemed a little like a bird claiming that it needed more sky. But Bush's loyalty to EMI had always been based on her trust and faith in a few people at the company, and there was nobody left with whom she enjoyed a close relationship or, she felt, fulfilled the brief of being an old school music person. The departure of Tony Wadsworth following the acquisition of the company by Terra Firma was a final straw. Indeed, there are unconfirmed reports that shortly afterwards Bush called Guy Hands and told him that this would be the first and last time she would ever speak to him, adding: "The only person I have dealt with at EMI is Tony Wadsworth and now he's gone you won't be hearing from me ever again."

Whatever passed between them Bush may have been amused to read a spoof memo that appeared in *The Sunday Times* of January 6, 2008, riffing on Hands' apparent lack of tact when it came to dealing with artists.

To: Kate Bush
From: Head of Album Scheduling
Re: Productivity

Dear Ms Bush
As you will have seen in the recently circulated training DVD "EMI and You: Working Together (A Bit Harder)", we expect our artists to produce an album every two years. Given the 12-year gap that preceded *Aerial*, I'm sure you've already realised that to keep up your average, we are expecting six albums from you in the next 12-month period. Please let me know if you anticipate any problems with this. On a related matter, that song on *Aerial*, 'Mrs Bartolozzi', about the woman who cleans the whole house thoroughly and puts all the clothes in the washing machine - you

know the one: "It took hours and hours to scrub it out" – is it based on a real person? If so, could you ask her to send in her CV?

Many thanks

That EMI was sold to Universal Music Group in November 2011 for £1.2bn presumably was all the evidence Bush required that she had made the correct decision to keep the power over her music located as close as possible to home. For a woman who already enjoyed almost unprecedented latitude in the industry, she acknowledged that the shift to independent label owner/manager was, "in many ways, probably quite a subtle change . . . I've always had a lot of creative freedom since my third album, but now I don't have to refer to people at the record company for certain decisions that I might have before. With something like [the 'Deeper Understanding'] video, I really wanted to direct it without being in it and make it like a short film as opposed to a music video. That might have been something the record company would have questioned before."[14]

The existence of 'Cloudbusting' and many of her other 'short films' provide something of a counter-argument to this claim. In any case, the video – a ham-fisted, melodramatic, overly-literal pudding of a thing starring Robbie Coltrane, Noel Fielding and Frances Barber – suggested that perhaps a bit of record company interference might not have been such a bad idea after all. 'Deeper Understanding: The Movie' stands as perhaps one of her most ill-conceived and downright poor pieces of work across all the creative disciplines.

However, in general her disassociation from EMI made sound creative sense. It allowed her not only full executive power over her work in a time of flux, but also to exercise even greater degrees of control over how she was presented publicly. Leading to the release of *Director's Cut* the media was fed a steady drip-feed of information, all of it carefully orchestrated. A small number of new photos heralded the return of Theatrical Bush after the organic, naturalistic portraits of *Aerial*: mostly we saw her as Serge Eisenstein, wild and kohl-eyed, wielding scissors in the cutting room and looking more than ever like a figment of Tim Burton's imagination. In other widely-reproduced pictures she wore an over-sized pleated white collar, like those worn by circus clowns, and was seen with and without a feline friend. In another, she was dressed in Tibetan national costume.

The album itself was a lavish artefact, coming as a digital download, a standard CD with a beautiful case-bound book, a two-disc vinyl album, and as a three-disc deluxe package containing *Director's Cut*, the newly re-mastered *The Red Shoes*, and *The Sensual World* (which, oddly, had not been remastered). Much of the corrupted fairytale imagery in Tim Walker's accompanying photography ("visual concept and direction by Kate", in case we were in any doubt) was directly inspired by the cut-and-paste modernism of Max Ernst's 1934 graphic novel *Une Semaine de Bonté*.

In terms of promotion, she put her shoulder behind the record and pushed. Hard. *MOJO* magazine screamed 'Kate Bush: The Only Interview!' Well, not quite. Not even close, in fact. She worked *Director's Cut* and later *50 Words For Snow* like a pro, talking to anyone and almost everyone on websites, magazines, radio stations, in the foreign and US press, via Skype, on the telephone and, occasionally, assenting to the old-fashioned medium of a face-to-face interview, but in the latter case only when it was for radio.

We heard her voice on prime-time Saturday night television, sending luck to *The Mighty Boosh* comic Noel Fielding as he offered a game interpretation of her 'Wuthering Heights' routine for *Let's Dance For Comic Relief*. And although it wasn't her hand on the tiller – "Social networking doesn't appeal to me," she said, a statement aspiring to almost Olympian levels of obviousness. "I'd rather spend my time doing other stuff"[15] – Kate Bush as a collective public entity now embraced Twitter, Facebook, Spotify and iTunes. *Director's Cut* streamed online pre-release and a new website was launched with considerably more information on it than the last one (as well as more opportunities to spend lots of money). She seemed to have softened her previously rather disapproving view of computers; correctly harnessed, she realised that new technology could create the illusion of increased accessibility and a much higher profile without necessarily requiring her to give away anything precious. In fact, building a presence in the virtual world offered her the chance to retreat even further in the real one. "We're all in this very transitional period," she said. "It could allow artists to have a much more direct communication with their audience. I've developed this philosophy where I kind of want the focus to be on my work."[16]

The only real oddity about it all was a routine and by now familiar one: the absolute absence of Bush as a physical entity. There wasn't a single glimpse of her in the flesh, either on TV, at a public event, via an unapproved photograph, or even in her own video. The delineation between 'star' and human seemed total. There was a person portrayed occasionally in a handful of very carefully constructed scenarios playing the role of 'Kate Bush'; and there was a woman living her life below the sight lines. They were the same, but the one gave the other plenty of room. A happy and necessary accommodation, perhaps, but there remained a suspicion that the pressure of living up to a past image may have caused a rather extreme reaction. Privacy was one thing for an artist; invisibility another. In the period between 1993 and 2011 Bush had, quite consciously, become an inanimate star, a vanishing siren.

For those meeting and working with the woman rather than the mythical recluse, there came a familiar chorus avowing her extraordinary ordinariness. Mica Paris recalls Bush as a "grounded lady gassing away" on the phone, demanding to know why Paris wasn't getting more spots on Jools Holland's TV show. "She's not eccentric at all, she's incredibly normal," says Paris. "What's unusual is that she is a female who creates everything and knows exactly what she wants. It's her own genre, there's no one else in it. It's the same with Prince. When you're in a studio with him he's a master and a total professional, and very focused. They're my heroes because you never know what's going on in their personal lives – ever – and they've kept their sanity because of that. What was interesting about seeing her in the flesh was seeing that she's a beautiful lady. She has beautiful skin and great hair. She still has that youthful look, she'll stay young forever. She still has that sort of innocence in her face. It's really interesting."

For Gadd, a veteran observer of rock music's great and good, "She took care of me the way she tried to take care of her songs. She's got a great family, her engineer has been there for years, it was a really nice situation. She treated me great. She always wants to make sure you're comfortable, that you're not tired or hungry."

Reviews for *Director's Cut* ranged between lukewarm and bewildered, encompassing qualified raves and the odd howl of protest. In general, it was an indulgence which was duly indulged, both by fans and critics. The warm response to an unusual project was gratifying, and further proof that – no matter how long she stayed away or what path she chose to take – there remained large numbers of people who would be prepared to go with her. The album debuted and peaked at number two in the UK charts, selling just under 35,000 copies in its first week on sale. By that time Bush was long gone, knee deep in the freshly fallen snow of her own imagination.

★ ★ ★

What almost nobody knew during the period she spent promoting *Director's Cut* was that Bush was already more than halfway through recording her next album even as she was discussing the last one. One afternoon in early May 2011, BBC journalist John Wilson visited her home to record an interview for the Radio Four arts show *Front Row*. At the same time, unbeknownst to almost all, elsewhere on the premises Elton John was recording his vocal for a new song called 'Snowed In At Wheeler Street'. That day Bush told Wilson, "I'm working on a new record, all kinds of bits and pieces, really, in different stages." Asked whether the new album would be conceptual, she said "I don't know yet."[17]

She was, as ever, holding her cards close to her chest, and indeed was not averse to telling the odd untruth in the name of secrecy. By now the idea of making a seasonal record was fully formed. As a writer, Bush has always been capable of harnessing the elements to powerful effect, and on 'December Will Be Magic Again', 'Under Ice' and 'Moments Of Pleasure' she had displayed an occasional penchant for capturing the crisp, cold essence of winter. She planned to return to that theme, and this time stay longer. "It's one of those things I've wanted to do for a long time," she said. "I've just loved the idea of doing a sort of seasonal record. I suppose you could call it wintery, but it's more specifically about snow."[18] It would make a neat counterpoint to the second side of *Aerial*, which traced a summer's day in the country.

So yes, she might have admitted to Wilson that this mysterious album dusted with snow was loosely conceptual. However, her habitual evasiveness wasn't entirely premeditated. Work on the new record progressed much more quickly than she expected, partly due to the fact that, because of its theme, it imposed its own deadline - winter or bust! - but also thanks to the creative rush she had experienced completing *Director's Cut*. Already in a focussed and imaginative space, for the first time in her life she went from completing one record straight into making another.

As more time passes it becomes easier to see *Director's Cut* as a necessary stepping stone to *50 Words For Snow*. It opened a new door to her creativity, boosted her confidence, and made her "feel more buoyant, just in terms of moving on".[19] She described that record as finishing off a cycle, closing a circle.

But if *Director's Cut* brought with it a sense of completion, it also contained within it a vibrant sense of new beginnings. She had become reacquainted with space on *Aerial*, but that process asserted itself more fully on *Director's Cut*. In many ways, its entire *raison d'être* was a celebration of absence, an exercise in the art of leaving things out. Also crucial was the idea of giving the songs room to breathe by extending them; 10 out of 11 tracks on that record are longer than the originals, many of them considerably so. The entirely reconstructed versions of 'Moments Of Pleasure' and 'This Woman's Work', in particular, could be regarded as gateway songs to the next record. "I achieved space in those tracks, and then I went straight into this album, where it felt like a really natural journey into these new songs where the space had already been created, in a way, by having gone through that process on the previous album."[20]

Equally as significant to the album as the unifying wintery theme was this clear intent to write long, involved pieces, unhurried and full of room. On first listening to *50 Words For Snow* it sounded as though some songs were meandering on their own accord, almost as though they were provisional and unstructured. With time, it became abundantly clear that the length of the songs, most particularly the first three, was no accident. She wanted the listener to "go on a longer journey", she said, by allowing the story more time to develop.[21] "I've been trying to move away from what I felt was a more straightforward pop-song structure. And particularly with this album, I've pushed it further, in that the song structures have opened up and they're much longer. To me, it's an evolving process. It's just stepped into a different stage."[22]

In an inspired state of mind and already on a roll in the studio, she felt a sense of "elation"[23] at being able to write from scratch rather than wrestling with her old work. 'Among Angels' had arrived three years previously and, given the timing, the lyric, and the exquisite sense of loss, love and doubt in the music, it's hard not to hear it as a song composed in response to the death of her father in 2008. Everything else was written post-*Director's Cut*. She found herself returning to an older, more traditional methodology: sitting at the piano, working through the music over and over again, finding the right words and melodies, practicing, honing, feeling. It was very much a return to how she wrote many years ago: only two songs of the seven on *50 Words For Snow* could be said to start from the rhythm up, or could in any way be regarded as synth-based studio constructs.

The first to come was 'Lake Tahoe', inspired by a story told to her by a friend about a woman during the Victorian era who fell into the huge freshwater alpine lake in the Sierra Nevada. According to local legend, she still occasionally rises up to the surface briefly before disappearing again. Clearly, the old themes and images were still capable of driving her into action: the lure of water, the otherworldly, time-shifts, lost spirits trying to find their way home. She recalled two further long pieces arriving in the space of two days. "The difficult thing was actually learning them!"[24]

This organic, old school ethos was carried through to the recording process. The journey between the song as written and the song as recorded was shorter and less torturous than at any time since the late Seventies. She put the piano pieces to tape in long, live single performances, tracking the instrumental part then adding her vocals. On 'Lake Tahoe' she was nearing the end of the 11-minute take when her finger slipped from the key and left a little pocket of silence; on 'Among Angels' she started on the wrong chord and softly muttered "no". Both mistakes were left in. It was a small thing in itself, but indicative of a rather profound new commitment to preserving the mood and the moment.

In the studio Bush had developed a firm routine, working Monday to Friday during the day away from all distractions, and using her computer only in the evening to attend to business. She devoted most of the rest of her time to family life. She would no longer leap on each idea as soon as it arrived; instead she waited for the correct 'work' moment to come, and if the idea proved strong enough it would still be there for her to access. "I have a lot of commitments as a mother, and there are things I don't want to bypass," she said. "I love spending time with my son. The way I set out to be a mother was that he came first and my work would fit around that. It means I don't always get a lot of sleep, but I feel really privileged that I can do a lot of my work at home."[25] There may well be parents who raise more than a single eyebrow at the sound of a non-touring multi-millionaire artist who has released a mere four albums in the past 20 years voicing her apparent difficulties in balancing the rigours of work with the demands of raising a teenage son. Such matters are personal and always relative. Certainly, one of the reasons for her ongoing lack of appetite for touring is the disruption it would cause to the routine stability of her domestic life, while her need to find an acceptable way to work is key to her ongoing ability to make music. "If I didn't have a studio in my home I probably wouldn't be able to work," she said.[26]

Having long ago shrugged off all the accoutrements and distractions of making a record in a commercial studio, her working circle had shrunk to miniscule proportions. On what became the first track, 'Snowflake', three of only five people involved were Bush, her partner and their son. One of the others was Del Palmer, her ex-partner, engineer and closest music ally for nearly four decades. It could hardly have been more in-house and home spun.

Steve Gadd was once again invited to play drums on all tracks aside from 'Among Angels', which was left rhythmically unadorned, featuring just Bush, her piano and strings. "There was some space between [*Director's Cut*] and the new thing," says Gadd. "She might have had some ideas while we were working on the first one, but when I went back the first project was done and she was beginning the second one. With this record sometimes it was just Kate playing piano and the vocal, and trying to construct a drum part based on what was there and what could be there thereafter. It could be slow, but you take it one step at a time and build it. It doesn't make any sense until it feels right musically. When it doesn't feel right I know what she's talking about. It was great to work with her on that level – she really *knows*. It raises my game working with someone with ears like that."

"Steve was working with just the piano and the voice, he was the next musician to come in," said Bush. "I'd put the long songs down in one take, there was a feel to them, and Steve had to work on top of that and tell where I was going to be going next. Some of these tracks were not easy, in terms of their structure. A lot of the songs I'd put the piano down already and a lot of it was arrhythmic. They sounded so good just with piano and drums, there was this very interesting feel that was happening."[27]

On the opening trio of songs on the record, theirs is the key relationship: Bush's piano and Gadd's endlessly nuanced drums define the tracks. Around them, painterly touches were provided by her trusted core of musicians. John Giblin and Danny Thompson added electric and acoustic bass,

Palmer dusted down his four-string to play – beautifully – on 'Snowflake', while Danny McIntosh played all the guitars with the lightest of touches.

Into this sealed world of family and old friends guest musicians briefly came and then departed. Andy Fairweather Low, nowadays frequently in demand among rock's premier league, added an arresting vocal counterpoint to 'Wild Man'. Elton John snuck in for a day in May and quickly nailed the vocal on 'Snowed In At Wheeler Street', despite insisting that he didn't want to hear the track before he arrived. Bush was overjoyed to finally work with a musician she had loved since childhood. "I just think his performance on it is so great, so emotive," she said. "I'm just completely knocked out. I was so excited that he agreed to do it. It was really written for him, so I didn't know what I would have done."[28]

Stefan Roberts and Michael Wood came to sing on 'Lake Tahoe'. Roberts had been part of the Choir of Magdalen College Oxford, whose choristers had appeared on 'Lyra'. Wood had sung previously on 'A Coral Room' and was one of three members of Waynflete Chamber Choir who had added their voices to the new recording of 'Moments Of Pleasure'. The atmospheric, textural orchestral arrangements by Jonathan Tunick were recorded – as ever – at Abbey Road.

She worked right up to the wire in order to get the album ready for a 2011 release, all too aware that if she missed her deadline she would have to wait another year to put it out. "I think in a lot of ways I was driven, because otherwise I would have had to wait and release it next winter, which I really didn't want to do."[29] Then again, part of her simply wanted to keep going. "The imagery kept coming," she said. "I think I could easily have written another album's worth. I certainly wasn't lost for inspiration."[30] Stephen Fry came to record his part as Professor Joseph Yupik on the title track on September 2, 2011, just 10 days before the album's existence and impending arrival was officially announced, and a mere nine weeks before it was released. Bush was still writing the words to the track 10 minutes before he arrived. Fry, a stalwart of the *Blackadder/ Comic Strip* axis of actors whom Bush had known since the early Eighties, was chosen because "I needed someone who had a great voice of authority, so when they were saying silly-sounding words it would still have a sense of being important. He was, really, the only man for the job."[31]

An inveterate tweeter, after he'd completed his work on the song Fry tweeted that he had just done "a lovely, amazing recording thing with a lively amazing musician. Wish I could say more but bound by secrecy for the moment". Said Bush, "I asked him to try and keep quiet about it. It's difficult now with the internet not to give everything away when something comes out, whether it be a record or a book or a film."[32]

Ten days later, amid growing rumours and an online leak of the simple, appropriately wintery cover art, the release of *50 Words For Snow* on Fish People was officially announced, scheduled for November 21, 2011. The same day Fry was able to finally reveal his secret – via Twitter, naturally.

★ ★ ★

If *Director's Cut* was all about closing the circle, *50 Words For Snow*, on the other hand, is as opened-out as anything Bush has ever done. It marks a final severance, perhaps, from anything that could be called pop or even rock music. Her music has less and less to do with the games of rhythmic repetition and hooks which obsess those genres. Instead, she has worked her way to the fringes, into the realms of chamber-jazz, ECM and contemporary classical music, where diffuse melodies ebb and flow, meander and evolve. She is moving out into the wilds, increasingly a companion in spirit if not always in sound to Scott Walker and Mark Hollis, John Martyn at his most stretched and abandoned, or Van Morrison on the extraordinary *Common One* album: going deeper, further.

The music on *50 Words For Snow* is full of space but there is more going on than might at first be apparent. It is at once both simple and very complex. At times there are echoes of 'The Ninth Wave', but here the water is deeper and the ice floe is moving slower. It unravels like an old fashioned vinyl album: side two, containing the final four tracks, is rather more upbeat and the rhythm more accentuated - aside from on the closing 'Among Angels', which returns to the album's foundation stone of Bush and her piano. It is this haunting sound which defines side one, consisting of a three-song suite of quite extraordinary beauty.

Within seconds of 'Snowflake' starting with a soft flurry of piano the listener has been pulled through the wardrobe and is immediately aware that Bush has created a distinct song-world for this album. The first voice we hear is that of her son, Bertie. Although not a chorister, his clear, pure tone suggests he might have been. As the atmospheric narrative about this fragile, transient creation drifting through the sky towards some unnamed destination progresses, there comes a powerful awareness of a mother's sadness at a child growing into adulthood. "I wrote 'Snowflake' specifically for him and for his voice," she said. "There was a strong parallel in my mind between the idea of this little snowflake and that fact that Bertie will soon lose this high, pure voice as he gets older. There seemed to be a link between the brief time his voice will be like this and the brevity of the snowflake."[33] And yet, wherever he lands, "I'll find you".

If the emotional connection on 'Snowflake' hits home hard, it's the music rather than the vocal interplay between mother and son which carries the momentum. Bush's dextrous piano is joined later by Del Palmer's prowling bass and Gadd's splashes of rhythm, and together they conjure a moonlit ride through a white-out, where peace comes dropping slow and every sense is heightened, every sound amplified.

"The world is so loud" is a lament which drifts over the rest of an album largely devoted to the power of stillness. The world *is* too loud; it also wants to know too much. Lyrically, *50 Words For Snow* consistently seeks to preserve mystery, to exalt the unknown, to leave much unsaid. Snow is deployed as the great elemental transformer in a world which now seeks to understand everything. It imposes stillness and almost instant change, it is both beautiful and unsettling, playful and destructive. Bush uses these snowscapes as a playground for myths and secrets, the hidden world, for exploring transient but powerful feelings.

'Lake Tahoe' is another gothic ghost story, another time-shifting narrative about a mysterious lady in a lake and the sad dog left behind, dreaming of her return. Musically, it's an astonishingly clever and accomplished piece of work, beginning with the choral voices of Stefan Roberts and Michael Wood soaring softly over piano and strings. The high tones of the stately, Schubertian male voices rub against Bush's lower pitch, a neat gender switch and an effective textural device, but after three and a half minutes the mood and music shifts: rooks craw in the background, a sound of "desolation",[34] and the song takes on a dark, bluesy tone, becoming a slow, lowering Bolero between the piano and Steve Gadd's intense, rolling rhythm. Beautiful touches emerge as from a sea mist: a tense, taut string line; a smudge of woodwind; a vaguely Middle Eastern melody; a sinister death rattle. Bush's abrasive cry of "Snooowflaaaaake!" recalls the desperate "It's meeeeeeeee!" from 'Under Ice'.

At almost nine minutes comes that little gap in her piano track, partly covered by a breathy gasp from Bush, as though the singer has momentarily slipped a leg through the ice. The song powers from there to its climax, becoming heavier, more pressing. The climactic "You've come home" is thrilling, Bush hooting in the fog before falling, spent. It will, in time, come to be regarded as one of her greatest achievements.

'Misty' starts in the same vein, a two-chord piano pattern with the angular propulsion of Dave Brubeck's 'Take Five'. It is a strange song even by Bush's extraordinary standards, and although it has several moments of transcendent beauty, it is not an entirely successful one. Describing a fleeting tryst between a female – in interviews Bush refers to her as both a "girl" and a "woman" – and a snowman, she admitted, "It's a silly idea, but I hope there's tenderness, and it's quite dark. I hope I've made it work, but in a lot of ways it shouldn't."[35]

'Misty' dares to flirt with outright ridicule but it's the darkness and sense of loss that lingers. There is, we learn early on, blood on a hand, but where has it come from: the hymen? Menstruation? Something more sinister? Or less? Mostly, 'Misty' seems to be concerned with the mystery of love, the power of fantasy and the transience of sex, describing a Saturday night coupling which by Sunday morning has become nothing more than a damp patch on the bedclothes – and her man isn't just detumescent and heading gingerly for the door, he's actually melted.

Stretching to almost 14 minutes, the song's structure is genuinely challenging. Indeed, at times it almost loses its way, although some unexpected echoes of the distant past light a path through. The bluesy breakdown which begins with her singing "I turn off the light" directly recalls 'The Man With The Child In His Eyes', almost certainly unintentionally. There are further parallels with that song, not only in the music and melody, but also in the idea of a mysterious nocturnal visitor, the unabashed carnality, the meshing of the real and the imagined.

After three songs and 35 minutes, 'Wild Man' is the first track on *50 Words For Snow* that could be classed as being remotely close to pop music. It has electric bass, synthesisers, meaty backing vocals and a defined rhythm, all of which it wears gracefully and lightly. There is a slight hint of Grace Jones's muttered menace in the semi-spoken word verses, and also a vague suggestion of Yoko Ono, while the faintly Eastern motif which runs throughout recalls *Lodger*-era Bowie. Coming out of the radio in the early winter of 2011 it sounded neither dated nor especially contemporary. Simply beautiful.

'Wild Man' is mythopoeic, a literal hymn to the legend of the Yeti or Abominable Snowman which also explores private concerns far closer to home than the uncharted wilds of the Nepalese peaks. In this original twist on the archetypal story of the hunter and the hunted, it doesn't require a huge interpretative leap to see Bush as the wild man, up in the metaphorical mountains, chased by the pack and covering her footprints in the snow. "They want to know you, they will hunt you down / Then they will kill you . . ." The only solution, it seems, is to run away.

The preservation of mystery, the protection of myth, the desire not to put a name on and a cage around everything is classic Bush territory ('King Of The Mountain' told a similar tale) and one which has obvious personal resonance. She lamented the ease at which Google and YouTube could obliterate centuries of delicious uncertainty. "In our contemporary world, things of mystery are even more precious than they were before the internet and I think it would be really terrible if that mystery was taken away from us," she said. "It's really important."[36]

Elton John joined the party on 'Snowed In At Wheeler Street', a song born from Bush "looking for an original approach to tackle reincarnation, and that déjà vu feeling you get".[37] Both musically and in its lyrical theme of eternally thwarted love, it feels a little like a companion piece to 'Never Be Mine', only on an epic scale. The camera pans out over months, years and centuries to track two lovers, forever coming together throughout history (in Ancient Rome, classical Paris, during World War II and in the London smog), and forever pulled apart by forces apparently beyond their control.

It opens with an oddly hesitant, unresolved melody and throughout throbs rather than sears, never quite seeming to get going. Compared to the powerfully muted delicacy surrounding it, both the music and the emotions it carries feel somewhat overwrought and shrill, particularly during the crash-bang-wallop finale, which barely avoids a rather dubious element of manufactured hysteria. The sense of mystery that so pervades the rest of the record here descends towards the obvious and overstated: "At 9/11 in New York I took your photograph" is not one of Bush's most graceful lyrics, neither does the lovers' story evolve or offer any resolution. And although she raved about the power of John's deeper vocal, the blend between the two voices isn't an especially convincing one.

At times like these the relative speed in which she completed the project seems most apparent; it's not hard to imagine a better version of 'Snowed In A Wheeler Street'. Like the title track which follows, it also takes too long – eight minutes – to get where it's going. '50 Words For Snow' is a much more enjoyable ride, though. Gadd's eager drum pattern, John Giblin's syncopated bass and Danny McIntosh's heavily treated guitar create a churning momentum which recalls 'The Dreaming'. The song unfolds under a dark sky and in the centre of some whirling snowstorm, where the lights of home are no longer visible. There is a pleasing mischievousness and terrific invention in the increasingly outlandish descriptions of snow ("blackbird Braille", "mountainsob", "ankle breaker", "Shnamistoflopp'n", "terrablizza"), each one delivered by Stephen Fry resolutely playing Stephen Fry. The chorus really sticks as a chorus should, and it's heartening to hear a little of the old rhythmic pulse pushing the music. On the down side, the song is too much beholden to its title concept: cramming in a whole 50 words for snow means it goes on far longer than it should. After five minutes there are still "22 to go", and yet this enjoyable but essentially slight track has by then all but exhausted its possibilities.

'Among Angels', written some years earlier, "has nothing to do with snow whatsoever, but I felt that it had its place in there atmospherically".[38] The shortest song on the album at 6:49, it opens with a brief false start, a muffled aside, and then begins with just Bush and her piano. Moving "in and out of doubt", it addresses love, hope, death, belief, struggle. It could be about her father, but it could just as easily be a song for a friend in need, or a son. 'Among Angels' contains strong echoes of her pre-*The Kick Inside* compositions, particularly the unreleased 'Something Like A Song' on the passage that begins "I might know what you mean when you say you fall apart". She spends five minutes circling the whisper of a melody before catching it towards the end, with the help of a gorgeous swelling orchestral arrangement. Elegant, exquisite, show stopping.

The seven tracks on *50 Words For Snow* are embedded in myth, mystery and legend, but in subsequent interviews Bush very skilfully deflected any attempts to discuss what those songs actually meant to her. She was happy to talk prosaically about the genesis of 'Lake Tahoe' or 'Wild Man', but at the point of direct personal connection she pulled up the drawbridge. There are Wheeler Streets in Birmingham, Seattle, Cambridge and New York State – does it matter which one relates to the song? Bush certainly wasn't letting on. And as ever, she was wary of any critic imposing Grand Themes on her music – a suggestion that the album was a song-cycle encompassing birth, life and death was rapidly dismissed. A song about a ghost in a lake in Nevada was, apparently, no more or less than that; a song about a Yeti was nothing more than a slap on the wrist to human arrogance and its desire to know everything. At the moment when the discussion moves to *why* she might want to write a song about a sexual encounter with a snowman, the meaningful conversation stops and the music begins. It's just as well, then, that engaging in the mysteries of interpretation is one of the great joys of the album. It has its flaws, but the best parts only grow more extraordinary the more and the closer you listen to them.

It took the release of *50 Words For Snow* to really illuminate the relative slightness of *Director's Cut*. Bush had discovered yet another new way of being innovative, charting her own course without paying any heed to the current musical discourse. "She is not afraid," says Steve Gadd simply. "She's all about the art of it. I've never done another project like it. Her music is unique and beautiful and artistic. It was hard work but very fulfilling."

Any sense of disappointment, if it could be called that, was faintly felt rather than overt, and had more to do with what the album wasn't than what it was. It appears we have seen the last of Bush as a truly visionary *popular* artist. "I feel that there's a naturally evolving process I've moved through that means I'm gradually moving away from pop music," she said.[39] Although many of the sounds and styles she pioneered in the Eighties were now in vogue, she made no attempt to engage with them. She expressed vague gratitude that she was regarded as an influence on the likes of Florence + The Machine and Bat For Lashes, but she clearly had zero interest in exploring their music or working with them. The inclusion of Andy Fairweather Low, Elton John and Stephen Fry on the album showed no great progression in her central influences since the Eighties – Bush takes a very cloistered approach to seeking out new music. And although she revealed she had bought a Gorillaz album, such bands are highly unlikely to have an influence on the music she makes from hereon in. *50 Words For Snow* is wrapped in a beautiful veil of sadness, soft and sensuous. It is a thing of wonder, but we were also surely entitled to miss the sheer joy, the big rapturous 'O', the affirming yelp and euphoria that propelled much of her previous recorded work. It is also, of course, an album with inbuilt restrictions on its use – as the nights grow lighter and the days longer it starts to feel almost redundant. Like Christmas, its time comes but once a year.

★ ★ ★

50 Words For Snow was released on November 21, 2011 as a digital album, a standard CD in a case-bound book, and as a vinyl double album. As usual, it looked superb. "How she puts the album together sonically and visually – with photographers, images – is pretty amazing," says Steve Gadd. "It's the whole package."

It received almost uniformly terrific reviews from all around the world. Critics found their advance copy of the album was accompanied by an extremely daunting sheaf of legal documentation promising death or its close equivalent on anyone who dare breathe a word of its contents online or share the music 'by any means whatsoever or hereafter devised'. Such scare tactics had the desired affect of preserving the sense of anticipation until very close to its release date, and it certainly didn't deter anyone from engaging with an album which required something close to total immersion to really appreciate.

The general discourse about Bush suddenly seemed healthier, more relaxed, much more music-centric. The fact that she had released an album just six months previously, for which she had granted several interviews and generally been as visible as she ever has been, meant her first album of new material for six years stood a far greater chance of being discussed on its own merits rather than as part of the narrative of "the return of the weirdo recluse". There was some of that, but generally the air seemed a little clearer.

50 Words For Snow entered the UK album charts at number five on the first week of release, selling almost 50,000 copies in that period, a very respectable figure at a time of industry slump; it also became one of the best-selling vinyl albums of the year. The business had changed almost immeasurably since she had first arrived in early 1978, but Bush had surfed the shifting tides with a kind of regal detachment. Her latest album extended her unbroken string of Top 10 albums in the UK to 11 (including *The Whole Story*) since *The Kick Inside*, and meant she now had released top five albums in five different decades.

Once again she put her full weight behind the record. There were billboards posted in major cities, a TV ad voiced by Stephen Fry, even a couple of brief official statements about things other than music. The first reassured everyone who saw her heavily wrapped up in a fur hat and coat in the handful of promotional photos that she was not wearing a dead animal; the other was a heartfelt protest about continuing Chinese oppression in Tibet which was causing monks to set themselves alight in protest. A few cynics raised an eyebrow that her humanist streak moved her to make a rare public announcement the week before an album came out; everybody else put it down to a quirk of timing.

It was a case of from famine to feast. Post-*50 Words For Snow*, the myth that Bush "rarely gives interviews" could forever be banished. There were scores of them, most of which gave little or nothing away and often said the same thing in so similar a fashion you began wondering whether she was working from a script. Generally she sounded warm, relaxed and happy, often breaking out into a smoky laugh. Politely but firmly preserving her privacy, she did occasionally reveal the odd titbit of extracurricular information.

She no longer danced. She read reviews of her work because "I do like to know what people think, but you do have to be strong".[40] She was a fan of Duncan Jones's smart sci-fi movie *Source Code* and retained a passionate commitment to preserving the album format. She rarely travelled, despite the many exotic locations mentioned on *50 Words For Snow* and, yes, she believed in Yetis. "I do, actually. Why not? Why should we know about everything that exists in the remotest parts of this planet?"[41] Her desire to feature Bertie in her music – "I've always involved my family and friends in my music, and he's the new member of the gang"[42] – was clearly going to be ongoing, and meant that she had to be expected to discuss him to a certain degree. We learned that he played the violin and was "quite musical. He's good at a lot of things".[43] He liked his mother's music but was also "one of my greatest critics".[44]

She claimed she would love to release a DVD collection of her videos at some point, but in the continued absence of such an artefact fans had to make do with three very different animated films, created to accompany segments from 'Wild Man', 'Misty' and 'Lake Tahoe'. The first featured a glimpse of Bush wrapped in fake furs amongst atmospheric swirls of white and dark shadows, depicting an expeditionary force climbing the mountains in search of mystery.

The second was a piece of stop-frame animation named 'Mistraldespair' which, perhaps rather literally, visualised the tryst between the snowman and the woman. 'Eider Falls At Lake Tahoe' was the longest film at five minutes, a simple and haunting piece of shadow puppetry tracking the dog's journey over land and water to be reunited with its owner. Puppets and shadow theatre, it transpired, were very much at the front of her mind.

This tumult of activity in 2011 put her firmly back in the spotlight, and the ongoing reverberations kept her public profile on a medium heat well into 2012. Her image took up half of the front page of the *Guardian* in early January, the day after she was nominated for a Brit award for Best Female Artist. Less than 48 hours later she was also splashed all over another newspaper, this time when it was revealed that a stalker had broken into her home shortly after Christmas. Having flown to the UK with a £3,000 ring bought from Tiffany's in New York, 32-year-old American Frank Tufaro arrived at Bush's property in Devon with the intention, he claimed, of proposing to her. When he realised nobody was at home, he broke a window and clambered inside. After wandering around for 10 minutes, he left the property and was arrested near the house shortly afterwards by a police team supported by a helicopter unit. He was detained under the Mental Health Act and deported back to the United States.

Perhaps the wider subtext that lurked behind that unwelcome (but not unprecedented) intrusion had prompted some of the changes which had already taken place in the personal life. As soon as *50 Words For Snow* was completed, her mill house in Theale went on the market for £2,500,000. She had bought a new home some time previously, a rambling, historic, three-storey, nine-bedroom house by the riverside in a picture postcard Oxfordshire village, which had been put on sale in July 2009 for £6,500,000. There were smaller external buildings which could, in time, serve as studios.

Releasing two albums in one year inevitably changed things. The release and promotion of *Director's Cut*, swiftly followed by *50 Words For Snow*, ensured that her music had become less burdened by the extraneous issues of her mythical stature and her "silence". That particular spell, or curse perhaps, seemed finally to be starting to wear off. As it did so, the path leading to further work seemed less uncertain. Where only a few years previously it was up for debate whether Bush would ever release any new music again, at the age of 53 she seemed re-engaged with her muse, fully back in the world and in the process of writing a third act to a career which, it had become obvious, had no serious modern precedent. Deep in the drifts of her imagination, she appeared as alive to the wonder of the world as ever, even if that world was getting louder at the same time as her music seemed destined to immerse itself in something closer to silence.

She professed that she would like to work quicker. She felt, improbably, that she was only just getting the hang of making records, and hinted at further treasures to come. "I feel very proud of this album in a way that I haven't since my first record," she said. "What I think is really interesting, in a strange kind of way by doing *Director's Cut* it was almost like finishing off a cycle. It feels to me like [*50 Words For Snow*] has begun a new phase. That's what it feels like. In some ways this feels like the beginning of my music from now on. I'd like to have a break and then make another album. I've got a few ideas . . ."[45]

She most certainly had, and it transpired that they would eventually take her not to the studio, but to somewhere few observers imagined she would ever return: back to the stage.

14

Before The Dawn. . . & Afterwards

ONCE again, it was Peter Gabriel who threatened to give the game away. Not content with revealing to the world, back in 2000, that Bush had become a mother, 14 years later Gabriel's loose lips almost sunk the launch of the biggest bombshell in recent musical history.

Talking to this writer on February 26, 2014, about his new concert film, *Back To Front*, the conversation turned to Gabriel's old friend and duet partner. "We send each other records and cards but I haven't seen her for quite a while," he said, adding, "Kate has been quite well buried away, but there are rumours that her hiding away might be interrupted for a little while in the near future." He smiled. "It would be lovely."

When pushed on the detail Gabriel, somewhat reluctantly, clammed up, but here was the very first public inkling, some four weeks prior to 'Before The Dawn' being announced, that Bush was already committed to the most ambitious undertaking of her career. As it was, her secret remained the preserve of a trusted few until the morning of Friday, March 21, 2014, when it was announced via her website that popular music's most reluctant live draw would be performing 15 shows at London's Eventim Apollo throughout August and September.

Even without Gabriel's hint, perhaps with hindsight it might have been possible to see it coming. By her own recent standards, Bush had continued to be 'present' following the release of *50 Words For Snow*. She made a public appearance, at the Dorchester Hotel, in June 2012 to pick up the Sky Arts Pop Award for her last album. Accepting the award from Tom Jones, who lurched painfully through the autocue with the aura of a man for whom reading aloud was indeed unusual, Bush was a beguiling bundle of nerves and gratitude. She produced a crumpled piece of paper to make a short, gracious speech, singling out Danny McIntosh and Bertie for particular praise. Her son, now almost 14 and with a vibrant crop of ginger hair, sat in the audience, chaperoned by Terry Gilliam.

To mark the 2012 London Olympics, which began a few weeks later on July 27, Bush subjected 'Running Up That Hill' to the *Director's Cut* treatment, dropping it a semitone, extending the backing track to accentuate the rhythm and adding a new vocal. Even at this stage there were murmurings of a live comeback, persistent rumours that Bush would appear at the event's opening or closing ceremony to perform the remix in person.

In fact, her participation extended to making a video involving Jude Law, to be screened at the closing ceremony. Bush was, however, ultimately unhappy with the results and pulled the film, proving that even A-list film stars weren't spared the cutting room floor should her work not live up to her expectations. In the end, the new audio of 'Running Up That Hill' was played at the ceremony as drummers patrolled the arena, footage of great Olympic achievements was displayed on the screens, and a group of dancers assembled a huge pyramid of white boxes in the centre of the park.

"I called her up after the ceremony and she answered the phone," says Brian Bath. "I was surprised I got through. I said, 'I thought there would be thousands of people calling you,' but she said, 'No, you're the only person who has bothered to call!'" The remix gave Bush her first top ten single since 2005, reaching number six in the UK charts in August 2012. By the time she had collected her CBE from the Queen during a Windsor Castle investiture ceremony in April 2013 – "Now I've got something really special to put on top of the Christmas tree," Bush said in a prepared statement, though she swept past waiting reporters afterwards without comment – she was already in the early stages of planning 'Before The Dawn'.

Bush gave no interviews following the announcement, nor in the run up to the concerts, during the shows themselves or in their immediate aftermath. As a result, the all-pervading 'why' which hung over this momentous undertaking was left largely to the mercy of idle speculation. She acknowledged the question only briefly, with glib good humour, in her programme notes. "In March 2013, I said to Bertie, 'Shall we do some shows?' He said, 'Yes, absolutely!' I really wanted to do something different from working on another album and felt a real desire to have contact with the audience that still liked my work."[1]

And that was it. It was, deliberately, thin gruel for those who had waited 35 years for Bush to reach this decision, but her words contained crumbs of clues nonetheless. Bush's vaulting leaps of creativity have most often occurred within strict and rather limited physical parameters. "Part of her really relies on the family, the protective cocoon, and yet another part of her is so adventurous creatively and so willing to just depart completely from the box that she's been put in and stretch the fabric of time and space," says Charlie Morgan. "It's an interesting and total dichotomy [between] her day-to-day life, which is relatively cosseted, and yet her creativity being without boundaries."

For the longest time that dichotomy raised the odds against her playing live. Now it seemed to encourage it. Her son's involvement was key. With Bertie now in his mid-teens, performing live had become an endeavour which, far from taking Bush away from her family commitments, could instead enrich them. Bertie had firm aspirations to be an actor – he had recently sat exams for the London Academy of Music and Dramatic Art – and part of Bush's change of heart was wrapped up in her obvious pride in showcasing him publicly as an emerging actor and singer. 'Before The Dawn' was conceived as something that mother and son could embark upon as a shared adventure.

"I can see that Bush obsession working again in [Bertie]," said his uncle, John Carder Bush. "He wants to be an actor, I think, and he's got the self-confidence to do it."[2] In a touching reversal of the traditional parent-child dynamic, his youthful confidence radiated reassurance to Bush. "He gave me the courage to push the button," she told the crowd during the first performance of 'Before The Dawn'. "Thank you Bertie." The show, in many respects, was a very public demonstration of mutual devotion, a gift both from her to him, and from him to her.

Yet her stated desire to re-establish a direct connection with her audience was also significant. Bush has never craved adulation. She wants people to enjoy her music, but she genuinely does not have – and in this she is perhaps unique amongst performers at any level – the compulsion to be loved by a room full of strangers. Nevertheless, there was a sense that her need for privacy had bricked up the kind of ongoing creative dialogue with her audience which was far more positive than negative. Did her work now exist too much in a vacuum? If so, Bush felt compelled to break a spell of isolation that had worked perhaps just a little too well.

There was, certainly, no better time to consider restoring the myth to flesh and blood. With two recent records under her belt, both of which she had promoted heavily (if all but invisibly), she was match fit once more, and closer to the conventions of being a full time working musician than at any time since the early Nineties. Perhaps even more significantly, with her son now a young man and – as an aspiring thespian – actively seeking exposure rather than shying away from it, the need to form a protective shell around him had diminished. And, she may finally have pondered, if not now, then when? At least it would stop writers asking her about it whenever she consented to an interview.

Typically, once she had committed to the venture she poured every ounce of her creative energy into it. Selecting the right framework within which to present the show was crucial. 'Before The Dawn' was meticulously planned to counter-act many of the negatives Bush still associated with playing live. An extended residency at a single venue allowed her to approach the production with complete dedication to her vision, without the need to concern herself with the practicalities of different stages, variable acoustics and lighting rigs, as well as having to dismantle a highly complex set and reassemble it at a new venue every other night. A residency also, undoubtedly, suited her temperament. Performing live again would be hard enough without the rigmarole of negotiating new cities, hotel check-ins, security drills and privacy issues; it also afforded a minimum of domestic disruption.

Though she could have sold out the O2 many times over, Bush sought a medium scale theatre venue for an intimate ambience. She revealed that early design prototypes based on a huge hangar-like venue had made her feel "physically sick".[3] There would be no jumbo video screens flanking the stage, no over-sized buckets of soft drinks, no aroma of hot dog and chips drifting in from the foyer.

Happily, the schedule for the completion of a major refurbishment programme at the previously rather downtrodden Eventim Apollo, formerly the Carling Apollo and before that the Hammersmith Odeon, coincided almost exactly with the timeline for the shows. As the location for her last full concert on May 14, 1979, it was also a space where she felt comfortable. For most major artists, returning to the same venue you played on your last tour would be a worrying sign of career stasis. For Bush, several decades beyond such considerations, it was "the perfect setting".[4] With its comfortable 4,000 capacity and revamped old school charm, the venerable theatre perfectly suited her needs. It was also handy. The Apollo is situated in west London, easily accessed by the M4 and M40 motorways that lead west out of the city towards her house near Abingdon in Oxfordshire. For the duration of 'Before The Dawn', Bush would be in familiar surroundings and a mere hour's drive from home.

If the choice of venue turned out to be a nod to nostalgia, creatively it was clear that Bush viewed whole swathes of her past largely as another country. She decided early on that the focus of the show would be relatively narrow. All but three of the songs performed in 'Before The Dawn' were taken from *Aerial* and *Hounds Of Love*. She had said several times that she felt the two records were linked by certain similarities of sound and spirit, while their two conceptual suites – 'The Ninth Wave' and 'A Sky Of Honey' – lent themselves to a sustained visual experience. Dramatic, interlinked and already highly visual, they are the two pieces of her own work for which she has most often expressed satisfaction, a rare enough emotion for Bush, who tends to look back with exasperation rather than contentment.

As well as seeking a thematic fit, she must have also given consideration to what material would most suit her voice, something that counted against revisiting her first four records and weighted the show towards more recent work. In the end, songs from only two more of her nine studio albums were included – two tracks from *The Red Shoes* and one from *50 Words For Snow*. 'Never Be Mine' was part of the set list for the opening night, slotted between 'Top Of The City' and 'Running Up That Hill', but it was never performed. Similarly, 'Moments Of Pleasure' and 'A Coral Room' were also rehearsed, intended initially to form part of the encore, but they were eventually cut. There were rumours that Bush had performed 'Wuthering Heights' during the warm-up show, held for family and friends on the Sunday before the opening night of 'Before The Dawn', but this was not the case. A photographer was present at this show and a carefully chosen selection of pictures was distributed to the media on opening night through the photo agency Rex Features. In every other respect, the warm-up concert mirrored every one of the public shows.

★ ★ ★

'Before The Dawn' was conceived by Bush as a three-hour immersive stage show split into two acts and three parts. To fulfil her vision, she handpicked individuals who had made an impression on her from her frequent forays into London's theatreland. Lighting designer Mark Henderson, a veteran of some of the biggest productions in the West End and on Broadway, was a key early appointment, as was set designer Dick Bird, who boasted equally impressive credentials in the world of theatre, opera and ballet.

Old friends were also called into service. David Munns, her supporter and confidante for over 30 years, was on hand to offer advice and scout venues. David Garfath – who had directed 'Running Up That Hill' almost 30 years before – was hired to shoot the filmed sequences for 'The Ninth Wave', in which Bush would portray the real life ordeal of the suite's protagonist, lost at sea and awaiting rescue.

These were some of the most fraught days of pre-production. Wearing a custom made life jacket, and with her "little light" shining, Bush spent up to six hours at a time in the 20-foot flotation tank at Pinewood Studios, growing cold, impatient and finding increasingly inventive ways to swear. Virtually anyone else would have lip-synced to a pre-recorded vocal, but Bush was insistent that the filmed sequences would show her singing live in real time while immersed in the water. The effect was eventually achieved using microphones hidden in two inflater tubes on the life jacket, although the Method approach left her with mild hypothermia and a ticking off from her doctor.

When it came to the music, Bush assembled a group of highly experienced session men notable for their impeccably understated professionalism, capable of providing a rock-solid musical foundation for her voice, as well as coping with the considerable nuances of these songs and the theatrics they often demanded. She recruited Peter Gabriel's regular guitarist David Rhodes, long-time Bush bassist John Giblin, classically trained new age guitarist Frissi Karlsson and regular Pink Floyd collaborator Jon Carin on keyboards and programming. The rhythm, the beating heart of the show, would be supplied by larger than life French percussionist Mino Cinelu and redoubtable drummer Omar Hakim. The sole remaining links in the chain stretching back to 'Tour Of Life' were Irishman Kevin McAlea, on keyboards, accordion and Uilleann pipes, and Bush herself, who played piano on only two songs.

Of the five singers in the Chorus, who as Bush's principal dramatic foils adopted various personae throughout the production, four were recruited from the stage and musical theatre. Sandra Marvin, Jacqui DuBois, Jo Servi and Bob Harms were experienced actors and session singers, with particularly strong soul, R&B and gospel roots. The other Chorus member was Bertie.

Her determination to shoot for the very best calibre of collaborator had not faded with time. She invited Adrian Noble, formerly creative director of the Royal Shakespeare Company, to co-direct with her. Rather than someone who would come in and seek to radically alter her overall vision for the piece, Noble's role became that of genial facilitator, ensuring that Bush's ideas reached the stage in the best shape possible, finessed with his own inspirational touches and creative eye for detail.

She also enlisted the help of acclaimed English novelist David Mitchell, author of *Cloud Atlas* and *The Bone Clocks*, and a Bush fan of longstanding. "It's so inspiring that an artist in her field just keeps getting better," Mitchell told me shortly before 'Before The Dawn' opened. "I thought *50 Words For Snow* was pretty much her best album, and I thought that about *Aerial*. Perhaps *The Red Shoes* and *The Sensual World* were just a little bit more hit and miss, but even then they're brilliant albums. She fulfils the Three Great Albums rule. If you've got three five-star albums then you're in the pantheon as one of the greats – there's only a handful of artists who are there. She has *Hounds Of Love*, *The Dreaming*, *Aerial*, and *50 Words…* That's four!"

It's no surprise that Bush and Mitchell hit it off, and embarked on an occasional correspondence. They are both risk takers who share an uncanny ability to access different worlds, their imaginations unfettered by the limitations of binary absolutes: living and dead, male and female, past and present, reality and fantasy – all appear as liquid concepts in their work. As the idea of playing live was starting to formulate, Mitchell invited Bush, via her agent, to the opening night of *Sunken Garden*, a '3D film opera' he had written with Dutch contemporary classical composer Michel van der Aa, performed at the Barbican between April 12 and 20, 2013. "To my great surprise she emailed me back, and said she'd love to go," Mitchell said. "I think she was thinking of 'Before The Dawn' even then."[5]

It was, Bush conceded, an "interesting bit of timing"[6]. Afterwards, she talked with Mitchell and Aa over a glass of wine. When the moment came to create the dialogue she felt was required to stitch together 'The Ninth

Wave' into a more unified narrative, she sought out Mitchell for his input. He described himself as a co-writer, used by Bush largely as a sounding board. "She sent notes and ideas, I knocked those into a first draft, she knocked them into a second draft, we were pinging back and forth six or seven times until Kate was happy," he said. "So I am her humble servant. I am an obedient cog in her majestic machine, no more than that, but it was so cool."[7] A purportedly humorous – though in reality, rather laboured – approximation of the pair's creative dialogue was spread over two pages of the programme.

Mitchell was just one such "cog" in an undertaking that involved a full 18 months of plotting, planning, revising, rehearsing and performing. Actors and singers were identified and auditioned by key company members, often without knowing what they were auditioning for. Such sensitive information was kept secret until after they had been hired, at which point they were asked, politely but firmly, not to breathe a word.

'Before The Dawn' would be credited to the KT Fellowship, a nice nod back to the days of the KT Bush Band, and all of Bush's discourse regarding the process made reference to "we" this and "our" that. At the end of the final performance, during 'Cloudbusting', the entire cast and crew came onstage for their curtain call, in recognition of their collective effort.

Putting the show together in a former school building, the warm, creative, familial atmosphere recalled the spirit that had fuelled 'Tour Of Life'. Bush split the enterprise into distinct departments. The band rehearsed in one space, the designers worked up their ideas in another, while the technical team managed the logistics from their office in the same building. There were puppeteers in the old gymnasium, and costume fittings were held in the art department. One source recalls Bush obsessing over every detail, down to the design of the – beautiful – tickets. "Driving us mad," they sighed, not unkindly. Even the programme was a glorious artefact, painstakingly created to resemble some ancient parchment dragged up from the depths of the ocean.

It was all classic Bush, obsessively detailed, utterly idiosyncratic and veiled in secrecy. In an age of full disclosure she somehow managed to retain the trump cards of mystery and surprise. Given the scale of the production and the number of component parts required, this may well have ranked as her most impressive piece of subterfuge yet. David Mitchell explains it thus: "People who work with her are persuaded by her wish for privacy and tend not to talk out of school."

"It was a family secret we had to sit on for a long time," added John Carder Bush. "But that's always been how it is. She's always very careful not to release any information about anything . . . [Even] I had no idea what to expect."[8]

The pains taken to preserve the magic were not in vain. No ingénue when it comes to the machinations of the music industry, Bush has always understood the importance of making a full blooded impact, and the eventual announcement of 'Before The Dawn' in March 2014 blindsided everyone in the industry. The lack of PR overkill was a clever PR stratagem in itself, using Bush's old school mystique as a unique selling point. And it worked. It would be hard to overstate the quivering excitement which accompanied the initial news of her return. Even five months before the opening night, 'Before The Dawn' had become the outstanding musical event of 2014, if not the decade. By comparison, David Bowie's surprise return the previous year with *The Next Day* after a ten-year silence looked almost humdrum.

Even before the shows went on general sale, a further seven dates were added, stretching the run from August 26 to October 2. The tickets – which ranged in price from £49 to £135, with hospitality packages stretching into several hundreds of pounds – were subject to strict restrictions. No more than four could be sold to one applicant for each concert, and the buyer had to be present on the night with photographic identification. Intended to prevent scalping, it was much the same system that Tom Waits had used a few years earlier for his own, equally oversubscribed UK shows. Some 80,000 tickets went on sale to the general public at 9:30 am on Friday, March 28. Later that morning, Bush's PR, Murray Chalmers, issued a brief statement to confirm that the whole lot had sold out within 15 minutes.

The media coverage was frenzied and somewhat relentless. For those who dimly remembered 'Wuthering Heights' and 'Running Up That Hill' it must have all been slightly baffling. For those who felt that Bush had perhaps never quite received her due as one of the most significant artists of the past half century, the flood of attention was gratifying, if not always terribly profound. In the days leading up to the show itself the focus on all things Bush surged to epidemic proportions, a seemingly endless production line of profiles, commendations and archive pieces; lists of favourite songs, videos and costumes; tributes from writers, musicians, artists, old friends; glossy magazine features, radio pieces and speculative shots at what the shows may or may not feature; feminist critiques of her career, the odd dire warning that she could never pull it off, and one worried middle-aged male critic opining that it would be "unbecoming" to see a 56-year-old woman attempting to do something as subversive as dance.

The BBC broadcast a newly commissioned hour-long documentary, *The Kate Bush Story: Running Up That Hill*, featuring contributions from Elton John, David Gilmour, John Lydon, Tricky, Stephen Fry and a whole host of others. Two major photographic overviews were published: *Kate Bush* by Guido Harari and *WOW* by Gered Mankowitz, and their joint exhibition ran at Snap Galleries in London for the duration of the 'Before The Dawn' residency. Her songs were all over the radio and almost all of her albums found their way back into the charts. Bushmania is not too strong a phrase.

Throughout it all, Bush uttered not one single word to any media outlet whatsoever, though in the run up to August 26 a request appeared on her website. "It would mean a great deal to me if you would please refrain from taking photos or filming during the shows. I very much want to have contact with you as an audience, not with iPhones, iPads or cameras. I know it's a lot to ask but it would allow us to all share in the experience together." Back, again, to the importance of preserving that undiluted "connection" between her and her audience.

At the venue itself, the application of this charmingly worded 'request' was somewhat more stringent. Prior to the show's commencement an announcement repeated the entreaty over the PA system, and anyone wielding a camera or phone during proceedings (as well as before the concert and during the interval) was swiftly admonished by Apollo staff. But the desired affect was achieved. This was one post-millennial event that really rewarded physical presence and total, non-virtual immersion; only a few, very brief snippets of footage of the shows eventually leaked on to the internet, and they were a pale echo of the live experience. For once, the combined forces of the internet and social media could not even begin to hint at the real thing.

★ ★ ★

For 22 nights over the late summer and early autumn of 2014, the residents of Hammersmith grew used to having Bush around. Hotels reported roaring trade. Local pubs like The Swan became impromptu fan HQs. On show nights the theatre was encircled by an ad hoc community of fans, touts, chancers, celebrities, crazies, fast food sellers and unofficial merchandise vendors. A maze of crash barriers guided the audience in a zig-zagging line towards the doors, while above their heads the marquee proclaimed: THE KT FELLOWSHIP PRESENTS BEFORE THE DAWN SOLD OUT.

For opening night, Tuesday, August 26, the agents and enablers who had been so quiet in public had, in private, done their job. Among those in attendance were David Gilmour, Bjork, Grace Jones, Lily Allen, Marc Almond, Chrissie Hynde, Holly Johnson, Michael Ball, Frank Skinner, Gemma Arterton and Anna Calvi, the latter pair whisked immediately afterwards to the BBC's *Newsnight* studio to attempt to explain what they had just witnessed. There were rumours on live blogs and Twitter that Madonna had slipped in and out unnoticed, although David Bowie was definitely not there, despite whispers to the contrary.

The A-list love-in continued at every show throughout the run. Elton John, Paul McCartney, Johnny Depp, Ricky Gervais, Jimmy Page, Daniel Craig and Kylie Minogue were among the hundreds of famous faces who lined up to attend, many more than once. Some nights Bush lingered to mingle in the VIP room; other nights she left straight away. "I was reassured Kate is a night owl and she wanted to say hello," said one visitor, the singer Toyah Wilcox. "It was almost overwhelming to see her after such an incredible performance. She wrapped her arms around me and kissed my face. We had a bit of catching up to do, the last time I saw her son Bertie he was six years old, now he is a man."[9] Bush remained less than enamoured of any opportunist photographers, who saw only the top of her head, wrapped in a scarf, as she arrived at the venue each day in the back of a black car, slipping into the building in mid-afternoon.

Each night the doors opened at 6:15pm and business was brisk. Inside, fans stocked up on official merchandise. Alongside the usual T-shirts, posters and programmes were somewhat more imaginative items. A *Hounds Of Love* mug selling for £13.50; a 'Cloudbusting' pendant at £30; a 'Before The Dawn' Rescue Kit for £45.

The foyer was an eager, edgy crush. After all the months of hype and speculation, the moment of reckoning was nigh. The nervous tension was acutely palpable, as though 4,000 people were about to watch a cherished family member walk across a high wire. As the stage time of 7:45 approached, the audience filed into the auditorium, soothed by the languorous sound of Eberhard Weber's ambient bass. The imposing stage, bathed in a deep blue wash of light, displayed an impressive array of instruments, amps and microphones; the drums seemed to dominate, as they would on much of the music to follow.

At last, the house lights dimmed and the sampled voice of Bush's late healer, Lily Cranford, spilled from the speakers, reciting the modern variation of the Gayatri Mantra, one of the oldest Vedic Sanskrit mantras. The seven-piece band walked on and kicked into 'Lily', the plush, deep, rhythmic groove, sleek yet punchy, setting the musical tone for the early part of the show.

'Lily' is a banishing ritual, a song of protection, throwing out a "circle of fire" from which Bush could draw strength to perform. More prosaically, it was the kind of song that perfectly suited her richer, fuller, more soulful voice. As the pulse of the song steadied and began to throb, and without toying overly long with the audience's hunger for gratification, Bush emerged from the rear right of the stage leading a kind of spiritually enlightened conga line, heading up the Chorus, the five-strong ensemble of singers and actors who would collectively act as her foil through the subsequent three hours. She was dressed in a black silk shirt, a long black coat, extravagantly fringed and tassled, and loose black trousers. A silver necklace with a pendant hung around her throat. Her feet were bare, and her tousled hair tumbled down her back. She looked both entirely ordinary and utterly remarkable: powerful, fierce, radiant, a benevolent Gothic goddess, stretching out her arms to the crowd in a gesture of welcome and inclusion.

Predictably, her mere physical presence earned the first of numerous ovations. She grinned, stepped to the centre of the stage, opened her mouth and, at long last, sang. Though early on there were clear traces of nerves in her singing voice – which quickly dissolved as she hit her stride – it was immediately apparent that her vocals remained astonishingly potent. As she drew sparks from the words "fire" and "darkness", the first two killer notes of the show, the anxiety in the audience – as least as pronounced as that of anyone on stage – dissolved. Suddenly everybody knew that this would work, and that it promised to be magical, and a wave of euphoria swept over the room.

When 'Lily' ended, a clearly delighted Bush shouted "Where've you been!" Her interaction with the audience each night was low key but finely judged. Her words were simple but heartfelt, and she articulated her gratitude and acknowledged the significance of the occasion without recourse to either cheap sentiment or gushing indulgence.

In any case, her face spoke more eloquently than her brief speeches. The theatrical distance deployed throughout 'Tour Of Life' was again in evidence on 'Before The Dawn' whenever the dramaturgy demanded it, but during the opening six songs in particular – performed straight, without any artifice, against a simple display of diamond lights – Bush appeared unguarded and guileless, reacting genuinely to each moment and allowing her joy to spill out. She smiled and joked with her band, slipped to the side of the stage to glug a bottle of water, and responded disarmingly to the energy of the crowd.

After 'Lily' came the familiar cry: "It's in the trees, it's coming!" 'Hounds Of Love' breezed rather than burned, its sense of quivering urgency never as taut as it might have been, but it still sounded rapturous. She tinkered slightly with the chorus melody and threw in a new line, an entreaty to "tie me to the mast". The phrase, pickpocketed from Greek mythology, underlined the enduring power of love's siren call, while acting as a piece of subliminal scene-setting for the upcoming 'The Ninth Wave'.

It's fair to say that 'Joanni' would not have been high on most people's dream Kate Bush set list, but even a middling, somewhat hesitant song from *Aerial* gained vigour in this context. The sampled peal of the bells of Rouen cathedral chimed as Bush hummed and declaimed in French. The message conveyed – not for the first or last time – was one of feminine power and strength. 'Top Of The City', another unlikely inclusion, had undergone a far more remarkable metamorphosis, transformed from a largely overlooked track on a widely unfancied album to a high-stepping highlight. Bush sang it with extraordinary versatility and passion, rising from a serene whisper to a soulful howl, throwing herself into the song with raw, transported physicality. She did not dance during 'Before The Dawn', at least not in the manner that she once had, but she swayed, swooped and side-stepped, her movements still animated by a supple grace. The entire show was put together with a dancer's understanding of space and spectacle.

The still sleek 'Running Up That Hill', cleaving closely to the 2012 remix, sounded wonderful. As the musicians located its rolling rhythm and quicksilver synthetic pulse, Bush waggled a coaxing finger and purred "Come on, baby." Her other post-Millennial hit, 'King Of The Mountain', was another early high point, its chimeric reggae churned up into a thick, satisfyingly propulsive broth.

The song marked a key moment in 'Before The Dawn', a hinge between the straight gig and the theatrics to come. As 'King Of The Mountain' pushed onward, the atmosphere turned increasingly inclement and Bush evolved from smiling earth mother to lowering Prospero, summoning the coming tempest. At the tumultuous, drum-heavy climax – "the wind is whistling", and then some – percussionist Mino Cinelu stepped forward to the centre of the stage and began whirling a traditional Maori wind instrument, the *purerehua*, on a rope around his head. Bedlam ensued. Lights flashed, thunder crashed, an immense storm rolled out from the four corners of the theatre and the sound of some terrible collision engulfed the audience. Those in the rows closest to the stage were showered with hundreds of scraps of yellow tissue paper, a rain of golden confetti, each piece adorned with the verse from Tennyson's *The Coming Of Arthur*, the poem which had given 'The Ninth Wave' its name.

An emergency signal rent the darkness, and a curtain fell in front of the stage. The switch in mood was abrupt, unsettling and hugely effective. From something close to a conventional rock show, 'Before The Dawn' had adjusted its priorities. Even the terrain had shifted, lurching from the sky-scraping peaks of city, hill and mountain to the darkest depths of the ocean.

'The Ninth Wave' began with a brief piece of film, written by Bush and Mitchell and titled 'The Astronomer's Tale'. Projected on to the curtain, it was partly a technical necessity, allowing the stage to be prepared for the coming drama, and partly a piece of slightly clumsy exposition. In a call to the coast guard, an amateur astronomer, played by Kevin Doyle (known to many as Molesley from *Downton Abbey*), explained that he had picked up a distress signal from a ship called *Celtic Deep*. Somewhere off the coast there was, we learned, a vessel sinking fast.

When this short monologue ended and the curtain rose, the stage had been spectacularly reset. The band and Chorus were now framed within the skeletal ribs of a sunken ship, the lighting shadowy and subaquatic, throwing out deep greens, blues and misty shafts of silvery light. Bush appeared on the screen at the back of the stage singing 'And Dream Of Sheep' live to camera, one of the sequences filmed months earlier at Pinewood. Surrounded by sea, spot lit by watery moonlight, she looked appropriately vulnerable as she sang one of her most bewitching ballads. Through it all her emergency beacon bleeped, like a tiny heartbeat.

For 'Under Ice' the stage floor was transformed into a rippling sea of waves and Bush returned to the stage in the flesh, now clad in a Navy greatcoat, liberally buckled, buttoned and belted. The band locked into the song's oppressive rhythm, perfectly articulating its chilly claustrophobia. Bush was alternately swallowed and given up by trapdoors in the stage, while on screen her likeness remained in the water, highlighting the duality of 'The Ninth Wave'. Throughout the piece, the filmed portions represented the reality of the woman in the water, watching, hoping, waiting, drifting, not quite alive but not yet dead. Onstage, her visions of the past, present and future were played out.

Chainsaw's burred and axes cut into the water, but rescue proved short lived. The Chorus – transformed into Lords Of The Deep, a cabal of sinister, skeletal fish people clad in bony masks and heavy netting, their forked tails somehow demonic – spirited Bush into the hands of the Witch Finder for 'Waking The Witch', a piece of vividly disturbing theatre. Jo Servi excelled as the grand inquisitor, masked and dreadful. Surrounded by a terrifying cacophony of condemnation, Bush lurched, screamed and gasped for air, before repeated cries of "get out of the water!" brought the diabolical persecution fantasy lurching back, once again, to reality, as a rescue helicopter thundered overhead.

The pilot's radio communication, written by Mitchell and voiced by Paddy Bush, explained that the crew of the *Celtic Deep* had been picked up safely, as well as "all but one of the passengers". For several minutes a virtual helicopter strafed the audience in the stalls, the deafening roar of its blade rotation and its harsh white search spotlight pinning people to their seats. The woman it was seeking in the darkness was more than just an anonymous face on the screen. The dramatisation of 'Watching You, Without Me' radically extended the remit of the song by painting in some of the crucial details of her life. This sad, subdued lament now made explicit the uncomfortable truth that even as one person is battling through their own dark night of the soul, life around them continues in all its staggering and glorious mundanity.

The song was now framed by a comic vignette in which Bertie, as the woman's brattish son, Ben, and Bob Harms, as her husband and his father, played out a scene of domestic normality in their living room. The pair niggled over a lost work portfolio, watched football, cooked (and burned) dinner, teased, taunted and sofa surfed. Bush seemed to be aiming at something akin to the everyday fly-on-the-wall humour of the hit BBC TV show *Outnumbered*, while much of the dialogue betrayed her fondness for the very English wordplay and ribaldry of *Blackadder* and *The Young Ones* – "Captain Hilarious strikes again!" – but, in both its script and execution, the scene fell flat.

Eventually, mercifully, Bush drifted into view, hovering ghostlike behind her family to sing 'Watching You, Without Me', present but unheard and unseen. The skew-whiff mini-set created for this tableau was wonderful. Lamps flickered and a television slid from one end of the building to the other, as though the room were acutely attuned to Bush's electric, poltergeist aura even if the human occupants remained oblivious.

'Jig Of Life' was a musical tour de force, all hard Celtic rhythm, with Kevin McAlea excelling on the Uilleann pipes. Jay, Bush's eldest brother, made an appearance in black and white on a video screen, reciting the Irish-toned poem he had written for the original track. For 'Hello Earth' a huge buoy, bathed in the red light of emergency flares, ascended from the waves. In one of the most unforgettable images of 'Before The Dawn', Bush tried again and again to escape the water and reach its refuge, only to be pulled back each time by the Lords Of The Deep, determined to drag her below the surface.

While this was happening, a couple of stagehands assembled a short ramp that led up from the floor of the auditorium to the right hand side of the stage. As the song's stunningly sombre choral passage rang out, an inert Bush was lifted from the waves, carried slowly down the ramp and into the audience. The funeral procession then paused in the aisle. Any member of the audience lucky enough to be in the first few rows on this side of the theatre was thus afforded an intimate view of Bush, lying prostrate, six foot in the air, so close you could see her thick make-up drenched in a sheen of sweat. As a voice implored her to "go deeper", her eyes suddenly snapped open, and she was lead through the side door of the auditorium and out of sight. The crowd, as one, seemed to exhale. It was spellbinding, genuinely operatic, and as darkly dramatic (and strikingly contemporary) as any modern staging of *The Ring* or *Parsifal*.

The buoy slipped away and the stage flooded with the golden light of a new dawn, both literal and metaphorical, setting the scene for a lilting, truly lovely acoustic rendition of 'The Morning Fog'. When Bush re-entered the auditorium and made her way back to the stage, she was no longer in character. Behind and around her the musicians and Chorus, shorn of their fish heads, tails and all sense of menace, swayed to the music and danced gracefully with one another, their smiles and their song acting as a balm to all that had come before.

'The Morning Fog' was a gift of gratitude which transcended 'The Ninth Wave', reaching out to reflect on the entire experience of staging 'Before The Dawn', and her return to performing. When Bush sang "I love you better now" she gestured to the audience and smiled. To the list of family members included in the lyrics at the end of the song she added "son", and when she talked of her "brothers" and "sisters", she held out her arms to the men and women around her onstage, extending the embrace of family to include the KT Fellowship. It should have been corny. Perhaps on one level it was. But experienced at first hand, it was also deeply felt and undeniably moving.

Within the song's warm, beatific glow the terrible spell cast by 'The Ninth Wave' receded and was broken, bringing an end to one of the most extraordinary pieces of imaginative theatre ever staged by a popular musician. And that was only Act I.

★ ★ ★

During the 20-minute interval, the stage was hidden behind a lush red curtain adorned with a feather motif, an early clue that the mood of the next phase of 'Before The Dawn' would be very different from the first.

The band had now shifted to the left hand side, with Bush among them, seated at the piano. Trees had sprouted around her, and the effect was of some kind of magical, Narnian forest. Though she had changed clothes she was still all in black. Now she wore a long and rather mystical looking overcoat, embroidered on the sleeves and cuffs with gold, amber and silver patterns and topped off with feathered epaulettes. Her hands, feet and forehead were bejewelled. She could have passed for Persian royalty.

A vast set of Moorish doors, 30 foot high, now dominated the stage, like the gateway to a fairy tale. They creaked open and a wooden artist's mannequin and its puppet master entered, both central figures in 'A Sky Of Honey'. (Only at the end of the final show did Bush reveal that the 'puppet' was actually played by an actor, Charlotte Williams, hidden inside the suit. "She kept saying to me, 'We'll make a fuss of you on the last show,' and she did," said Williams.[10] Bush described her that night as "our secret weapon".)

The sound of birdsong, piano and the sampled voice of the young Bertie – taken from *Aerial* – ushered in 'Prelude', which half way through shifted key from the major to the minor, introducing the aura of vague disquiet which constantly threatened to unsettle this otherwise perfect summer's day.

As a vast screen stretching across the rear of the stage projected slow motion images of birds in flight, Bush began 'Prologue', transformed into a ten-minute tour de force. The music was stunningly beautiful, dominated by her rippling piano and John Giblin's airy, lyrical bass, and lifted by a new, jubilant coda which featured Bush singing "Ding dong, ding dong, ding dong / Shake it down, break it down" and harmonising with the peal of distant bells.

Before 'An Architect's Dream', the huge doors were removed. A vast canvas screen descended stage right, in front of which Bertie appeared as the artist, taking over the role played on the album by Rolf Harris. Clutching his palette and brushes, with his smock, straw hat and ragged red beard (which he had been allowed to grow only with permission from his school), he appeared to be channelling his inner Van Gogh. As he grappled with his painting on the canvas, the puppet, Chorus and Bush weaved around him, "watching the painter paint".

The mood, now established and sustained throughout the majority of 'A Sky Of Honey', was slow, stoned, dream-like. The lighting cast the stage in rich, golden tones, translucent blues and deep reds, nature's bounty blending with the glorious smudge of a Turner painting. The music demanded something different from Act I, and the band duly played with lithe, bright nuance and extraordinary grace, while Bush wrapped herself around the songs, her voice a perfect fit for the relatively recent material.

Dramatically, where 'The Ninth Wave' was a complex series of set pieces, the shift in mood, media and perspective constant and deliberately jarring, 'A Sky Of Honey' was a truly unified piece of work, the songs eliding in a seamless progression. It allowed for full immersion. For the audience, this was an hour in the presence of an intense stillness, punctuated by the occasional flurry of activity or arresting image. Nothing much happened for most of it. The puppet child skittered around anxiously, Bertie wandered about with his brushes, birds trilled, suns sank and moons rose as the texture of the day shifted. The effect was hermetic and hypnotic, like being lulled into a serene trance where every sense still remained highly attuned. It was a pitch-perfect realisation of one of her most sublime pieces of work.

'Sunset' was simply outstanding. Kevin McAlea's accordion casting a richly romantic spell, its organic push-and-pull meshing with Giblin's burbling bass as it climbed towards a rattling climax. Cinelu's percussive power pushed the song "all the way up to the top of the night", and as Bush's sang in her sultriest, most headily perfumed purr, it was impossible to conceive that her voice had ever sounded better. Her risk-taking instincts, too, remained primed. On 'Aerial Tal' she mimicked the song of the blackbird, head bobbing, elbows wide, lips pecking, every inch of her a bird. 'Somewhere In Between' was revealed conclusively to be one of her great pop compositions, a gliding kiss of a song and a sensuous exploration of an enduring preoccupation with the liminal spaces.

As the blood red sun sank behind her, Bush slipped away in its wake, leaving her fine new song, 'Tawny Moon', to be performed by Bertie. A bluesy, rhythmic construction, it was at odds with the rest of 'A Sky Of Honey', and closer to something Bush might have recorded in the mid-Eighties. Bertie declared, "Ladies and gentlemen, we present to you tonight: the moon!" and a vast, silver orb rose slowly on the screen behind him.

Paying homage to the "queen of bedlam", the song marked the point at which 'A Sky Of Honey' began to hurtle towards its climax. The sunshine had engendered an atmosphere of sensual lassitude; nightfall brought new, more dangerous forces to the fore. Since 'Sunset' the trajectory of the music had been rising again, circling back towards the elevated terrain explored in the show's beginnings. As a deeply rhythmic 'Nocturn' gave way to 'Aerial', a new day had broken and the morning bells were ringing out (there were *a lot* of bells in 'Before The Dawn'). Bush was roused from slumber, impatient, ready to "get up on the roof". The band and Chorus were by now decked out in startling bird masks. Welcome to the dawn chorus.

There was a new tension to the music, which at one point throbbed like some New Age interpretation of Frankie Goes To Hollywood's 'Relax'. Over an angry squall of guitar and a heavy artillery of drums, Bush and David Rhodes engaged in a haughty, erotically charged stand-off, circling each other like hunter and prey, lover and killer. As Rhodes strutted, Bush wailed about her "beautiful wings", which she indeed now had, big, black things fixed on to her epaulettes by members of the Chorus. As the music pushed harder and harder, up and up, on the final stroke of the final song she was hitched up and suspended above the stage. Airborne at last.

For the encore Bush returned alone, as herself. After thanking the crowd for their "wonderful, warm and positive response", she sang 'Among Angels' at the piano. It took a few moments to realise that following the extraordinary drama at the denouement of 'A Sky Of Honey', the piano now had a tree growing out of it. It was an impeccable rendition, note perfect, the utter purity of her voice reducing the theatre to silence. It was also a timely reminder that, for all the theatrics, if Bush were 'just' a singer she would still be unique. That she was so much more besides seemed almost unfair on everyone else.

As the applause receded she spoke. "We hope you enjoyed the show." Uproar. "Does that mean yes?" The band returned for 'Cloudbusting', transformed now into a martial clap along, slack with the collective release of tension but buoyed by sheer goodwill. Bush grinned and waved, perhaps allowing herself to finally savour the feeling of being surrounded by something that seemed very, very close to love. And one wondered, not for the first time, just why she would spend 35 years denying herself – and us, dammit – access to such a uniquely uplifting experience.

★ ★ ★

It was almost impossible to write about 'Before The Dawn' without getting wrapped up in the emotion surrounding its wider narrative. The immensity of the occasion did not lend itself easily to the subjective critical view, especially for writers filing overnight reviews. The critical response was overwhelmingly positive. *The Independent* called it "stunning, undoubtedly the most ambitious, and genuinely moving, piece of theatrical pop ever seen on a British stage." *The Guardian* described it as "spellbinding", the *NME* "phenomenal". And on and on and on, wave after wave of adulation from around the globe. It might well have been the most widely reviewed performance of all time. Despite the occasional equivocations, the heady expectations, it could safely be said, were more than met.

For those who wished to seek out codes, messages, threads and influences, there was plenty to chew on. 'Before The Dawn' touched upon angels, Celtic myth, reincarnation, motherhood, circadian rhythms, saints, birds, steampunk, *The Tempest*, *Ulysses*, *War Horse*, Hammer Horror, *Doctor Who*, witchcraft, JMW Turner, *Pinocchio*, *The Hogsmill Ophelia*, the end of childhood, and much else besides. For those who simply wanted to sit back and goggle at the sheer spectacle, the rewards were no less rich. Like the best theatrical experiences, it did not just live on as a fond memory but took on new shapes, expanded and realigned itself as the extent of its ambition sunk in.

Was it flawless? Not remotely. Was it sometimes ridiculous, baffling and borderline embarrassing? Of course. For all its use of cutting edge technology and its corps of high end collaborators, there was still room in 'Before The Dawn' for the defiantly home grown, the slightly half-baked, the deeply, defiantly personal. Bush did not return to the stage after so long a time only to impose limits on the extent to which she could give free rein to her imagination.

Musically, some quibbled over the lack of 'hits' in the set list, but what was actually delivered was something deeper and surely more satisfying. The lack of spontaneity in the set and its inflexibility from night to night was hardly a surprise, given the theatrical nature of the show and Bush's determination – unchanged in the 35 years since 'Tour Of Life' – to leave nothing that happened onstage to chance. Still, the solo piano slot in the first encore, where she performed 'Among Angels' each night, might have provided an opportunity to air a different song from time to time. Perhaps the already rehearsed 'Moments Of Pleasure' or 'A Coral Room', or 'This Woman's Work', 'Breathing' or 'Under The Ivy'.

Many fans would have been delighted to have seen a whole show performed this way, but her desire to deliver much more than simply a conventional rendition of her best known songs was, in her mind, precisely the point of playing live. The fruits of her ambition didn't always hit the sweet spot. The purpose of the mannequin which darted nervously – and pleasingly enough – around the stage throughout 'A Sky Of Honey' was never quite apparent, nor would it have necessarily been to the detriment of the piece had it got lost in the woods. 'The Astronomer's Tale' felt similarly extraneous, while the kind of dialogue that works so well in David Mitchell's novels did not translate particularly effectively to a theatrical production.

There was evidence to suggest that Adrian Noble ceded to Bush on the major directorial decisions, otherwise the hammy am-dram domestic scene which prefaced 'Watching You, Without Me' would surely have been cut or rewritten. "HP and Mayo" might have been "the badgers' nadgers" *chez* Bush, but her attempt to transpose the lively cut and thrust of domestic badinage to the stage was a flop. Coming directly after the overlong helicopter interlude at the end of 'Waking The Witch', the skit contributed considerably to a momentum-sapping, tension-leaking lull in the middle of the otherwise superb 'Ninth Wave'.

That scene, and Bertie's West End rendition of 'Tawny Moon', gave some credence to the suspicion that 'Before The Dawn' was partly designed as a vast shop window display for the talents of Bush's son. If Bertie McIntosh was a slightly too-shrill presence in his principle dramatic roles, and perhaps not yet the singularly gifted actor and singer he may well become, the self-possession, professionalism and sheer chutzpah exhibited by a 16-year-old in the face of such intense scrutiny could not fail to impress. And after all, had it not been for him, it's entirely likely the show would never have been staged at all.

It would be all too easy to adopt a default position of contrarian cynicism in the face of the undiluted *gush* that defined much of the discourse surrounding 'Before The Dawn', but in the end this was a show of such sustained quality it reduced any nominal competition to rubble. Like many of Bush's landmarks, its minor failings were woven into its wider triumph, inextricably linked to the unique vision that dreamed it all up.

Though 'Tour Of Life' seemed by comparison a somewhat callow and charmingly analogue undertaking, there were some echoes to be heard in 'Before The Dawn'. When Bush took flight at the end of 'A Sky Of Honey', she picked up the distant thread of 'Kite', during which she was winged and borne aloft by her dancers. (The wind effects at the end of the same song now seemed like a gentle zephyr compared to 'The Ninth Wave''s mighty roar.) A fat, blood-soaked sun had now hung heavy over both her live shows, and on the same stage. Jay once again read poetry, Paddy had a dramatic part, and her love of costume, spectacle and absurdist British comedy had not diminished over time. And as she had done 35 years previously on 'Hammer Horror', she was not averse to pre-recording her vocals if the visual context demanded it.

One of the most pleasing aspects of 'Before The Dawn' was the way it united so many aspects of her career, and renewed public interest in the broad sweep of her work. In the week that the show opened, Bush became the first woman to have eight albums in the UK's Official Albums Chart at the same time. Two were in the top ten: *The Whole Story* compilation at six, and *Hounds Of Love* at nine. *50 Words For Snow* (20), *The Kick Inside* (24), *The Sensual World* (26), *The Dreaming* (37), *Never For Ever* (38) and *Lionheart* (40) were the others. It was historical feat; only The Beatles and Elvis Presley had charted more albums simultaneously.

'Before The Dawn' also had the effect of reanimating much of her recorded work. Bush reclaimed *Hounds Of Love* from the dread grasp of 'classic' album status, bringing it vividly to life at last. Many listeners would now be inclined to give the neglected *The Red Shoes* fresh attention, while *Aerial* was starting to be more recognised as one of her major works, and 'A Sky Of Honey' arguably her masterpiece.

If the shows were significant in moving the critical focus of Bush's career away from the early albums and towards more recent material, they also, at last, created a vibrant new visual frame of reference for a woman who had often felt constrained by the difficulties of living up to the striking series of creative personae she developed as a younger artist. The shows felt like a declaration of sorts: this is who I am, and it is not who I was. The mix of elevated art and unabashed humanity and vulnerability felt unforced but also important. 'Before The Dawn' very publicly reaffirmed her existence as a living, breathing, very physical entity after years – decades – of rarefied quasi-invisibility.

Performances on September 16 and 17 were filmed for posterity, and at the end of the final concert on October 2, amid the bows, bouquets and ovations, Bush said, "This is our last show – for a while, anyway." A couple of weeks later she wrote about the "surreal journey" she had been on. The emotional charge seemed to have taken her by surprise. "The really unexpected part of it all was the audiences," she wrote on her website. "Audiences that you could only ever dream of. One of the main reasons for wanting to perform live again was to have contact with that audience. They took my breath away. Every single night they were so behind us . . . I just never imagined it would be possible to connect with an audience on such a powerful and intimate level; to feel such, well quite frankly, love." It turned out she had created a piece of work with a social function. 'Before The Dawn' prompted strangers to interact, encouraged numerous displays of naked emotion, and simply made those who saw it feel better.

All the immediate indications suggested that she enjoyed the experience and regarded it as a success, though it had not been without its stresses. On the release of the *Before The Dawn* live album in 2016, I interviewed the late bass player John Giblin about the intense and some-times euphoric experience of working on the shows. "Kate does nothing by halves," he said. "Everyone involved knew that! Working with Kate for me has always been about the unspoken: 'Gimme the energy. Gimme something to move the song on'."

The rehearsal process, Giblin recalled, was "Very complex. Kate was under very intense pressure from the off. Every element demanded her time and energy. Every tiny detail was under Kate's control, always, and as the rehearsals developed, each of the elements would be vying more and more for more of her time. Frustrating for all parties, as only one person knew the answers. That one person had to be there in the room for it to work." Once the production "went live", the perennial headache during the twenty-two-night run concerned "Timing! The timing of the cues, the ends, the song dynamics. If there was a technical hitch, we improvised. On opening night it was euphoric, of course. This was no ordinary concert, [but] everyone concerned was a pro, and everyone knew their job. It was never going to be less than well-executed."

In theory, 'Before The Dawn' opened up a host of potential future possibilities. One useful comparison is with Leonard Cohen, whose return to the live arena in 2008 after an absence of fifteen years heralded a triumphant third act which lasted until his death in 2016 and delivered three superb studio albums, four live records, three DVDs and a new *Greatest Hits* collection. His stage comeback revived and recontextualised a career which was revered but somewhat dormant and in need of a little post-millennial polish.

Unlike Cohen, whose business manager had embezzled all his money, Bush was not forced onstage by unfortunate circumstances, but the impact of her returning to the spotlight presented a similar opportunity for exploring new outlets and fresh contexts for her work. At 56, she appeared in her prime. Having generated the kind of career momentum which can last years, 'Before The Dawn' needn't have been a self-contained event.

But Bush rarely, if ever, follows neatly scripted plot points. The aftermath of 'Before The Dawn' did not turn out to be the beginning of a new chapter after all. Instead, with the benefit of hindsight, it clearly marked the triumphant conclusion of a cycle which began with *Aerial* in 2005. Viewed from a distance of ten years, it made perfect sense to see it that way; as an ending of sorts, rather than a beginning.

Following the final curtain call in Hammersmith, the sound of silence descended once again. On the first night there had been a group party near the venue after the concert. On the final night? "I went home!" said Giblin. There was a period of rest, then post-production. The musical content from the show was finally released in November 2016 as a triple live album. Running to 155 minutes, with the addition of 'Never Be Mine' taped at a rehearsal performance, *Before The Dawn* was a welcome souvenir but not an especially commercial proposition, nor one designed to draw in anyone beyond the diehard fanbase. An accompanying single-disc compilation of concert highlights would have made an interesting parallel release.

Even with the live album in circulation, ten years after the fact the full sweeping ambition of the 'Before The Dawn' residency remained a secret to anyone who hadn't attended the shows – a group which comprised the entire planet, minus around 100,000 people. According to a source who worked on filming selected nights for the intended concert movie, the visual footage of 'Before The Dawn' will remain forever unreleased on DVD because Bush was unhappy with the way she looked in it.

★　★　★

The hope that the relative surge in activity by Bush between 2011 and 2014 would usher in a period of increased visibility and productivity proved to be wishful thinking. In the following decade notable events occurred within her working world, but there was no new music, no public appearances, no meaningful creative movement to report. Which is not to imply that Bush was not busy making new work during this time; simply that we did not see or hear any evidence of it.

Nor is it correct to suggest that the narrative has not moved forward. Some of that post-millennial polish and generational rejuvenation which so benefited Leonard Cohen did indeed come to pass. These days, an artist is not necessarily in control of how and when their music gains from a timely turbo boost. In the age of instant access, when it has never been more true that all music is new music for *someone*, and when a fresh contextual twist can reignite even the most sedately slumbering career, the music of Kate Bush is constantly being heard – and re-examined – anew. While she did not consciously make any major moves towards mainstream pop culture, that world turned its head towards her just the same. Indeed, large parts of the industry began engaging with her music for the very first time.

Much of this movement was attributable to her association in 2022 with the hit Netflix show, *Stranger Things*. Some years before that happy meeting occurred, however, Bush was already working hard on finding new ways to re-present her music publicly to her greater satisfaction.

The idea that Kate Bush is an artist who by nature is disinclined to spend time looking backwards is one of the tenets of this book. I would argue it is a philosophy which served her particularly well during what we might call her imperial phase, between 1980 and 1990. Yet that theory has been challenged repeatedly since 2010, a period defined by a significant amount of catalogue curation, an activity in which she showed a marked disinterest previously.

First came *Director's Cut* – perhaps a more meaningful project than anyone at the time realised, in its efforts to bring fresh creative impetus to older material. Then came the live shows, an arena in which it is natural for an artist to interrogate their back catalogue, reshaping it and teasing out new narratives. Further historic curation, this time on the page, came in December 2018, when Faber and Faber published *How To Be Invisible,* a thematically arranged compilation of Bush's lyrics with an introduction written by her friend, the author David Mitchell. This was a hands-on project for her – she made the selections herself. The paperback version, published in 2023, even featured a new introduction written by Bush.

At the same time, the first instalment of what has become a major overhaul of her back catalogue occurred. In November 2018 Bush began releasing all her studio albums on both vinyl and CD in new individual editions, remastered by her alongside James Guthrie, and issued via her own Fish People label. Regarding *Aerial*, one pressing piece of business was excising any trace of Rolf Harris following his incarceration for a number of sexual assaults against underage girls; he died, thoroughly disgraced, in 2023. Bush's son Bertie replaced Harris's parts on the remastered edition of the album.

Released simultaneously were two CD box set collections and four vinyl box sets, the latter titled *Remastered In Vinyl: I – IV*. These encompassed all her studio albums, including *The Whole Story*, repackaged to cover *The Kick Inside* to *The Dreaming*; *Hounds Of Love* to *The Red Shoes* (which was now presented as a double album); and *Aerial* to *50 Words For Snow*. The fourth box set was *The Other Sides*, a newly compiled rarities collection gathering together almost all of her B-sides, remixes, non-album tracks recorded for films and compilations, plus one previously unreleased track, 'Humming', from the mid-1970s.

This extensive undertaking ensured that Bush's entire catalogue was available once more in physical form, sounding as she wished it to. Re-released via her own label, it also affirmed her ownership of the work, a principle she had strived to retain since the very beginning. Given Bush's dedication to overseeing every detail, the reissue programme would have required significant reserves of time and energy.

The enthusiastic revisionism didn't stop there. In February 2023, Bush announced that Fish People was working with a new distribution partner. The state51 Conspiracy was taking over from Warner Music Group to distribute her post-1980 releases worldwide, and the entire catalogue in the United States. The initiative may have been given added impetus following the newfound interest in her work in America. All her studio albums were (re-)re-released on vinyl and CD in November 2023 via state51, each one featuring the 2018 remastering work by Bush and James

Guthrie. Special coloured vinyl editions were made available only through independent record shops. As part of the same initiative, first *Hounds Of Love* and then *The Dreaming* were released in "special illustrated presentations" titled the *Baskerville Edition* and *Escapologist Edition*, respectively. These featured arresting new cover artwork from Timorous Beasties, the creative design company that had worked with Bush on 'Before The Dawn'. In addition, a lavish boxed edition of *Hounds Of Love*, titled *The Boxes Of Lost At Sea*, presented the album over two vinyl records.

Partly, no doubt, this careful and very beautiful shoring-up of all her existing material was simply a pragmatic response to the state of the music industry in the 2020s, where revenue streams had to be fished rather more smartly and regularly than of old. The merchandise portal on the Kate Bush official website is certainly well-stocked these days, offering clothing, art prints, bandanas, cushion covers and even an umbrella for sale.

Yet this was also, perhaps, the true legacy of the 'Before The Dawn' residency. Having presented her post-1985 catalogue onstage for the first time, Bush had the breathing space and inclination, finally, to look back over almost 50 years' worth of recorded work. What she has not yet done, unlike Bob Dylan, Neil Young and David Bowie – albeit posthumously in the case of Bowie – and so many more of her peers, is radically re-construct the narrative of her career by compiling copious 'new' albums from old material, unearthing endless out-takes, demos, alternate versions and live cuts to herd onto vast legacy box sets, and generally repaving the road she has travelled with layers of added context in a manner which ultimately re-shapes the way in which we regard entire eras of an artist's evolution.

To put it more simply: each Kate Bush album is still the same Kate Bush album it always was. The catalogue remains the catalogue. The body of her work has not grown. It has simply been subtly reconfigured and, in the case of some albums, made widely available again in her preferred format: vinyl. It is housekeeping, albeit very stylish housekeeping, rather than fresh construction work or intensive archaeology.

★ ★ ★

Looming over this in-house activity was an unexpected plot twist that pitched the past headlong into the frenetic present. The one truly headline-worthy piece of news which occurred in the ten years after 'Before The Dawn', was that Kate Bush finally broke into mainstream American music culture. The last time she was on the radar of US listeners in any meaningful sense, artists were expected to tour the States relentlessly in order to penetrate the national consciousness. In more recent times, it was possible to do it through a screen. The key concession on her part was simply allowing it all to happen. Granting permission for others to use her work for the enablement of their own artistic expression has not always been Bush's way. This time, the power of Yes was reclaimed from 'The Sensual World' and sent into action.

Stranger Things is a soulful 1980s-set supernatural sci-fi drama created by Matt and Ross Duffer (known as the Duffer brothers), which has aired on Netflix since 2016. Bush was apparently an existing fan of the show, which makes sense. Its themes resonate with several of her own interests: parallel worlds, childlike wonder, mystery, horror, suspense and hope.

For the fourth series, the production team sought a song to convey the doggedly individualistic personality and existential struggles of one of the principal young female characters, Max Mayfield. Early on, the music supervisor on *Stranger Things*, Nora Felder, hit upon 'Running Up That Hill' as a prime candidate (Winona Ryder, a regular cast member, insisted she had been dropping hints in this direction for the past several years by repeatedly wearing Kate Bush T-shirts on set).

The song, said Felder, who like the show is American, "Immediately struck me with its deep chords of the possible connection to Max's emotional struggles. The song was important not just to the storyline, but the symbolism of the 'deal with God' lyric was significant which made it perfect for Max's theme. . . in the face of Max's painful isolation and alienation from others, a 'deal with god' could heart-wrenchingly reflect Max's implicit belief that only a miracle of unlikely understanding and show of support could help her climb the hills of life before her."[11]

The feeling was that the song could hold meaning for the character and ensure its emotional impact throughout the series would grow deeper and ever more profound. The request to license 'Running Up That Hill' was made through Wende Crowley, Sony Music Publishing's SVP of creative marketing, film and television. Everyone involved did their homework. They knew there was a good chance Bush might say no, and so left nothing to fate. Says Felder: "I sat with my clearance co-ordinator and laid out all the scripted scenes for song uses that we knew of at that point. Knowing the challenges, we proceeded to create elaborate scene descriptions that provided as much context as possible so that Kate and her camp would have a full understanding of the uses. . . When we finished, we were on edge, but excited and hopeful."[12]

"Kate Bush is selective when it comes to licensing her music and because of that, we made sure to get script pages and footage for her to review so she could see exactly how the song would be used," said Crowley. Eventually, satisfied, Bush granted permission. "The deal took longer than normal to secure because of the uniqueness of the use and how many times it is played over this season in multiple episodes," said Crowley.[13]

What these negotiations make clear is that the use of 'Running Up That Hill' on *Stranger Things* was considered in great depth by both the showrunners and Bush herself; it was not done cheaply. It also suggests that Bush had a fair idea that allowing the song to feature in such a popular show would make some sort of wider impact.

The series aired in May 2022. As it unfolded, and 'Running Up That Hill' became more intrinsically associated with Max's story, so interest around it grew. Despite being almost forty years old, the music and production sounded remarkably fresh in its modern context. Furthermore, the messages it transmitted proved mutable, positive and thoroughly current even beyond the immediate context of the character and the show.

And so 'Running Up That Hill' began to climb. In the era of streaming and download, when everything is already out there, primed for immediate access, there was no need to re-release the track as a single. It took off on TikTok, and in the early summer became the most streamed song on Spotify in the United States, the United Kingdom, Canada, Australia and many more global markets.

On 10 June 2022, 'Running Up That Hill' reached number two on the UK Singles Chart, leapfrogging its previous peak of number three in 1985. The determining of chart placing had become a matter of some confusion in recent times, with various 'weightings' for different kinds of tracks, as well as different modes of access, brought into play. 'Running Up That Hill' was the most popular song that week in the UK, ahead of 'As It Was' by Harry Styles, but initially fell afoul of a chart rule which penalised older songs being streamed. This bylaw was made with the (not unreasonable) intention of ensuring current material released by contemporary artists was not squeezed out of the picture by long-established songs from the old guard.

However, there was now considerable momentum growing in the media and wider populus for Bush to get to number one. The rather formidable sounding Chart Supervisory Committee duly responded by granting the record an exemption from the "accelerated chart ratio" rule due to its ongoing sales resurgence. In essence, they bent the rules simply because Kate Bush is Kate Bush and nobody wanted a riot on their conscience. On 17 June, 'Running Up That Hill' gave Bush her second British number one single, forty-four years after 'Wuthering Heights' became her first. In doing so, she surpassed Tom Jones's forty-two-year gap between number ones and broke two further records, too. At 63 years and 11 months, Bush supplanted Cher as the oldest solo female artist to top the charts. She also achieved the record for a single which had taken the longest time to reach number one; the thirty-seven-year wait for 'Running Up That Hill' to peak beat the previous record, held by Wham!'s 'Last Christmas', by a year.

It was a similar story in America – except there, this was all happening more or less for the first time. By the end of July, 'Running Up That Hill' had reached number three on the US Billboard Hot 100, surpassing its original peak of 30 in November 1985, to become Bush's first US Top 10 hit. In its wake, many of her albums, particularly *Hounds Of Love* and *The Whole Story*, enjoyed a huge resurgence there and worldwide.

Such a remarkable and unexpected success story was impossible to ignore. Bush broke cover to undertake a breezy and typically unrevealing phone interview with Emma Barnett for *Woman's Hour* on BBC Radio 4.

"What is really wonderful is that this is a whole new audience," she said down a rather crackly line. "In a lot of cases they had never heard of me, and I love that."[14] She also issued periodic and very enthusiastic statements via her website as the song surged.

As Bush acknowledged, as well as expanding her geographical reach, *Stranger Things* introduced her to an entirely new demographic. In one message on her site, she noted that her music had received a "whole new lease of life" brought about "by the young fans who love the show."[15] Though most entrenched aficionados of her music were nothing but delighted at this outcome, a few long-term devotees muttered and shook their heads. For some, this highly excitable "discovery" of Kate Bush by a largely younger audience felt shallow and fleeting; somehow unworthy. It's doubtful Bush felt the same. The work of an artist endures through successive generations finding, listening to and loving their music. It was exciting to witness Bush being discovered by many for the first time, and fascinating to observe which elements of her, and her work, this newly energised listenership connected with.

The *Stranger Things* youthquake was a very 2020s tremor. It shook the summer of 2022 for a few weeks then quickly subsided. Yet there were notable aftershocks. The most visible, perhaps, was Bush's 2023 induction into the Rock 'n' Roll Hall of Fame.

Founded in 1983 and located in the blue-collar heartland of Cleveland, Ohio, the Hall of Fame is overseen by the grandees of US rock culture, among them Jann Wenner, founder of *Rolling Stone* magazine; Ahmet Ertegun of Atlantic Records and Seymour Stein of Sire. In 2023, it celebrated its fortieth year of passing canonical judgement on the *rox populi*, offering a kind of faded denim "quality" mark. Setting itself up as the ultimate arbiter of worthy music, in reality the institution represents legacy building at its most sluggish. Light years behind the curve, it tells us nothing we don't already know.

Bush's nomination in 2023 was her fourth since 2018. On this occasion she was granted entry, primarily due to the resurgence of 'Running Up That Hill', which played heavily in the video presentation of her career, shown at the ceremony. Having made no new music in the period since her first nomination and the last, her "body of work" and "innovation and superiority" – among the Hall's lofty criteria for inclusion – had not altered one iota. It was simply that, thanks to a TV show, the gods of American commerce now deemed her credentials to pass muster. She published a well-meaning note of gratitude shortly before the ceremony and, of course, stayed at home. It was left to Outkast's Big Boi to collect her award and make a speech, "like the White House press secretary". Perhaps Bush's greatest fan, he had also fulfilled the dream of collaborating with her. In Cleveland, Big Boi reiterated his awe at her work and urged her to release the track the pair had been working on for, seemingly, several years: "I sent you three versions; pick one!" St Vincent performed a reverent 'Running Up That Hill'. Beyond all the essentially meaningless hullabaloo, the event did nothing to harm her growing profile in the United States.

★　★　★

Away from this biz business, Bush continued, as was her custom, to reveal little of her interior life. Her son, Bertie – so ecstatically hymned on *Aerial* and given a central role in 'Before The Dawn' – was now a grown man in his mid-twenties. Having graduated from Oxford University with a degree in physics, Albert McIntosh was now undertaking postgraduate research abroad.

At home, between bouts of gardening and perhaps other forms of nurturing creativity, Bush connected with her fans whenever there was a morsel of news, communicating via short posts on her website which read like notes pinned on the village noticeboard. They varied in tone and content, from gushing gestures of thanks and gratitude, to points of order. In one posted in January 2019, she felt compelled to correct the perception that she was a supporter of the Conservative Party, having previously expressed admiration for the Conservative prime minister, Theresa May. In a telephone interview promoting the *Before The Dawn* live album, published in 2016 in the Canadian magazine *MacLean's*, she said: "We have a female prime minister here in the UK. I actually really like her and think she's wonderful. I think it's the best thing that's happened to us in a long time. She's a very intelligent woman but I don't see much to fear. I will say it is great to have a woman in charge of the country. She's very sensible and I think that's a good thing at this point in time."[16]

Two years later, when the remastered reissues and the publication of *How To Be Invisible* brought about a flurry of press attention, she issued a "clarification": "It seems the quote keeps being used and so I'd like to present my side of the story. Over the years, I have avoided making political comments in interviews. My response to the interviewer was not meant to be political but rather was in the defence of women in power. I felt he was putting a really negative slant on powerful women, referring to a witch hunt involving Hilary Clinton. In response I said that we had a woman in charge of our country, and that I felt it was a good thing to have women in power. I should have been clearer when I then said it was the best thing that had happened to us for a long time – because I greatly disliked the behaviour of the previous PM [David Cameron], who at that point I felt had abandoned us and everybody felt angry and let down. Again with no response from me to the latest resurfacing of this article, it could make it seem like I am a Tory supporter which I want to make clear I am not."[17]

Her annual Christmas message in 2023 was uncharacteristically bleak: "I'd always hoped that the human race would become more spiritual, gentle creatures as we moved into the future but it has proved to be the absolute antithesis. The world is at war while the planet burns. . .What is going on? I'm among a group of friends who don't watch the news any more. It now seems to be a global trend. Of course we want to stay informed but sometimes elements of the visual reporting feel horrifically voyeuristic. I've tried to write this piece three times so far, looking for something positive to focus on, but that's been hard to find."[18]

As well as turning away from the carnage of a world gone wrong, her mood may have been adversely affected by two very painful personal losses. The great Scottish bass player John Giblin died from cancer in May 2023, aged 71. He had first worked with Bush on *Never For Ever*, and had been involved with her music ever since, last playing with her in the 'Before The Dawn' band. It was the end of a deeply important friendship. "I loved John so very much," she wrote. "He was one of my very dearest and closest friends for over forty years. My world will never be the same again without him."[19]

The death of Del Palmer on 5 January 2024, also aged 71, was another almost incalculable loss. Outside of Bush's family, Palmer represented perhaps the strongest living link between the past and the present. They had been young lovers, bandmates, romantic and musical partners through the height of Bush's fame, exes and old friends. His creative input, first as a bass player, then as an engineer, ran through almost all of her music. "It's hard to know what to say," Bush wrote in tribute, no doubt desiring to keep much private. "It's going to take a long time to come to terms with him not being here with us. . . I am going to miss him terribly."[20]

In a more positive development, Record Store Day UK announced Bush as its official ambassador for 2024, a largely symbolic position previously held by, among others, Taylor Swift, Elton John and Noel Gallagher. This felt like a continuation of the vinyl-centric advocacy of the reissue projects. Vinyl, Bush said in a statement, "Encourages people to listen to albums, an art form that I've always thought can be treasured in a unique way. An album on vinyl is a beautiful thing, given a strong identity by its large-scale artwork. There's a much more personal connection with the artist and their work." On April 20, she released a special 10-inch Record Store Day edition of 'Eat The Music', the song originally scheduled to be the first release from *The Red Shoes* before it was replaced by 'Rubberband Girl'. Finally, it had found its moment.

As for the matter of writing, recording and releasing new music, to guess what may lie ahead remains the ultimate fool's errand. The standard rhythms of the industry are alien to her. Bush has for the longest time made music away from any sense of outside pressure or stimulus. It is highly unlikely that the speed or methodology of that process would be affected one way or another by a strange collision with a teenage TV show: the idea of "capitalising" on the success of 'Running Up That Hill' would not have been given serious consideration.

Whatever her intentions, age should not present any barrier to further creativity – musicians are now routinely working into their late seventies and eighties. Perhaps Bush has said all she wishes to say; if so, she has crafted a catalogue of rare beauty which will continue to yield new and surprising treasure to anyone who hears it. The hope remains, however, that she continues to work on new music in private, and that she will one day invite us to listen. Stranger things have happened.

Epilogue 2024

This Woman's Work

IN 2008, when I started conducting interviews for the original edition of this book, Kate Bush's friend and former engineer Haydn Bendall told me, "I'm ashamed that she isn't regarded more as a national treasure." If it was a debatable sentiment even then – as far back as 2006, viewers of BBC Two's *Culture Show* had voted Bush seventh in a poll to find the top ten living British icons – in the years since it has, indisputably, been rendered obsolete.

In 2014 alone many miles of column inches were devoted to shoring up the evidence. As the *Financial Times* music critic Ludovic Hunter-Tilney wrote during his review of 'Before The Dawn', "So esteemed is she in Britain that she's gone beyond the status of national treasure to something even more cherished. The French have Marianne, their symbol of republican liberty. The British have Kate, as decent as a cup of tea, as mysterious as Stonehenge."[1]

The resurgence of 'Running Up That Hill' in 2022 sparked much more of the same. Bush had in some respects reached a point beyond criticism, which is never a particularly healthy place for any artist to arrive at. Usually, as with David Bowie, it takes death for that process to begin, smoothing the more complicated and less easily eulogised edges of a creative life to arrive at something altogether less complete, and less interesting. There was also the danger, post-*Stranger Things*, that she might become too closely associated in the wider public perception with a single song, to the detriment of an appreciation for the rest of her catalogue.

Bush's long periods of inactivity and highly curated catalogue perhaps make it easy to draw broad conclusions. People look at her, or a version of her, and see many different things.

A timely side effect of the successes of 'Before The Dawn' and then 'Running Up That Hill' in 2022, was to be reminded of just how many constituencies she speaks to, and which claim her. Her cultural resonance ripples out from the core to embrace multiple music genres, as well as the worlds of film, television, fashion, comedy, literature and queer discourse.

Even for those who still seek to confine her achievements within the most narrow, gender-specific spectrum of popular music, Bush has built a vibrant legacy. Ever since the arrival of her contemporary Toyah Wilcox in 1979, it has been *de rigueur* for virtually every emerging female artist to either cover Bush's songs, cite her as an inspirational heroine, or be compared to her.

'Before the Dawn' had offered her extended "family" of musical offspring a rare opportunity to assemble in numbers. Bjork, PJ Harvey, Natasha Khan of Bat For Lashes, Lily Allen, Florence Welch, Sophie Ellis Bextor, Alison Goldfrapp, Grace Jones, Cerys Matthews, Alison Moyet, Anna Calvi, Annie Lennox, Kylie Minogue, Adele, Ellie Goulding and KT Tunstall were all in attendance, each of them owing, to varying degrees, a creative debt to Bush. Those who couldn't make it, such as Tori Amos and St Vincent sang her praises in the *Running Up That Hill* documentary, while Solange Knowles started performing a soulful 'Cloudbusting' in her live shows. In the years since, those who continue to acknowledge her influence through their work include Lana Del Rey, Fiona Apple, Lady Gaga, Olivia Rodrigo, Janelle Monáe, Anohni, Lorde, Tracey Thorn and Joanna Newsom. Early in 2024 the winners of BBC Sound of 2024, The Last Dinner Party, recorded a cover of 'Army Dreamers' for a radio session.

This traffic has largely flowed in one direction. When it comes to making music, Bush is, by nature, a self-sustaining creator. She has made no serious attempt to engage with the majority of the acts she has influenced, yet she is still regarded as the *grande dame* of outsider artists the world over. Though not entirely without credence, it is a limiting view, reducing Bush (and her peers) to little more than a smattering of vocal eccentricities and what is usually defined, rather vaguely and chauvinistically, as "kookiness".

In the meantime, much of what she does remains under-examined.

Her work as a producer is still enormously under-recognised, a point well made by Lauren Mayberry of Chvrches in the tribute film aired at the Rock 'n' Roll Hall of Fame. *Hounds Of Love* and *Aerial*, to pick two examples, are masterclasses in dazzling sound manipulation.

She knows how to make pop music. Her best known songs are commercial enough to have crossed into the repertoire of prime time mainstream television, not only on *Stranger Things* and *I Hate Suzie*, the latter using 'Under The Ivy' to dramatic effect, but also on shows such as *The X Factor, The Voice* and *American Idol*. Indie and alternative rock bands are equally in her thrall. Futureheads had a Top 10 hit in 2005 with 'Hounds Of Love' (later remixed by Mystery Jets) and Placebo tackled 'Running Up That Hill'. Nada Surf have covered 'Love And Anger', Ra Ra Riot 'Suspended In Gaffa', and the Decemberists 'Wuthering Heights'.

She is a folk heroine, a beacon of contemporary prog, trance and psych rock, and an avatar of occult resistance for underground counter-cultural rock acts such as Coil. Countless dance acts have sampled or covered her songs; among them The Prodigy, Utah Saints, E-Clypse, David Vorhaus and Blue Pearl. She is beloved in the worlds of R&B and hip hop. Prince was a fan and collaborator. Tupac Shakur was an admirer, and nu-soul singer Maxwell covered 'This Woman's Work', presumably with the best of intentions. Tricky called her music "My bible. It sounds religious to me. She should be treasured more in this country than The Beatles."[2]. Her Hall of Fame "Spokesperson", Big Boi, is a raving devotee of longstanding. "She was so bugged out, man! My uncle would explain what the songs stood for, like 'The Man With The Child In His Eyes' and all that shit."[3] He remains "infatuated" with her.

Big Boi had made the pilgrimage to Hammersmith for 'Before The Dawn'. Among the many valuable aspects of the residency, it provided a very public context for Bush's various constituencies to assemble, teasing out distinct enclaves of friends and collaborators (those "spokes" again), and providing a handy primer for revealing where she goes hunting for her ideas.

Big Boi was among representatives from some of music's most indi-vidualistic bands, among them Orbital, Pulp, Pet Shop Boys, Suede, Prefab Sprout, Groove Armada, Killing Joke, Simple Minds and Sparks. They were joined by sturdy pillars of the rock establishment. Perhaps more than most, the likes of Elton John, Paul McCartney, Peter Gabriel, David Gilmour and Jimmy Page recognised not only how hard it was to remain relevant across a span of four decades, but also to do so while retaining artistic control and maintaining the very highest creative standards.

Many other guest list luminaries at 'Before The Dawn' worked in film and theatre, and, on some level, recognised in Bush a kindred spirit. Among them were Kiera Knightley, Daniel Craig, Stephen Fry, Jude Law, Miranda Richardson, Kirsten Dunst, Orlando Bloom, Rachel Weisz, Gemma Arterton, Ian McKellen and Vanessa Redgrave. Directors Steve McQueen, Danny Boyle and Paul Greengrass came, as did Michael Ball and Andrew Lloyd Webber from the world of musical theatre. The British comedy establishment were also out in force. Her beloved *Monty Python* was represented by Terry Gilliam and the late Terry Jones. Tim McInnerney from *Blackadder*, who starred in the video for 'This Woman's Work', and old friends Lenny Henry and Dawn French attended, as well as Noel Fielding, David Walliams, Jo Brand, Bill Bailey and Frank Skinner.

As far back as 2005, designer Greg Myler used Bush's daring stylistic shifts as the bedrock of his Milan show. She remains an enduring icon in the world of fashion, nominated in the British Style category for the 2014 British Fashion Awards. In September 2014, Phoebe Philo opened her Céline show with 'This Woman's Work', clad in a Kate Bush T-shirt she had bought days earlier at the Eventim Apollo. Stella McCartney and Kate Moss also attended concerts. British fashion designer Hussein Chalayan said, "Her appeal is not so much about the way she dresses – despite all those amazing costumes – but about her ideas and her work."[4]

Perhaps of all those in attendance, the most telling presence was that of the authors, among them Jeanette Winterson, Neil Gaiman, David Mitchell and Philip Pullman. Winterson was not alone in being moved to pen an article praising Bush's talent, originality and integrity. "Through all her experiments with herself she remains clearly and cleanly the self that she is," she wrote. "She's doing the work of her soul and if we like it, that's grand, if not, she's doing it anyway."[5] Four years later, in the introduction to *How To Be Invisible*, David Mitchell wrote: "One paradox about Kate is that while her lyrics are proudly idiosyncratic, those same lyrics evoke emotions and sensations that feel universal. Literature works in similar mysterious ways. . . These fiercely singular songs, which nobody else could have authored, are also maps of the heart, the psyche, the imagination. In other words, art."[6] For comedian Jo Brand, "She doesn't do what she's told and as a woman in the music industry at the time she started, that was revolutionary."[7]

The revolution continues. It is remarkable just how far and wide her influence has stretched. Like David Bowie, Bush's impact has grown more powerful with time and has travelled far beyond the realm of music.

These days, again in common with Bowie, she is identified first and foremost by many as a queer icon. Always a meaningful artist for the LGBTQ+ community, who relate intensely to so much of her work without Bush ever having had to explicitly state her advocacy, the connection was reaffirmed through 'Running Up That Hill' re-entering the culture in 2022. The song's desire for fluidity, resilience and empathy, to experience and seek to recognise all sides of the human experience – not least, one might argue, in terms of challenging orthodoxies around sex and gender – in order to better understand both ourselves and one another, hit hard and deep with a contemporary audience for whom binaries are increasingly blurred; particularly, perhaps, with the younger generations engaging with her music for the first time.

The span of her influence speaks to the qualities that lie beneath the surface appeal of Bush's work, distinct from catchy tunes, funny costumes, weird videos and viral sensations. Admirers from all walks of life and numerous disciplines have responded over almost 50 years to the unabashed openness of expression, the singularity of vision, the concealed steel and the sheer uniqueness of what she does and how she does it. They recognise that before Kate Bush, there was no Kate Bush. She is *sui generis*. There are few comparisons that make sense; any that do resonate relate to a certain common sensibility rather than a particular look, feel or sound. We might mention Angela Carter, Mark Hollis, Bjork, Stanley Kubrick, Scott Walker, Roald Dahl, Delia Derbyshire, Terry Gilliam, Joni Mitchell, Tim Burton, David Bowie, Wendy Carlos. Inimitable individualists and demanding mavericks, unfettered by time or trends, fearless and futuristic, all of whom paint vividly idiosyncratic pictures and work in the realm of dark imagination, sly humour and deep emotion. They roam lands that belong to neither the adult nor the child; or rather, belong to both.

Who is she? Not a pop star, that's for sure, or if so only partially, and by default. Bush sees music as an integral part of a much greater tapestry; she is, at heart, a storyteller. "That's what I started doing when I was a little girl," she said. "That's what turned me on, that's the buzz: writing a story."[8] At her best she is our greatest poet of the senses and the psyche. She brings to life through her music every twitch, every neuroses, every love, every tingle, every ache, every muscle, every unseen demon, every remembered angel, every recalled taste, touch and smell. At her least effective, of course, she can be painfully sincere, naïve, twee, ridiculous, overly-literal and rather clumsy, but such rare missteps have proved a price worth paying. Over ten albums and two ground-breaking live productions she has sought to re-sensualise the human experience, to break down the barriers between the heart and the mind, the body and the spirit, the living and the dead, the sea and the sky, winter and summer, day and night, man and woman. In doing so, she reveals herself without barriers.

It's a generous gift from such an otherwise determinedly concealed individual. Bush's intensely private nature is not a fiction, but it has been misinterpreted. The notion that she ekes out a remote, otherworldly existence is a nonsense which increasingly seems to be accepted as such, yet she remains an intriguing study in contradictions: her physical world is relatively confined yet her imaginative universe is boundless; she likes people yet craves privacy; she is proud of her work and wants her audience to hear it, yet hates selling it; her music is both candid confession and armour-plated shield. These tensions have at times made her life difficult. In particular, the artist who has relished dissolving binary opposites in her work – fusing the synthetic and the earthy, the childishly innocent and the overtly erotic, the real and the phantastic, the ancient and the modern, the male and the female – has for much of her career struggled to resolve the core clashes between privacy and fame, and reality and image. As a result, there has often been a confusion of perception about who she really is. "There is a figure that is adored," she once said. "But I'd question very strongly that it's me."[9]

The astonishing response she received at every 'Before The Dawn' show and the outpouring of affection that accompanied the trajectory of 'Running Up That Hill' may have since persuaded her otherwise – but at other times, when she has been at her most remote and objectified, it's natural to wonder whether Bush has been cursed by success. "I've thought about that a lot, because I was so proud of signing her and not letting her go into the studio [too soon], and so I was obviously somewhat conscious of that," Bob Mercer told me in 2008. "But no. I think Kate is Kate and fame didn't crack her at all. Kate has had the career that she would have liked to have had."

Her music has never been about the pursuit of fame. She survived the post-'Wuthering Heights' period of invasion, intrusion and immense self-consciousness, but it's little wonder that she spent the ensuing years steadily backing away from that utterly unexpected and bewildering entrance, gradually carving out more and more elbow room in order to safeguard her own sense of identity. Her very authorly isolation, that charmed realm of silence beloved of all storytellers, was doggedly seized from instant pop stardom, its attendant objectification and ceaseless demands for more, more, *more*. It is perhaps her greatest achievement and fiercely protected. She simply couldn't have done what she has without it.

Within that "circle of fire", Bush has sought to keep alive her connection to the terribly fragile surge of wonder and possibility which she first glimpsed as a young girl. In doing so, she has re-shaped the world. Periods of prolonged invisibility have only served to make her more impactful. The *Stranger Things* episode and its aftermath was simply the latest proof that, whether physically present or in absentia, she remains an active and positive agent for change. We see and hear Kate Bush only very rarely; we also see and hear her everywhere.

Acknowledgements

I would like to thank everyone who agreed to answer my questions for this book. They include:

Christine Ashley, Stewart Avon Arnold, Ian Bairnson, Brian Bath, Haydn Bendall, Steve Blacknell, Joe Boyd, Nina Brown, Richard Burgess, Richard Campbell, Ian Cooper, Adam Darius, Geoff Emerick, Peter Erskine, Martyn Ford, David Garfath, Chris Hall, Paul Hardiman, Paul Henry, John Henshall, David Jackson, Vic King, Robin Kovac-Mueller, Daniel Lanois, Nick Launay, Steve Lillywhite, Colin Lloyd-Tucker, Bruce Lynch, Peter Lyster-Todd, Gered Mankowitz, Pat Martin, Oonagh McCormack, Bob Mercer, Max Middleton, Charlie Morgan, Shealla Mubi, Jimmy Murakami, Borimira Nedeva, Concepta Nolan-Long, Randy Olson, Hugh Padgham, David Paton, Susanna Pell, Morris Pert, Andrew Powell, Nick Price, Steve Sanger, Alan Skidmore, Brian Southall, Jeremy Thomas, Sean Twomey, Tony Visconti, Tony Wadsworth, John Walters, Jane Wilkinson, Janet Willmot, Brian Wiseman and Youth.

Thanks also . . .

To all those who helped facilitate the interviews, and to Jon Kelly for talking in such depth about his work with Kate Bush for another of my projects, an interview which was of much use here.

To Peter Fitzgerald-Morris at *Homeground* magazine, and Sean Twomey of the *Kate Bush News & Information Service* for their assistance and advice. Thanks to Marcel Nahapiet

To my original editor, Chris Charlesworth, and to David Barraclough and Claire Browne for their valued input on the 2024 update; thanks to Gordon, for reading and responding to early parts of the book, and to Stan for all his help. Particular thanks to the late Johnny Rogan for his attention to detail.

And finally, a huge thank you to all my family – primarily my wife, Jen, and our three children, for their love, patience and understanding.

Notes & Sources

All the quotations in the book are derived from interviews conducted by the author unless indicated otherwise in the text or marked with a reference number corresponding to the sources listed below. All footnotes are denoted by an asterisk and are listed at the bottom of the relevant page.

INTRODUCTION:
1. *Q*, November 1989
2. *Personal Call*, BBC Radio One, 1979
3. Bob Mercer, interview with author
4. *Q*, December 1993
5. *Hi-Fi & Record Review*, December 1985

CHAPTER 1:
1. *Cathy*, John Carder Bush, 1986
2. *Personal Call*, BBC Radio One, 1979
3. *Evening Standard*, September 5, 1980
4. *Sounds*, August 30, 1980
5. Max Middleton/Brian Southall, interviews with author
6. Unedited interview with MTV, November 1985
7. *Musician*, Autumn 1985
8. ibid
9. ibid
10. ibid
11. *Sunday Telegraph*, July 6, 1980
12. http://gaffa.org/dreaming/ied_3.html
13. Introduction to *Cathy*, John Carder Bush, 1986
14. http://gaffa.org/cloud/subjects/john_carter_bush.html
15. *Profiles In Rock*, CITY-TV, December 1980
16. ibid
17. *Sunday Telegraph*, July 6 1980

CHAPTER 2:
1. *Friday Night, Saturday Morning With Desmond Morris*, BBC 2, November 21, 1981
2. *Kate Bush: A Visual Documentary*, Kevin Cann and Sean Mayes, Omnibus Press, 1988

3. Interview Picture Disc, 1985
4. *Electronics & Music Maker*, 1982
5. *My Beliefs*, October 1978, http://gaffa.org/reaching/i78_mb.html
6. *Melody Maker*, March 1978
7. *Flexipop*, September 1982
8. Connie Nolan-Long, interview with author
9. *Cathy*, John Carder Bush, 1986
10. *Flexipop*, September 1982
11. *My Beliefs*, October 1978, http://gaffa.org/reaching/i78_mb.html
12. *Woman's Hour*, BBC Radio Four, February 21, 1979
13. *Musician*, Autumn 1985
14. Interview with Tony Myatt, Kate Bush fan convention, November 1985
15. *Musician*, Autumn 1985
16. *Kate Bush: The Whole Story*, Kerry Juby, Sidgwick & Jackson, 1988
17. *Sounds*, March 11, 1978
18. *Kate Bush: The Whole Story*, Kerry Juby, Sidgwick & Jackson, 1988
19. *Trouser Press*, July 1978
20. *New Statesman*, February 7, 2005
21. *You* magazine, October 22, 1989
22. *Trouser Press*, July 1978
23. *Personal Call*, BBC Radio One, 1979
24. *Pop On The Line*, BBC World Service, November 22 1998
25. *Sound International*, September 1980
26. *Sounds,* August 30, 1980
27. *Kate Bush: The Whole Story*, Kerry Juby, Sidgwick & Jackson, 1988
28. *Sounds*, August 1980
29. *The Multi-Coloured Swap Shop*, BBC 1, January 20, 1979
30. *Personal Call*, BBC Radio One, 1979
31. *Record Mirror*, October 7, 1978
32. *Flexipop*, September 1982
33. ibid
34. *Q*, November 1989
35. *Sunday Mirror*, Inside The Private World Of Kate Bush
36. Interview Picture Disc, 1985
37. *Superpop*, February 10, 1979
38. *Nationwide*, BBC One, April 4, 1979
39. *Flexipop*, September 1982
40. ibid

CHAPTER 3:

1. *What Kate Did Next*, http://gaffa.org/reaching/i85_what.html, 1985
2. *Personal Call*, BBC Radio One, 1979
3. *The Dreaming* Interview Disc, CBAK 4011, 1982
4. *The Mark Radcliffe Show*, Radio Two, November 7, 2005
5. *Kate Bush In Concert*, German TV, April 1980

6. *Electronics & Music Maker*, 1982
7. *Sounds International*, September 1980
8. *Woman's Hour*, BBC Radio Four, February 21, 1979
9. *Friday Night, Saturday Morning With Desmond Morris*, BBC 2, November 21, 1981
10. *Electronics & Music Maker*, 1982
11. *Crawdaddy*, 1974
12. ibid
13. *New Musical Express*, October 1982
14. *Radio & Record News*, February 1978
15. VH-1 Special, 1990
16. *The Peter Powell Show*, Radio One, October 11, 1980
17. ibid
18. *Tune-In*, Christmas 1978
19. *Razzamatazz*, ITV, July 14, 1981
20. *Electronics & Music Maker*, 1982
21. *Sounds*, August 30, 1980
22. *Kerrang*, February/March 1984
23. VH-1 Special, 1990
24. *Tune-In*, Christmas 1978
25. *Sounds*, August 30, 1980
26. *New Musical Express*, October 1982
27. *Melody Maker*, June 3, 1978
28. *Nationwide*, BBC One, April 4, 1979
29. *The Dreaming* Interview Disc, CBAK 4011, 1982
30. ibid
31. *Musician*, Autumn 1985
32. *Homeground*, Summer 2007
33. *Musician*, Autumn 1985
34. *Homeground*, Summer 2007
35. *Musician*, Autumn 1985
36. *Record Mirror*, October 7, 1978
37. *Hot Press*, November 1985
38. *Nationwide*, BBC One, April 4, 1979

CHAPTER 4:

1. *Musician*, Autumn 1985
2. *Radio & Record News*, February 1978
3. *Sounds*, March 11, 1978
4. *Kerrang!*, 1982
5. *The Multi-Coloured Swap Shop*, BBC One, January 20, 1979
6. *Record Mirror*, February 25, 1978
7. *Melody Maker*, June 3, 1978
8. *Kerrang!*, February/March, 1984
9. Both quotes from Brian Bath, interview with author

10. Peter Lyster-Todd, interview with author
11. *Q*, November 1989
12. ibid
13. *Kate Bush Club Newsletter*, No. 5, 1980
14. *Sounds*, August 30, 1980
15. ibid
16. *Homeground*, Summer 2004
17. *Kate Bush In Concert*, German TV, April 1980
18. *New Musical Express*, March 1978
19. *Hot Press*, November 1985
20. *Sounds*, March 11, 1978
21. *Homeground*, Summer 2004

CHAPTER 5:

1. *Kerrang!*, February/March, 1984
2. *Pulse*, December 1989
3. *Q*, November 1989
4. *Tune-In*, Christmas 1978
5. *News At Night*, MTV, January 1990
6. *Radio & Record News*, February 1978
7. *Trouser Press*, July 1978
8. *Melody Maker*, November, 1978
9. ibid
10. *Lionheart* promotional cassette, EMI-Canada, 1978
11. *Melody Maker*, November, 1978
12. *Sounds*, August 30, 1980

CHAPTER 6:

1. *Smash Hits*, May 1980
2. *Musician*, Autumn 1985
3. *Kate Bush: The Whole Story*, Kerry Juby, Sidgwick & Jackson, 1988
4. *Homeground*, Summer 2007
5. ibid
6. *Homeground*, Summer 2004
7. *Nationwide*, BBC One, April 4, 1979
8. *Record Mirror*, March 24, 1979
9. *Nationwide*, BBC One, April 4, 1979
10. *Homeground*, Summer 2007
11. *Nationwide*, BBC One, April 4, 1979
12. ibid
13. *Smash Hits*, May 1980
14. *Smash Hits*, September 1979
15. *Kate Bush: The Whole Story*, Kerry Juby, Sidgwick & Jackson, 1988
16. *Homeground*, Summer 2007
17. *Q*, November 1989

18. *Record Mirror*, September 1981
19. *Kate Bush In Concert*, German TV, 1980/ 'Getting Down Under With Kate Bush', *Record Mirror*, 1982
20. *Musician*, Autumn 1985
21. *Sunday Telegraph*, July 6, 1980
22. *Poppix*, 1982
23. *Homeground*, Summer 2007
24. ibid
25. *Musician*, Autumn 1985
26. *Company*, January 1982
27. *Sunday Telegraph*, July 6, 1980
28. *New Musical Express*, October 20, 1979
29. *Homeground*, Summer 2007
30. *Musician*, Autumn 1985
31. *Homeground*, Summer 2007

CHAPTER 7:

1. *The Women Of Rock*, 1984
2. *Nationwide*, BBC One, April 4, 1979
3. *Sounds*, August 30, 1980
4. *Kate Bush: A Visual Documentary*, Kevin Cann and Sean Mayes, Omnibus Press, 1988
5. *Smash Hits,* June 1981
6. *MuchMusic*, Canadian TV, 1985/*Electronics & Music Maker*, 1982
7. *Zig Zag*, 1980
8. ibid
9. ibid
10. ibid
11. *Razzmatazz*, ITV, July 14, 1981
12. *Hot Press*, November, 1985
13. *Guardian*, October 12, 1989
14. *Record Mirror*, October 7, 1978
15. *The Best Of Kate Bush*, EMI Music Publishing, 1981
16. *Record Mirror*, September 6, 1980
17. *The Peter Powell Show*, Radio One, October 11, 1980
18. *Fachblatt Musikmagazin*, November 1985

CHAPTER 8:

1. *Record Mirror*, September 1981
2. ibid
3. *Musician*, Autumn 1985
4. ibid
5. *Electronics & Music Maker*, 1982
6. *Mix*, 2006

7. *Melody Maker*, October 16, 1982
8. *Record Mirror*, September 1981
9. *Kate Bush Club Newsletter*, No. 12, October 1982
10. *Record Mirror*, September 1981
11. 'Getting Down Under With Kate Bush', *Record Mirror*, 1982
12. *Company*, January 1982
13. *Q*, November 1989
14. *Electronics & Music Maker*, 1982
15. Preview of *The Dreaming*, Radio Two, September 13, 1982
16. *Kate Bush Club Newsletter*, No. 12, October 1982
17. *Homeground*, Summer 2007
18. *Company*, January 1982
19. Paul Hardiman, interview with author
20. *The Women Of Rock*, 1984
21. *Hi-Fi For Pleasure*, August 1983
22. *Fachblatt Musikmagazin*, November 1985
23. Interview with Tony Myatt, Kate Bush fan convention, November 1985
24. *MuchMusic*, Canadian TV, December 1985
25. *Homeground*, Summer 2007
26. *Kerrang!*, 1982
27. *Q*, November 1989
28. ibid

CHAPTER 9:

1. *Kate Bush Club Newsletter*, No. 14, Autumn 1983
2. *You*, October 22, 1989
3. Interview Disc, CBAK 4011, 1985
4. *Kate Bush: The Whole Story*, Kerry Juby, Sidgwick & Jackson, 1988
5. *MuchMusic*, Canadian TV, November 1985
6. The *Times*, August 27, 1985
7. *Kate Bush Club Newsletter*, No. 13, Summer 1983
8. *What Kate Did Next*, http://gaffa.org/reaching/i85_what.html, 1985
9. *Fachblatt Musikmagazin*, November 1985
10. *Hot Press*, November 1985
11. Unaccredited radio interview, July 29, 1983
12. *Daily Mirror*, March 21, 1990
13. *You* magazine, October 22, 1989/*Daily Mirror*, March 21, 1990
14. *Kate Bush Club Newsletter*, No. 14, Autumn 1983
15. ibid
16. ibid
17. *Classic Albums*, Radio One, January 26, 1992
18. *The Dreaming* Interview Disc, CBAK 4011, 1982
19. Interview with Tony Myatt, Kate Bush fan convention, November 1985
20. *Kate Bush Club Newsletter*, No. 17, Winter 1984
21. *Homeground*, Summer 2007

22. *Classic Albums*, Radio One, January 26, 1992
23. ibid
24. *Musician*, Autumn 1985
25. *Homeground*, Summer 2007
26. *Musician*, Autumn 1985
27. Interview with Tony Myatt, Kate Bush fan convention, November 1985
28. *Classic Albums*, Radio One, January 26, 1992
29. Q, November 1989
30. Interview by Doug Alan, November 1985
31. Q, November 1989
32. Q, December 1990
33. Unaccredited US radio interview, 1989
34. Q, 20th Anniversary issue, October 2006
35. *Zig Zag*, November 1985
36. *Hot Press*, November 1985
37. *Kate Bush Club Newsletter*, No. 21, Winter 1987
38. *Mojo*, December 2005
39. *Melody Maker*, October 21, 1989
40. *Blitz*, September 1985
41. *Classic Albums*, Radio One, January 26, 1992

CHAPTER 10:
1. *You*, October 22, 1989/*Daily Mirror*, March 21, 1990
2. http://ebni.com/byrds/newsbwidc2.htm
3. *YTV Rocks*, Canada, December 1989
4. *Melody Maker*, October 21, 1989
5. *International Musician*, December 1989
6. *Musician*, February 1990
7. *Tracks*, November 1989
8. VH-1 Special, 1990
9. *Melody Maker*, October 21, 1989
10. *Reaching Out*, 1989
11. *The Sensual World* Press kit, CBS America, 1989
12. WFNX radio, Boston, Autumn 1989
13. *Pulse*, December 1989
14. *International Musician*, December 1989
15. *Options,* March/April 89
16. *Melody Maker*, October 21, 1989
17. ibid
18. ibid
19. ibid
20. *Raw*, issues 32/33, November 1989
21. From 'Rocket Man' single sleeve
22. Q, HMV Special mini-edition, 1990
23. ibid

24. *Los Angeles Times*, January 29, 1990
25. Capital Radio, September 1989
26. Q, HMV Special mini-edition, 1990
27. *Homeground*, Summer 1996
28. *Future Music*, November 1993
29. ibid
30. *Homeground*, Spring 1994
31. Q, 20th Anniversary issue, October 2006
32. *Vox*, November 1993
33. ibid
34. *Front Row*, BBC Radio Four, November 4, 2005
35. *Associated Press*, November 17, 1989
36. *Future Music*, November 1993
37. *Rock World*, October 1993
38. Q, December 2001
39. *Mojo*, December 2005
40. Q, December 2001

CHAPTER 11:

1. *Musician*, Autumn 1985
2. *Melody Maker*, 1983
3. ibid
4. *Classic Albums*, Radio One, January 26, 1992
5. Unedited interview with MTV, November 1985
6. *Good Morning With Anne And Nick*, BBC One, April 1994
7. ibid
8. *Musician*, February 1990

CHAPTER 12:

1. BBC Radio 2, July 4, 1996
2. *Kate Bush Club Newsletter*, December 1995
3. *Vox*, November 1993
4. Q, December 2001
5. Q, December 1993
6. *Thank You For The Days*, Mark Radcliffe, Simon & Schuster, 2009
7. Q, December 2001
8. ibid
9. *Mojo*, December 2005
10. *Front Row*, BBC Radio Four, November 4, 2005
11. *The Mark Radcliffe Show*, BBC Radio Two, November 7, 2005
12. Q, December 2001
13. ibid
14. *Mojo*, December 2005
15. ibid
16. ibid

17. *Rolling Stone* (France), February 2006
18. *Front Row*, BBC Radio Four, November 4, 2005

CHAPTER 13:

1. *Front Row*, The Presenter's Cut, BBC Radio Four, May 5, 2011
2. *The Times*, April 30, 2011
3. *NPR*, August 19, 2011
4. *Interview*, June 2011
5. *Pitchfork*, May 16, 2011
6. *MOJO*, June 2011
7. *Radcliffe and Maconie*, BBC Radio 6music, May 23, 2011
8. *NPR*, August 19, 2011
9. *MOJO*, June 2011
10. *Pitchfork*, May 16, 2011
11. *MOJO*, June 2011
12. *Radcliffe and Maconie*, BBC Radio 6music, May 23, 2011
13. *Radcliffe and Maconie*, BBC Radio 6music, May 26, 2011
14. *Pitchfork*, May 16, 2011
15. *Radcliffe and Maconie*, BBC Radio 6music, May 26, 2011
16. PRI's *The World*, November 15, 2011
17. *Front Row*, The Presenter's Cut, BBC Radio Four, May 5, 2011
18. *MOJO*, December 2011
19. *MOJO*, December 2011
20. *Sirius XM*, OutQ Radio, December 8, 2011
21. *Front Row*, BBC Radio Four, November 22, 2011
22. *Independent*, November 18, 2011
23. *the Quietus*, November 13, 2011
24. *Radcliffe and Maconie*, BBC Radio 6music, December 12/13, 2011
25. *Irish Times*, May 6, 2011
26. *Front Row*, The Presenter's Cut, BBC Radio Four, May 5, 2011
27. Interview with Jamie Cullum, Avro.nl, December 6, 2011
28. *MOJO*, Decemeber 2011
29. *Washington Post*, November 18, 2011
30. *The Lauren Laverne Show*, BBC Radio 6music, November 24, 2011
31. *MOJO*, December 2011
32. *The Australian*, October 29, 2011
33. Interview with Jamie Cullumm, Avro.nl, December 6, 2011
34. *Classic Rock Presents Prog Magazine*, Issue 22, December 2011
35. *Front Row*, BBC Radio Four, November 22, 2011
36. *MOJO*, December 2011337
37. *Classic Rock Presents Prog Magazine*, Issue 22, December 2011
38. Interview with Jamie Cullum, Avro.nl, December 6, 2011
39. *The Lauren Laverne Show*, BBC Radio 6music, November 24, 2011
40. Interview with Jamie Cullum, Avro.nl, December 6, 2011
41. *Radcliffe and Maconie*, BBC Radio 6music, December 12/13, 2011

42. *Irish Times*, May 6, 2011

43. *Radcliffe and Maconie*, BBC Radio 6music, December 12/13, 2011

44. *Irish Times*, May 6, 2011

45. *Front Row*, BBC Radio Four, November 22, 2011

Steve Gadd and Mica Paris were interviewed by the author for a piece that appeared in *Uncut*, January 2012

CHAPTER 14:

1. *Before The Dawn*, programme notes

2. *Sunday Times*, October 12, 2014

3. *Before The Dawn,* programme notes

4. *ibid*

5. *New Statesman*, October 2, 2014

6. *Before The Dawn*, programme notes

7. *New Statesman*, October 2, 2014

8. *Sunday Times*, October 12, 2014

9. *Toyah Wilcox website*, https://toyahwillcox.com/toyahs-blog-oct-2014/

10. *Faeries and Enchantment, Winter* 2014

11. *Variety,* June 1, 2022

12. *ibid*

13. *ibid*

14. *Woman's Hour*, BBC R4, June 22, 2022

15. *www.katebush.com*, June 4, 2022

16. *Maclean's*, November 28, 2016

17. *www.katebush.com*, January 8, 2019

18. *www.katebush.com*, December 23, 2023

19. *www.katebush.com*, May 16, 2023

20. *www.katebush.com*, January 10, 2024

EPILOGUE:

1. *Financial Times*, August 27, 2014

2. *MOJO*, July 2003

3. *Times*, October 22, 2005

4. *Vogue,* August 26, 2014

5. *Guardian*, August 22, 2014

6. *How To Be Invisible*, Introduction, David Mitchell, Faber, 2018

7. *Big Issue*, August 22, 2014

8. *Front Row*, BBC Radio Four, November 4, 2005

9. *Details*, March 1994

Selected Bibliography

Numerous newspapers, magazines and web pages were enormously helpful during the writing of this book. Most notably, *Homeground* magazine has been a longstanding and always fascinating source of both hard information and strongly felt opinion on Kate Bush. There are several dedicated Bush sites on the internet, and in particular the *Kate Bush News And Information Service* and *Gaffaweb* are both invaluable destinations for any Bush fan. The following books have also proved particularly useful:

- *The Best Of Kate Bush*, EMI Music Publishing, 1981
- *Cathy*, John Carder Bush, 1986
- *The Complete David Bowie*, Nicholas Pegg, Raymond & Hearns Ltd, 2002
- *Dylan: Behind The Shades*, Clinton Heylin, Viking, 1991
- *The Illustrated Guide To Kate Bush,* Robert Godwin, Collector's Guide Limited, 2005
- *Kate Bush: An Illustrated Biography,* Paul Kerton, Proteus Books, 1980
- *Kate Bush And Hounds Of Love,* Ron Moy, Ashgate Publishing Limited, 2005
- *Kate Bush: A Visual Documentary*, Kevin Cann and Sean Mayes, Omnibus Press, 1988
- *Kate Bush Biography*, Fred & Judy Vermorel, Target Books, 1980
- *Kate Bush: The Biography*, Rob Jovanovic, Portrait, 2005
- *Kate Bush: The Whole Story*, Kerry Juby, Sidgwick & Jackson, 1988
- *Performing Democracy: Bulgarian Music And Musicians In Transition*, Donna A. Buchanan, University Of Chicago Press, 2006
- *The Secret History Of Kate Bush*, Fred Vermorel, Omnibus Press, 1983
- *Thank You For The Days*, Mark Radcliffe, Simon & Schuster, 2009
- *The Third MOJO Collection*, edited by Colin McLear and Jim Irvin, Canongate, 2003
- *Waiting For Kate Bush*, John Mendelsshon, Omnibus Press, 2004

Selective Discography

ALBUMS & EPS

The Kick Inside (1978)

'Moving', 'The Saxophone Song', 'Strange Phenomena', 'Kite', 'The Man With The Child In His Eyes', 'Wuthering Heights', 'James And The Cold Gun', 'Feel It', 'Oh To Be In Love', 'L'Amour Looks Something Like You', 'Them Heavy People', 'Room For The Life', 'The Kick Inside'.

Lionheart (1978)

'Symphony In Blue', 'In Search Of Peter Pan', 'Wow', 'Don't Push Your Foot On The Heartbrake', 'Oh England, My Lionheart', 'Full House', 'In The Warm Room', 'Kashka From Baghdad', 'Coffee Homeground', 'Hammer Horror'.

On Stage EP (1979)

'Them Heavy People', 'Don't Push Your Foot On The Heartbrake', 'James And The Cold Gun', 'L'Amour Looks Something Like You'.

Never For Ever (1980)

'Babooshka', 'Delius (Song Of Summer)', 'Blow Away (For Bill)', 'All We Ever Look For', 'Egypt', 'The Wedding List', 'Violin', 'The Infant Kiss', 'Night Scented Stock', 'Army Dreamers', 'Breathing'.

The Dreaming (1982)

'Sat In Your Lap', 'There Goes A Tenner', 'Pull Out The Pin', 'Suspended In Gaffa', 'Leave It Open', 'The Dreaming', 'Night Of The Swallow', 'All The Love', 'Houdini', 'Get Out Of My House'.

Hounds Of Love (1985)

'Running Up That Hill (A Deal with God)', 'Hounds Of Love', 'The Big Sky', 'Mother Stands For Comfort', 'Cloudbusting', 'And Dream Of Sheep', 'Under Ice', 'Waking The Witch', 'Watching You Without Me', 'Jig Of Life', 'Hello Earth', 'The Morning Fog'.

The Whole Story (1986)

'Wuthering Heights', 'Cloudbusting', 'The Man With The Child In His Eyes', 'Breathing', 'Wow', 'Hounds Of Love', 'Running Up That Hill (A Deal With God)', 'Army Dreamers', 'Sat In Your Lap', 'Experiment IV', 'The Dreaming', 'Babooshka'.

The Sensual World (1989)

'The Sensual World', 'Love And Anger', 'The Fog', 'Reaching Out', 'Heads We're Dancing', 'Deeper Understanding', 'Between A Man And A Woman', 'Never Be Mine', 'Rocket's Tail', 'This Woman's Work', 'Walk Straight Down The Middle' (CD and cassette only).

This Woman's Work (1990)

Box set containing Bush's first six studio albums in their entirety, plus:

Disc 7

'The Empty Bullring', 'Ran Tan Waltz', 'Passing Through Air', 'December Will Be Magic Again', 'Warm And Soothing', 'Lord Of The Reedy River', 'Ne T'Enfui Pas', 'Un Baiser d'Enfant', 'Under The Ivy', 'Burning Bridge', 'My Lagan Love', 'The Handsome Cabin Boy', 'Not This Time', 'Walk Straight Down The Middle', 'Be Kind To My Mistakes'.

Disc 8

'I'm Still Waiting', 'Ken', 'One Last Look Around The House Before We Go . . .', 'Wuthering Heights', 'Experiment IV', 'Them Heavy People (Live)', 'Don't Push Your Foot On The Heartbrake (Live)', 'James And The Cold Gun (Live)', 'L'Amour Looks Something Like You (Live)', 'Running Up That Hill (A Deal With God)', 'Cloudbusting', 'Hounds Of Love (Alternative)', 'The Big Sky (extended remix)', 'Experiment IV (extended remix)'.

The Red Shoes (1993)

'Rubberband Girl', 'And So Is Love', 'Eat The Music', 'Moments Of Pleasure', 'The Song Of Solomon', 'Lily', 'The Red Shoes', 'Top Of The City', 'Constellation Of The Heart, 'Big Stripey Lie', 'Why Should I Love You?', 'You're The One'.

Live At Hammersmith Odeon (1994)

'Moving', 'Them Heavy People', 'Violin', 'Strange Phenomena', 'Hammer Horror', 'Don't Push Your Foot On The Heartbrake', 'Wow', 'Feel It', 'Kite', 'James And The Cold Gun', 'Oh England, My Lionheart', 'Wuthering Heights'.

Aerial (2005)

Disc 1

'King Of The Mountain', 'π', 'Bertie', 'Mrs Bartolozzi', 'How To Be Invisible', 'Joanni', 'A Coral Room'.

Disc 2

'Prelude', 'Prologue', 'An Architect's Dream', 'The Painter's Link', 'Sunset', 'Aerial Tal', 'Somewhere In Between', 'Nocturn', 'Aerial'.

Director's Cut (2011)

'Flower Of The Mountain', 'The Song Of Solomon', 'Lily', 'Deeper Understanding', 'The Red Shoes', 'This Woman's Work', 'Moments Of Pleasure', 'Never Be Mine', 'Top Of The City', 'And So Is Love', 'Rubberband Girl'

50 Words For Snow (2011)

'Snowflake', 'Lake Tahoe', 'Misty', 'Wild Man', 'Snowed In At Wheeler Street', '50 Words For Snow', 'Among Angels'

Before The Dawn (2016)

Disc 1

Act I: 'Lily', 'Hounds Of Love', 'Joanni', 'Top Of The City', 'Never Be Mine', 'Running Up That Hill', 'King Of The Mountain'.

Disc 2

Act II: 'Astronomer's Call (Spoken Monologue)', 'And Dream Of Sheep', 'Under Ice', 'Waking The Witch', 'Watching Them Without Her (Dialogue)', 'Watching You Without Me', 'Little Light', 'Jig Of Life', 'Hello Earth', 'The Morning Fog'.

Disc 3

Act III: 'Prelude', 'Prologue', 'An Architect's Dream', 'The Painter's Link', 'Sunset', 'Aerial Tal', 'Somewhere In Between', 'Tawny Moon', 'Nocturn', 'Aerial', 'Among Angels', 'Cloudbusting'.

OTHER NOTABLE APPEARANCES

Big Country: *The Seer* (1986). Sings on 'The Seer'.

Alexandre Desplat: *The Golden Compass Original Soundtrack* (2008). Sings 'Lyra'.

Peter Gabriel: *Peter Gabriel* (1980). Sings on 'No Self Control', 'I Don't Remember' and 'Games Without Frontiers'.

Peter Gabriel: *So* (1986). Sings on 'Don't Give Up'.

Go West: *Dancing On The Couch* (1987). Sings on 'The King Is Dead'.

Roy Harper: *The Unknown Soldier* (1980). Sings on 'You (The Game Part II)'.

Roy Harper: *Once* (1990). Sings on 'Once'.

Prince: *Emancipation* (1996). Appears on 'My Computer'.

Alan Stivell: *Again* (1993). Sings and plays on 'Kimiad', which she also produced.

Midge Ure: *Answers To Nothing* (1988). Sings on 'Brother And Sister'.

Various Artists: *Brazil Soundtrack* (1993). Sings 'Brazil'.

Various Artists: *Castaway: Original Motion Picture Soundtrack* (1987). Sings 'Be Kind To My Mistakes'.

Various Artists: *Comic Relief: Utterly, Utterly Live* (1986). Sings 'Breathing' and duets with Rowan Atkinson on 'Do Bears?'

Various Artists: *Common Ground: Voices Of Irish Music* (1996). Sings 'Mná Na h-Éireann'.   383

Various Artists: *The Glory Of Gershwin* (1994). Performs 'The Man I Love' with Larry Adler.

Various Artists: *The Prince's Trust Collection* (1985). Sings 'The Wedding List'.

Various Artists: *The Secret Policeman's Third Ball: The Music* (1987). Performs 'Running Up That Hill (A Deal With God)' with David Gilmour and band.

Various Artists: *She's Having A Baby Soundtrack* (1988). Sings 'This Woman's Work'.

Various Artists: *Two Rooms* (1991). Sings 'Rocket Man'.

Index

Singles releases are in roman type and albums are in italics.